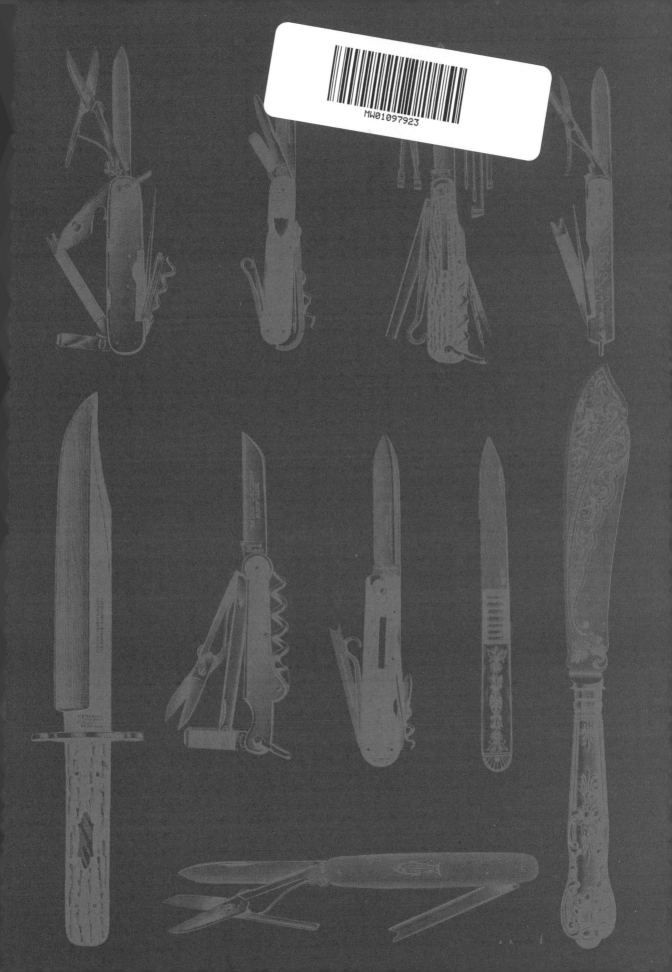

The Sheffield Knife Book

A History and Collectors' Guide

Geoffrey Tweedale

19th-century sport's-knife, marked Needham, Hill Street.

The
Sheffield Knife Book

A History and Collectors' Guide

Geoffrey Tweedale

The **Hallamshire** Press 1996

The colour photography in this book is mostly the work of the author, who also took a few of the black and white photographs. Captions in the book therefore usually refer to location, not provenance. Most of the black and white illustrations are from Sheffield City Library's collection or from trade catalogues loaned to the author. Besides those individuals mentioned in the preface, the author would like to thank Sheffield Newspapers, Richardson Sheffield and Stanley Tools.

© 1996 The Hallamshire Press

Published by The Hallamshire Press
The Hallamshire Press is an Imprint of
Interleaf Productions Limited
Broom Hall
Sheffield S10 2DR
UK

Typeset by Interleaf Productions Limited
Printed by Saik Wah Press Pte. Ltd, Singapore

British Library Cataloguing in Publication Data
  Tweedale, Geoffrey
    The Sheffield knife book : a history and collectors' guide
    1.Knives - England - Sheffield - History 2.Knives - England
    - Sheffield - Collectors and collecting
    I.Title
    683.8'2'0942821

  ISBN 1874718113

Contents

Preface   7

Part One: The Rise and Fall of Knife City   11

  1 Prologue   13

  2 Crucible Steel and Knifemaking up to 1860   19

  3 Sheffield and America   27

  4 Making Knives in the Golden Age   37

  5 Patterns and Styles   63

  6 Zenith and the Beginnings of Decline: 1860–1914   99

  7 The First World War and Its Aftermath, 1914–1939   117

  8 Boom and Bust, 1940–1990s   131

  9 Retrospect   141

Part Two: Sheffield Knifemakers   149

  A Note on Identifying and Dating Sheffield Knives   307

  Places to Visit   311

  Sources   313

  Further Reading   315

To Thomas Brady (1953–1994),
who loved Sheffield crafts

Preface

A GENERATION AGO, almost everyone regarded the words 'Sheffield' and 'knives' as virtually synonymous. 'Sheffield' and 'quality' meant the same thing, too. The evidence was on our dining room tables and also in our pockets, as almost everyone carried a Sheffield pocket-knife. In fact, owning such a knife was once one of the dreams of every schoolboy. It was certainly mine and I have fond memories of my first pocket-knife. It was like 'The Knife' described in a *Just William* story: 'a magnificent affair with four blades, a corkscrew, a file and a thing for getting stones out of a horse's hoof'. Like most schoolboys, it was not long before I had managed to cut my fingers on the blades, and not long either before I had lost it. This knife was soon replaced by another, even more deadly weapon: a small Sheffield Bowie knife in a sheath. This proved useful for performing imaginary acts of heroism (and for less brave acts, such as carving chunks out of tree bark), before it too was either lost or laid to one side. I never imagined as a boy that I would one day study cutlery seriously. That would have seemed inconceivable to me then, for I soon began to share the common view of knives: that they had little appeal or interest.

It is not that we underrate knives—we all admit their usefulness—rather that most of us are indifferent to them, as we are to most everyday objects. Quite simply, we take knives (and other cutlery products) for granted. It follows that anyone who shows an interest in the history, design and use of knives is usually regarded as, at best, an eccentric, or at worst, as someone who should be given a wide birth. Even amongst collectors, knives are not usually near the top in popularity. Unlike Sheffield Plate and silverware, it seems that knives are simply not regarded as 'art'. They have therefore been relatively little studied and have only very recently been collected—even in Sheffield.

Yet some twenty-five years later, for various reasons, I found my interest in the subject reawakened. I had visited Morton's cutlery shop on West Street in Sheffield to see if I could still buy a traditional hand-crafted Sheffield knife. The shop assistant handed me a knife such as I had not seen before (except in museums): it was a hunting-knife in which the blade locked as it opened. What was so striking about this knife was not this mechanism, ingenious though this was, but the quality of the knife: the blade was mirror-polished, and the knife had milled scales, a shield, a shackle and a richly-coloured stag (horn) handle. Running along the back of the knife was an ornate chased pattern cut into the spring and the blades. It seemed impossible that such a lovely work of art was entirely made by hand, but such proved to be the case. It was a surprise to discover that there were still craftsmen in Sheffield capable of making such knives in the 1980s.

This knife, made by Stan Shaw, revived all those boyhood memories of Sheffield knives. It also reminded me of how little I knew about the history of the industry. I resolved to interview some of the remaining craftsmen and find out more about a subject which I had previously only learned about second-hand from books. Later I decided to write something of my own on the history of the Sheffield knife.

It did not take long to discover that the number of historians interested in the cutlery industry is

almost as low of the number of surviving craftsmen. This is partly because history is still a relatively
snobbish discipline, far more concerned with the
so-called 'great events' of politics and religion than
with industry and craftsmanship. The fact that
knife (and tool) manufacture was a comparatively
small-scale British industry even in its heyday, has
also played some part in its neglect. In America,
books on the history of the cutlery industry have
been proliferating in recent years, but in the UK
there are only two major studies of the subject. The
first is Godfrey Lloyd's book, *The Cutlery Trades*.
Although it was published as long ago as 1913, it
is still the standard work on the theme. Only one
attempt has been made to update Lloyd's work:
Joseph Himsworth's, *The Story of Cutlery*, published in 1953. Apart from a few local history
publications, the subject in the 1990s is more forgotten than ever. The historian or collector has no
readily available source of information on Sheffield
knives.

   This book aims to fill that want. It provides
information and an overview of what was once the
world's greatest cutlery centre and its most famous
product. It is slightly different in approach from
past publications on Sheffield cutlery, because it
highlights themes that have not previously been
well treated. Lloyd's account, for example, although
still essential reading, is somewhat dry, as perhaps
one would expect from an economist. To be sure,
Himsworth provides a more lively read and he had
the advantage, as the owner of a cutlery business,
of direct experience of the industry. But he was
more concerned with the overall evolution of cutlery than with the specifics of Sheffield knife
manufacture.

   Looking at these publications and others, it has
always seemed strange to me that they have said so
little about the Sheffield firms that made so many
marvellous products. So I hope that this book,
while not entirely superseding those older accounts,
will provide a better picture of knifemaking as an
industry. It describes some of the manufacturing
processes involved in knifemaking and provides
details on Sheffield patterns and trade marks—
facts that will be useful for the collector. I have

also tried to reveal the story behind the leading
companies and say something about the individuals who ran them. Above all, I have tried to bring
into the picture the life-blood of the industry—the
thousands of workers, many of them very highly
skilled (but poorly paid), who are now completely
forgotten. They were part of an industrial system
that was as hard and unforgiving as the material
with which they worked, but their products are a
testament to their wonderful courage and skill. I have
tried to show something of these products—their
manufacture, design, and marvellous workmanship—again something that has not been well
illustrated before. This has not been easy, now that
so many of the best examples of Sheffield craftsmanship are now in the hands of private collectors
(often in America). Perhaps one day, someone with
far more time and greater resources than myself
will be able to do a better job.

   This book concentrates entirely on Sheffield
knives. This should be emphasised at the outset,
because inevitably this has meant ignoring some of
Sheffield's most famous products. Silverware and
holloware, razors, saws, scythes, files, and many
other quintessentially Sheffield tools, which may
be broadly classified as 'cutlery', are not included
in this book. Nor have I been able to include every
type of knife, such as machine knives, DIY knives
and surgical knives. That I have had to exclude
them is a tribute to Sheffield's remarkable diversity, for it is no exaggeration to suggest that each
product demands a book to itself.

   Cutlery is a deceptive subject, at once thoroughly
mundane and straightforward, yet enormously
complicated beneath the surface. It is an industry
with its own language and craft freemasonry. In
writing this book, I have been able to draw on over
fifteen years' experience in studying and writing
about the subject; yet, this is almost insignificant
compared with the knowledge and experience of
those who have been involved in making knives all
their lives. Fortunately, I have been able to tap that
experience through my contacts with Sheffield cutlers
and industrialists over the years. I am particularly
grateful to Stan Shaw and several other little mesters,
such as Graham Clayton and Rowland Swinden,

for explaining knifemaking to me in such great detail. Harold Osborne, Edith and John Wragg, and Eileen Armitage also made available to me their reminiscences of their fathers' work. Others, notably Ruben Viner and John Price, have helped by describing their experiences at the other end of the spectrum, as businessmen. Roger Inman provided much helpful information, besides showing me the latest technology in knife manufacture at Harrison Fisher's Eye Witness Works. Gordon Ragg of Granton Ragg Ltd also kindly helped with my company profiles, as did Jack Taylor of Elliot's. Naturally, they bear no responsibility for the accuracy of the text or my opinions on the history of the industry.

For help with the illustrations in the book, I must thank W.A.D. Glossop and Frank Hudson for the kind loan of various artefacts and catalogues; Doug Watson for lending several fine Sheffield knives; Philip Hansen for helping me track down so many obituaries; David Jenkins for information on the Harrison family; Bernard Callan for his help with the Sandersons; David Sier for making available some of the Weston Park collection; Julie MacDonald for access to the Cutlers' Company; and Margaret Oversby, who provided information on the Saynors. Finally, Sheffield City Library and Archives must be thanked for allowing me to plunder their holdings of photographs (which have been expertly copied by Cynthia Woodhouse). In fact, the Local Studies Library in Sheffield deserves special mention as an exemplar of what a local history library can and should be. Its resources are a tribute both to a socialist local authority dedicated to the ideal of public services, and to years of patient cataloguing and collecting by librarians and archivists. Writing this book would have been immensely more difficult and far less enjoyable without Sheffield Library's resources and the help of Sylvia Pybus, Doug Hindmarch, Mike Spick, Alison Cooper, Pat Clark, Helen Askham, Maureen Bailey, Sue Hulse and Sue Linton. Finally, Pauline Climpson and her staff at the Hallamshire Press ensured that the book moved smoothly through to publication.

Geoff Tweedale
Manchester 1995

Part One

The Rise and Fall
of
Knife City

1

Prologue

THE HEYDAY of the Sheffield knife industry was in the nineteenth-century. During this period—covering almost a hundred years from the end of the Napoleonic Wars in 1815 to the outbreak of the First World War—the city's cutlers produced some of the finest knives ever made. To be sure, there have been other 'golden ages' of cutlery manufacture in medieval England and on the Continent of Europe. However, it seems safe to say that no other cutlery centre (either before or since) has ever been able to match Sheffield in the range, volume, quality and craftsmanship of the knives it produced.

What brought this unique industry into being? Whatever it was must have had very ancient roots, for even by the nineteenth century, Sheffield cutlery manufacture had a history that went back hundreds of years. As one industrial reporter stated in about 1880:

> Sheffield has been so completely identified with the cutlery manufacture during a time which, as the law books have it, 'the memory of man runneth not to the contrary', that no account of the trade itself would be acceptable which did not include a considerable reference to its ancient locality. It is one of those cases, in which, from

View of Sheffield by William Ibbitt in the 1850s. The Sheffield cutlery industry was then the largest in the world and also one of the oldest.

long association of ideas, the place and its productions seem to couple themselves naturally in our minds, and cannot be separated. Nottingham lace, Staffordshire pottery, Manchester cottons, Kidderminster carpets, Coventry ribbons, and many other specialities of the same kind, down to Burton ale and Cheshire cheese, are 'familiar in our mouths as household words', but Sheffield cutlery is the oldest and most familiar of them all.

Knives were undoubtedly made in the Sheffield region well before written records began: or as the local chronicler, Joseph Hunter, put it, 'in the mists of antiquity'. The first documentary evidence actually linking Sheffield with cutlery manufacture dates from 1297, when a cutler surfaced in the local tax returns. Almost fifty years later a Sheffield knife was amongst the King's possessions at the Tower of London. Thereafter, Sheffield and knives are linked in several medieval documents and books, though the references are scattered and rarely supply any details. Geoffrey Chaucer's description of his miller of Trumpington in *The Reeve's Tale*, mentions a 'Sheffield thwitel' (or whittle) a straight, wooden-handled knife carried in a waist-belt. Chaucer's words have been cited so often in books about Sheffield that they have almost been worn out by overuse. However, they do show that Sheffield knives were beginning to edge their way into the national consciousness.

By Tudor times, the Sheffield region was certainly gaining a reputation as a centre for knife production. In about 1540, the topographer John Leland remarked on the 'many smithes and cuttelars' there. In 1590, one writer described 'women's wittes' as being like Sheffield knives: 'for they are sometimes so keene they will cut a haire, and sometimes so blunt they must goe toe a grindstone'. Peter Bales, the author of *The Writing Schoolmaster* (1590), claimed that 'a right Sheffield knife [was] best for cutting quills', and in doing so made one of the first allusions to Sheffield's reputation for quality. Besides these literary sources, archaeologists, sifting through the mud on the banks of the Thames in London, have recovered a number of Sheffield knives dating back to the fourteenth century. Some of these finds are now in

Cutlers' Hall. One notable knife, probably made by Sheffield cutler Jonathan Creswick in about 1630, demonstrates a growing mastery in metalworking and bone carving that shows how much the industry was developing.

However, the knife industry around Sheffield was certainly a very small one. Moreover, it also had competitors, both at home and overseas. London cutlers had been manufacturing knives since at least the twelfth century and had soon established a guild for their cutlery industry. It was the dominant English centre for knife manufacture in the Middle Ages and beyond. Cutlery manufacture also existed as a distinct and significant trade in several other places, such as Salisbury, Thaxted (Essex), York and Birmingham. Abroad, continental cutlers probably surpassed the efforts of any English centre both in material and workmanship. France was one of the foremost cutlery nations and its knife manufacturers in Paris, Thiers, Nogent, Langres and Chatellerault were at least as long-established as those in Sheffield. The German cutlery industry around Solingen was not quite so old—it seems to have begun in the fourteenth century—but it organised rapidly and by the sixteenth century goods of the highest quality and workmanship were being produced there.

The prospect of Sheffield ever overtaking any of these competitors would have seemed a distant one up to the early 1700s, though the cutlery trades continued to expand in Hallamshire (the ancient district containing Sheffield). After operating for a time under the lords of the manor, in 1624 a craft guild, the Company of Cutlers, was formed to govern the industry. It admitted freemen, controlled apprenticeship, issued marks, and had the power to check that goods were made to the required standard. When the Company was formed about 500 names were on its register, which meant that only London and possibly York surpassed Sheffield in cutlery manufacture. On its formation, the Cutlers' Company claimed—accurately, enough—that Hallamshire supplied 'most parts of this kingdom' and also 'foreign countries'. On the other hand, the technology of knifemaking was primitive. It was very much a cottage industry (in fact, some of the

The Great Mark Book, Cutlers' Hall. The Company of Cutlers has a continuous run of trade mark registers from 1614, attesting to the industry's ancient roots.

Water power was a vital asset to the emerging knife industry. At Kelham Island, Sheffield's main waterway, the River Don, passes over a weir close to James Dixon's Works.

region's cutlers practised their craft in outlying rural areas). Knife blades were forged in smithies that were often in out-buildings and lean-tos. With only a hearth and bellows, a 'stithy and stock' (an anvil on top of an oak stump let into the ground), and a trough for hardening and tempering, the Hallamshire cutler forged his blades with only a few simple tongs and hammers. Even had the output from these forges been greater, it looked doubtful whether Sheffield would ever be able to market large volumes of knives. The reason: it was one of the least accessible towns in England. Even in the nineteenth century, travellers spoke of Sheffield as being 'embosomed in a range of lofty hills and moorlands . . . nestling in a hollow, its coverlid of black smoke resting closely upon it and around it'. How could such an isolated place become the leading knifemaker in the world by the nineteenth century?

A number of factors made this possible: the region's natural advantages; inspired innovations in metal manufacture; the skills of its workers; new forms of industrial organisation; and the growth and exploitation of domestic and overseas markets.

As the demand for knives began to grow in the eighteenth century, Sheffield had one great advantage not possessed by its provincial rivals, such as Salisbury and Thaxted: the availability of water-power and suitable sandstones for grinding. Sheffield, a town built at the confluence of several rivers and brooks (the Don, Rivelin, Loxley, Porter and Sheaf) and surrounded by hills, could hardly have been better situated in an age of water-power. Its rivers and their tributaries were not major waterways, but this was an advantage as it meant they could be dammed easily and at frequent intervals. Soon the Sheffield region became the most intensive user of water power in the country, perhaps in Europe. By 1740, roughly 90 mills had been built in the area, two-thirds of them for grinding; by about 1850, the number of mills was well over a hundred. These mills could operate grindstones, forge-hammers and rolling mills and were a vital foundation for knife manufacture. The Peak Moors that provided some of the water for these mills also yielded another important raw material—sandstone for the

grinding wheels. This sandstone could even be mined on the fringes of Sheffield itself at places such as Brincliffe Edge.

Coal to operate the forges and ironworks was also available nearby. Iron (and later steel) was the knifemaker's most important raw material and its manufacture had long been established in the region. We know that in 1160, monks in Lincolnshire had erected forges to the north of Sheffield. Cutlery, and the future steel industry, were therefore linked with the rise of charcoal iron manufacture, which nurtured skills in smelting, forging and the use of water power. In steelmaking itself, Sheffield learned to walk before it could run, since in the beginning, strange to say, the town did not make steel. That was imported. Then after 1650, Sheffield began copying a method that was in use elsewhere— cementation—which produced 'blister' steel. This was usually Swedish iron, carbonised in charcoal in conical structures (rather like pottery kilns) that were known as cementation furnaces. By the mid-nineteenth century, over 200 of these furnaces were dotted over the Sheffield industrial landscape. After the iron had been cooked for a week in charcoal, it was 'converted' into a crude type of steel: the curious blisters that formed on the bars giving the product its name.

Forge welded (or 'fagotted'), these bars could be made into 'shear' steel. This helped diffuse the carbon in the bars (since the take-up of carbon from the charcoal during cementation was not very even) and produced a steel with superb cutting properties—the slag inclusions providing microscopic serations on the edge. Shear steel became legendary for its sharpness.

As Sheffield's technological mastery of iron and steel manufacture slowly began to unfold, knife-making itself became a more specialised and skilled occupation. The small-scale (sometimes rural) nature of the industry had provided a great springboard. In the early days of knife manufacture, cutlers needed to be all-rounders, able to forge, grind and assemble an article from start to finish. These were 'the ancient Hallamshire cutlers', who, in the nineteenth century, were to assume an almost folkloric status—the kind of craftsmen who prided themselves that they could go into a workshop and go through all the processes themselves. They developed a virtuosity that began to raise the quality of Sheffield knives above the ordinary. In the beginning, Sheffield had a reputation for providing the cheaper qualities of cutlery, leaving the kudos of producing for the high-quality market to Londoners. But Hallamshire cutlers soon began invading the top end of the knife market by starting to work with precious metals, such as gold and silver, and expensive hafting materials, like ivory. The records of the Cutlers' Company in 1625 show that local knives worth five shillings or more had to be damasked, inlaid or studded with nothing less than sterling silver; while the Company records and parish registers show a number of specialist goldbeaters and silversmiths. By the eighteenth century, Sheffield was already showing signs of the expertise in working metals that would allow it, after the 1740s, to dominate not only the manufacture of steel and knives, but also plated silver manufacture.

Linked with these growing skills was the expansion of the multitude of industries that orbited around knifemaking (and steel manufacture). Scissorsmiths and shearsmiths were active in the Sheffield area by the early seventeenth century; so too were filesmiths, nailmakers, forkmakers and razormakers; and buttonmaking had also appeared as a sideline for the cutlers. The manufacture of small metal boxes for tobacco, snuff and trinkets had begun as a specialist craft by the late seventeenth century. This spread of related trades continued to grow, so that by the end of the eighteenth century, makers of, *inter alia*, saws, anvils, lancets, household metalware and many other cutlery products could be found in Sheffield directories; for by then, many of these trades were entirely town-based. This was a crucial transformation, because as knifemaking became more sophisticated it needed the help of pearl, ivory, and horn suppliers and cutters for handle materials; it needed acid etchers to decorate

the blades; mark makers to provide the punches to stamp them; buffers to polish them; paper manufacturers and case-makers to package goods; glassmakers to supply crystals for silverware, and so on. As these trades slowly concentrated and expanded in the town, the knife industry was able to operate on the principle of the division of labour. Sheffield became, as one Victorian industrial correspondent put it in 1844, 'one great workshop for the production of cutlery and edge-tools—a huge factory which scatters its separate departments in different parts of the town, but still retains them all, like so many links in a chain'. This form of industrial organisation, operating through so many different skilled industries within such a small locality, was to give Sheffield enormous economic strength over its rivals.

Communications with the outside world were improving, too. By 1826, the River Don was made navigable as far as Tinsley, improving links with the capital, and through it with overseas markets. It also gave better access to the supplies of Swedish iron ore. Not that Sheffield's isolated situation had prevented its cutlers from selling their wares far afield. During the seventeenth century, the marketing of Sheffield cutlery was launched through wholesalers and merchants in London, Liverpool and Hull, who were supplied by Hallamshire chapmen, hardwaremen and factors. No one in Sheffield then described themselves as a merchant. However, the substantial growth in the cutlery trades in the eighteenth century triggered a search for new markets. Sheffield's own merchants and factors appeared—the Shores, Broadbents and Roebucks—who began trading directly with the Continent and even the American colonies.

The result of all these changes was that by about 1740, the Sheffield knife industry was poised to take full advantage of a technical innovation provided by an obscure Doncaster clockmaker.

Teeming crucible steel at Thos Turner's, c. 1900.

Crucible melting hole at Abbeydale Industrial Hamlet.

2

Crucible Steel and Knifemaking up to 1860

USUALLY THE STEEL in an old Sheffield knife hardly concerns most people who handle or collect old knives. That is a pity, for every time we pick up an old Sheffield knife, we are holding not only a cutlery antique, but also a piece of steelmaking history that is every bit as interesting as the knife itself. In fact, the type of steel, its temper and durability were the first considerations of nineteenth-century knife users. How would the steel cut? How long would it hold its edge? How much resharpening would it take? These were the questions that were uppermost in their minds, and it was Sheffield's ability to satisfy knife-users in this respect, by supplying the world's best steel, that was at least as important as the skill of its cutlers.

As we have already stated, the first steel Sheffield used for its knives was imported, though slowly the town began to make its own material by the cementation process from imported iron. But by the early 1740s, Sheffield was ready to take a big leap forward, with the work of Benjamin Huntsman (1707–1776), a Quaker clockmaker from nearby Doncaster. In about the 1730s, Huntsman was a man with a problem: how could he make a more satisfactory and uniform material for his clock springs than his customary blister steel? Remember such steel contained slag, which made it unreliable in such critical applications. By the 1740s, when he had moved to Sheffield, Huntsman found a brilliant answer. Like most great ideas, it was surprisingly simple. Why not, he thought, break up blister steel and melt the pieces in a clay pot (a crucible). Liquefy it, in other words, so releasing the slag (which could be skimmed off), thoroughly mixing the carbon, and allowing the

metal to be poured into a mould. When he did this, Huntsman produced the world's first steel ingot and discovered the ideal product for knives (and edge-tools). Huntsman's crucible steel (which was also, incidentally, often called 'cast steel') gave Sheffield the chance to lead the world in steel (and knife) manufacture for more than a century.

A crucible steel furnace, the only one in the world, can still be seen at Abbeydale Industrial Hamlet, an industrial museum on the outskirts of Sheffield. The furnace, in the corner of the Hamlet, is a somewhat nondescript stone building, not much bigger than a small stable. The interior contains a row of holes cut into the stone floor against the far wall; some shelves supporting a number of large, white clay pots; and several odd-looking implements: a large rusty funnel, some long pairs of tongs, a narrow iron receptacle standing upright in the floor and held together by rings and wedges, some old steel ingots, a broom and pan. It is not an impressive scene.

Do not be misled. Making crucible steel was a far from simple operation. Like making knives, the job took years to learn and the skills were in the *hands* and *eyes* of the furnacemen. The boss was the head melter, who could 'read' the carbon in the steel simply by looking at the crystalline fracture of an ingot. He was backed up by, amongst others, the 'puller-out' of the crucible from the fire-hole; and the potmakers, who mixed the clay for the crucibles by treading it for hours with their bare feet. This is not to forget the cellar-lads, who helped beneath the furnaces and fetched one of the most important raw materials for the process—beer, from the pub outside the factory gates.

Watching crucible steel being teemed (a procedure that could still be seen in Sheffield as late as 1972) must have been fascinating. The scene at Thos Turner's (shown in the photograph) is described as follows in the company's own words:

> The two chief men employed—the head-melter, or teemer, and the puller-out—will have each assumed leggings and apron, made of layers of sacking saturated with water, and each will have on the right hand a bag, also of wet sacking, which serves the purposes of a large glove. The puller-out slips aside the top of the furnace, plunges his tongs into the fiery recess, and, with no little dexterity, raises the crucible and deposits the glowing mass on the iron floor. Should his apron happen to catch the crucible it bursts into flames, but these are readily extinguished by a few pats with the wet sacking covering the right hand. Meanwhile, the head melter will have seized the crucible with another pair of tongs, and then there is a sight which is worth going to Sheffield to see. The lid having been removed, the teemer raises the crucible to the height of the mould in which the ingot is to be made, and proceeds to pour in the molten metal. The appearance of the inside of the crucible at this moment can be compared only with that of the fiercest suns. The glow is intense, the heat is felt all over the room, while as the crucible is tilted over the mould there comes from it a stream of what has been described aptly as 'liquid sunlight'
>
> No less striking, however, than the glow of the metal is the pose of the teemer, by whom the operation is performed... The crucible weighs 27lbs, its contents about 56lbs, and tongs 19lbs. All this he must raise and have under such perfect control that, notwithstanding the weight and intense heat, he can pour the molten metal into the mould—which produces an ingot 3-in. square and 30-in long—so that none of the metal will touch the sides until it reaches the bottom of the mould. Should the sides be touched first, the metal would instantly 'set' where it touched, and there would be serious flaws in the ingot. So the stream of 'liquid sunlight', scattering its showers or sparks all around, must flow in an absolutely even and constant stream in the exact centre of that three square-inches of space, until the contents of the crucible have been entirely transferred to the mould.

Little wonder that such men soon came to acquire an aura of glamour. One is struck by how long the process took—over a week to make the blister steel alone, to say nothing of the melting operations and the forging into bars or rods. Only then did crucible steel arrive in the hands of the blade forgers, grinders and cutlers. At first they seem to have taken a dislike to the product, which in the forge and on the grinding wheel was so unlike the older shear steel. In fact, it was the French who were one of the biggest customers for crucible steel in the 1770s. But after their initial conservative reaction, Sheffield cutlers, too, soon began to appreciate crucible steel's finer qualities. The product gave almost as fine an edge as the legendary shear steel, but it was much more uniform, because it did not contain slag. This made it far more robust and it could be used for tools as well as blades. It was ideal, in fact, for the heavy duty Bowie knives and sport's-knives in which Sheffield was later to excel. Corkscrews, punches, saws and screwdrivers could now be added to knives and serve as useful tools.

Sheffield's cutlery craftsmen swore by crucible steel, especially when it was hand-forged. Sometimes the quality was variable. After all, there was no science of metallurgy in the nineteenth century. Modern chemical analysis, however, shows that most crucible steel was remarkably 'clean'—a tribute to the purity of the base material, the top-quality Swedish iron, which Sheffield crucible steelmakers used religiously. Analysis of surviving knife blades has shown that the old craftsmen also achieved a wonderful accuracy in their judgement of carbon content—all done without pyrometers or any technical aids. Each class of cutlery had its own temper. The range for blister and crucible steels would be as follows:

	Carbon %
Shear-steel table-blades	0.08/0.95
Shear-steel carvers	0.80/0.95
Cast-steel table-carvers	0.08/0.95
Cast-steel carvers	0.80/0.95
Ordinary-steel table-knives	0.45/0.50
Ordinary-steel carvers	0.45/0.50
Cast-steel pocket-knives	0.80/1.00
Cast-steel razors	1.40/1.50

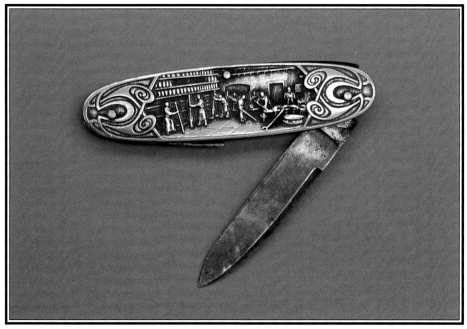

A pocket-knife illustrating, appropriately, the manufacture of the material from which its blades are made—crucible steel. (Weston Park Museum).

Sheffield cutlery firms would usually buy crucible steel in rods from the steelmakers, ready for forging into blades of various sizes. In the nineteenth century some crucible steelmakers specialised in cutlery steel. These included William Jessop & Sons, S. & C. Wardlow and Kayser, Ellison & Co. We know that certain prominent cutlers favoured a particular steelmaker. George Wostenholm, for example, often bought steel from Thos Firth, one of the most famous names in Sheffield steel. So important was the quality of the steel to some cutlery manufacturers, however, that they began making it themselves. Thos Turner, for example, melted its own steel at its Suffolk Works. Joseph Rodgers also eventually made its own crucible steel in the late nineteenth century.

Huntsman's technological breakthrough went hand in hand with the growth of Sheffield's export markets and the steady increase of the home trade. At home, a growing industrial (but still mainly agricultural) society was demanding increasing quantities of fixed-blade knives for its crafts and industries and greater varieties of pocket-knives. Abroad, America was emerging as the major market (its development is considered in a separate section), but Sheffield knives were also in demand in Spain, Portugal, South America and in other countries of the world. Merchants competed with each other to supply these booming markets. In the first decade of the nineteenth century, it was estimated that one half of Sheffield's cutlery output was sent overseas.

Periods of unprecedented activity, however, such as in 1809–10, invariably gave way to slump. War, speculative ventures by merchants, the fluctuations of foreign currencies and markets, even the seasons, caused a boom and bust syndrome (or 'hunger and burst system', as contemporaries described it) to develop. The post-war boom after the ending of the Napoleonic war in 1815, which saw a spectacular rush of knives to America, was soon followed by a slump in 1818; or as Joseph Hunter put it, 'glut, dismay and disaster'. Trade ground to a standstill and many workers were

SHOE KNIVES

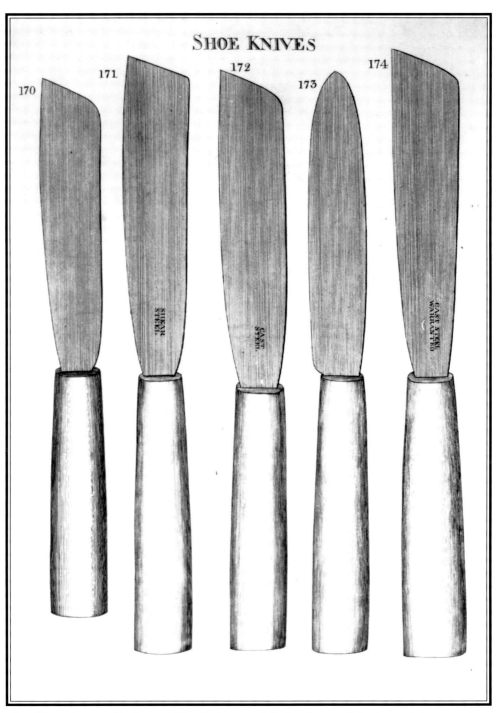

Crucible steel was an ideal material for blades, especially for those made for heavy-duty use, such as these early 19th-century Sheffield shoe-knives. 'Cast Steel Warranted' was often stamped on such knives as a mark of extra quality.

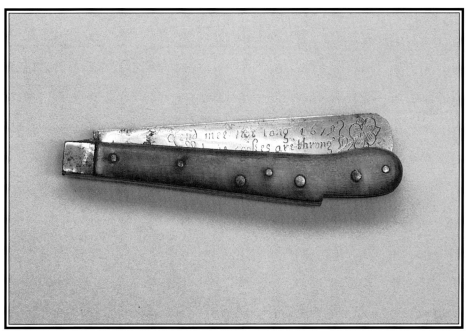

Folding knife by Thomas Wilson (1679), with the following advice inscribed on the blade:
Let mee not long/wher cookes are throng. *(Weston Park Museum).*

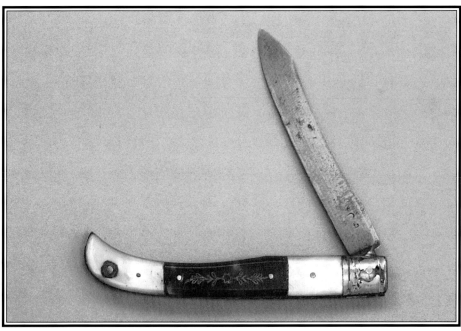

An early folding-knife (c. 1760), probably made by Edward Steel,
showing the growing skills of the 18th-century cutler. (Weston Park Museum).

thrown onto poor relief. Trade picked up again after 1820, but then there was another speculative trade boom in 1825, followed by almost continuous depression for six years. Overseas demand, especially from America, greatly improved matters from 1832. Cutlery manufacture began expanding again, until what the *Sheffield Iris* described as 'the glorious year of prosperity 1835'. Cutlery manufacture, however, remained a highly irregular business over the next decade and by the early 1840s destitution was once more widespread amongst Sheffield workers.

Gradually, after the 1840s, these cycles stabilised and in the 1850s prosperity had returned to the cutlery trades. Anyway, the ebb and flow of trade made little difference to the general trend of cutlery output and numbers employed. Both were steadily upward. The value of Sheffield exports of cutlery rose from about £2 million in 1835 to over £3 million in 1840.

Unfortunately, no statistics are available on the growth of Sheffield's knife industry: we have no means of knowing how many knives the town produced; nor do we have accurate figures until the mid-nineteenth century of how many knifemakers worked in Sheffield. However, trade directories do survive. These are far from perfect sources, since they were not always very reliable and makers could be enumerated in several categories. However, they can be used to tell the story in broad outline.

The 1787 Sheffield trade directory has a classified listing of knifemakers in and around the town. It enumerates:

Pen- and pocket-knife makers	96
Common pocket- and penknives	148
Spotted-knives	76
Stamped brass, white metal and metal-framed knives	38
Table-knives	71

A Sheffield directory for 1849 shows a substantial increase in these figures and some new specialisations can be seen emerging:

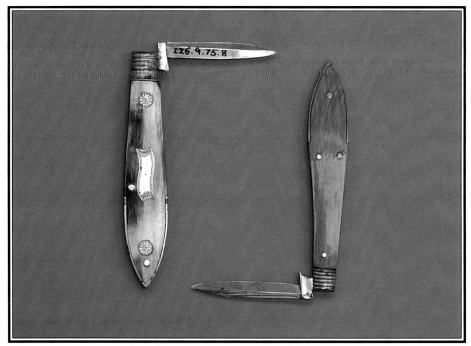

Two pen-knives by Joseph Rodgers (1775). Crucible steel allowed the production of fine, sharp and durable blades for cutting quills. (Weston Park Museum).

Pen- and pocket-knives	328
Shoe-, butcher's-, bread-, and cook's-knives	36
Silver-, fruit-, and dessert-knives	27
Table-knives	200

Detailed statistics on the number of knifemakers employed in Sheffield are not available until well into the nineteenth century, but one source (Thomas Allen's, *A New and Complete History of the County of Yorkshire*) gives the following statistics for the late 1820s: 2,240 table-knifemakers; and 2,190 spring-knifemakers. Some 2,000 workers were also involved in the plated trade. By 1851, another source states that the numbers in the table- and butchers'-knife trade had increased to 3,750; and in the spring-knife trade to 4,000. By the mid-nineteenth century, Sheffield had the largest group of cutlers in the world, easily surpassing all other centres of knife production.

Amongst the multitude of little mesters, some leading knifemakers were beginning to emerge. The industry remained a handicraft, but nevertheless there were some advantages in having large groups of workers in one location. Joseph Rodgers & Sons typified the change: before 1800, this business had operated in a traditionally small way in a backstreet in the town centre; by 1850, it had moved to the Norfolk Works and employed well over 500 workers. Meanwhile, George Wostenholm, a cutler from equally humble roots, had launched the Washington Works in 1848. His workforce, too, numbered in the hundreds by the 1850s. Mappin's Queen's Cutlery Works and James Dixon's Cornish Place Works were equally prominent establishments. By now, these firms had an international reputation, especially in the USA.

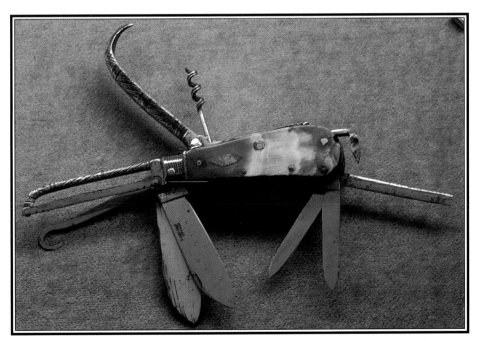

Early 19th-century horseman's knife by Joseph Rodgers, demonstrating Sheffield's rapid progress in the making of multi-blade knives. (Weston Park Museum).

*By the 1850s, Joseph Rodgers' Norfolk Works had become easily the largest
cutlery factory in the world.*

*Invoice for a cutlery business in Orchard Street, 1838. The owner was (Sir) John Brown,
who used cutlery as a springboard for a world-famous steel business.*

3

Sheffield and America

THERE WAS an inevitability about the growth of the nineteenth-century Sheffield knife industry (just as there was a certain inevitability about its decline a century later). The town had a stranglehold on the manufacture of crucible steel until at least the 1850s; its natural advantages, the availability of water-power and grindstones, were great; and it had a resourceful and very hard-working band of knifemakers. These factors alone ensured a successful future for the Sheffield cutlery industry from the 1830s.

However, Sheffield did not just grow modestly in the early years of the nineteenth century: it grew spectacularly. The population of Sheffield Parish grew from 62,275 in 1821, to 91,692 in 1831, then to 111,091 in 1841. Contemporaries knew why. Wrote a local worthy, Arthur Gatty, in *Sheffield: Past and Present* (1873): 'Nothing can account for the sustained prosperity of Sheffield, and the very large increase of its population from 1821 to 1831… except the American demand'.

The development of Sheffield's American trade, in both knives and steel, soon overshadowed its business with other countries before the 1850s. Indeed, in some years exports to the New World eclipsed even those to the domestic market. In certain periods, it is not too much to suggest that Sheffield industry revolved around America.

This Anglo-American connection, though now long forgotten, should not be that surprising. Whilst Sheffield was perfecting its knife industry, America was an undeveloped country, but it soon began growing with remarkable rapidity and offered a huge potential market. The country's population grew from 9.6 million in 1820 to over 23

million in 1850. Since the Americans had neither the knowledge nor the skilled workers (in those days they amounted to the same thing) to produce cutlery for themselves, it was inevitable that they should seek to buy their knives from Sheffield. The American settler and frontiersman had plenty of uses for a good knife—and so too did the native American!

Sheffield cutlers seized eagerly on the opportunities offered by this market. In some ways it was their finest hour. Despite their town's isolation and despite the difficulties of journeying to America at that time (a sea voyage could take weeks and a safe arrival was never guaranteed), some Sheffield cutlers became almost as well known in New York as they were at home.

No one knows when the American link began, but by time of the American War of Independence it had already acquired considerable significance. The War was said to have 'created much alarm in the town', especially amongst Sheffield merchants and factors who had opened up a trade with the east coast of America since the 1760s. America's new-found independence, however, did not bring economic self-sufficiency. By the start of the nineteenth century, its trade with Sheffield was growing again. A third of the town's manufactured goods were said to be going to America and a third of the town's working population of 18,000 was apparently involved in the American trade.

The Napoleonic War was again bad for business, but when hostilities ended in 1815 a boom period began as American industrialisation began. In the 1820s and 1830s, although there were periodic slumps and setbacks, the trend in Sheffield's

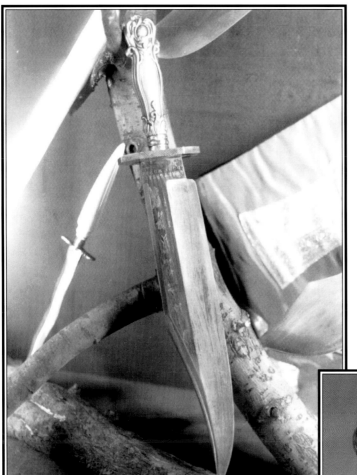

Massive Bowie knife made by John Walters' Globe Works in about the mid 19th century. Handle and blade are about 20 inches long. The trade marks on the blade are described on page 287.

Close-up of the handle of the Walters' Bowie knife. (Cutlers' Hall).

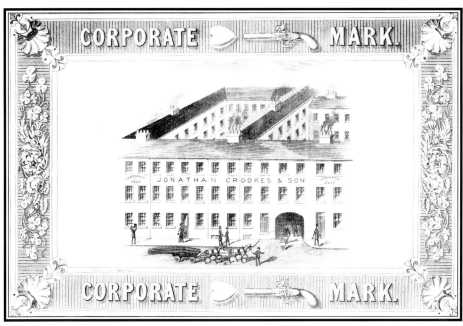

Jonathan Crookes was one of the first Sheffield knifemakers to exploit the American market.

American trade was firmly upward. William Cobbett noted sanguinely in his *Rural Rides* (1830) that Sheffield knife manufacture was one sector of British trade where there was 'no fear of rival-ship…[since]…as long as [the Americans] continue to cut their victuals, from Sheffield they must have the things to cut it with'. He added: 'If the people of Sheffield could only receive a tenth part of what their knives sell for by retail in America, Sheffield might pave its streets with silver'. Even so, almost all the successful Sheffield knifemakers in this period, Greaves, Butcher, Mappin, Dixon, Marsh, Turner, Wostenholm, Rodgers, Sanderson, and J. Crookes, made large fortunes in the trade. Soon the south Manhattan hardware district of New York was home to a growing number of Sheffield repre-sentatives of these leading houses. Often a leading partner of a firm resided permanently in America; later the biggest Sheffield firms recruited their own American agents and often had their own offices.

The dramatic growth of this trade was exempli-fied by William Greaves & Sons, manufacturers and traders in all types of cutlery and steel. A self-styled American merchanting house, Greaves used the profits of the transatlantic business to build the Sheaf Works in 1823—regarded by contempo-raries as the first custom-built centralised factory in Sheffield. According to Gatty, when it was in full operation in 1826, 'it gave a new impulse to the system of our local manufacture'. Other factories flourished on American orders: though less grand, they still looked across the Atlantic for their orders and their names proudly announced the fact: Atlantic Works, Boston Works, Manhattan Works, America Works, Brooklyn Works, and Washington Works. The latter, launched by George Wostenholm, grew into one of the biggest knife factories in Sheffield almost entirely on the back of the American trade.

What type of knives did Sheffield export to America before the Civil War? No official statistics exist to tell us in detail, though surviving knives in museums and in the hands of collectors provide some clues, as do comments in the few available written records. Table-knives obviously figured largely in Sheffield's shipments to America, with firms such as Sanderson and Marsh Bros sending large quantities. Kitchen- and butchers'-knives

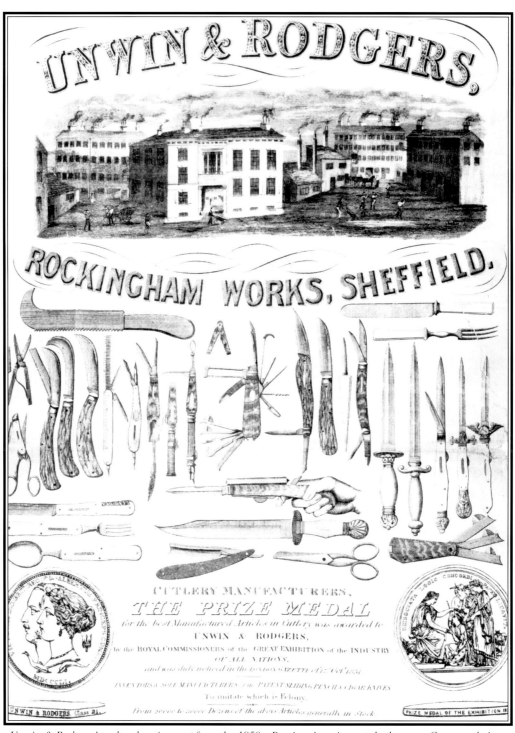

Unwin & Rodgers' trade advertisement from the 1850s. Bowies, American-style daggers, Congress knives and the self-defence pistol-knife show the US market dominating Sheffield output at this time.

were also much in demand, supplied by makers such as John Wilson. Tools such as shoe-knives, farriers'-knives, oyster-knives, and palette-knives were needed for a whole range of jobs in the New World. On the American frontier, the term 'trade-knife' had other connotations: it could refer to the knives traded (bartered) to the American Indians. Often these were Sheffield knives: some no more than ordinary butchers'- or kitchen-knives, which the Indians adapted to their own use; others were sold specifically by Sheffield cutlers to the fur-trading companies with the native American in mind. In the 1830s, there are recorded instances of Sheffield firms responding to the demand on the frontier for Indian scalping-knives!

The other large category of knife shipped to America was the pocket-knife. Almost all types of this knife found a ready sale in the USA after the American Revolution—from the simple Barlow (which is described later and which was exported to America from the late eighteenth century), to the most complicated sportsman's knives. No doubt, the majority of knives exported were simple folding knives, such as jack-knives, but as purchasing power grew in America, the finest qualities of multi-blade knives were sold. Many Sheffield patterns, such as the Congress knife, were directly inspired by the Americans.

Another large market in the USA was for weapons. The country came into existence through a victorious war, gained large parts of its territory through war, and was to secure its national unity through a bloody civil war—hardly surprising, then, that in the days before Colt and Winchester, America was a receptive market for all types of daggers and 'self-defence' knives. American demand in this area was to exert a profound influence on Sheffield cutlers. It led to the development of one of the most famous of all knives—the Bowie knife. Comments cutlery historian and dealer, James F. Parker: 'When you hold a Bowie you are not just holding a mere tool, but a tool and weapon that opened the [American] western frontier, and it's as much a part of the western folklore as the Peace-maker Colt or '73 Winchester. It preceded both!'.

The Bowie knife story began on 19th September 1827 on a Mississippi River sandbar near Natchez.

At what was quaintly described as 'an interview' to settle an 'affair of honour' (in other words a duel) James Bowie, a land speculator, successfully (and it is claimed heroically) defended himself with a large hunting knife made for his brother. The incident, known as the Vidalia Sandbar Fight, hit a nerve with the American public and attracted enormous popular interest, a fascination that has continued for some to this day. Soon the Bowie knife became an American craze and everyone wanted a knife like Bowie's. James Bowie's dramatic death at the Alamo in 1836 only served to fire the legend and glamour of his knife even more. The stylistic evolution of the Bowie knife is discussed in greater detail later (see chapter 5): here we will confine ourselves to the commercial development of the Bowie-knife trade.

The earliest Bowie knives were made by the American custom knifemakers of the day—blacksmiths, surgical instrument makers, and cutlers, but it was not long before Sheffield began to hear about James Bowie. No one knows when news of the sandbar incident reached Sheffield, but with the town's extensive American contacts it would not have taken long. Soon Sheffield cutlers were ready to supply the demand. The trade began to take off in the 1830s, then expanded in the 1840s, reaching a peak in the decade before the American Civil War. In fact, the English town grew to dominate the Bowie-knife trade. The reasons for its success are readily apparent. The USA had no crucible steelmakers and its cutlery industry was in its infancy. Moreover, Sheffield could draw on a large number of ancillary trades: hafters, die-stampers and acid-etchers, to embellish these new knives. It had already developed extensive marketing contacts with American buyers; and last, but not least, Sheffield craftsmen, largely because of their lower wages, were able to make knives much cheaper than American cutlers.

Who made Bowie knives in Sheffield? This is not an easy question to answer, since so little documentation has survived on the cutlery industry before 1860. Also, of course, most Sheffield Bowie knives made in the early nineteenth century were exported to America. There was, after all, little need in Yorkshire for a weapon that was designed

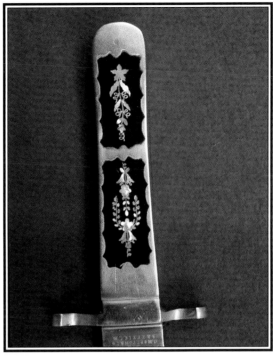

19th-century Sheffield Bowies were often notable for their craftsmanship and decorative work. Maker: J. Morlion. (Weston Park Museum).

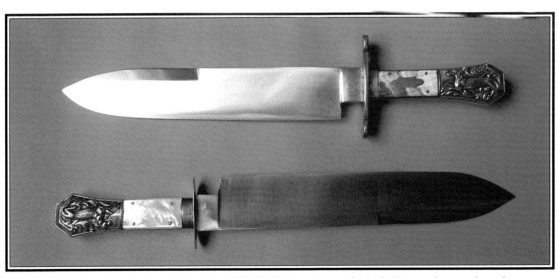

Spear-point Bowies from the heyday of Sheffield's American trade, hafted in grey horn and pearl. The makers are unfortunately unknown. (Cutlers' Hall).

for combat with desperadoes and Red Indians! Moreover, there is no separate category in Sheffield trade directories for Bowie-knife makers—it was simply just another knife at that time, and few specialists in the Bowie trade bothered advertising. However, it is possible to get some idea of the leading makers by examining surviving artefacts and simply observing which names tend to recur in private and public collections. This knowledge can sometimes be combined with information from Sheffield directories and trade advertisements.

At the risk of destroying some of the mystique of the knife, it should be stated at the outset that technically the Bowie is not a very interesting object. Bowie knives were relatively easy to make and any Sheffield cutlery firm worth its salt, especially the makers of table- and butchers'-knives, could try their hand at this line—and many did. Perhaps more important in the early days of the Bowie-knife business was a firm's ability to sell the knife: in other words, did it have the range of commercial contacts necessary to get these knives into the hands of the American customer and still make a profit? This may explain why some of the

earliest entrants to the Bowie-knife trade were firms which did merchanting as part of their business: companies such as William Greaves, Thos Turner, Thos Tillotson, W. & S. Butcher, John Walters, and Coulson, Jukes. Other Bowie knife 'makers' also seem to have been merchants, though in different cities (such as London or Birmingham) or on the other side of the Atlantic. This may account for the fact that many undoubtedly Sheffield-made Bowies before 1850 were apparently stamped by makers which cannot be traced in the local Sheffield directories. For example, the names 'Alexander' or 'Manson' or 'Gravely & Wreaks', which are stamped on some Sheffield knives of this era, are probably American import brands. Other names, such as Westa and James Rodgers ('Celebrated Sheffield Cutlery'), cannot be found in Sheffield listings, suggesting that they too were either London distributors/retailers or American importers. Further research may clear up the exact location of these knifemakers or merchants.

Nevertheless, very high-quality Bowie knives, especially those with acid-etching and fancy 'furniture', demanded a certain degree of specialisation.

The Globe Works of John Walters, one of the suppliers of Bowie knives to America before 1865.

William Butcher (c. 1791–1870), alongside his brother Samuel, was one of the town's most successful traders with America in the early nineteenth century. Bowies and razors were his speciality.

NAME	PLACE/WORKS	DATES
Edward Barnes & Sons	Wheedon Works, Edward Street	1833–1876
J. & J. Beal	Red Hill Works	1850–1950
Henry C. Booth	Norfolk Works, Norfolk Lane	1856–1876
Brookes & Crookes	Atlantic Works	1858–1957
Robert Bunting (& Son after 1852)	Regent Street	1825–1876
James Burnand	Leicester Works	1850–1930
W. & S. Butcher	Eyre Lane, Furnival Street	1725–1946
John Clarke	Harvest Lane	1848–1986
John Coe	Albion Works	1849–1888
Charles Congreve	Arundel Street	1833–1841
Jonathan Crookes	Eldon Street	1827–1914
Corsan, Denton & Burdekin	Eyre Street	1852–1862
Coulson, Jukes & Co	Change Alley/ Carver Street	1856–1868
Enoch Drabble	Bailey Street	1833–1839
Fenton & Shore	Division Street	1833–1862
Wm. Greaves & Sons	Sheaf Works	1724–1850
Samuel Hancock	Mazeppa Works	1841–1914
Ibbotson, Peace	Eagle Works, Russell Street	1845–1862
Thos Ibbotson	Charles Street	1839–1864
W.F. Jackson	Sheaf Island Works, Pond Hill	1852–1862
John Hinchcliffe	Hermitage Street	1839–1862
John Lingard (also Joseph & Robert)	Peacroft	1852–1876
Mappin Bros	Queen's Cutlery Works	1810–1903
George Nixon	Mount Pisgah	1841–1864
Joseph Rodgers & Sons	Norfolk Works	1724–1975
William Shirley	Crescent Works/ Boston Works	1860–1879
Slater Bros	Beehive Works	1858–1990
Thos Tillotson	Coalpit Lane	1825–1862
Unwin & Rodgers	Rockingham Works	1833–1910
John Walters	Globe Works	1841–1865
Wingfield, Rowbotham	Tenter Street	1825–1898
George Wostenholm	Washington Works	1745–1983
(George) Woodhead & (Joshua) Hartley	Lambert Street/ Howard Street	1841–1884
Samuel C. Wragg	Furnace Hill	1817–1852

Table 1. Sheffield Bowie Knife Makers.

So it is not surprising that a select number of firms seem to have been particularly involved with this trade. They are listed in Table 1., which gives an indication of when they were active (unfortunately, dates can only be approximate, since Sheffield trade directories were not issued annually and are far from complete anyway). It should be noted that this listing is not exhaustive: it merely attempts to show the most prominent firms who were active in the Bowie-knife trade before the 1860s.

Interestingly, it was some of the smaller Sheffield makers who first began specialising in Bowie knives and dirks for the American market. Robert Bunting, based in Regent Street by 1833, was making

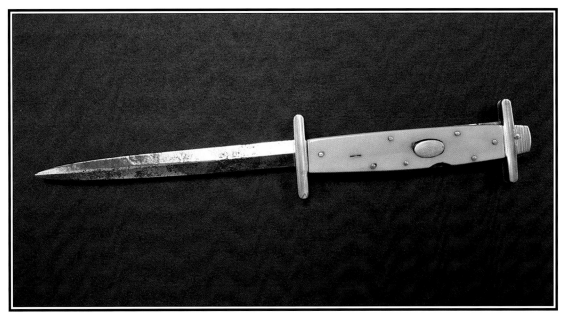

Folding dirk, with press-button in the ivory handle and locking blade. This style of 'self-defence' knife was much in demand in the USA in the early ninteenth century. Unidentified maker. (Weston Park Museum).

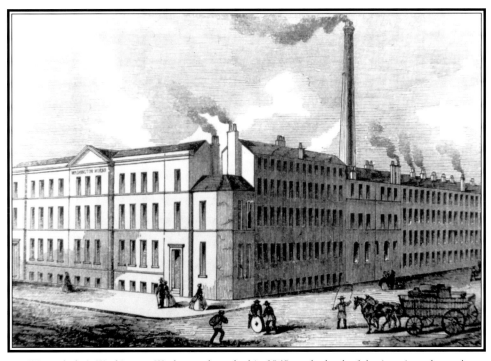

Wostenholm's Washington Works was launched in 1848 on the back of the American demand.

'Self-Defence' knives by that date. Charles Congreve, who made some of the finest folding Bowies, was active in Gell Street, also in 1833. By 1839, John Hinchcliffe, was listed in directories at 20 Earl Street as a maker of 'dagger, American, Indian, and Self-Defence Knives'. Samuel C. Wragg, who was one of the town's leading dirk makers, also seems to have been active by the 1830s. After the 1850s, as the Bowie trade reached its heyday, several other makers were describing themselves as dagger and Bowie makers: for example, Abraham Leon, H.C. Booth, William Shirley (with his 'Celebrated OIO Cutlery') and George Woodhead. An Unwin & Rodgers' trade advertisement in the 1850s shows that this firm was particularly active in the manufacture of Bowie knives: a full range of Bowies, both folding and fixed-blade, are shown. This was the maker which had the inspired idea of having the best of both worlds by combining a knife and sidearm in its patented breech-loading pistol-knife (advertised in 1839). Presumably, if the pistol failed or the shot did not kill, then the spear blade did the rest. Again, America was probably the major market for such pistol-knives. One wonders how many saloon-bar arguments in the Wild West were settled with a shot from a Sheffield pistol-knife or a lunge from one of Unwin & Rodgers' Bowie blades.

The front-runner in the early days of the Bowie-knife trade (William Butcher) was later eclipsed by the undoubted leader in the manufacture of Bowie knives—George Wostenholm. His knives, stamped I*XL, reached an unprecedented level of craftsmanship at this time and they are naturally highly valued by collectors. At an American auction in 1992 a large I*XL Bowie, made for the Centennial Exhibition in Philadelphia in 1876, fetched $120,000. Surprisingly, Joseph Rodgers does not seem to have made a special play for this market until after the 1850s, though when it chose to do so it soon made its presence felt. Joseph Rodgers' Bowies are amongst the finest made, with marvellously ground blades and superb styling.

The Bowie-knife trade reached its peak in the 1850s, as did Sheffield's crafts skills in making these knives. This was also a decade in which Sheffield's American trade reached its height. Tariffs were still at a relatively low level, the US cutlery industry was still puny compared to the mighty Sheffield firms, and Americans still needed large quantities of cutlery. For the little mesters, the 1850s was a period of almost unlimited demand from Brother Jonathan. It was a golden age.

4

Making Knives
in the Golden Age

NOW THAT we have sketched in something of Sheffield's rise as the knife capital
of the world by the 1850s, we can examine
in more detail how that success was achieved. A
discussion of Sheffield's methods of knife fabrica-
tion, the organisation of the trades, the layout of
the factories, and the attitudes of its businessmen
and workforce are crucial for an understanding of
its brilliant successes: they also say much about the
industry's later failures.

What did a visitor to Sheffield see in the mid-
nineteenth century? Perhaps it might be more
apposite to ask what they did *not* see, since almost
everyone agreed that their first impression of the
town was one of smoke. Noted one tourist (as
reported in the *Sheffield Independent*, 4th January
1871): 'Pleasantly as is the city located, covering
as many hills as Rome, the aspect of the place as
viewed from the railway bridge is by no means
attractive. A thousand tall chimneys belch forth the
thick smoke from a thousand fires, and the sun
makes an almost useless effort to penetrate the
combined vapours which settle heavy and black
upon the grimy city'. Once visitors had penetrated
the gloom, they were met by the sight of an industry in which hand-labour predominated. A trade
journalist remarked in *Great Industries of Great
Britain* (1886):

> The general conditions of the [cutlery] trade have
> altered very little within the last generation. Few
> points of novelty are presented, and no new and
> startling departures, such as have revolutionised
> other trades, have occurred in this… The visitor
> to a cutler's shop will see nothing striking or won-
> derful, only a few workmen filing, hammering,

drilling, and fitting parts together, with a deftness
and quickness which only long practice, aided by
hereditary aptitude, could give. The tools they
use are simple and old-fashioned; the shop is
meagre of all appliances and aids to labour; their
own manner shows surly independence and
reserve.

Although there were countless variations on the
theme, the manufacture of a knife followed a set
routine: forging, grinding, hafting, assembly (cutler-
ing), polishing and, finally, packing and distribution.

As we have mentioned, crucible (or shear) steel
was bought as rods or strips (less often as blanks)
and the first job was to transform this material into
the desired shape. It is important to realise that in
the early nineteenth century there was no specialised
steel available for punching, blanking out and
machining blades in large quantities. So *every*
blade was hand-forged. In scores of small workshops around Sheffield (often in backyards),
forgers would heat up the steel in their fires and
hammer it into shape. This was man's work, performed with quite rudimentary equipment. One
contemporary correspondent, Henry Palmer, gives a
good description of the blade forger's work:

> The solitary forger's hearth, discovered in a tran-
> quil thoroughfare, might at first sight be easily
> mistaken for a small stable which had suffered a
> severe gunpowder explosion, but a second
> glance reveals the simple materials required to
> produce all that is essential in a good knife—a
> rod of steel, fire, hammer, water. Such are the
> elements out of which Mr Ruskin's 'masterful'
> magician will in a few moments present you
> with a table-blade, perfect in shape and symme-
> try, hard as adamant as to edge, pliable as a cane

Forging pen-knife blades.

as to temper, and requiring only the grinder's touch and the cutler's hafting to be fit for the table. The forger's first operation is moulding ('mooding' as he calls it) or shaping, which is done before the length of blade required is severed from the strip of steel which he holds in his hand. The steel in a table knife ends at the base of the blade; at that point a small strip of wrought iron is welded to the steel, and forms what is called the bolster—that is the shoulder cap which meets the handle—and the 'tang', or tail, which runs down the centre of the haft. Every person given to after-dinner meditation must

have noticed at the base of the blade of his knife a shaded outline like a large thumb print. This mark indicates the union of the iron with the steel, a process which is called 'shooting', and is performed jointly by the forger and his assistant. The next stage is 'tanging', and consists in shaping the bolster and tang by the aid of small dies and appliances with which the anvil is fitted. The blade is now complete in shape, but has to be straightened, marked (with the manufacturer's name or other brand), hardened and tempered, the whole operation being comprehensively called 'smithing'.

Forging is one of the most difficult crafts to write about in retrospect. The job was learned rather than taught and no nineteenth century forger ever committed to paper a description of his work. Forging was also one of the first manual crafts to disappear after the Second World War and by 1980 there were only two traditional forgers left in the trade. The last working forger was George Watts at Kelham Island, who died in 1985. The forger's job was to shape the steel, and some were so skillful that in, say, the manufacture of a butcher's blade they would be able to thin the steel out towards the edge of the blade—thus reducing the work for the grinder. Without any measuring aids, they turned out thousands of blades of the required size and shape—often so accurately, that the blades could be placed against each other and show no difference. But as retired forger Bill Winfield makes plain (in his interview in Jenkins' and McClarence's book, *On the Knife Edge*), the job involved more than that. The forger put extra quality into the steel by repeatedly hammering it: 'flogging' it, until the atoms of the metal were compressed and manipulated to give an unmatched cutting edge. Some Sheffield cutlers still rate hand-forged crucible steel as the ideal material for knife blades, despite the wonders of modern steels. That opinion may be simple conservatism: on the other hand, that view, expressed by craftsmen who have been working Sheffield steels for fifty years or more, has to be respected. Certainly, there still seems to be nothing quite like an old Sheffield pen-knife or razor for cutting one's finger accidentally.

After forging, the knife blade was almost ready for the grinder. However, another procedure still needed to be completed: *hardening* and *tempering*.

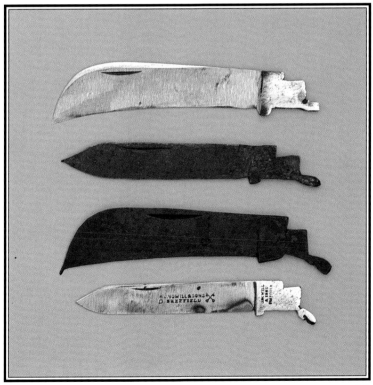

Hand-forged pocket-knife blades. Note the 'neb', projecting from the tang of the knife. It gave the forger something to grip and was later removed at the grindstone.

*Stan Shaw hardening a
blade in Paul Harding's
forge in Garden Street.
The colour of the hot
blade is used as a guide
to the correct temperature.*

This was another highly skilled operation, carried out in the forge without any measuring instruments. In hardening, the steel blade was heated to a predetermined temperature (from about 600–900°C, or 1100–1650°F), then plunged (quenched) in a bath of oil or a mixture of oil and water. The operation sounds very simple, but it was only so in the most skilled hands. The correct temperature was essential for the later quality of the knife blade; and the blade itself could warp (or 'skeller') if it was not quenched in the right way. The blade was now like glass and very brittle. Tempering allowed the blades to remain hard enough to take a cutting edge, yet restored a measure of flexibility, so that the knife was not too brittle. It was done by heating the blades slowly to a lower temperature (250–300°C, or 480–570°F) and quenching again. Contemporaries regarded the skillful execution of these processes with something approaching awe, since there was much that was mysterious about them. In fact, it seems that the forgers themselves could not always explain the scientific principles involved. For example, in the nineteenth century it was known for Sheffield cutlers setting out for the

*Stan Shaw tempering a blade by quenching it in a
bucket of oil. The process restores elasticity to the knife
blade and is another skilled job.*

New World to take barrels of local water with them because of its 'magical' properties—though it is doubtful whether it made any difference to the quality of the blades.

Now it was the turn of the grinders, glazers and buffers to transform the forged blade into an almost finished item for the cutler. The men who earned a living hunched over rapidly revolving grindstones were a special breed, even in an industry where difficult working conditions and hard labour were regarded as a fact of life. In grinding 'hulls' around the town, grinders sat astride their 'horsing', methodically working their way through piles of knife blades, holding first one then another against the stones in a shower of sparks and screech of metal. The job demanded stamina and a keen eye: one lapse of concentration could be disastrous for the fingers, and this was apart from greater dangers such as bursting stones and the problems caused by inhaling dust and steel particles. Again, grinding needed special skills and the processes were far from straightforward: in fact, there were several grinding stages. Rough grinding took out the hammer marks and scales caused by forging; whitening allowed the grinder to shape and polish the blades with greater accuracy; rough- and fine-glazing on wooden grit-covered wheels gave them their first (and sometimes final) polish; buffing (on leather-covered wooden wheels, dressed with polishing powder) gave them a high finish. The most expensive blades were given a final polish on wheels which were coated with an iron oxide (crocus): it was hard work for the polishers, but it gave the blade a finish like a mirror.

Rowland Swinden, almost the last hand-grinder working in Sheffield in the early 1990s, once described to me some of the intricacies of his job—the technicalities of which had not changed for centuries:

> Anybody can soon learn how to do a bit of grinding and put an edge on a blade, but the trick is getting a quality finish, with no bumps and irregularities on the blade. I've always said that most people could grind a blade, but could they grind

Pocket-knife grinding at Needham, Veall & Tyzack's Eye Witness Works.

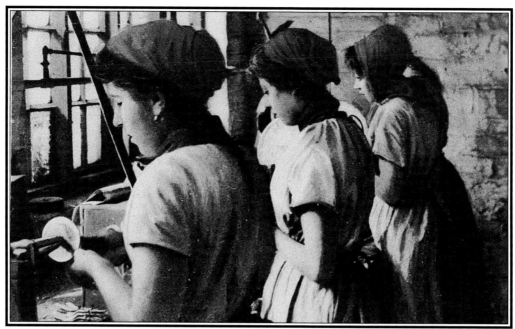

The Sheffield cutlery industry depended upon a vast army of female workers, especially in the buffing trades, in which a knife (or other cutlery product) would be given its final high polish.

it at a price where you could've earned a living? See, in the old days, they never wanted to pay any money. If you didn't do the work, somebody else would—a little bit cheaper. You had to be quick.

Grinders had to work to very close tolerances, especially in pocket-knife grinding, where sloppy work could make things difficult for the next man down the manufacturing line. Rowland stresses the problems involved:

I was a couple of years doing roughing out before I was allowed to finish a blade. And it is difficult. A blade's forged and on the edge it's left at about anything from $1/16$th to $1/8$th of an inch thick, and that's got to be taken down so that it'll take an edge and hold an edge. So there's very little difference between getting it too thin (or thick) and having it just right. Bear in mind that when I grind, I don't put the final edge on: I take it down to a thin edge, so that it's got to be glazed, it's got to be polished (which will take a little bit more off), and you've got to have the experience to know that by the time that other work's been done, it will then go on the whetstone and hold an edge. And remember that the blades are all different shapes and you can make a mess of one by not putting a flat side on it. You've got to have a nice, flat finish on the grinding for appearance.

Ground and polished, the blades were now ready for the 'cutler'—the craftsmen who did the final processes on a knife. For table-knives, one of the main finishing procedures was fitting the handle ('hafting'). The extraordinary variation in knife-handle shapes and in the hafting materials used, meant that this section of the cutlery trades is not easily described. Handles could be made from rosewood, cocobolo, horn, stag, bone, ivory, mother-of-pearl, porcelain, metal and silver. Sambar stag, the outer covering from the shed antlers of Indian deer, was one of the most popular materials in Sheffield. In 1887, it was estimated that 72,000 stag handles and scales were produced weekly for the spring-knife and table-knife trades. Buffalo horn was another popular material, which made attractive and durable knife handles. For the most

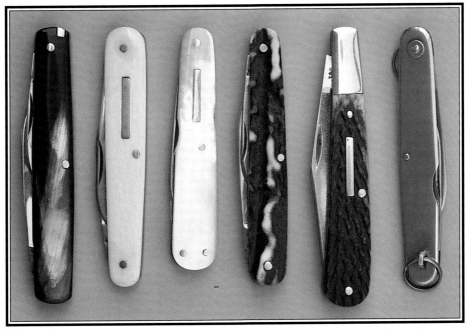

Pocket-knife hafting (handle) materials. Left to right: buffalo horn; ivory; pearl; genuine stag; bone (jigged and coloured to look like stag); metal (sometimes known as 'engine-turned').

expensive knives, ivory, mother-of-pearl, and tortoiseshell were commonly used. The cutting of these materials constituted an industry in its own right in the town. Firms specialised in, say, horn cutting or pearl cutting. Both were skilled occupations, industries within industries, as necessary to the knife trade as the steelmakers and forgers.

Even when the horn was carted to the cutler, there was still a good deal of work left to do. Natural materials are not a standard size like plastics (which at this time had made no inroads into the industry): they were all shapes, in fact, and one of the jobs the cutler had to do before he pinned it to a knife was to flatten the covering material, pull it straight and scrape it so that it fitted snugly to the inner scale. Stag and some other natural materials (such as tortoiseshell) needed boiling to soften them before manipulation. Then the scale would have to be pinned before the handle tried to resume its normal shape.

Pinning the handle to the inner scales called for a special tool—a fiddle drill (also known as a

Cutting elephant tusks at Joseph Rodgers in the 1840s.

Rodgers' legendary ivory store at the Norfolk Works.

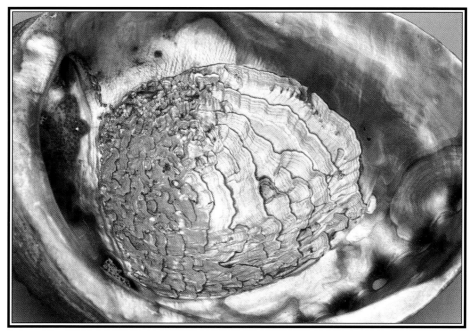

Abalone shell. An attractive hafting material, abalone is rarely used because of its expense and the difficulty in shaping it. The shell is very fragile and skilled hands are required to pin it to a knife.

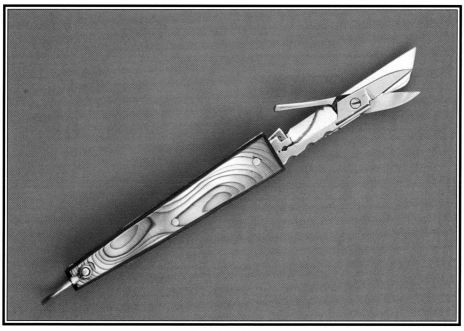

Manicure-knife with abalone handle. Maker, Stan Shaw.

One of the most traditional of the cutler's tools is the parser. The technique, which is ideally
suited to drilling delicate materials (such as pearl), is now almost extinct. The two-legged parser
routs out a shield-hole (nameplate) in the handle of a pocket-knife, using the various templates.

parser). This consisted of a boring stick with a
leather bow, a breastplate, and a bobbin-drill. By
wrapping the leather thongs around the bobbin,
and inserting the other end in his breastplate for
support, the cutler could 'whip' the tool like a
child's top and rapidly drill holes for the rivets. An
ancient tool, the parser had several advantages: it
was fast, efficient, needed no power, and was perfectly adapted to working delicate materials such
as pearl. It came into its own in shielding, when the
cutler cut a hole in the handle of the knife for a
nameplate. In this procedure, the cutler used a two-
legged parser, which cut out the hole using a
template. Even in the 1990s, no more simple and
efficient tool has been found for drilling fragile
materials such as pearl.

Shielding was a procedure that was often carried
out in the assembly of pocket-knives—which was
traditionally regarded as one of the most skilled of
all the cutlery trades. According to *The Ironmonger*,
reporting on a tour of Mappin's in 1856: 'There are
several branches of the cutlery business in which a
few weeks' apprenticeship suffices to enable even

Henry Hinchcliffe assembling a pocket-knife at
Thos Turner's in about 1900. This was recognised as
one of the most skilled jobs in the cutlery trades.

The parts for a three-
blade pocket-knife:
blades, springs, inner
scales, bolsters and
buffalo horn outer
covering. From such
humble materials the
cutler created an object
of utility and beauty.

boys to earn pretty good wages. But in the [spring-knife] fitting department it requires an apprenticeship of full seven years to give a young man even a decent knowledge of his business'.

The reason that pocket-knife assembly was such a skilled occupation was partly because of the enormous variations in patterns. At Mappin's it was noted that the firm 'manufacture some 12,000 different patterns of spring-knives, many of them, moreover, with several variations'. What made the job doubly difficult, though, was the fact that Sheffield pocket-knives grew to be enormously complex, as the town's manufacturers revelled in the demand for multi-blades—knives with innumerable blades and instruments. Buttonhooks, scissors, punches, gimlets, awls, saws, can-openers, needles, pickers, tweezers, stonehooks and almost every type of blade imaginable could find their way into a Sheffield multi-blade knife. All these parts had to function perfectly, like a small machine. As Stan Shaw, one of the greatest exponents of the craft has stated: 'All multi-blades are

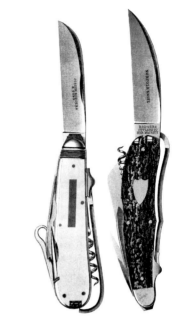

Sport's-knives, such as these examples made by cutlers at Joseph Rodgers, were amongst the most difficult knives to assemble. Each knife had to 'walk and talk' (open and close properly).

In assembling a pocket-knife the cutler used a selection of hammers.
Sheffield craftsmen were skilled enough to make most of these tools themselves.

difficult to make—it's like packing a suitcase, everything has to go in the right place'. This was achieved then, as it is now, with careful drilling, filing and fitting, using only the simplest tools. A selection of hammers, files, drills, a vice and a small anvil (or stiddy) was all that was needed.

The cutler's ideal was a pocket-knife which would 'walk and talk' (open and close easily) but the pitfalls in achieving this were many. I have described some of them in my book on Stan Shaw. Any excessive strain on the scales when the knife was rivetted together (which could be caused by poor alignment or not having the drill holes in the outer covering wide enough), could result in the pearl or ivory handle cracking or shattering. If the springs and blades were not tempered and set correctly then the knife blades would be either too difficult to lift (and also snap back too suddenly on the fingers), or they would be 'lazy'. The blade kick's height was also crucial: too low and the user would be unable to get their fingernail in the nail mark; too high and the point of the blade would be raised dangerously above the body of the knife when it was shut. The kick could be adjusted by filing, but even then the cutler needed to take care that this was not overdone, otherwise the blade edge would be blunted as it shut on the spring (see diagram, page 64). When *The Ironmonger* reporter visited Mappin Bros, he saw:

> …a so-called double-box sporting knife in process of fitting up. There were forty parts to be put together, the knife containing nineteen useful articles, such as a wood-saw, a cock-heel, a hollow gouge, a button-hook, a nail file, a pen blade, a pocket-blade, a corkscrew, a punch, a gimlet, a sacking needle and another needle, a lancet, a picker, tweezers, a pair of scissors, and some other articles. All these articles were furnished ready-made to the fitter, with all the other necessaries to put them together, yet we are apprised that it would take him ten days to finish the knife!

This may have been an exaggeration, but certainly the job of assembling a pocket-knife took

Rivetting a pearl scale to a pocket-knife. The fragility of pearl meant that this could only be done by very skilled craftsmen.

The outer edges of the inner scales of the best knives were milled for decoration. The fine lines were cut into the brass with a small wheel.

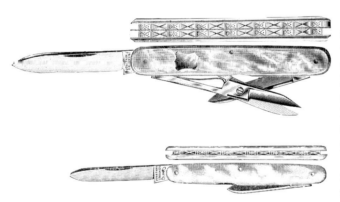

Knives with a 'fancy back' made by Jonathan Crookes. The marks were cut into the steel with a file.

Occasionally, the pocket-knife cutler would add something extra on the very best knives. Prior to the final assembly, he would decorate the springs and blade backs with chased patterns; this was known as fluting, or workbacking. It was done by clamping the blades and springs in the vice, then laboriously filing a pattern into the steel. It needed a skilled hand to do the job quickly and, of course, mistakes were impossible to rectify.

A whetting, to give the knife its sharp edge; a final inspection either by the cutler or the boss; and then oiling and wrapping sent the knife on its way to the customer. Packaging was relatively unsophisticated in the early nineteenth century and knives were often simply wrapped in brown paper parcels (though the paper was often acid-free and protected the blades from rust—an important consideration if the knives were being exported). Later a whole industry grew up in Sheffield supplying cardboard boxes and labels for the cutlery firms. The bigger firms usually had a separate section for packing, which was staffed by women. Eventually,

much time and patience. It was once calculated that even a simple two-blade penknife required some seventy or eighty separate operations. For a four-bladed knife, there were no fewer than 154 different operations!

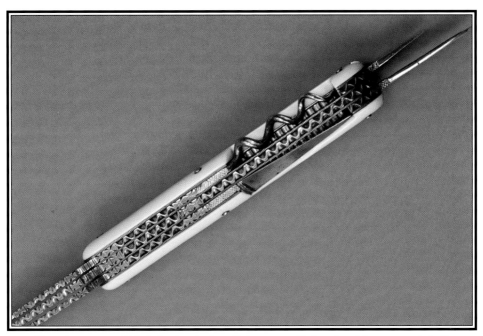

Chased springs and blade backs of a late 19th-century Christopher Johnson sport's-knife. (Weston Park Museum).

Girls packing pocket-knives.

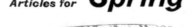

Some firms specialised in supplying the knife trade with blades, scales and springs. One of the largest was Henry Innocent.

too, boxmaking firms which specialised in expensive presentation cases in mahogany and other woods, appeared. Greaves, the casemakers, in Sidney Street is an example.

Very little advertising was done by Sheffield manufacturers. Individual makers were unable to afford much in the way of display and instead they relied upon their ancient name and trade marks. Even the largest manufacturers gave little thought to pushing their products through advertisements in the trade and popular press. They might occasionally pay for an advertisement in a trade directory, or mount an exhibit at a trade fair (such as the Great Exhibition of 1851), or print a catalogue, but most relied simply on the quality of their products and the activities of merchants and wholesalers to get their goods to market. Cutlery showrooms in Sheffield were unknown—so much so, that when Rodgers opened one in the 1820s, it caused a sensation and blocked Norfolk Street with sightseers.

Describing knife manufacture as simply a series of technical operations, however, scarcely does justice to the complexities of the knife industry in Sheffield. To catch its fuller atmosphere we need to say something about how the industry was organised, both economically and socially.

Despite the world-wide fame of its knifemakers, it was not an industry dominated by large factories. A popular journal, *The Penny Magazine* (1844), described how Sheffield industry was composed of:

> …separate branches, [which] are only united in respect to the larger merchants and manufacturers. These manufacturers buy the steel from one or more firms, have it forged by another or several others, ground by others, and finished by others; or they will purchase ready-made goods from smaller manufacturers; or they sometimes advance money to workmen to purchase material, and then agree to give a certain price for the articles. In short, there are several modes of conducting the manufacture, but the factory system is not one of them. By this we mean, that there is no large building, under a central authority, in which a piece of steel goes in at one door, and comes out at another converted into knives… Nearly all the articles of cutlery made at Sheffield travel about the town several times before they are finished.

Courtyard view of Butcher's Wheel in Arundel Street. Such large factories were essentially tenements, in which many trades and craftsmen would rent a workshop.

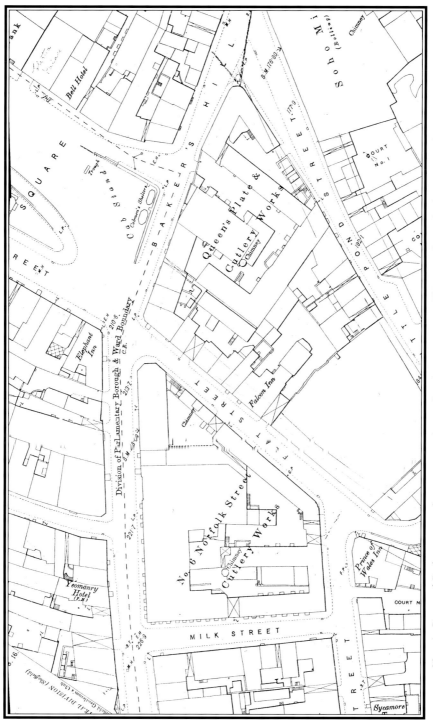

Mappin Bros and Rodgers were close to each other and to the town centre. This map shows the factories as they were in 1889. They had all been demolished by the inter-war period.

In other words, Sheffield itself functioned as one large factory, in which all the tasks involved in making a knife were extensively subdivided amongst many independent makers. At the heart of this system was the little mester (the individual manufacturer) who rented a workshop and perhaps employed one or two apprentices or workers. Such a man might work as a knifemaker (a cutler) but he usually only specialised in one type of knife and would never make all the parts for that knife himself or carry out all of the manufacturing operations. By the mid-nineteenth century, the idea of a cutler in Sheffield manufacturing a knife from start to finish was alien to the industry. Knifemakers would rely on other craftsmen or small firms scattered around the city. For example, some manufacturers supplied parts—forged blades, scales and various tools—whilst others provided an ancillary craft, such as mark-making or acid-etching.

Outworking and subcontracting were at the heart of this system and were very extensive. Small-scale manufacturers, some working in their own homes, would take orders wherever they could, sometimes working to a system of ''liver and draw'. Materials would be advanced by a factor at the beginning of the week, and the finished knives would be exchanged for an agreed price a few days later (in other words, 'deliver the goods and draw the money'). Meanwhile, larger manufacturers could employ outworkers whenever things got busy; if business was not so good, then the outworkers could be discarded at no cost to the manufacturer. The big knifemakers, such as Mappin and Rodgers, could also insulate themselves from fluctuations in the market in this way by renting out space to outworkers within their own factory, and then setting them on and laying them off as they chose.

It is therefore very difficult to say what constituted a 'firm' or a 'factory' at this time. The Sheffield directories and local maps show that many knifemakers operated from a 'works', but these were mostly backstreet affairs, which employed

THE QUEEN'S CUTLERY WORKS.

Mappin Bros' Queen's Cutlery Works was one of the top five firms in the cutlery industry by the 1850s.
The engraver cannot hide its tenement-style character.

Jessop & Smith, cutlery forgers. The Sheffield knife trade was extensively subdivided, with factories usually specialising in a single job—such as supplying the trade with forged (but not finished) blades.

a small number of workers. A 'works' might only employ twenty or so (sometimes less) and some of these might be outworkers. The factory would often be a few rooms in a tenement block, surrounding a courtyard, with an arched entrance to the street (the usual layout for a modest Sheffield factory). A works which employed more than a hundred would be unusual and only a very few makers—Mappin Bros, Rodgers, Wostenholm, Butcher's and Dixon's—employed hundreds of workers by the end of the 1860s. But even in these factories the outwork system predominated. William Harrison, one of the partners of Harrison Bros & Howson in Norfolk Street, told an official commission in 1865: 'Much of our work, probably half is done off our premises by outworkers in small places. Most large cutlery factories, I should say, have part of their work done out in this way . . . We have all our grinding done off our premises; the men are perhaps in a dozen different wheels'.

A large knife factory in Sheffield would therefore resemble a rookery, with all kinds of trades

Frank J. Hurst (1878–1957) was typical of the skilled craftsmen that allowed Sheffield's great knife industry to function. He worked as a pearl and ivory fluter in Cambridge Street and when he retired he was probably the last little mester working at this skilled craft.

Pattern book of Frank Hurst.

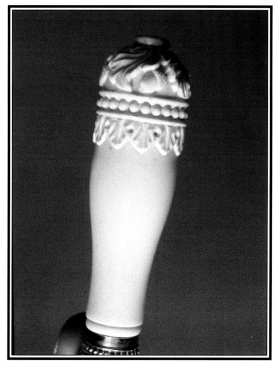

An example of the ivory carver's skill. The handle of an old Sheffield Bowie knife. (Cutlers' Hall).

and workers finding a rented home there. For example, Wragg's Advance Works in the 1880s was a home for Ralph Brough, George Hartley, and William H. Kavanagh—all independent spring-knife makers—and George Tandy & Son, a comb manufacturer. Brookes & Crookes' Atlantic Works was the address of Albert Oates, a sport's-knife maker with own mark (CURRENT, registered 1855); and also Joseph Westby, who was in the same trade. These makers controlled their own output, though they rented space from the main factory owners and also no doubt did work for them as the occasion arose.

Thus, the knife collector who cherishes a knife made by a particular maker should appreciate that it could have been made almost anywhere in the town (and of course was never made entirely by one man). Obviously, any contemporary estimates of the work's rolls for the larger factories must be highly approximate. Knife factories in Sheffield,

both large and small, were essentially a hodge-podge. Extensive mechanisation, apart from steam engines for supplying power for the grinding and polishing wheels, was non-existent. In fact, the installation of any machinery would have been difficult, because of the haphazard way the factories had developed. The plans of the largest works show that as trade expanded, workshops were added or adjacent works were taken over as needed.

This hive of industry gave Sheffield enormous strength as a knifemaking centre. While manufacture remained a handicraft, Sheffield knifemakers proved highly flexible at producing an almost infinite variety of knives. Whether the same organisation and attitudes could respond to the advance of the modern factory system was a question that was not even on the agenda in mid-nineteenth century Sheffield—though even then, it was apparent that the system of manufacturing knives in the town was far from perfect.

For the workers, it is true, the outwork and sub-contracting system had advantages that even a worker at the end of the twentieth century might envy. First, the Sheffield knifemaker could feel he (or she) was their own boss. Workers who rented space within a factory or wheel had considerable independence. At Harrison Bros & Howson, one of the partners observed: 'The men . . . work only as they please, and sometimes do not come in 'til 11am. That is why cutlers do not like working in America, because there they have to be in the factory each day regularly'. The first day of the working week in the Sheffield trades was known as 'Saint Monday' and was regarded as an unofficial holiday. It was often spent in the pub (or in sleeping off the weekend's excesses). Cutlers would then work harder during the rest of the week to make up lost time. Sometimes workers would have already been paid for their knives in advance—in which case, they would call them 'sours', because they were not very pleasant to do. (Conversely, knives for which payment was promised were called 'sweets'.)

The independence of Sheffield's cutlers was one of their most striking characteristics. It was nurtured further by the fact that the knifemakers' position could not be undermined by machinery (at least, not before the 1850s), nor by unskilled labour brought in from outside the town. Their position was further strengthened by powerful trade unions, such as the Operative Company of Spring Knife Cutlers, which were able to control the supply of labour to maintain good wages. The unions were not above terrorising their employers by 'rattening' (the wilful damage of machinery by various acts of sabotage, which could include the use of gunpowder) if their demands were ignored. These 'outrages' had become a national scandal by the 1860s and required investigation by a government commission.

Sheffield's system of knife manufacture also had other drawbacks, both for the workers and their employers. Working hours were irregular, depending on the state of trade, but in some of the domestic trades (where women and children were employed) a working day could last for thirteen or fourteen hours. The large manufactories worked about ten hours a day on average. Wages too, varied, most men being paid by the piece. When times were prosperous wages rose, but outwork bred insecurity and misery when business was bad. Little mesters and outworkers were obviously at the mercy of factors and factory owners, who could ruthlessly play off one group of workers against another, by auctioning work to the lowest bidder. In these conditions, knifemaking became a 'sweated' industry, which set employer against employee, and artisan against artisan, so that eventually wages were sometimes no longer enough to support even the most basic level of subsistence. Bitterness and poverty were the result. There were cases of hard-working cutlers, who had died of malnutrition!

The fact that steel was such a tough material and because the industry was based on hand skills, with very little mechanisation, meant that working conditions were often appalling. Not all the cutlery trades were unhealthy, but at its worst the Sheffield knife trade killed large numbers of men. For some death was sudden: a momentary loss of concentration might result in a child or man being pulled into the factory's shafts, bands or pulleys; or a grindstone might suddenly explode (a constant fear), the fragments cutting down and mutilating anyone in their path. For others, death would be more insidious, especially in the grinding hulls (a word which had originally meant, perhaps aptly, a sty), where sandstone and steel particles hung thick in the air and were inhaled by the grinders. Contemporary published accounts of working conditions for Sheffield grinders make shocking reading. The government's Children's Employment Commission (1865) noted the high mortality caused by grinders' disease (silicosis):

> The cause of this disease is, first, the irritation produced by the metallic and gritty particles inhaled in grinding…and, next, the constrained position in which the men labour. To this must be added the working for many hours in a badly ventilated room, and the very unpleasant smell produced by the friction of the steel on the grinding stone. When at work, the grinder sits astride of what he calls his 'horsing'; this is a low, narrow wooden bench; his elbows rest upon his

knees, and his head, particularly when employed on very small articles, is bent over the stone. The position is a very injurious one and when long continued, is calculated most unquestionably to induce pulmonary congestion. Again, in many of the heavy branches, such, for example, as table-knife grinding, the men work in the coldest weather without either coat or waistcoat, with their handkerchiefs off, their shirts open and their chests fully exposed; and this too in a room every bit of the glass from the windows of which has been removed, that the light may not be obstructed by the splashing of the water rendered dirty by the grinding stone. The work is very laborious, the men perspire freely, and in this condition they will often leave the hull without putting their clothes on, and recklessly lounge about in the yard even in weather…bitterly cold. Inflammation of the lungs, pleurisy, rheumatic fever, and diseases of the heart, are consequently not infrequent among them.

The Commission found that the average age of death for a grinder in the cutlery factories was rarely above forty, and often it was below thirty. Equipment for dust extraction was slowly being introduced, but the fragmented nature of the industry meant that progress was slow. In any case, the grinders often disregarded safety measures because they were paid high wages as compensation and did not want to see their danger-money reduced.

Even aside from the grinding hulls—some of which, inspectors admitted, were 'more like dog kennels than anything'—most workshops were poorly lit, inadequately ventilated and heated, and had the most basic sanitary facilities. Foreign visitors, although they were captivated by Sheffield skills, were shocked by the factory life in the town. They found that the forges and workshops which made their gleaming knives were often no more than 'old rookeries', which were badly-lit, cramped and difficult of access. One American wrote (in the *Sheffield Independent*, 4th January 1871), after watching two forgers expertly hammer out a knife blade for him:

> I must say, in all frankness, that while by the system of labour pursued in Sheffield, absolute perfection in its manufactures is obtained, humanity is proportionately degraded. The minute subdivision of labour gives no chance for the cultivation of

the mind, and man becomes almost as much of a machine as the forge or the hammer he uses. Thus, it follows that the principal resort of the labourer after working hours is the alehouse; his principal enjoyments, beer and tobacco.

The knife and steel trades were indeed steeped in drink (as was the rest of the country). In 1831 it is known that Sheffield and its surrounding districts could boast about 1,500 licenced premises. Whenever money could be earned easily and while working hours were irregular, the local pub was the first port of call—after all, cutlery was dusty and thirsty work. Sometimes, though, cutlers would drink even before the working day began, calling in for a 'stiffener' to help them through the morning. For many knifemakers, social life revolved around the pub: it provided solace and a refuge from the conditions described above, though it also ruined many before their time.

For the leading manufacturers, of course, life could be very different. One of the attractions of little mesterdom was that it offered the chance to become very wealthy. Cutlers such as Frederick Mappin, George Wostenholm and John Rodgers had soon made unprecedented fortunes. Mappin could afford a residence in London as well as in Sheffield; Wostenholm and Rodgers were amongst those manufacturers who marked their wealth by moving to stately houses in the leafy suburbs of Abbeydale and Sharrow. Wostenholm, for example, by the 1860s had already bought up a substantial estate at Kenwood, modelled on the townscapes he had admired in America. These men, though they were usually trained as working cutlers, soon occupied an orbit far higher than that of their workforce. Henry Coward (later a knighted musician), who was trained as a cutler at Wostenholm's Washington Works in the nineteenth century, has given us a vivid portrait of industrial relations at the firm. He recalls that 'there was a tremendous difference between the men in the factory and those in the office or counting-house, who were a class apart from the men; consequently, the intimates of the principal [George Wostenholm]…were unapproachable by the mere 'hand' except on the business of the firm'.

Kenwood, the country house built for George Wostenholm in the early 1840s. The American trade had brought Wostenholm unprecedented wealth, though his fortune was not typical in the industry.

Aside from the industry giants, such as Wostenholm and Rodgers, most cutlery factories were small-scale and often no bigger than a modest house. This is Bocking's cutlery factory in Gell Street, established in 1838.

Nevertheless, these men were exceptional and most cutlery manufacturers did not become as wealthy—which is not perhaps surprising, given that the number of really big firms in the trade was quite small. Even the wealthiest Sheffield cutlers could not compare themselves with the big British cotton, coal and engineering magnates. As the historian Sally Taylor has emphasised, a significant proportion of manufacturers lived in 'respectable' workingmen's districts such as Crookes and Walkley, not far their own workforce. Most of them were still practical men, who had received the same education as their workers. Few were gentrified and for most, their own business, which was typically quite small, was their main interest in life. A few of the more prominent took the office of Master Cutler when it was offered to them, and some had a taste for freemasonry, but only rarely did they enter politics or occupy leading civic roles. The typical knife manufacturer was also Sheffield born and bred. Occasionally, an outsider from London (e.g. Robert Mosely) might decide to take up cutlery manufacture in the town. Some occasionally came from even further afield, such as the Barnascones from Switzerland, but in the early nineteenth century, the town's cutlery industry was a self-contained and very parochial world. In R.E. Leader's words, in the nineteenth century Sheffield cutlery was still a very 'homely' industry, which retained many of the attitudes of the days when cutlery manufacturers were 'respected because they forged their own blades in the little smithies behind their cottages and, far from being knights or baronets, were spoken of and to by their Christian names, without even the prefix of "Mr" '.

Speaking very broadly, there was as yet a very close identification of interest between the manufacturer and artisan. This was despite the atrocious working conditions, the strikes, the Sheffield Outrages, and the undoubted class differences between the workers and the wealthiest manufacturers. Industrial relations in the golden age of Sheffield knifemaking were usually good—or as contemporaries were fond of saying, 'cordial'. Firms could be highly paternalistic: Joseph Rodgers,

in particular, was an assiduous promoter of good relations with its workforce. The depth of its paternalism can be savoured in the account in the *Sheffield Mercury*, 28th November 1840, of a ceremony at the Norfolk Street Works when the Rodgers' workmen presented a large gold cup to their employers. The cup, proferred by an eighty year-old workman—one Thomas Jennings, of 'tottering limb' and 'humble gait'—was an expression of the employees' 'attachment' to Rodgers, 'from a conviction of the honourable and gentlemanly conduct evinced by them to us their workmen'. Even so flinty a character as George Wostenholm had managed to nurture a spirit of paternalism similar to his rival. On 28th December 1855, the workers at the Washington Works organised a testimonial for George Wostenholm during which they presented him with silverware worth some 200 guineas as a tribute to his 'talents as a manufacturer, and their deep conviction that his energy, integrity, perseverance and enterprise, have very largely contributed to give to Sheffield cutlery manufacture its proved supremacy'.

A recurring feature of these exchanges of 'goodwill' between managers and workers in the cutlery industry was the pride in, and respect accorded to, long-service records. Publicity material, company histories and newspaper reports for the leading firms almost invariably mention those workers whose connection with the firm (like their bosses) went back several generations. The themes of loyalty, sobriety, hard work, thrift and dedication were reinforced by numerous examples of cutlers who had been with a single firm for many decades. In 1840, for example, at Rodgers there were 520 workmen whose divided services amounted to 4,600 years. Examples of individuals who had been with a company for fifty years or more were not unusual, though few could match the record of William Smith, who joined Rodgers in the 1850s. When he died in 1931, aged ninety, he had worked at Rodgers for seventy-eight years!

What united masters and men above all other considerations was an obsessive concern with quality and a belief in craftsmanship.

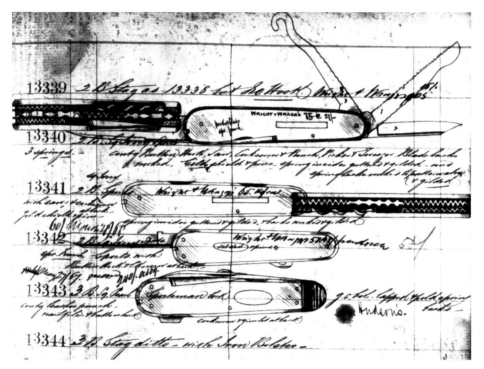

To keep track of so many patterns, Sheffield makers would sometimes copy the design of a knife into a pattern book. If it was ordered again, the cutler had a record. This is a page from a Wostenholm pattern book, 1861–70, when the Sheffield knife industry was nearing its peak in quality and technical virtuosity. (Sheffield Archives).

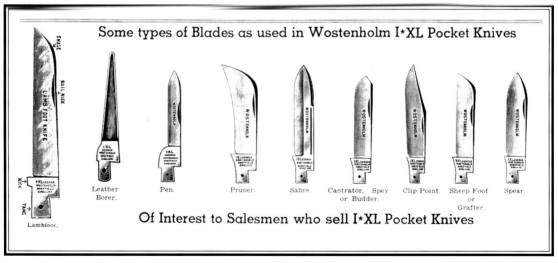

A 20th-century printed Wostenholm catalogue shows a few of the most popular types of knife blade.

5

Patterns and Styles

IN THE NINETEENTH CENTURY, a knife was an important purchase, far more so than at the end of the twentieth century, when an object with a true cutting edge plays far less part in our everyday lives. A good knife was required to be efficient, to look good, and also be durable. Naturally, a knife was required to perform a wide variety of tasks and if it could be offered in a similar range of patterns and styles, so much the better. In fact, in the nineteenth century the range of knives sold was never wider. In the era before standardisation and mass production, Sheffield makers revelled in supplying almost anything that was required: in fact, the whole outwork and subcontracting system was geared to allow the town to become a 'universal provider' of all types of knives.

Our information on Sheffield knives in the nineteenth century is derived from two major sources: contemporary pattern books, catalogues, and trade literature; and the knives themselves, which have survived either in private hands (kitchen drawers, antique collections) or in museums. Both testify to the extraordinary variety of knives produced in Sheffield. To give one example: in about 1900, Joseph Rodgers produced a trade catalogue for its travellers and offices. It showed well over a hundred pages of knives, with some of the pages having as many as a dozen different patterns. The town did not 'invent' these knives: as in almost any human activity, there is nothing new under the sun, and many of the ideas utilised by Sheffield cutlers had their precursors. Nevertheless, Sheffield cutlers did make their own innovations and, as we shall see, they took some of the traditional designs as close to perfection as possible, given the craft

nature of the technology. Quite how they did so must remain a mystery, since there were no knife 'designers' in the nineteenth century. Individual cutlers perfected the designs, perhaps responding to the demands from a particular customer or market, or more probably to their own intuitive feel for what was required in a given situation. Occasionally, a new style might be noted for future reference in the company pattern book—some of which, grimy and faded, have survived to the present day. Or a firm might keep 'pattern-stock'—an example of every knife it had made. But more often, much of the knowledge was held in the cutler's head and hands and often died with him.

Cutlers, though, did work to a definite range of patterns and types, even if describing their various and often bewildering classifications is difficult. No definite rules existed. For example, the Rodgers' catalogue, referred to earlier, groups sport's-knives and fleams in the penknife section. Some knives were evidently classified by Rodgers by common usage (thus the biggest classification of folding-knives was under the heading, 'pocket-knives'); others by the shape (or material) of the handle or blade; and some were known inside the company by a specific pattern (with each knife having a separate number). However, it is evident from surviving trade catalogues that the leading firms did not care to split too many hairs when they were selling knives: they kept things fairly simple. (The Rodgers' catalogue had only four main headings: these were pen-knives, erasers/desk-knives, pocket-knives, and table cutlery.) I have adopted a similarly broad classification and divided Sheffield knives into two simple categories: folding-knives and fixed-blade

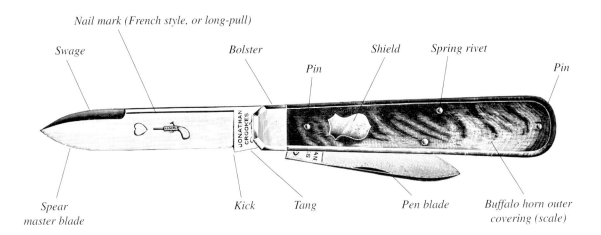

Nail mark (French style, or long-pull)

Swage   *Bolster*   *Shield*   *Spring rivet*   *Pin*

Pin

Spear   *Kick*   *Tang*   *Pen blade*   *Buffalo horn outer*
master blade   *covering (scale)*

knives. To these I have added a third, which strad-
dles both classifications—exhibition knives. In this
chapter, I have not attempted to give an exhaustive
compilation of Sheffield knife-types, but have
merely tried to give an idea of some of the major
varieties.

Folding-knives

Perhaps the first knife that demonstrated the potential
of Sheffield's steel and its cutlers was the pen-knife.
The word pen-knife is now used to describe almost
any kind of pocket-knife, but in the nineteenth century the term was more specific: it referred to a
delicate knife (generally with one or two blades,

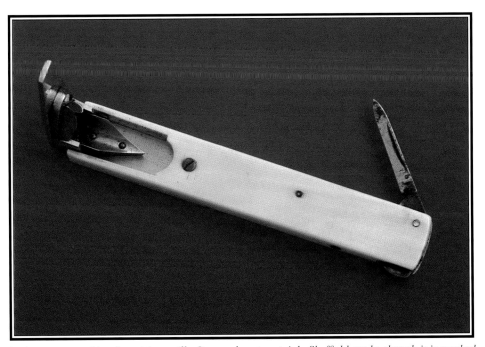

*An ivory pen-machine for cutting quills. It was almost certainly Sheffield-made, though it is marked
with the name of a London retailer.*

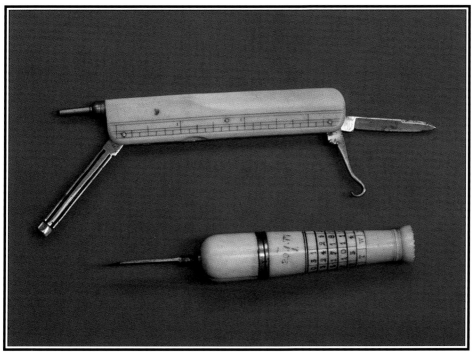

19th century ivory pen-knives, one with a rule, the other with a calendar. (Weston Park Museum).

sometimes more) which was designed to cut and shape quill pens. Sketchley's *Sheffield Directory* (1774), which categorises pen- and pocket-knife makers separately, lists sixty-six pen-knife cutlers, some of whom specialised in a particular type of knife. The handle material—stag, ivory, spotted horn (which was horn stained to resemble tortoise-shell)—was usually the characteristic makers used to differentiate themselves.

Traditional quill knives had extremely slender blades used for slitting the quill and they were often single-bladed. By the 1820s, however, the penknife trade had expanded in Sheffield and there were three times as many cutlers in this sector as there had been fifty years earlier. Their knives had become more sophisticated and now sometimes had two or three blades and were double-ended. Making such slim knives—most were only about $2^{1}/_{2}$ inches long—was a highly skilled job. So, too, was manufacturing a pen-machine, a device patented by the London inventor Joseph Bramah, which appeared on the scene by the 1830s. The machine

19th century pen-knives for cutting quills and an eraser knife.

LOCKWOOD BROTHERS LIMITED, SHEFFIELD.

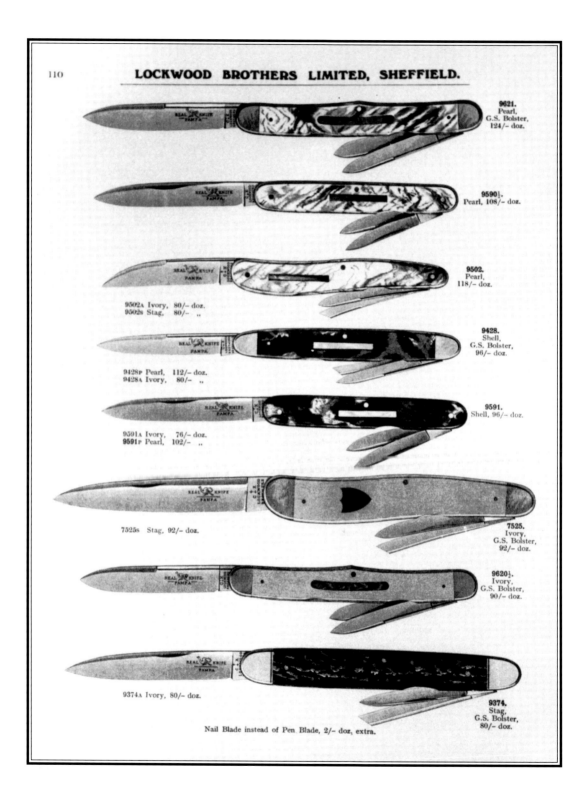

9621.
Pearl,
G.S. Bolster,
124/- doz.

9590½.
Pearl, 108/- doz.

9502.
Pearl,
118/- doz.

9502A Ivory, 80/- doz.
9502s Stag, 80/- „

9428.
Shell,
G.S. Bolster,
96/- doz.

9428P Pearl, 112/- doz.
9428A Ivory, 80/- „

9591.
Shell, 96/- doz.

9591A Ivory, 76/- doz.
9591P Pearl, 102/- „

7525s Stag, 92/- doz.

7525.
Ivory,
G.S. Bolster,
92/- doz.

9620½.
Ivory,
G.S. Bolster,
90/- doz.

9374A Ivory, 80/- doz.

9374.
Stag,
G.S. Bolster,
80/- doz.

Nail Blade instead of Pen Blade, 2/- doz, extra.

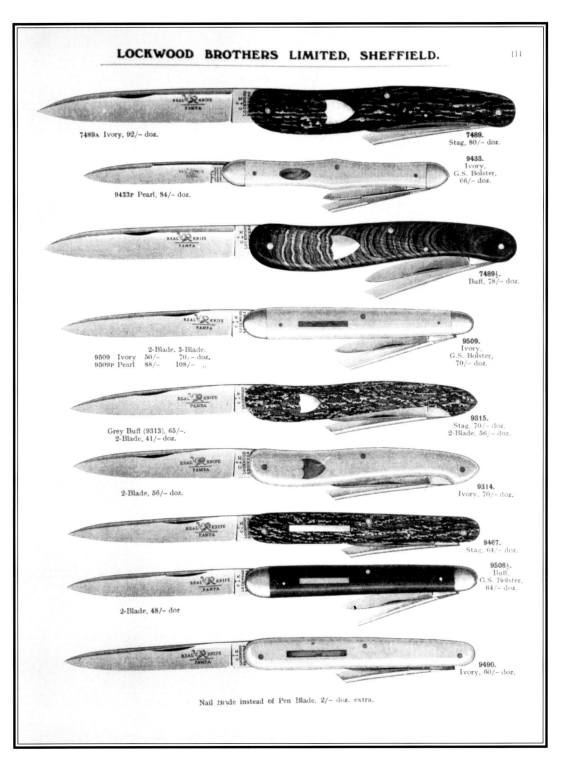

7489A Ivory, 92/- doz.

7489.
Stag, 80/- doz.

9433.
Ivory,
G.S. Bolster,
66/- doz.

9433P Pearl, 84/- doz.

7489½.
Buff, 78/- doz.

2-Blade. 3-Blade.
9509   Ivory   50/-   70/- doz.
9509P Pearl   88/-   108/- „

9509.
Ivory,
G.S. Bolster,
70/- doz.

Grey Buff (9313), 65/-.
2-Blade, 41/- doz.

9315.
Stag, 70/- doz.
2-Blade, 56/- doz.

2-Blade, 56/- doz.

9314.
Ivory, 70/- doz.

9467.
Stag, 64/- doz.

9508½.
Buff,
G.S. Bolster,
64/- doz.

2-Blade, 48/- doz.

9490.
Ivory, 60/- doz.

Nail Blade instead of Pen Blade, 2/- doz. extra.

A variety of whittler patterns in ivory, pearl, horn and stag. 'Whittler' is an American term; to Sheffielders the knives were three-blade pen-knives.

is operated rather like a cigar cutter, using paired blades in a V-shape which are pressed down onto the end of an inserted quill against a nib-shaped template. The point of the quill is then slit using a pen-knife blade and the point trimmed with a cutter adjacent to the nib-shaping slot. Many of Sheffield's foremost makers, such as Joseph Rodgers, Harrison Bros & Howson, and Joseph Mappin, made pen-machines. The device may not look very impressive from our own viewpoint: nevertheless, it was a complicated business making one and pen-machines (and pen-knives) were a good source of profit for Sheffield cutlers. Often they started these firms on the road to greater things. The invention of the steel-nibbed pen during the early nineteenth century caused the decline of the pen-knife, but pen-knives and pen-machines evidently remained popular with customers who disliked a scratchy steel nib and so Sheffield cutlers continued to make and advertise them. (They also, incidentally, made eraser knives, which were needed whatever the type of nib, and also propelling-pencil knives). Of course, plenty of uses could be found for a fine blade and that was not forgotten either. Many knives continued to carry a pen-blade after that.

The term pen-knife also embraces other types of knife: such as whittlers, lobsters, and Congress knives.

'Whittler' is a term used by modern collectors and knife-users for a three-blade penknife, which looks at first glance to be fairly straightforward in design. Whittlers have a large blade in one end, and two cutting blades of equal length in the other. They have two springs. But what is unusual about a whittler is that the large master blade is extra thick and works off *both* springs. The whittler was a premium-priced knife, because of the difficulty in making it. Many have a centre divider, which tapers to nothing just beyond the centre rivet. Whittlers can range from small, delicate knives for ladies, to larger versions, which can be used for

something dear to Americans' hearts—whittling wood—a pastime which is part of American folk-lore. In *The United States Magazine* (March 1857), one worthy described how:

> The Yankee boy, before he's sent to school,
> Well knows the mystery of that magic tool,
> The pocket-knife. To that his wistful eye
> Turns, when he hears his mother's lullaby;
> His hoarded cents he gladly gives to get it,
> Then leaves no stone unturned till he can whet it;
> And in the education of the lad,
> No little part that implement hath had;
> His pocket-knife to the young whittler brings
> A growing knowledge of material things.

Carving wood may not have been as popular in England, though several Sheffield firms made

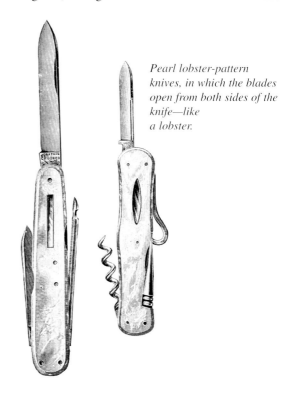

Pearl lobster-pattern knives, in which the blades open from both sides of the knife—like a lobster.

The beak-shaped Wharncliffe blade in a serpentine body—a design pioneered by Joseph Rodgers.

whittlers (which appear in catalogues as 'three-blade pen-knives'), not least because they found a ready market in the USA. Joseph Rodgers made them in its well-known Wharncliffe pattern, with a serpentine handle and curved master blade. The history of this knife is interesting. According to the local antiquarian Joseph Hunter—who described the Wharncliffe as 'the handiest knife for the pocket that has ever been invented'—it was designed one day after dinner by Rodgers' noble patron Lord Wharncliffe and his kinsman Archdeacon Corbett.

Another premium-priced knife made by Sheffield cutlers was the lobster. This pen-knife has blades at both ends, and on top and bottom of the knife, so that when the blades are opened it resembles the claws of a lobster. To allow the lobster-knife to operate in this fashion the knife's spring is split. The pattern is said to have been the invention of Sheffield cutler James Crawshaw (see Part Two). Considering the degree of difficulty in making a lobster—it has always been regarded as the knife which sorted out the men from the boys in cutler-ing—it would not be surprising if Sheffield had designed it, though no conclusive evidence can be provided. Certainly, it was a popular Sheffield style, despite its expense (they were usually the priciest knife in a firm's range). Lobster knives are usually small, not over about three inches long, and delicate. Often made of pearl or ivory, it was easy to break the scales with rough handling, or to strain the springs by opening too many blades at once. They were, however, popular as a ladies' knife or as a waistcoat accoutrement: for that reason they were often made with scissors and a manicure blade.

A Sheffield pen-knife that sold well in America was the Congress knife, which had a handle that curved like a crescent. No one has discovered why this pattern was so named, though we do know that it became popular before the American Civil War. Sheffield exported many Congress knives to the USA, especially to the Southern states, where they seem to have been sold almost exclusively. Besides the gently curving handle, other distinguishing features were squarish corners on the bolster, a universal sheepfoot master blade, and four or more

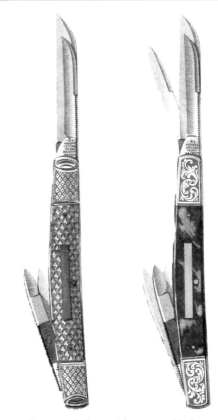

Congress knives, with engraved bolsters. The one on the left is silver-mounted; the one on the right is gold-mounted. A premium knife made by Joseph Rodgers.

blades. Some Congress knives had eight blades, making the pattern very definitely a top-of-the-line model. Sheffield makers such as Joseph Rodgers lavished much attention on their Congress knives by producing them with ornate, engraved bolsters. The firm made a four-bladed Congress knife, 'silver mounted'; and a six-blade version, 'gold mounted'.

One of the most popular patterns of pocket-knife was the sleeveboard. It seems to have derived its name from its shape, which resembles the small ironing boards once used for sleeves.

FRUIT KNIVES

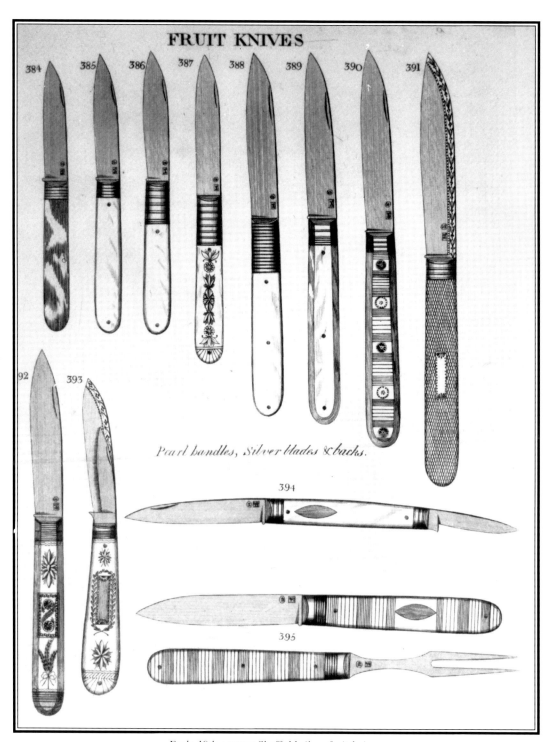

384 385 386 387 388 389 390 391

92 393

Pearl handles, Silver blades & backs.

394

395

Early 19th-century Sheffield silver fruit-knives.

According to cutlery historian Bernard Levine, on the night when US President Abraham Lincoln was assassinated in 1865, he was carrying a six-bladed ivory-handled Congress knife. It was marked, 'William Gilchrist's Celebrated Razor Steel', and may have been Sheffield-made (though no Wm Gilchrist seems to be listed in directories of that time). The knife is now in the Library of Congress.

A discussion of pen-knives opens the way to the even wider vista of other types of folding knives. No one could ever supply a complete list of all the patterns. As Thos Turner stated in 1902: 'To the varieties of such knives now made there is practically no end. It is calculated that at different times no fewer than 10,000 different patterns have been produced at the Suffolk Works alone, and the average number kept there in stock or 'to order' will be from 2,000 to 3,000'.

The simplest folding-knife does not even have a spring, but can be made with a handle and a single blade, with the latter opening and closing with a single pivot pin. These knives are sometimes referred to as 'penny knives'. The majority of Sheffield folding-knives, however, operated on a spring, and ranged from delicate silver fruit-knives to large and fearsome folding-dirks.

The production of silver folding fruit-knives was fully underway in Sheffield by the late eighteenth century and united two branches of local industry—the silver trade and knifemaking—in an endeavour that was always dear to Sheffield hearts: the production of a high-quality product. Silver fruit-knives were luxury items intended to be used in the dainty task of cutting fruit (obviously, the silver blade did not rust, like carbon steel, or tarnish so easily). Birmingham and Sheffield soon dominated the field. The skill and imagination of their cutlers reached a zenith in the Georgian period, when silver fruit-knives were simple in design, yet elegant and tastefully decorated.

Georgian and most Victorian fruit-knives are single-bladed, though some had a second blade for coring apples or removing seeds. A few were made as knife-and-fork pairs: half-opening one of the pair allowed them to be separated. The quality of Sheffield fruit-knives remained high in the Victorian

Silver fruit-knife made by Atkin & Oxley, Sheffield, in 1834.

era. Knives were made in exotic shapes, in pearl and tortoiseshell, and sometimes the scales were decorated with pin work (piqué). By this method, tiny silver pins were painstakingly let into the pearl scales producing a dazzling effect. Scales were also shielded, carved and engraved. Several Sheffield makers achieved a high reputation by specialising in silver fruit-knives, though the master in the Victorian era is recognised as John Y. Cowlishaw (see Part Two). Naturally, the advent of stainless steel destroyed the silver fruit-knife trade after the First World War, though by then many of the craftsmen who had produced such marvellous pieces were either dead or in decline too.

One of the most popular Sheffield folders was the jack-knife—a sturdy and simply made pocket-knife, which usually had a single blade in one end of the handle (though some jack-knife patterns had two blades). Again, no one has ever offered a satisfactory definition as to why these knives are so named, though some have suggested a link with the mythical Jacques o'Lieges, a Flemish cutler who came to Sheffield in the sixteenth century. This is more fancy than fact and more probably the name simply derives from the traditional English word 'jack', meaning labourer or sailor. Certainly, the term 'jack-knife' covers a wide variety of types. For example, folding hunting-knives are recognisably jack-knives. Some knives in the nineteenth century had 'jack' in their actual name. Perhaps the best example is the 'Jack Tar' knife. Thos Turner supplied nearly half a million of these knives to the Admiralty in the late nineteenth century. They described it as follows:

> The pattern of this knife is a very old one. The end of the blade is an inch in width, and quite blunt, the original idea being, apparently, that the sailor should not be tempted to use his pocket-knife as a stabbing instrument in any quarrels…The other feature of the knife is that the strong pin by which the blade is held in its place stands above the 'bolster', so that if the blade should get loose at any time the sailor can himself rivet it tight again. Jack's knife is, indeed, an indispensable possession…[with which]…he eats his dinner, for Jack is not allowed the luxury of a table knife and fork, he scrapes the paint off a boat, he cleans an iron rail, cuts his plug tobacco, and does innumerable

other things besides. So it is that…the 'Jack Tar' knife is almost the strongest pocket-knife made.

Generally, the term jack-knife has fallen into disuse in England (though it is used more in America), and to most people jack-knives are simply pocket-knives.

Aside from the original penknife, no Sheffield pocket-knife was more well known in the early nineteenth century than the Barlow knife. This was a cheap, sturdy pattern intended for young boys—though, of course, this did not prevent it from being used by adults. Barlows had one or two blades, but their chief characteristic was a long bolster (which added extra support for the blade and so made a stronger knife). Often the bolsters carried a name or trade mark. Barlow knives and the cutlers who made them were indigenous to the Sheffield area. The most important was Obadiah Barlow, who founded a business which made

Jack-knives from a Jonathan Crookes' catalogue. The top knife with the square-ended blade is a sailor's-knife and would have been similar to Turner's 'Jack Tar' knife.

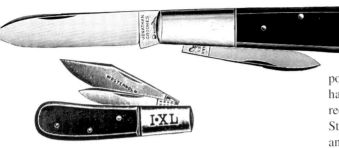

*Barlow knives by Jonathan Crookes and Wostenholm.
The long bolster on this knife was its characteristic
feature.*

The Adventures of Huckleberry Finn (1885), Huck mentions a 'bran-new Barlow worth two bits in any store'. Most of the big Sheffield firms exported Barlows, though the profits on them seem to have been thin. A director at Wostenholm's recalled: 'We used to send [Barlows] to the United States in casks. We made little or no profit on them, and…were always behindhand with orders'.

Barlow knives until the end of the eighteenth century. The family used its own name as a trade mark, which no doubt increased its association with the knife. By the time this business ceased trading in 1798, other makers were beginning to take up its manufacture. These included the Furness family of Stannington, whose knives were widely sold in America in the nineteenth century. The Barlow was immortalised by James Fenimore Cooper in *The Pioneers* (1823), and by Mark Twain in *The Adventures of Tom Sawyer* (1876). In

Many single-ended folding knives were aimed at the farmer or gardener. Usually hafted in stag, horn or wood, they contained one or perhaps two of these following specialist blades: a fleam for bleeding animals, a lambfoot blade for trimming sheep's hooves, a castrator (spey) blade for cattle, a pruning blade for crops, and a budding blade for plants.

Larger folding knives, for more serious purposes, often, though not always, had a locking mechanism. As the single master-blade opened, a sneck (or latch) locked it in place, so that it would not shut on the hand in actual use. Thumb pressure on the back-spring then released the blade, so that it could be closed. Some lock-knives in the early nineteenth century were designed primarily as

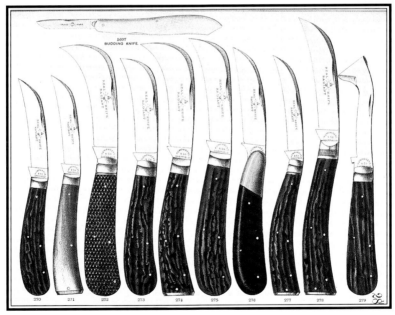

*A selection of pruning-knives for the Victorian gardener from a W.R. Humphrey's catalogue.
The knife on the right is a timber scriber (or rase-knife) for marking wooden objects,
such as packing cases or barrels.*

Fleams for bleeding animals.

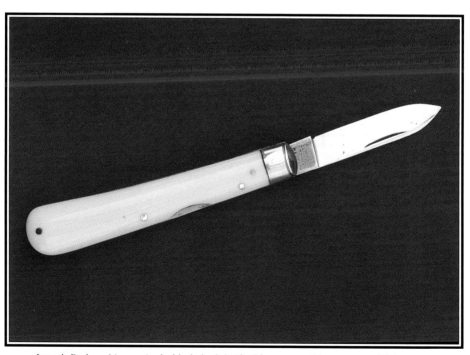

Joseph Rodgers' ivory single-blade lock-knife. I have seen this pattern, with its stout, short blade, described as a wool knife.

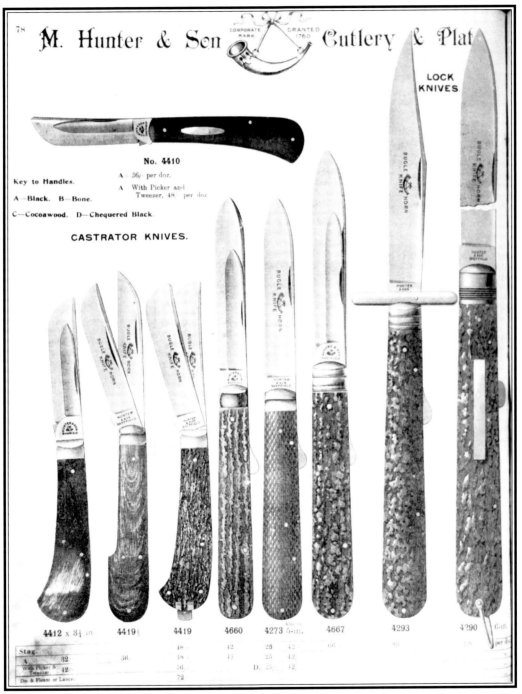

M. Hunter & Son Cutlery & Plat

CORPORATE MARK — GRANTED 1760

LOCK KNIVES.

No. 4410

A — 36/- per doz.

A With Picker and Tweezer, 48 per doz

Key to Handles.

A—Black. B—Bone.

C—Cocoawood. D—Chequered Black.

CASTRATOR KNIVES.

	4412 x 3¼ in.	**4419¼**	**4419**	**4660**	**4273** 5-in.	**4667**	**4293**	**4290** 6-in.
Stag								per d
A	32	36	48	42	28 42	66	80	
With Picker & Tweezer	42		48	42	25 42			
Do. & Fleam or Lance			56		D. 25 42			
			72					

Besides castrator knives for the farmer, Michael Hunter also produced a variety of lock-knives. A simple locking device in the spring prevented the knife shutting on the hand. Thumb-pressure on the backspring then released the lock and allowed the blade to shut.

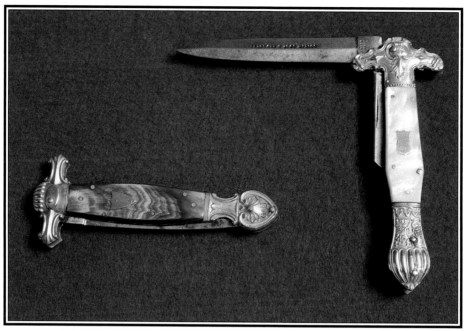

Folding dirks (sometimes known as folding Bowies) were made by Sheffield makers for the
American market between the 1820s and 1850s. They were often highly ornate,
so that stabbing someone could be done in style. (Weston Park Museum).

weapons. They were, strictly speaking, folding-dirks or daggers, though variants intended for the American market have often been labelled as folding Bowie knives. The Bowie, as we have seen, hit the headlines in the late 1820s. Not everyone, how-ever, wanted a heavy fixed-blade knife and a market for a foldable version developed. As with standard Bowie knives, which are discussed below, Sheffield makers were America's chief supplier. They recognised that even bigger sales were possi-ble if they catered for American tastes for decoration and patriotic sentiments. They made folding dirks from top-quality materials—ivory and pearl—and added fancy mounts and bolsters. American eagles, horses and cannons, and patriotic words (such as 'Liberty and Union', reflecting Daniel Webster's famous speech of 1850), adorned Sheffield folding Bowies. One of the most desirable motifs for col-lectors is the 'half-horse, half-alligator', which was sometimes stamped in relief on the nickel-silver pommels of these knives. This referred to the 'The

Hunters of Kentucky', a patriotic song from the War of 1812, which described the fearless 'Kentucky boys' as being 'half a horse, and half an alligator'. Folding Bowies made before 1850 are rare. Bernard Levine and Roger Baker comment: 'The Sheffield folding Bowie is fascinating in its historical lore, mechanical workmanship and elegant beauty. It is frustrating to search for these rare pieces of Americana. It can be devasting to the wallet to acquire one. However, even a single fine example can be considered a respectable collection'.

Somewhat plainer than these knives, is another version of the folding Bowie that was probably made somewhat later in the nineteenth century. The standard style has a clip-point blade which protrudes a few inches from the handle even when the knife is shut, making a sheath mandatory, but allowing the knife to be used for skinning and sim-ilar tasks. It can be opened fully at the push of a handle-button, which allows the blade to open and lock, and crossguards to fall into place. Since the

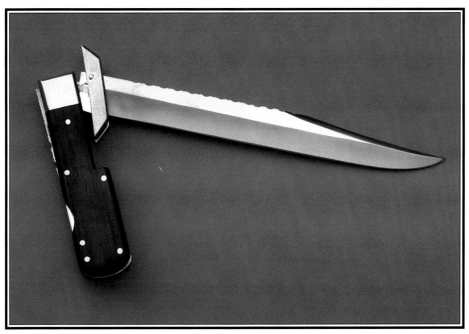

*Large folding Bowie knife, with push-button and locking mechanism. This style evolved in the late
19th century, after the heyday of the fixed-blade Bowie. This knife was made in the 1990s
by Stan Shaw, but is an exact copy from the old Sheffield patterns.*

usual blade length was about 15-inches when open, the knife could be used as a vicious weapon. Such folding Bowies operated by means of a spring mechanism concealed in the handle and making this work correctly needed much careful filing and adjustment by the cutler.

One of the most recognisable types of folding knife is the multi-blade—perhaps the best known example of which is the erstwhile sport's-knife (or, or to give it its more recent label, Swiss Army Knife) These knives had at least three blades, though often they had many more. They were sturdy, usually double-ended, and were distinguished by the fact that they contained special-purpose blades or tools (such as punches, saws and can-openers). A favourite Sheffield trick (copied in modern Swiss Army knives) was to file recesses into the knife's outer covering, into which could be slotted pickers and tweezers, even extra blades and scissors.

The Victorian era was the heyday of the multi-blade knife and Sheffield makers made some of the best examples. In fact, Sheffield cutlers arguably took the art of making multi-blades to unprecedented heights. Why was this? Part of the reason for Sheffield's superiority lay in the fact that Benjamin Huntsman had provided Sheffield with such a superb raw material. Crucible steel came into its own in a knife which needed rugged tools and blades. One should emphasise, too, the dense texture of Sheffield industry with its vast spread of ancillary trades in steel melting, forging, grinding, hafting, blade manufacture, etching, buffing, and assembly. It was this which provided the cutlers with the punches, corkscrews, files, augers, tweezers, hoofpicks, saws and countless other tools for a multi-blade. Finally, of course, one has to mention that by the 1850s Sheffield cutlers had developed remarkable skills in the difficult job of assembling such marvellous creations.

Sheffield multi-blades were produced in a bewildering variety of patterns—from the relatively delicate lobster, to the more robust 'gadget'-knife.

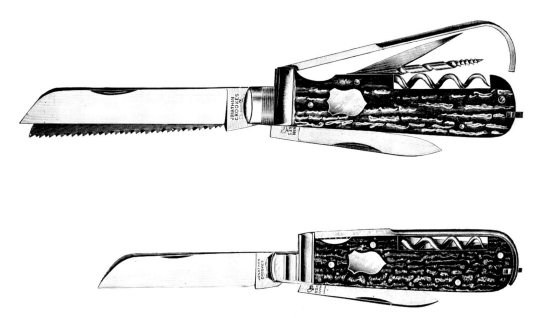

The horseman's-knife, with a hoofpick and other tools, was one of the most popular of Sheffield's multi-blades.

This diversity, and the evident skill that went into making them, has made multi-blades eminently collectable as antiques. The finest Sheffield multi-blade knives have an aesthetic appeal that often transcends their sometimes mundane uses.

Perhaps the most famous Sheffield multi-blade is the horseman's-knife—the one with the 'thing for getting stones out of a horse's hoof'. This knife has a hoofpick (sometimes called a stonehook), the hinge on which allows it to open 180°. When swung open, the pick usually reveals various tools—a corkscrew, gimlet and punch—on the back of the knife. The pick snaps shut by a kind of clawing action on the end of the knife. Leather punches are popular tools on horseman's knives, and occasionally some have harness bolts through the handle of the knife. These bolts could be unscrewed and used in an emergency to mend a torn harness or trace.

The Sheffield multi-blade reflects English social history. Some of the most complicated were made in a lobster pattern for the Victorian smoker. They had cigar clippers and long punches for opening up an airway in the tobacco before lighting up; cigar forks for holding short stubs without burning the fingers; pipe reamers and tampers; and pen- and manicure-blades. Often made in pearl and extremely difficult to assemble, they were a truly premium knife. Another popular multi-blade for the Victorian (or Edwardian) upper classes was the champagne pattern, which had a corkscrew on the back of the knife and a wire-cutter blade to help pop the cork. For the grouse moors, some sport's-knives combined corkscrews with other useful gadgets, such as cartridge extractors.

For those who worked harder for their living, other multi-blades were devised. Some, such as the horseman's-knife, were intended for farmer's and other manual workers. Besides hoofpicks and leather punches, some contained fleams; others had budding-knives. Screwdrivers, sacking needles, saws, heavy-duty files, awls, and rulers were also added in various combinations. By the end of the nineteenth century, a special-purpose cattle-knife—the stock-knife—had appeared. This seems to have developed first as an American pattern, though Sheffield soon followed the lead by producing it, too. Stock-knives were less bulky than

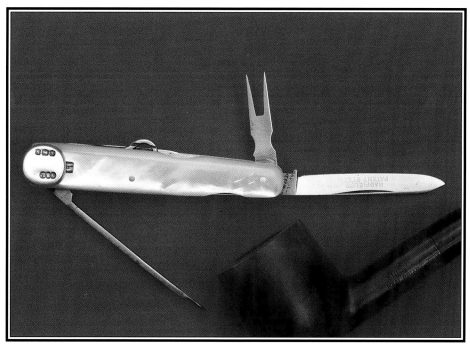

19th century smoker's knife, made in a lobster pattern with blades and tools opening from both sides of the knife. The maker is unknown, but intriguingly the master blade has 'Hadfield's Patent Steel' etched on it. Was this knife made for one of the city's leading firms, Hadfield's Steel Company?

A champagne knife with wire-cutter and nickel-silver handle.

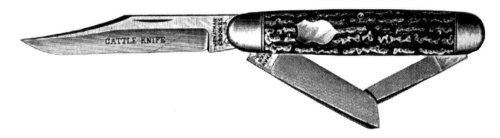

A cattle-knife with genuine stag handles, over $3\frac{1}{2}$ inches long.

SPORTS and HUNTING KNIVES

B152 One blade, leather borer, tin opener, screwdriver, and bottle opener. Nickel silver handle with shackle. Length (closed) 3½ inches.

7487 Officer's Knife. Two blades, tin opener, screwdriver, bottle opener, leather punch and corkscrew, nickel silver handle with shackle. Length (closed) 4 inches.

B204 Clip point blade, corkscrew, bottle opener, screwdriver and tin opener. Imitation stag handle with shackle, nickel silver bolsters and shield. Length (closed) 3½ inches.

B154 One blade, leather borer, tin opener, screwdriver, and bottle opener, imitation stag handle with shackle, nickel silver bolsters and shield. Length (closed) 3½ inches.

B1531DHSH Lock Knife. Imitation stag handle with shackle, clip point blade which locks when opened. Length (closed) 4½ inches.

B154C Clip point blade, leather borer, tin opener, bottle opener, and screwdriver, imitation stag handle with shackle, nickel silver bolsters and shield. Length (closed) 3½ inches.

By the 20th century, the sport's-knife had evolved into a general utility-knife or scout-knife.

the typical Victorian multi-blade (usually 3½ to 4 inches long), but were heavy-duty knives nonetheless. They had three blades: usually a spear or clip master-blade, with a spey and a lambfoot blade. Wostenholm's, however, made a version with four, which it called the I*XL farmer's-knife.

Sport's-knives followed social trends in other ways. The Sheffield multi-blade summons up a lost world when Britannia ruled the waves and intrepid Victorian soldiers and explorers marched across the globe. Brookes & Crookes, around the time that Britain was opening up the 'dark' continent, decided to produce a knife specially for explorers. They named it 'Stanley' and then sent the knife to the African explorer to whom it was dedicated. A trade journal, *The Implement and Machinery Review* (July 1882), reprinted Sir Henry Stanley's acknowledgement. He wrote:

> Looking at it from a traveller's view, and recalling to my mind all the pocket or belt weapons, tools, and useful things I needed while in Africa, I do think this splendid, artistic, beautifully made knife supplies a large number of those utilities in as compact and ready-at-hand a form as imagination could conceive. Within one frame, I have

a strong blade, which may be as useful as it may be harmful, a good saw, a gimlet, a file, screwdriver, and awl, the very names of which suggest a multitude of occasions they may be required for. My sails, tents, awnings, and clothes bags, with the aid of your brass foot measure, might easily, with the addition of thread and canvas, have been repaired; and my clothes, often rent by briar and bramble in the jungle, are brought to my recollection when I see your sewing needles and scissors. Your extractor also reminds me of times when I strained and tugged to extract a spoilt cartridge when life was depending on it. I see that there are other things there, but I think that I have told you enough to show that I think it a marvel of utility, for which accept my hearty thanks.

Other Sheffield multi-blades were made specifically for the Army and Navy. These were not usually designed as weapons, but as 'utility' knives, with corkscrews, punches and can-openers, as well as a strong master-blade. They probably evolved from the sailor's-knife, or early soldier's-knives. Thos Turner then made an army knife with a single blade; a 'square pike' for punching a leather strap, removing a stone from a horse's hoof, or making a hole in a board an inch thick; and also a

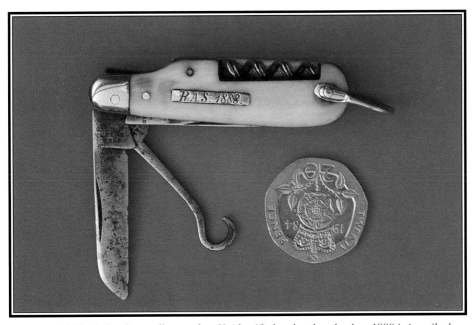

A Sheffield knife for the smallest pocket. Unidentified maker, but the date 1888 is inscribed on the shield.

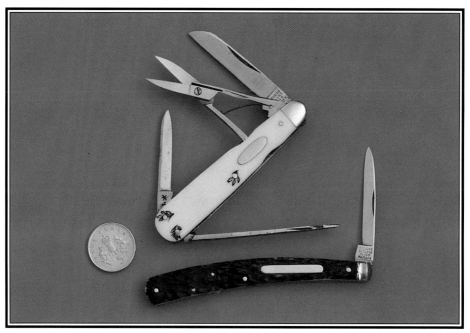

An ivory lobster pocket-knife and a stag pen-knife by Joseph Rodgers & Sons, both probably made before 1914.

can-opener, to prevent the soldier using his bayonet and blunting it. Joseph Rodgers made a military knife that had a pair of pliers in the end, perhaps for cutting barbed wire. Sheffield cutlery firms also made knives for that junior version of the Army—the Boy Scout movement, founded in the 1880s by Lord Baden-Powell. By the First World War, a scout's-knife had become a recognisable multi-blade style, often with four blades: ordinarily, a spear master blade, a punch, a can-opener, and screwdriver cap-lifter. The scout's-knife bore a strong resemblance to the 'utility'-knife, which became very popular in the twentieth century as an inexpensive version of the pricey Victorian multi-blade. It was usually described simply as a 'sport's-knife'.

Fixed-blade knives

In nineteenth century Sheffield directories, the pen- and pocket-knife makers were the largest single category of cutlers. Their products, because of their diversity and value, have also attracted the most attention from collectors. The latter have generally found multi-blades the most fun to collect. However, we should certainly not neglect fixed-blade knives, amongst which we can include kitchen- and butchers'-knives, trade-knives (i.e. industrial knives) and various weapons (such as the Bowie knife). Taken as a whole, the production of such knives—as regards unit output—probably surpassed that of folding-knives. Certainly, they have become the most important class of knives in modern times. Fixed-blade knives were also of vital significance for domestic and industrial life in the nineteenth century.

Table-knives became increasingly standardised in the nineteenth century. The old English style of scimitar blade had gradually become obsolete by the early nineteenth century, to be replaced by a more regular pattern. This had a blade which was broad and parallel-sided, with rounded tips. The majority of Sheffield table-knives were of this pattern by the mid-nineteenth century, though some

A selection of Joseph Rodgers' table-knives, mostly 19th century. (Weston Park Museum).

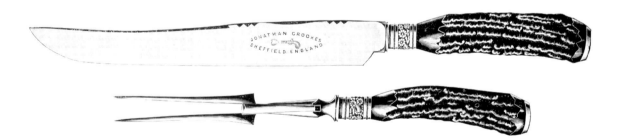

Genuine stag carving set by Jonathan Crookes, with silver mounts.

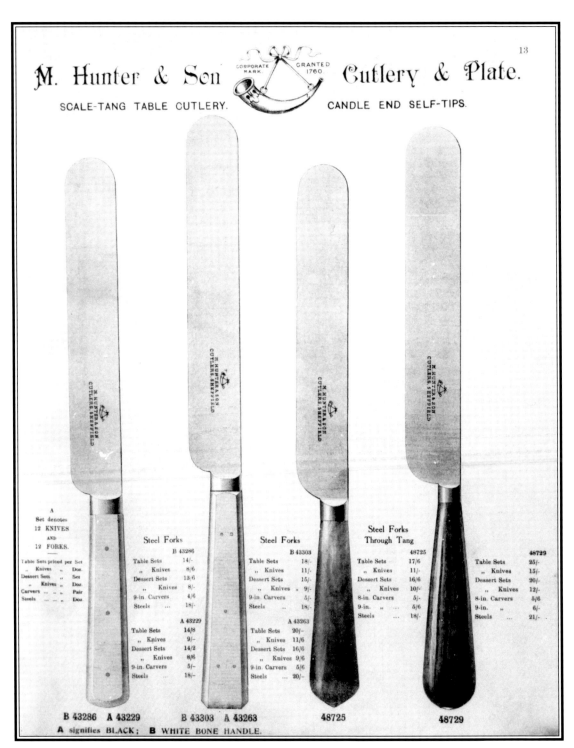

M. Hunter & Son — Cutlery & Plate.

CORPORATE MARK. GRANTED 1760

SCALE-TANG TABLE CUTLERY.   CANDLE END SELF-TIPS.

A Set denotes
12 KNIVES
AND
12 FORKS.

Table Sets priced per	Set
„ Knives „	Doz.
Dessert Sets „	Set
„ Knives „	Doz.
Carvers ... „ „	Pair
Steels ... ... „	Doz.

Steel Forks

B 43286
Table Sets	14/-
„ Knives	8/6
Dessert Sets	13/6
„ Knives	8/-
9-in. Carvers	4/6
Steels	18/-

A 43229
Table Sets	14/8
„ Knives	9/-
Dessert Sets	14/2
„ Knives	8/6
9-in. Carvers	5/-
Steels	18/-

Steel Forks

B 43303
Table Sets	18/-
„ Knives	11/-
Dessert Sets	15/-
„ Knives	9/-
9-in. Carvers	5/-
Steels	18/-

A 43263
Table Sets	20/-
„ Knives	11/6
Dessert Sets	16/6
„ Knives	9/6
9-in. Carvers	5/6
Steels	20/-

Steel Forks Through Tang

48725
Table Sets	17/6
„ Knives	11/-
Dessert Sets	16/6
„ Knives	10/-
8-in. Carvers	5/-
9-in. „	5/6
Steels	18/-

48729
Table Sets	25/-
„ Knives	15/-
Dessert Sets	20/-
„ Knives	12/-
8-in. Carvers	5/6
9-in. „	6/-
Steels	21/-

B 43286   A 43229   B 43303   A 43263   48725   48729

A signifies BLACK; **B** WHITE BONE HANDLE.

By the 19th century, table-knives had settled into a uniform style with broad, parallel-sided blades and rounded ends.

of the more expensive plated knives still followed the older designs. Most table-knives were made of crucible steel, though shear steel was occasionally used. The type of tang and bolster and especially the handle material were often the main distinguishing feature in manufacturers' catalogues. Table-knives were hafted in ivory, stag, horn, white bone and ebony. Bolsters, still forged as part of the blade, were fairly simple. After the 1850s, blades were increasingly fixed to the haft with a pin tang—a narrow, cylindrical shaft, which sometimes ran through the whole of the handle. Pearl was occasionally used for hafting table cutlery, especially for plated fish-knives and dessert-knives, which became an important line for Sheffield makers from the mid-nineteenth century to 1914, as the middle- and upper-class markets for such products expanded rapidly. Usually, these knives had carved handles and engraved blades.

Another important item at the Victorian dining table was the carving-knife. At that time, Sheffielders said that a manufacturer staked his reputation as a cutler on his carving-knives rather than on any other single article in his extensive lists. The carving-knives made by Joseph Rodgers were amongst the most celebrated and would stand comparison with many modern knives—though there were several makers who produced the finer qualities. Often they would be sold as part of boxed sets, with a matching carving-fork and also a steeling iron for sharpening the blade.

The different styles of carving and kitchen-knives merge into another important class of fixed-blade knife: the butchers'-knife. This knife was very important in the nineteenth century, when sticking, skinning and chopping meat were still hand-skills and when butchers' shops and abattoirs had little in the way of machinery. (The same could be said of fish markets, where a wide range of filleting-knives was needed.) This was where the hand-forged knife really came into its own. Many of the best butchers'-knives were produced from shear steel, because of its prized cutting properties. As Bill Winfield, an old hand-forger, remarked:

The hand-forged double shear steel stands out more than anything in cutlery. When you talk to

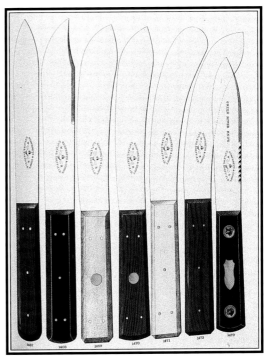

Butcher-style skinning-knives from W.R. Humphrey's catalogue. The American influence on Sheffield is apparent from the knife on the right, marked Green River Knife. This style of hunting-/skinning- knife was popularised by J. Russell's Green River Works in Massachusetts, Sheffield later copied the design. Giving it to someone 'up to Green River' euphemistically highlights one use for the knife on the frontier.

so many abattoir people and butchers they all say that you have a sharper knife if it is hand-forged. And when you see those serrated edge knives, they wouldn't look at them in an abbatoir. I don't go in butchers' shops, but you used to see butchers sharpening their own knives. Now, they're ready sharpened. They used to be bulky, but you'd have them ground to nearly a razor edge. Beautiful to cut.

Many of the leading Sheffield cutlery firms based their reputation on hand-forged butchers'-knives. Perhaps the two most prominent were A.J. Jordan and John Wilson, though there were several others, such as Rodgers, Petty, Oxley, and William Gregory.

A fascinating, but little-explored, facet of the cutlery world is the manufacture of trade-knives. These were industrial knives produced for the

LOCKWOOD BROTHERS LIMITED, SHEFFIELD.

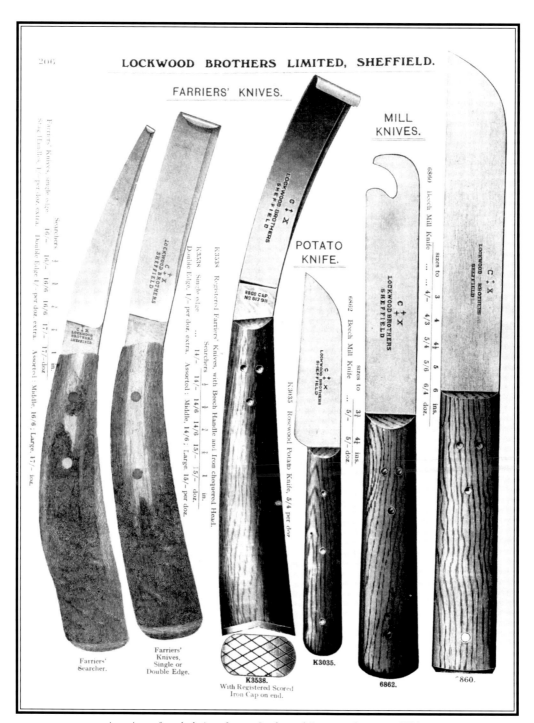

FARRIERS' KNIVES.

MILL KNIVES.

POTATO KNIFE.

Farriers' Knives, single edge
Stag Handle, 1/- per doz. extra. Double Edge 1/- per doz. extra. Assorted: Middle 16/6; Large, 17/- /doz.

Searchers	½	⅝	¾	⅞	1 in.
	16/-	16/-	16/6	16/6	17/-	17/- doz

K3533 Registered Farriers' Knives, with Beech Handle and Iron chequered Head.

Single edge

Double Edge, 1/- per doz. extra. Assorted: Middle, 14/6; Large 15/- per doz.

Searchers	½	⅝	¾	⅞	1 in.
	14/-	14/-	14/6	14/6	15/-	15/- doz.

K3538 Single edge

K3035 Rosewood Potato Knife, 5/4 per doz

K3035.

K3538.
With Registered Scored Iron Cap on end.

6862 Beech Mill Knife

sizes to	3½	4½ ins.
	5/-	5/- doz.

6862.

6860 Beech Mill Knife

sizes to	3	4	4½	5	6	6½ ins.
	4/-	4/3	5/4	5/6	6/4 doz.

6860.

Farriers' Searcher.

Farriers' Knives, Single or Double Edge.

A variety of trade-knives from a Lockwood Bros catalogue, c. 1920s.

craftsman, artisan and factory worker. Almost every Victorian industry needed its trade-knife. The leather industry alone was a customer for a huge range of knives, especially for the shoemaker. Raphael Salaman's scholarly study of leather-working tools illustrates something of the remarkable variety of knives needed in this trade alone. But a range of knives was also needed by the farrier, the plumber, painter, glazier, and linoleum cutter; the hatter and textile worker; the basket-maker—the list is almost endless. Sheffield also had a large export business in trade-knives, which meant tailoring them for specific tasks. Thus it was that, after the mid-nineteenth century, the town began producing plantation knives: pruners for tea and tobacco crops; rubber-knives for tapping trees; and sisal-knives. Matchets for hacking clearings for crops

were always in steady demand from tropical countries. Sheffield cutlers often made their reputation by specialising in a certain type of trade-knife: George Barnsley, for example, was highly regarded for his shoe-knives; and Edwin Terry concentrated on farriers'- and plumbers'-knives.

The most desirable fixed-blades in the eyes of modern collectors are those used as weapons. Ever since man developed the knife as a universal tool, he has also found it extremely useful as a weapon, both for slaughtering animals and for warlike uses against his fellow man. Surprisingly, although Sheffield has made its share of swords, bayonets and daggers (especially during the two World Wars), it has never been the leading maker of these products. In the nineteenth century, they were mostly made in London and Birmingham or

Sheffield Bowie knives with classic American decorative pommels. One has a horse's head; the other, the legendary half-horse/half-alligator motif, designed to cater for American patriotic sentiments. (Cutlers' Hall).

imported from countries abroad, such as Germany. Sheffield concentrated on higher quality cutlery and, it seems, left these more mundane items to its competitors.

Nevertheless, Sheffield manufacturers could still excel in the manufacture of weaponry and hunting knives whenever they were called upon to do so. In the nineteenth century, Sheffield's wide-ranging international trade called forth a large variety of such products: the American frontiersman needed his Bowie and 'self-defence' knife; the South American gaucho needed his dagger and matchet; and the Far Easterner needed his kris, dah and kukri.

The Bowie knife, the history of which we have already touched upon, is perhaps the most famous. But what exactly was a Bowie knife? Every year some American collector claims to have found one of Bowie's original knives or to have discovered some new fact about his life. Learned seminars discuss in portentous details the latest in Bowie folklore. Mostly it is just that—folklore—since the exact details of both Bowie's exploits and the precise

design of his knife are obscure. As we have seen in the section on folding knives, Bowies are varied in design and surviving examples show that there was no universal type. They could be long or short, light or heavy, and have single-edged or double-edged blades. Some had straight-backs, some had curved; some had clip blades, some were spear-pointed. They could be plain or decorated, and they could be made with or without a cross-guard. The earliest Bowie knives (often made by local American cutlers and surgical instrument makers) looked like crude butchers'-knives; later examples, such as those made in Sheffield, have a clip point (a piece taken out of the back of the blade to lessen its weight and increase its cutting qualities). Whatever the design, the Bowie knife was primarily intended as a weapon, and many of the finest examples are surprisingly light for their size. This was a reflection of first-class grinding and was done because the knife was designed to kill people. (A mistake made by many modern custom Bowie knifemakers is to make the blades too heavy and clumsy.)

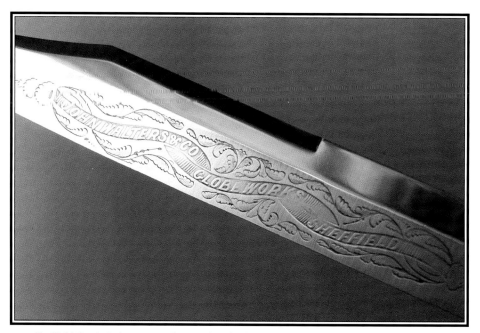

Sheffield Bowie knives were often acid-etched on the blade—another highly skilled craft.
The etch on the knife with the tortoishell grip (previous colour photo) allows us to identify the
knife's maker as John Walters. The knife, which is an exceptional example of a Sheffield Bowie
knife, was made at the Globe Works before 1865.

Besides the diversity of blade shapes, the most notable feature of Sheffield Bowie knives made in the knife's pre-1860 heyday is the astounding range of handle shapes and blade decoration. The town's cutlery infrastructure, with its die-makers, ivory carvers and acid etchers, allowed Sheffield Bowie knifemakers to become expert at making designs specifically for the American market. As they did with folding Bowie knives, they acid-etched their blades with American eagles and patriotic slogans. Etchings that referred to the Mexican War, the Gold Rush, and the Civil War (backing both Rebel and Yankee) were the commonest. Some acid-etched slogans pandered to the frontier myth and the penchant in some states for brawling, stabbing and knife-throwing. Some of the larger Bowies made in Sheffield were etched 'Arkansas Toothpick', a reference to the state that was described by one reporter as the 'headquarters of Bowieism', due to its lawless reputation. Sheffield Bowie knife makers also stamped and cast nickel-silver (sometimes known as German silver or 'white brass') into decorative shapes for the handles. The renowned 'half-horse, half-alligator' motif is again very much in evidence on fixed-blade Bowies of this pre-1860 era.

It is an indication of the abiding popularity of the Bowie knife that even when the trade went into decline after the 1860s—due mainly to the spread of firearms—the knife did not simply disappear. Gradually, it metamorphosed into a hunting-knife. Bowie knives continued to be produced by Sheffield makers up to 1914—indeed, the trade continued well into the twentieth century and even in Sheffield in the 1990s Bowie knives can still be bought in the city. This is perhaps surprising, given that Bowies do not make particularly useful hunting-knives: for skinning game, they are too thick and clumsy, and for chopping wood and brush they are too small. No doubt, many Bowies were (and are) bought by youngsters fed on its folklore appeal (not yet dimmed, even by Rambo) as a machismo weapon.

Bowies made later than the 1870s are usually easily distinguishable: they are often smaller than those from the golden age; are, of course, devoid of etching and fancy mounts; and they often have straight-sided handles, which taper slightly towards one end and have ball-shaped quillons at the other. Several Sheffield makers, such as Joseph Allen and Wostenholm, continued to send this plainer type of Bowie knife to the USA in the late nineteenth century.

That said, some Sheffield cutlers, notably Joseph Rodgers, continued to make premium-quality Bowie knives and fixed-blade dirks up to about 1900. The company's trade catalogue from around

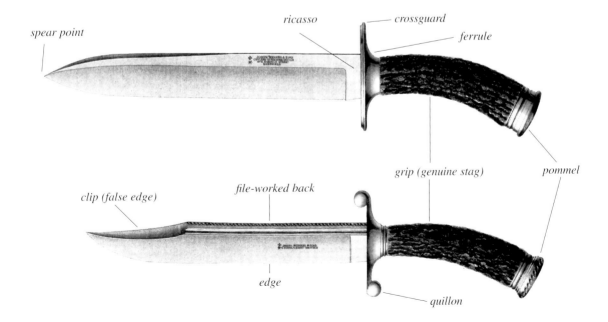

Plate 75

CHRISTOPHER JOHNSON & CO.,
MANUFACTURERS,
WESTERN WORKS, SHEFFIELD.

BOWIE OR HUNTING KNIVES.
ENGRAVED ONE THIRD SIZE.

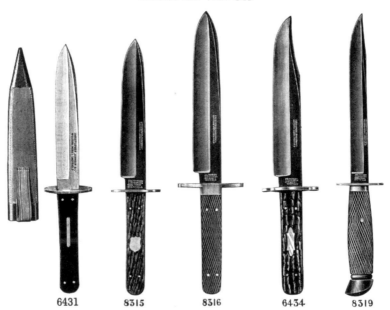

6431 8315 8316 6434 8319

No.	Price per doz.	
6431	62/	4 in. Black Horn Handle, 6 in. Blade, G.S. Guard, in G.S. Mounted Leather Sheath
8315	60/	4 in. Rosewood Handle, 6 in. Blade, G.S. Guard, in G.S. Mounted Leather Sheath
8316	86	4 in. Black Horn Handle, 7 in. Blade, G.S. Guard, in G.S. Mounted Leather Sheath
6434	76/	4 in. Stag Handle, 7 in. Blade, Steel Guard, in G.S. Mounted Leather Sheath
8319	196/	4¼ in. Ebony Handle, 7 in. Polished Blade, G.S. Guard and Ferrule, in Best Black Leather Sheath

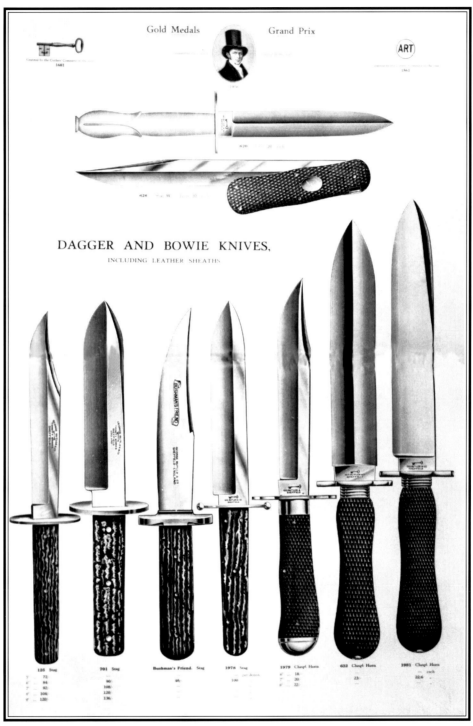

Pages from a Johnson catalogue (c. 1900) and a Butler catalogue (1936). Bowie knives became simpler in design and less ornate in finish after the 1870s.

Once Sheffield's US trade had passed its peak after the 1860s, the town's knifemakers soon switched their skills to satisfying the demand from some of the less 'civilised' corners of the globe. This 19th-century Beal dagger has palm trees, natives and a canoe. (Cutlers' Hall).

this time still gives a prominent place to Bowie knives. Many were in the later 'hunting-knife'-style of Bowie, but they were still superbly ground and had fileworked blades, and decorated handles and sheaths. It must also not be forgotten that, as the American market became closed to Sheffield makers, there was still plenty of business to be done in the Colonies. Joseph Rodgers, for example, illustrated several Indian-style daggers in its catalogue. Cutlers' Hall in Sheffield has a case of nineteenth-century daggers and other weapons by Rodgers, which demonstrate the superb standard this firm attained in grinding and finishing. One impressive folding spear-point knife, hafted in wood with a shackle, is nearly eighteen inches long! Two daggers with genuine stag handles and their scabbards are almost as impressive. Knives like these may have been destined for the Far East, besides America.

Customers in these markets did not usually have the purchasing power of the Americans. Nevertheless,

Sheffield cutlers applied some of the same techniques they had used in the USA to adapt their fixed-blades for these new markets. Cutlers' Hall has several knives made by Joseph Beal. Amongst them is, for example, an ivory-hafted kris, over a foot in length; and a Burmese dah, some twenty-seven inches long, complete with cable-wired grip. Beal's, too, utilised Sheffield expertise in acid-etching and stamping blades with decorative motifs. The Collection has two Mediterranean-style Beal daggers (both about ten inches long), both featuring decorations on the blade: one has a canoe, palm trees and natives; the other has ranchers chasing cattle, plus a tribe of natives around a boiling pot!

Exhibition-knives

Exhibition-knives—as Sheffield cutlers intended them to be—are in a class by themselves. These pieces were designed to show off the individual

Due to their rarity and the fact that they represent the summit of cutlery art, exhibition-knives in recent years have become highly prized by collectors. The oldest that have survived date from the early nineteenth century, when showpiece knives became yet another Sheffield speciality. Most of the leading firms, such as Mappin, Rodgers and Wostenholm, are known to have tried their hand at them before 1860.

Joseph Rodgers, with its keen awareness of marketing, became the leading maker of exhibition-knives in the 1820s and 1830s. It was such a knife, which caught the eye of the Prince Regent in 1821, and resulted in many orders. When Rodgers opened its showroom in Norfolk Street in 1822, customers were greeted by the sight of the largest multi-blade exhibition knife ever made (before or

Tiny multi-blade exhibition-knife (the body of which is only about an inch long, when closed), with over 50 blades and attachments. It was made by Herbert Lee in about 1920. (Weston Park Museum).

cutler's skills; or to advertise the merits of a particular firm. Some were literally 'shop-window' knives; others were produced for the big nineteenth-century trade exhibitions; and sometimes they were intended as presentation pieces for important dignitaries. Occasionally they appear to have been made simply (one imagines) for the challenge or for the pleasure of making something different in the cutler's own time (which may explain why some exhibition knives are not stamped with a maker's name). Whatever the reason they were made, perhaps the best definition of a showpiece knife would be this: it is a knife intended for display and not actual use. Within this definition, exhibition pieces could be giant or minute; they could be packed with a myriad of blades or have only one.

Joseph Rodgers' stand at the Great Exhibition, 1851.

since). This was the Year Knife, made in the form of a Maltese Cross, the arms of which bristled with a blade for each year. Commented the *Sheffield Independent*, 21st April 1821: 'It must be seen to be admired. We understand the above article is not made for sale, but that it will remain in possession of the inventors as a lasting specimen of what human ingenuity is capable of achieving. It occupied no more than nine months in making'. According to one source, the sole maker of the knife may have been Jonathan Crookes (see Part Two). Every five years new blades were added to the original 1,822 to bring it up to date (a tradition that has continued until quite recently).

The Year Knife has its place in the *Guinness Book of Records* as the world's largest knife, but other makers worked at the opposite end of the spectrum. According to a report in the *Sheffield Independent*—reproduced in a Mappin advertisement—in 1839 Mappin's produced an 'unrivalled specimen of Sheffield cutlery' that was clearly intended as an exhibition piece:

> The knife is only 3$\frac{1}{2}$ inches long, but it contains twenty-seven blades and instruments, the backs and exposed parts of which are all covered with fine gold, and the springs on which they work are so ingeniously constructed, that no motion whatever is observed in the action of opening or shutting the several blades. It is not in the number of blades and instruments introduced into a knife that its chief excellence consists, but in the adaptation of the several parts to the whole; their fitness for disposition; their compactness when united; and the harmonious finish they present. In all these qualities, Mr [Joseph] Mappin's knife is an unique and perfect specimen. The springs, inside and out, the bolsters, and all the exposed parts of this beautiful piece of workmanship, are covered with plate gold, the filing and fluting of which are as accurate as the most minute cameo, and of the highest possible finish. Within the broad end of the knife, there is a machine for making pens (of the kind for which Mr Mappin is so justly celebrated), the excellence of which essentially depends upon the nicest accuracy, which the maker has most successfully attained. The scales are of beautiful mother-of-pearl. At the back of the knife is a horse-picker, and other useful instruments. Chastity of design, exquisite workmanship, and high-finish, are the striking characteristics of this fine specimen of cutlery. The workman who manufactured this knife, has been employed upon it for the last sixteen weeks: and gold to the value of twenty pounds has been used in the making.

The development of foreign competition and the staging of world trade exhibitions encouraged the manufacture of display knives. The Great Exhibition at the Crystal Palace in London in 1851 was the landmark event. For many visitors, it was a defining moment in Victorian society—'the great subject throughout the country', as the Sheffield press put it—an event that for the first time demonstrated the giant strides made by Britain during the Industrial Revolution. The Sheffield newspapers treated their readers to a full description of the event over several days. Their verdict: that Sheffield trounced all-comers.

Many of Sheffield's leading knifemakers had displays: W. & S. Butcher, Mappin Bros, Unwin & Rodgers, Marsh Bros, George Wostenholm, and John Walters. Most of these makers had some kind of *chef d'oeuvre* to catch the public eye. Wostenholm, for example, had commissioned a fine set of ornate sheath knives and also displayed a selection of exhibition multi-blades. But overshadowing them all was the exhibit of Joseph Rodgers & Sons. Their huge octagonal glass case—more like a small greenhouse than a case—contained, in pyramid-fashion, three rows of highly-polished Bowies, pocket-knives and razors. If that did not make visitors gasp, then the knife surmounting that pyramid—a work of cutlery art surpassing any exhibition knife made then or since—almost certainly did.

It was a version of a *multum in parvo* or sportsman's knife, though it is doubtful if even the most energetic sportsman could have even lifted it, let alone put it in his pocket! In its open, upright, display position the knife was over two feet and six inches long and contained, so it was said, 75 blades and tools. (I have personally tried to count the items in the Norfolk Knife, which is now in Cutlers' Hall, and have totalled them provisionally at 74. Perhaps the reader would like to try this one day if they ever examine the knife. It is not an easy job.) A dazzling variety of punches, gimlets and

The Year Knife. (Stanley Tools).

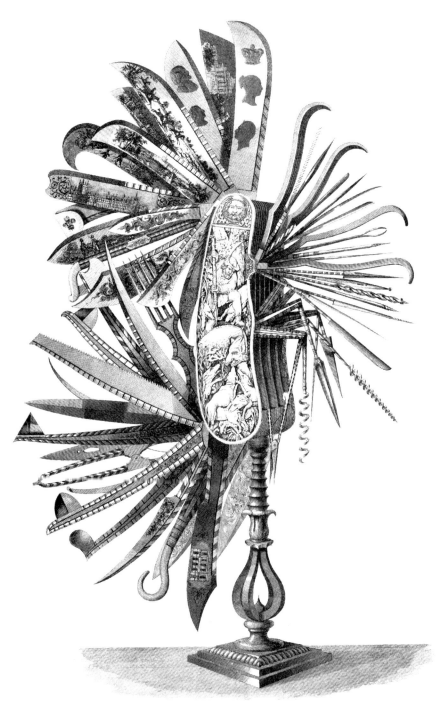

The Norfolk Knife, made by Rodgers for the Great Exhibition. After 1878, it was kept at the Norfolk Works, eventually being loaned for an exhibition at the Army & Navy Stores in London in 1935. When Rodgers fell on hard times in the 1960s, the Norfolk Knife was auctioned at Sotheby's in 1969 and bought by the Sheffield silverplate firm, Cooper Bros, who placed it on permanent loan at Cutlers' Hall.

*The carving on the Manila pearl scales of the Norfolk Knife was
executed by Charles Levesley. (Cutlers' Hall).*

hooks protruded from one side of the handle; while from the other, a series of master blades opened out like a fan, inviting closer inspection by the Victorian public. No doubt they were pleasantly surprised to find on the polished blades, acid-etched illustrations of, *inter alia*, the Crystal Palace itself, the Britannia Bridge, Windsor Castle, the Capitol in Washington, D.C., the Brighton Pavilion, and the heads of the Royal Family. Further decorative work enhanced the giant pearl scales.

We have few details about the creators of this giant work, christened the Norfolk Knife, or about its manufacture: however, scattered information indicates that the knife was made over a period of two years by William Bamforth and that the Manila-pearl carving on the scales was the work of

The superbly acid-etched views on the Norfolk Knife feature, inter alia, *The Capitol (Washington, D.C.),*
Sheffield College, and Albany. (Cutlers' Hall).

Charles Levesley (whose brother later ran Levesley Bros), who copied designs supplied by Wehnert. The total cost was £900—a considerable sum in the 1850s. The Norfolk Knife, however, was certainly the work of more than two men and was really a tribute to the countless cutlers at Joseph Rodgers & Sons.

The forging, grinding and tempering of some of these articles, such as the extra-long gimlets, corkscrews and springs, must have presented formidable problems to the Rodgers' cutlers. So, too, the fitting of so many articles into such a large knife. Yet the Norfolk Knife *springs* like an ordinary pocket-knife and all the parts fit together precisely. Ingeniously, the tools on the back of the knife are designed to drop into slots in the four giant hoofpicks as the knife is shut. Like all great works of art, one sees something new in the Norfolk Knife on each viewing. Besides the carved pearl scales (one depicting a boar hunt, the other a stag hunt) and skillful fileworking on the blade backs and springs, a particularly dazzling feature of the

Norfolk Knife is the acid-etching on the master blades and hoofpicks. These have been etched and polished with such precision and skill that the play of reflected light changes from black on white to white on black as you move around the knife.

Nor was this the full extent of Rodgers' display knives at the Exhibition. The Year Knife (now with 1851 blades) was wheeled out again. Rodgers also showed a pearl sport's knife with fifty-six blades and instruments—only $3/_4$" long! This was dwarfed by an ivory carving-knife and fork fifty-eight inches long (though for good measure this was also made in a $1^1/_2$" version).

Nowhere was John Bull's prowess over lesser, foreign mortals better demonstrated than in these exhibition knives. Little wonder firms such as Rodgers felt that no one could ever match them in the manufacture of a good knife. As Sheffield makers accepted their prize medals from the Great Exhibition judges, few would have imagined that within a few decades their leadership of the world cutlery industry would be under sustained threat.

6

Zenith and the Beginnings of Decline: 1860–1914

IN 1871, the leading trade journal, *The Ironmonger*, reviewed the history of Joseph Rodgers & Sons. Its article described the humble origins of the firm and its first tiny workshops in Sycamore Street, and then documented the rapid expansion of Rodgers into the nearby streets. 'The handsome and imposing frontage is in Norfolk Street', the journal told its readers, 'and the premises are, without doubt, for the purposes to which they are devoted, the most compact and complete in the world'. To many contemporaries, these last words might just as easily have described the Sheffield knife industry as a whole.

In the 1860s and 1870s, Sheffield was the dominant force in world cutlery. It was easily the most important centre of cutlery production in the United Kingdom and its factories employed the majority of the country's cutlers: in fact, by 1900 Sheffield monopolised the industry and virtually all the country's knifemakers worked in the town. Sheffield had emerged completely victorious over its older rivals in Salisbury and London. Sheffield also cast a long shadow, both in terms of quantity and quality, over the foreign centres of production in Germany (Solingen), France (Thiers), and New England (Massachusetts and Connecticut). No one knows how many knives poured out of Sheffield factories at this time: no official statistics and company records were kept. However, exports of hardware and cutlery, for which data exists, tell part of the story. They hit £4 million in 1857 and surpassed that amount for several years in the mid-1860s. The trade fell away slightly in the years up to 1870, but then the upward trend was resumed: exports reached a peak in 1872 when they registered £5 million. The world could still not get enough Sheffield knives. America was still a crucial factor in this strong export performance and trade reports show that the US trade still dominated the output of the town's cutlery manufactories.

With its cutlery factories in full swing, and its finest knives still carrying off the prize medals at industrial exhibitions, it must have seemed to Sheffield cutlers that it must always be thus. After all, how could it be otherwise, when many countries could not even melt their own crucible steel, and knife manufacture was still mainly a handicraft. As to the threat of foreign competition, most Sheffielders regarded the subject with disdain. Even seasoned journalists found it difficult to believe how the natural order could be undermined. *The Ironmonger's* 'artisan reporter' at the Paris Exhibition in 1878, having dismissed French and German cutlery as inferior and castigated the feeble showing of the Americans, asked:

> How was it that with the great facilities of machinery in America none of her sons could meet the Sheffield firms, and show scissors, razors or table cutlery, while the Sheffield firms of Rodgers & Sons, Wostenholm & Son, and John Wilson & Sons can keep agents in the United States and pay heavy import duties? I shall believe that the old town is not yet 'whipped' in the making of best cutlery, and so long as [its steelmakers], send steel from Sheffield, and some American makers advertise their goods as made from best 'English steel', I shall firmly believe that in good and cheap cutlery Sheffield will take some 'whipping'.

This would have been true enough if, as many Sheffielders expected, the world cutlery industry had stood still, but, of course, it did not. Even in Sheffield, changes were underway between 1860 and 1914. Although the humble Huntsman crucible continued to provide the cutlers with their raw material, elsewhere in the town the arrival of the bulk steelmaking processes of Bessemer and Siemens began having an enormous impact on the overall structure of the town's industry. Before 1860, Sheffield was regarded as essentially a cutlery metropolis, with steel a subsidiary activity. By 1900, the city was distinguished by its heavy steel trades, with cutlery and tool manufacture relegated to second place. As one reporter noted in 1884: 'the remarkable developments of the steel trade have long pushed the historic craft from its stool of honour'. The knifemakers were no longer the industry leaders in the city, and soon the fortunes of steelmakers such as Mark Firth, Thomas Jessop

and Sir John Brown dwarfed those that could be made in cutlery. The sea change had been signalled as early as 1860 by the Company of Cutlers, when it amended its rules to allow steelmakers to swell its ranks (and its coffers).

The arrival of cheap, mild steel, had other implications, since it opened the way to the production of low-cost Bessemer steel blades. This material did make some inroads into the Sheffield knife trade, though only to a limited extent. In Sheffield, the use of such steel was frowned upon and crucible (and shear) steel was still used almost exclusively for the finest qualities of knife. It was the same with handle materials. In the late nineteenth century, artificial handle materials were used more widely. This was due to the rise in the cost of raw materials, caused by an expanding market and limited supplies: for example, the cost of

Cutlers' Hall, home of the ancient craft guild of the industry. Stripped of its power in the early 19th century, the Company of Cutlers was revitalised after 1860 by the influx of wealthy steelmakers. It also found a new role for itself as the defender of Sheffield trade marks.

ivory doubled in price between 1879 and 1883, until it was fetching £1,000 per ton. By the 1870s, artificial materials, such as celluloid (introduced in the late 1860s) made their appearance. Vulcanite, ebonite, and xylonite also began replacing the traditional materials, even at some of the leading firms. For example, by 1879 Joseph Rodgers were manufacturing 'ebonite secure handled cutlery' and were predicting that man-made substances would soon replace ivory. Bone—the shin bone of beef cattle—was also used as a substitute for stag. Gouged (jigged) and dyed to resemble stag, it was very popular in America, and was also widely used in Sheffield by the twentieth century. Nevertheless, it was still felt in the trade that ivory, stag and pearl were the materials of first choice, especially for the highest qualities.

Not all makers were so choosy, especially abroad, where a seismic shift in world cutlery was to take place that would soon begin impinging on Sheffield's complacency. The tide began to turn in America, which for so long had been such a happy

hunting ground for the Sheffield knifemaker. Here a rival industry had been established in Connecticut and Massachusetts after the 1830s, by manufacturers such as Ames, Russell, Lamson & Goodnow, and Landers, Frary & Clark. These firms developed rapidly. American competition in certain classes of cutlery, especially table-knives, had been well underway before the Civil War. Sheffield manufacturers were naturally aware of this: even those that never visited America would have seen the worrying reports in the local newspapers in the late 1850s about the decline of Sheffield's table cutlery trade with America.

The Civil War marked a crucial divide. The Republicans immediately instituted a hefty tariff on imported goods (including Sheffield cutlery), launching a policy which by the end of the century would force English knives out of the American market. Government spending and currency inflation created a boom in the Northern states, which transformed the fortunes of the domestic cutlery manufacturers. Aided by the tariff, they were able

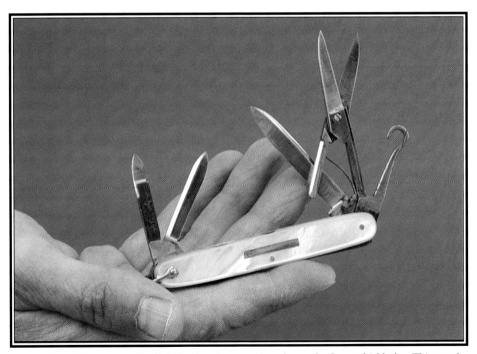

In the late 19th century, Sheffield knifemakers continued to make fine multi-blades. This pearl knife was made by Henry Hobson & Son in Queen Street, between about 1876 and the 1890s. The firm survived until the 1920s.

to take on Sheffield knifemakers for some of the more common goods, such as table cutlery. American purchasing power had been raised by the war, enabling US consumers to buy a better class of goods than Sheffield had been supplying. Meanwhile, the war disrupted the market for cutlery in the Southern states, which before 1860 had been one of Sheffield's best US markets for its common cutlery products. Social changes—the decline of the frontier culture, the subjugation of native Americans, the decimation of the buffalo, and, not least, the introduction of firearms—also ended the popularity of the Bowie knife. Not coincidentally, Table 1 (p.34) shows that many of the early Sheffield Bowie knife makers did not survive much beyond 1865. Money could still be made after the Civil War from the Bowie knife trade and there were some makers who did so, such as Brookes & Crookes, Slater Bros and John Clarke. But the golden age of the Bowie, and of Sheffield's American trade, had been ended by the Civil War.

After 1865, the US knife industry developed enormously. It was highlighted in the *Sheffield Independent*, 21st May 1878, with a feature on the Russell Cutlery Co. in Massachusetts, which was described as 'the largest in the United States'. The correspondent claimed that.

> …here the battle with Sheffield has been partly won. In 1834 all the table cutlery used in this country was imported from England. Today the English goods in this line have been entirely driven out of the American market, and only small exceptional parcels are being imported…The home market being secured, the trade is steadily extending into the foreign markets, notwithstanding the fact that the American table cutlery is dearer than the Sheffield articles. The reason why foreign nations are willing now even to pay a higher price for American cutlery of this particular description is because the goods made here are better shaped and better finished compared with the English table knife, which is clumsy and heavy.

How was this success achieved, especially since America was such a novice at the difficult art of knife manufacture? One might argue that it was Sheffield cutlers themselves—immigrants who took their skills across the Atlantic—who gave America such a good start. Certainly, Americans knew where to look when they needed good cutlers. As one immigrants' guide-book noted: 'Of foreigners, a Sheffield workman is preferred to all others, and if from the factory of Rodgers it is a sufficient introduction anywhere'. The number of Sheffield knifemakers who emigrated to America is unknown: however, it was a significant number and many did more than just settle as simple artisans. Some launched their own businesses. Table 2. (p.103) shows some of the more well known Sheffield cutlers in the New World. It is probably a partial listing. Some of these men became outstanding managers and business leaders. Perhaps the best example is the Platts family, whose leading light, Charles Platts (1838–1900), was trained as a knifemaker at Joseph Rodgers. He emigrated with his family to America in 1864, where he managed several concerns and then founded his own company, Western States Cutlery.

It would however be a mistake to suggest that the American knife industry was launched on Sheffield's back. After all, many Sheffield cutlers soon returned to their old 'hive', disillusioned and homesick, or their businesses failed. Others found that their old hand skills were of little use in a country which worshipped different gods. America, as a new country, was able to examine critically what was offered by the industry leaders and decide whether it was appropriate or not. They took what they needed from Sheffield and discarded the rest. In a country with labour shortages (and consequently high labour costs), Sheffield's laborious manual processes did not make economic sense. Instead, American manufacturers began using machinery. They were able to do so because the virtual absence of trade unionism, coupled with Yankee enterprise, allowed new ideas and technologies to flourish. In fact, Sheffield cutlers were responsible for some of them. An innovation that might have caused a strike or the bombing of a factory in Sheffield was welcomed enthusiastically in the New World. A major breakthrough was the drop-forging of knife blades, which eliminated Sheffield's laborious hand-forging.

FIRM	LOCATION	DATE	SHEFFIELD FOUNDERS
Rawson Bros	*Birmingham, Connecticut*	*c. 1846–1853*	*James Rawson*
Empire Knife Co.	*Winsted, Connecticut*	*c. 1856–1930*	*Gascoigne & Thompson*
New York Knife Co.	*Walden, New York*	*c. 1856–1931*	*Various Sheffield cutlers*
Northfield Knife Co.	*Northfield, Connecticut*	*1858–1929*	*Various Sheffield cutlers*
Booth Bros	*Sussex, New Jersey*	*1864–1909*	*Thomas Booth*
Clayton Bros	*Bristol, Connecticut*	*c. 1866–1906*	*William Clayton*
Cooperative Knife Co.	*Ellenville, New York*	*c. 1871–1876*	*Various Sheffield cutlers*
Turner & Cowlishaw	*Meriden, Connecticut*	*1873–?*	*Joseph Turner & William Cowlishaw*
J.W. Gardner	*Shelburne Falls, Massachusetts*	*c. 1876–1883*	*Joseph William Gardner*
Burkinshaw Knife Co.	*Pepperell, Massachusetts*	*c. 1881–1920*	*Aaron Burkinshaw*
Morris Cutlery Co.	*Grundy County, Illinois*	*c. 1882–1930*	*Albert & William Smith*
Hatch Cutlery Co.	*Bridgeport, Connecticut*	*1885–?*	*Fred Sackley*
C. Platts & Sons	*Gowanda, New York*	*1896–1905*	*Charles Platts & family*

Table 2. *Sheffield Cutlers in America.*

Eventually, knife blades in the USA would be stamped straight out from a steel sheet and then ground by machine. Of course, the quality was not as good as that of the best Sheffield blades, which was why Sheffield makers scorned the American methods, but it saved time, eliminated hard work, and reduced costs. Output soared.

Machine-made cutlery eliminated much of the customised nature of the ancient cutlery industry. The Americans began to reduce drastically the number of patterns available and became committed to standardisation; again, this was something that was anathema in Sheffield. The US manufacturer, though, was responding to a market which was far more willing than the European one to accept standardised goods. The American blueprint for success in knife manufacture was to concentrate on simple, mass-produced items, that could be advertised and sold in huge quantities and as cheaply as possible to the country's agricultural (but rapidly urbanising) population. To ensure these knives sold well, the American government continually raised the tariff barriers to keep out Sheffield imports.

American products—simple, but well-finished table- and hunting-knives—began pushing Sheffield out of the US market by the 1870s. Sheffield began to take a 'whipping'. Only in the highest qualities of pocket-knives was Sheffield able to hold its share of the market, as their manufacture had not yet succumbed to Yankee mechanisation. What spoiled even the pocket-knife market, however, was the rise of vigorous competition from Germany. Solingen also exploited mass-production methods and its low labour costs meant that it could compete effectively in America. It too embraced the ethos of cheap cutlery production to exploit America's mass market (helped along by a little counterfeiting of Sheffield's famous old marks!). A Sheffield business review in about 1887 raged against the 'ubiquitous Teuton, [who] not content with invading every commercial centre of the world, makes inroads into the very well-spring of the cutlery trade itself, and flaunts his meretricious wares in the windows of Sheffield shopkeepers'. But what was Sheffield to do about German and American competition?

Cutlery manufacture was partly mechanised by the Americans and Germans in the late 19th century, but in Sheffield traditional technologies were retained. This Sheffield table-knife cutler is finishing blades by hand in 1902.

It could still point to its virtues. First, there was the typical English pride in a handicraft job well done. A correspondent in *The English Illustrated Magazine* wrote in 1884:

> The best knives are, and always probably will be, made by hand, and the qualities which are necessary to this system are in Sheffield hereditary. In dexterity of handling, rapidity of execution, perception of results, and honest zest, the Hallamshire forger and grinder are unapproached by any foreign workman in the trade. With the latter the moral motive force is generally the bare necessity of earning bread and cheese; with the former there is the same incentive plus an inspiring local patriotism. Wherever foreign competitors have chipped Sheffield trade, the end has been adapting machinery to common work, as in America, or by stooping to the wholesale production of cutlery that won't cut, as in Germany.

Sheffield contempt for machinery is well highlighted by these comments. On other hand, the Sheffield industry itself was vulnerable to criticism. As the era of the mass-produced knife began to appear in America and Germany, Sheffield industry was beginning to look dated after the 1880s. No doubt Sheffield knives did look magnificent in the display or exhibition case, but the working conditions under which they were made did not. Sheffield was not filled with Ruskinite craftsmen, contentedly plying their trade in independent circumstances. The workforce was still poorly paid, treated in an arbitrary manner, and burdened by long hours in workshops that were often dirty and hazardous. Towards the end of the century, some of the leading Sheffield cutlery manufacturers and a few trade union officials, slowly began to pay serious attention to what was happening in the USA and Germany. The conclusions of their reports were virtually identical: although foreign products may not have equalled Sheffield's best, business organisation and working conditions abroad were far superior. This is what Robert Holmshaw, of the Sheffield Cutlery Council, saw in America in 1902:

> The workshops…were, with few exceptions, very good, being large, well-lighted, and heated by steam pipes…and there is no outworking. In an American factory a good stock of the raw materials used in manufacturing is kept ready for use—such as blades, handles, scales, springs and all other parts required in the making of a knife. This means there is no unnecessary waste of time…[as]…the employer's object is to turn out as much work as possible, and he knows that the best way to accomplish this is to make the workpeople as comfortable as possible, and place every means for rapid working at their disposal, with the result that the men can earn good wages under good conditions, and the employer is sure of an increased output. In Sheffield, as far as I know, only one firm has the same methodical time-saving system.

Sheffield's commitment to craft technologies also brought other problems. How could one small, isolated locality and a relatively small band of workers cope with the demand for knives from the whole of the industrialised world? Already by the 1880s, Sheffield was having difficulty in filling orders from Far Eastern and Australian markets. Even if Sheffield had fended off foreign competitors, it seems doubtful if it could have raised output sufficiently without introducing machinery.

In these circumstances, Sheffield's dislike for machine-made goods looks far less reasonable. In any case, the town had had no qualms about making money by producing low-cost knives: the rapid expansion of the American trade after 1815 had been partly built on low-grade cutlery—indeed, some localities around Sheffield, such as Wadsley, became notorious for it. The town's knifemakers also made the mistake of far too readily linking machine-made products with the slapdash and shoddy. No doubt many of Sheffield's criticisms of early mass-produced knives were entirely justified, but they forgot that technology does not stand still. The early machines were soon improved and superior designs were devised that would greatly raise the quality of mass-produced knives, maybe not to the heights of the old Sheffield knives, but certainly good enough for most customers.

Unfortunately, Sheffield's reaction to foreign competition was largely reactionary. An American who visited Joseph Rodgers in 1873 found that: 'They pride themselves on the age of their establishment

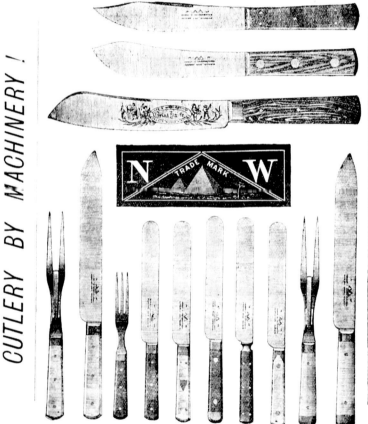

Nixon & Winterbottom were one of the few progressive firms in Sheffield. This advertisement from an 1876 Sheffield directory is probably the first to mention 'cutlery by machinery'.

and on the fact that they do not use improved machinery'. Not surprisingly, most of the other knifemakers in Sheffield, though they used some machines for sawing and cutting up materials, did little to mechanise their processes. Only a handful of firms made a real effort in this direction. The first knifemaker to absorb the message from abroad was James Drabble, who by the early 1860s had laid down machinery to compete with the Americans and Germans in table-knives. Another maker, Joseph Nixon (of Nixon & Winterbottom), had followed this lead at the firm's Pyramid Works by the 1870s. In 1880, Samuel Staniforth (c.1840–1910) began drop-forging table- and butcher-blades with a steam hammer at his Central Cutlery Forge in Carver Street. John McClory at the Eldon Works also made an unashamed bid for the market in 'cheap and middle-class goods' to compete with the Germans.

These were hardly dramatic developments in such a large manufacturing centre; and anyway most of these technologies had been around since at least the 1850s. By the 1890s, no factory in Sheffield was completely mechanised, and no attempt had been made to use machinery in labour-intensive branches of knife manufacture, such as pocket-knife assembly. Many of the pioneering firms did not fulfil their owners' expectations. Drabble ceased business by the end of the 1880s; Nixon & Winterbottom were taken over; McClory's survived, but remained a small business. Only Staniforth prospered, 'the demand for machine-forged blades [growing] at such as rate as necessitated constant extensions of plant'. Perhaps the demise of many of these low-cost makers confirmed Sheffielders' poor opinion of cheaper goods; more likely these businesses failed because the adoption of machinery was not sophisticated and wide-ranging enough to drive down costs.

A Brookes & Crookes' patent veterinary-knife, with Syme's Lancet, operating blade, searcher, scissors, forceps, flesh-needles, metallic probe, caustic and holder. It was made in scored horn, buckhorn, tortoiseshell, and nickel-silver.

Either way, despite the problems in America and Teuton skullduggery, Sheffield's knifemakers between 1880 and 1914 settled back into the routine of what they did best—producing high-quality, hand-made goods. Some firms threw themselves with renewed vigour into the quality market. Perhaps the best example of this is Brookes & Crookes, founded in 1858, which directed its efforts towards the luxury market. In particular, Brookes & Crookes' craftsmen devoted their skills to the production of superb sport's- and gadget-knives. *The Implement and Machinery Review* told its readers that Brookes & Crookes' knives were:

...got up in a great variety of patterns, with 'scales' of pearl, ivory, shell, stag and buffalo. Some of them are elaborately carved, the blades and instruments are of the best steel, and the backs of some of them are most skillfully worked. Here are sportsmen's knives which have carved on their rich, creamy-looking ivory scales, the Prince of Wales' feathers or some other design; the backs are chastely worked, and the springs being of different colours, a very pretty effect is produced. Another large knife of the same class has pearl scales; and one of its novelties is that it has no inside, the springs by an ingenious arrangement, acting as dividers between the different blades and instruments.

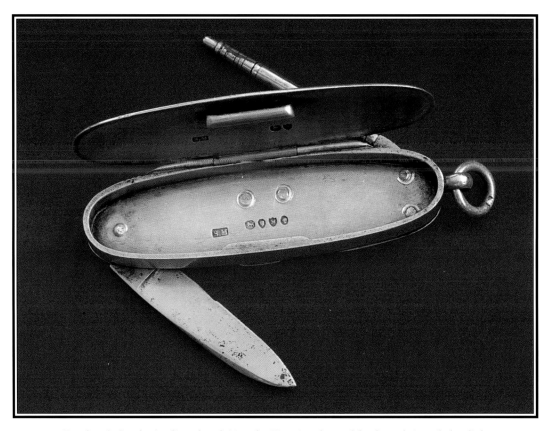

Brookes & Crookes' policy of exploiting the Victorian demand for fancy knives, led to links with London silver firms. This silver knife has blades by Brookes & Crookes and a propelling pencil by Sampson Morden & Co. of London, whose silver mark is inside the box (which may have been for snuff).

BEST CUTLERY, FROM THE CHRISTOPHER JOHNSON

BLADES WARRANTED, MANUFACTORY OF WESTERN WORKS, SHEFFIELD.

Sheffield's forte in the late 19th century was still in high-quality products rather than mass production. Superb sport's-knives in a huge range of patterns were still made in large quantities by firms such as Christopher Johnson.

This era was, in fact, the heyday of the Sheffield sport's-knife, when makers seemed to delight in lavishing on these knives all their available time and skills.

Vigorous foreign competition and the arrival of cheaper products also nurtured another defensive reaction in Sheffield knifemakers—an increasing commitment to trademark defence. Sheffield complaints about foreign makers, especially the Germans, stamping their inferior products as 'Made in Sheffield' or using fraudulent Sheffield marks, grew to a crescendo before 1914. In Sheffield's eyes it was bad enough marketing cheap, trashy knives: to then illegally stamp those products with a hallowed Sheffield mark, added insult to injury. As their blood pressure increased, Sheffield makers pressed the government to legislate. With the passing of the Trade Marks Act of 1875, some of their demands for protection were met. But the problem refused to go away. Sheffield became even more obsessional about trademark defence, a battle which drew in the Company of Cutlers (keen to find itself a new role after being stripped of its power earlier in the century), the Chamber of Commerce and many of the town's business leaders. Committees met constantly, Parliament was lobbied, delegations were sent abroad, and funding drives were launched. Many of the industry leaders, such as Rodgers and Wostenholm, regularly took foreign offenders to court. Alas, it proved largely futile. The counterfeiting of Sheffield marks continued unabated; so too did foreign competition.

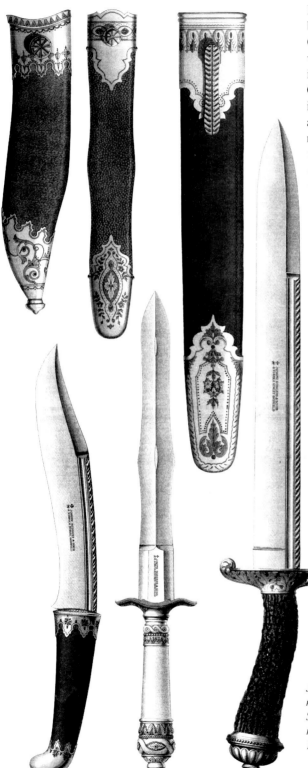

In fact, trademark defence proved to be a great blunder by the Sheffield knifemakers and by the Company of Cutlers. No doubt, trade marks were worth defending up to a point, but not if it meant ignoring the real reasons for American and German success—the modernisation of an ancient industry. There was always a touch of hypocrisy about the whole business, especially since it was not long before some Sheffield makers were importing blanks from abroad (which they then stamped 'Sheffield') to supplement their output. In trade marks as in everything else, Sheffield wanted the world to stand still.

To be sure, it was to be several decades before the weaknesses of the Sheffield knife industry became fully apparent. One factor that allowed Sheffield to avoid coming to terms with mechanisation was the growth of trade with new overseas markets. The central fact of Sheffield's overseas trade after 1860 was the swift decline of its trade with the USA, caused partly by the rise of that country's own knife industry and partly by punitive tariffs (the McKinley Tariff of 1890 having a particularly crippling effect). Sheffield had to look for other markets and by the 1870s this trend was well underway. Colonial markets in Australia, Canada and the Far East (especially India) became the favourite targets, as did South Africa and South America. Instead of Bowie knives, Sheffield trade catalogues began to sport Oriental daggers, matchets and tea-plantation knives.

These markets were not as prosperous as America; and Sheffield makers also found that they faced stiff competition from Germany and America. Nevertheless, countries such as Australia, where English manufacturers had preferential treatment, offered a huge and growing market. Australia imported an average of nearly £150,000 of British

Joseph Rodgers was one firm which exploited Colonial markets, where it had long had a good reputation. Some Far Eastern influence can be detected in its range of daggers and Bowie knives in the late 19th century.

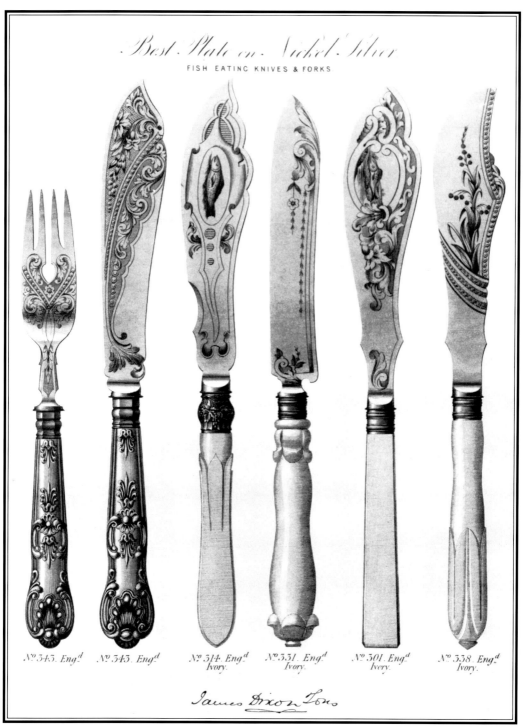

Best Plate on Nickel Silver

FISH EATING KNIVES & FORKS.

Nº 343. Eng.ᵈ   Nº 343. Eng.ᵈ   Nº 314. Eng.ᵈ   Nº 331. Eng.ᵈ   Nº 301. Eng.ᵈ   Nº 338. Eng.ᵈ
                                    Ivory.   Ivory.   Ivory.   Ivory.

James Dixon Sons

Sheffield's silver- and electroplate factories exploited the expanding middle- and upper-class markets for fancy eating cutlery. Fish-knives were a best-selling line for firms such as James Dixon.

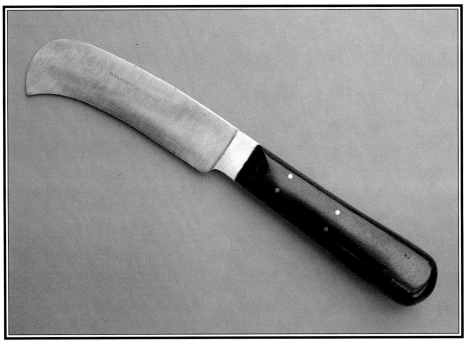

*A tea-plantation knife, made by an unidentified Sheffield maker in the 1870s. Sheffield began to
exploit the Far Eastern demand at this time as the American trade declined.*

cutlery each year in the first decade of the twentieth century—roughly double the amount that was sent to any other country. Such sales limited the damage caused by overseas competition and helped keep the Sheffield cutlery industry prosperous.

Another factor maintained Sheffield's place as the greatest cutlery centre in the world before 1914—the rapid growth of the silver- and electroplate trade. The trend can be seen in the employment figures for the industry in Table 3.

	1891	1911
Spring-knives	*5,800*	*4,700*
Table-knives	*4,850*	*4,500*
	10,650	*9,200*
Silver & plated	*5,300*	*10,600*

Table 3. *Employment in the Sheffield Knife
and Silver Trades.*

The silver and plated sector had been developing steadily since about the 1840s, as an offshoot of the cutlery industry. It fitted comfortably with the town's high-quality ethos. By the late nineteenth century, the dominant firms in this sector were Walker & Hall, Dixon's, Hutton's, Martin Hall, and Mappin & Webb. They grew rapidly as they supplied the Victorian and Edwardian dining room and parlour with tea- and coffee-services, claret jugs, cruet sets, cups, salvers and trays, cake baskets and entrée dishes. Some of these accoutrements were knives—fish-carvers, dessert-knives, lemon-saws, silver carving-sets and silver fruit-knives—and manufacturing them was something to which many of the knifemaking firms could adapt. Rodgers, for example, had launched a line in silver and plated goods by the 1860s. By the end of the century, nearly all the major knifemaking firms (with the exception perhaps of Wostenholm) were involved with the trade. This did their shareholders a world of good and kept the dividends of firm's

Firms such as Mappin & Webb which specialised in silver- and electroplate grew particularly rapidly after the 1880s. This view of the Royal Cutlery & Plate Works can be compared with the gloomy photograph of the same factory on page 225.

Needham, Veall & Tyzack's Eye Witness Works in the 1890s. The view looks impressive, due to a fair degree of artistic licence, but the map of the area (overleaf) shows that the cutlery industry around Milton Street was still small-scale and dominated by courtyards and tiny factories.

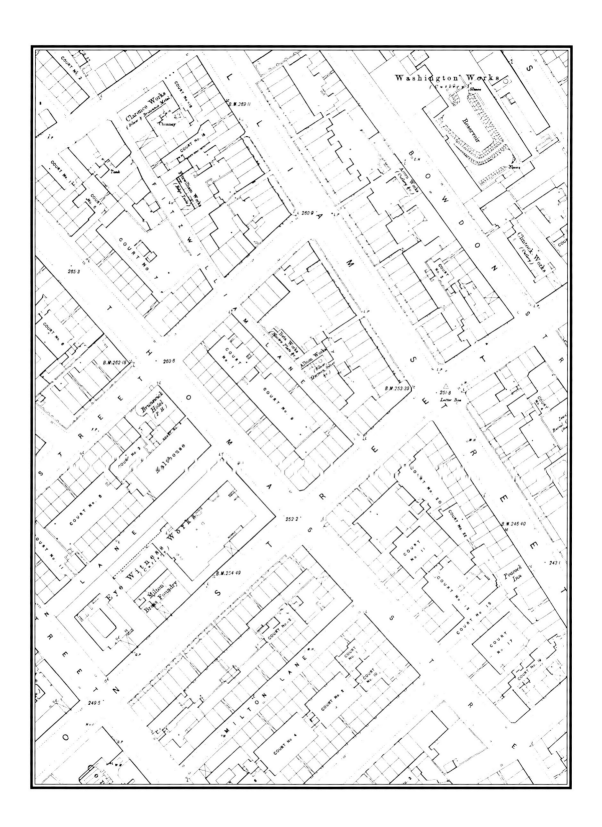

Company	Works/Address	Employees
Joseph Rodgers	*Norfolk Works*	*2000*
Walker & Hall	*Electro Works*	*800*
James Dixon	*Cornish Place Works*	*800*
Wostenholm	*Washington Works*	*700*
Butler	*Trinity Works*	*400*
Harrison Bros & Howson	*Norfolk Street*	*350+*
Martin, Hall	*Shrewsbury Works*	*350+*
Beal	*Red Hill Works*	*350*
Joseph Fenton	*Sykes Works*	*300+*
Turner	*Suffolk Works*	*300*
Mappin & Webb	*Royal Cutlery Works*	*250+*
William Hutton	*West Street*	*250+*
John Round	*Tudor Works*	*250*
Wingfield, Rowbotham	*Tenter Street*	*250*
Francis Newton	*Portobello Works*	*250*
James Deakin	*Sidney Works*	*200*
Southern & Richardson	*Don Cutlery Works*	*200*
Atkin Bros	*Truro Works*	*200*
Needham, Veall & Tyzack	*Eye Witness Works*	*150+*
Lockwood Bros	*Spital Hill Works*	*150*
Christopher Johnson	*Western Works*	*150*
John Wragg	*Advance Works*	*150*
Brookes & Crookes	*Atlantic Works*	*150*
A.J. Jordan	*East India Works*	*120+*
Thos Ellin	*Sylvester Works*	*100+*
Michael Hunter	*Talbot Works*	*100+*
William Gregory	*Howard Street*	*100+*
Wheatley Bros	*Eclipse Works*	*100+*
Mappin Bros	*Queen's Cutlery*	*100+*
John Batt	*Park Works*	*100+*
Maurice Baum	*Albert Works*	*100+*
Needham, Veall & Tyzack	*Eye Witness Works*	*100+*
Joseph Allen	*Oak Works*	*100*
Thos Renshaw	*Stand Works*	*100*
Parkin & Marshall	*Telegraph Works*	*100*
Francis Howard	*Aberdeen Works*	*80+*
Hides	*Hollis Works*	*80+*
John Newton	*Manhattan Works*	*40+*
R.F. Mosley	*Portland Works*	*40+*
John Sellers	*Arundel Street*	*40+*
Joseph Haywood	*Glamorgan Works*	*40+*
Deakin	*Tiger Works*	*40+*
John Petty	*Perth Works*	*40+*
Ibberson	*Central Works*	*40+*
John Clarke	*Harvest Lane*	*40+*

Table 4. *Leading Sheffield Cutlery Firms in 1890.*

Company	Works/Address	Employees
Walker & Hall	*Electro Works*	*2000*
Rodgers	*Norfolk Works*	*1500*
Dixon	*Cornish Place Works*	*1000*
Turner	*Suffolk Works*	*1000*
Hutton	*West Street Works*	*900*
Martin, Hall	*Shrewsbury Works*	*750*
Mappin & Webb	*Royal Cutlery Works*	*600*
Harrison Bros & Howson	*Alpha Works*	*600*
Wostenholm	*Washington Works*	*400*
Needham, Veall & Tyzack	*Eye Witness Works*	*350*
Atkin Bros	*Truro Works*	*250*

Table 5. *Leading Sheffield Cutlery Firms in 1914.*

such as Rodgers at respectable levels up to 1914. On the other hand, this prosperity masked underlying weaknesses in the core business of knifemaking. Certainly, the employment figures suggest that the city's knife industry had peaked before the First World War. So too does data for employment at the leading firms (shown in Tables 4 and 5). These figures can only be approximate (since they are gleaned from the trade press and newspapers and are sometimes estimates), but they do show that the rankings had altered significantly between about 1890 and 1914. By the First World War, the knifemakers had clearly passed their peak in terms of employment, while the silver firms were clearly reaching theirs.

The picture, of course, is painted retrospectively. At the time, few Sheffielders had doubts about their great knife industry. It was an Empire on which the sun never set.

Table-knife cutlers at Walker & Hall's Electro Works, photographed for a commemorative booklet produced by the company, c. 1918. Such traditional hand-technology became a liability for the industry during the War, when Sheffield was unable to step up its output to meet Government orders.

7

The First World War and Its Aftermath, 1914–1939

BOTH BEFORE AND DURING the Great War, Sheffield was the armoury of the nation. It was the home of Vickers, Brown, Cammell, Firth and Hadfields—the great arms conglomerates which supplied the front line with guns, shells and armour-plated ships. In fact, the special steels produced by Sheffield were one of the most important materials in the ensuing carnage. The phrase 'blood and iron' summed it up well; or more accurately, from Sheffield's viewpoint, 'blood and steel'.

The Great War brought unprecedented expansion for the Sheffield steel industry as vast new works' extensions were made and workers poured into the city. One would have imagined that the same trends would have occurred in the knife industry: after all, knives, bayonets and cut-throat razors were all standard issue for the British Tommy, to say nothing of supplies to overseas Allies. But the impact of the war on the knife industry was to prove decidedly mixed.

At the outbreak of war, many of the cutlery firms moved into high gear as the first contracts for clasp-knives, bayonets and spoons arrived. The surgical instrument-makers, not surprisingly, soon found their order books bulging. The Government completely cleared out the stocks of razors for the Army and the city's firms soon found themselves working overtime. The sword trade, which had largely been in the hands of Birmingham and German makers, also returned to Sheffield, once military personnel began demanding more than mere ceremonial weapons.

In the first year of the war, Sheffield knifemakers were also busy exploiting what was the city's greatest innovation in the cutlery trade since the advent of crucible steel—the discovery of stainless cutlery. This owed most to Harry Brearley (1871–1948), the director of the Brown-Firth Research Laboratories, who, in the course of his researches in 1913 into high-tensile alloy steels, discovered a chromium steel which was remarkably impervious to almost all corrosive influences. This new steel was low in carbon and contained about twelve percent chromium (an element which had the happy ability of forming an oxide film on the steel's surface, which resisted corrosion). Soon Brearley ensured that blanks of stainless steel (or 'rustless' steel, as it was also known in the beginning) were given a trial by the city's leading knifemakers. R.F. Mosely's and Ibberson's were pioneer users.

At first stainless steel did not seem a promising material for knife blades: it was so hard, it was virtually impossible to forge by normal methods and the traditional craftsmen took a dislike to it. However, with a little perseverance in forging the blades by power, satisfactory progress was made and the first stainless table knives appeared in the autumn of 1914. The new steel, manufactured by Brearley's employer, Thos Firth & Sons, caused a sensation. As Brearley remarked: 'The steel, once declared dead and well nigh worthless, was made an absorbing topic of conversation among cutlers and steel-makers, and the subject of newspaper comments'. On 3rd July 1915, for example, the *Sheffield Independent*, reported that: 'There is an increasing demand for table knives made of the new rustless steel and half a dozen firms are now making the latter material'. By 27th November, the newspaper stated that: 'Rustless and stainless table

There is nothing unusual about this hunting-knife, except that it once belonged to Harry Brearley.
It was presented to him by an Antarctic explorer, G. Taylor, in 1911—so it is not stainless!

cutlery is growing more and more popular week by week'.

Unfortunately, this promising development was nipped in the bud. Stainless steel proved ideal for another purpose—making aero-engine components—and this was judged to be of greater strategic importance than rustless knives. Since supplies of ferro-chromium were scarce, the Government immediately restricted its use in the cutlery industry. A rapidly developing sector of the knife industry immediately went into eclipse, until the restriction was lifted at the end of the War.

The War also hit other sectors of the cutlery industry. The mighty Sheffield silver- and electroplate firms: Walker & Hall; Dixon and Mappin & Webb, found that the market for luxury goods soon evaporated. Observed the *Sheffield Independent* (6th August 1915): 'The luxury trades of Sheffield, such as the best-class electroplate, have suffered severely because of the period of economy which has been encouraged throughout the country'. Many of the craftsmen from these firms either enlisted (at Mappin & Webb 250 staff had joined up, at Walker & Hall 335) or soon found jobs in the

big Brightside steel works, where wages were higher and there was plenty of overtime. Many never returned to their old jobs. Some of the electroplate firms adapted readily to war work. For example, Walker & Hall made thousands of table- and clasp-knives, and also supplied copper driving-bands for shells. Wm Hutton's subsidiary, the Sheffield Flatware Co. (the ownership of which was shared with Dixon; Walker & Hall and Barker Bros), did a profitable business making forged shell-heads and steel baseplates. Generally however, the profits of the electroplate firms were badly affected by the war.

It also hit the top-end makers in the knife trade. Firms such as Joseph Rodgers and George Wostenholm found that the market for their high-quality spring knives disappeared rapidly. Money could be made in the trade, but only by turning out the cheaper qualities, which did not fit the ethos of these firms. Rodgers' profits fell during the War from about £20,000 a year to £12,000. Wostenholm's profits also declined, as its directors lamented that the war was 'making havoc with the cutlery trade'. One Wostenholm director even described life in the trenches as 'paradise' compared with the wartime cutlery trade.

In some ways, the war was a leveller, because it allowed some of the smaller firms to expand. A good example is Viners (then known as Viener's). Once the leading members of this firm had been released from internment (caused by their German origins), they swiftly moved into munitions manufacture. Bullet-proof alloy-steel helmets—up to 36,000 a week—were turned out by the firm, using an ingenious pressing and stamping plant. As production was stepped up and the plant was worked day and night, items such as exploder containers and breastplates were also manufactured.

Plenty of cutlery orders were also available at the beginning of the war. The Army was demanding a million-and-a-half cut-throat razors, and with Germany now out of the international cutlery market, orders began to arrive from the Colonies and America. However, these orders cruelly emphasised the deficiencies of the Sheffield knife trade. The old hand-methods were simply not up to the job of producing in bulk. As the *Sheffield Daily Telegraph*, 16th February 1915, commented: 'The suspension of the German cutlery industry has had the effect of bringing a flood of inquiries from America and the home market to Sheffield for huge quantities of cheap goods, but many orders had to be rejected through inability to increase local output and because purchasers expected to get goods at German prices'. Soon Sheffield cutlers fell six months behind with their orders and there was a shortage of both workers and materials. The Company of Cutlers had to launch a public appeal for razors, when the city's firms proved unable to meet the Army demands. The impact of the failure of the industry to modernise in the years before the war was now being felt. At the heart of the problem was the lack of mechanisation.

An exhibition of cutlery at Cutlers' Hall, in February and March 1915, rammed the point home. It was organised by one of the more progressive knife manufacturers, Walter Tyzack of Taylor's 'Eye Witness' fame, who was keen to push the industry towards a more mechanised future. The pocket-knives and table cutlery (and

razors and scissors) in the exhibition were piquant, to say the least—they were all German-made. As the *Sheffield Independent*, 13th February 1915, remarked: 'The exhibition of German cutlery now being held at the Cutlers' Hall is a revelation in price and finish of articles'. Sheffield cutlers found themselves fighting a war on two fronts, both military and commercial.

The message was not lost on some of the leading manufacturers, who, in the aftermath of the exhibition, organised conferences between manufacturers and workmen to discuss what was to be done. These meetings, such as at Cutlers' Hall in March 1915, chaired by the Master Cutler, W.H. Ellis, brought to the surface many of the long-standing criticisms of the Sheffield industry. Walter Tyzack stated that:

> …he was not much of a believer in the making of cheaper goods, and would not encourage rubbish, but there was a call for a cheaper class of goods. The factory system that had grown up in Sheffield was wrong entirely, and the method of a firm doing for itself everything from A to Z, when it might be more profitable for one firm to do certain things for the lot, was wrong. There would have to be more specialising and making a feature of certain classes of work. As regarding the adoption of machinery, there was great room for improvement.

Tyzack himself had set an example at Needham, Veall & Tyzack by installing German machinery at the Pond Hill Works to manufacture a basic design of Army knife. With mechanisation, less experienced workers—boys, girls, even the blind—could make knives.

However, not all the big knifemakers were so well-disposed towards the introduction of machines. There was little sign that Rodgers did much to mechanise during the war. Wostenholm's were full of good intentions and brought some fresh blood into the company through the appointment of a new director, Frank Colver, who made a start on a much-needed overhaul of the company. But when Colver drew up plans at the end of the war to install machinery for pocket-knife manufacture, he was bitterly opposed by some of the older members

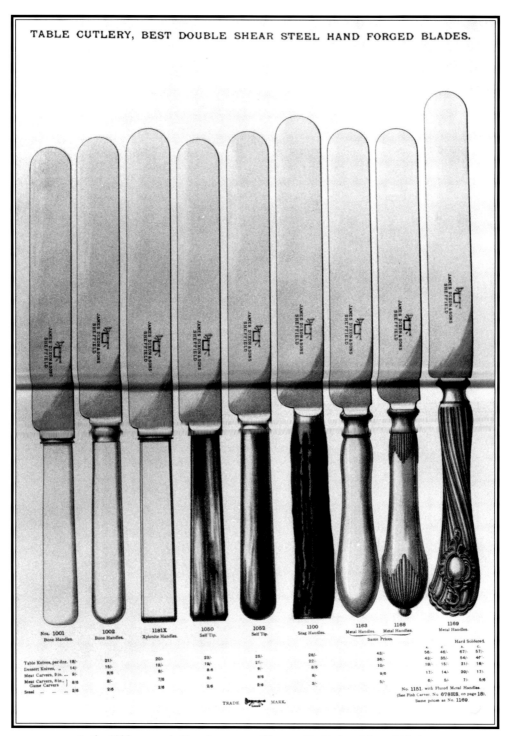

TABLE CUTLERY, BEST DOUBLE SHEAR STEEL HAND FORGED BLADES.

In the 1920s, many knifemakers were still committed to hand-forged blades,
sometimes made from shear steel.

of the company. It was probably this opposition to machinery, coupled with the decline in the demand for luxury articles, which did most harm to the Sheffield knife industry in the long run.

The basic structure of the knife industry was not much altered by the War. A glance at the Sheffield trade directories for these years shows that the knife trade was still dominated by a large number of small firms. Some Victorian firms fell by the wayside during the War: nevertheless, by 1918 over a hundred pocket- and sportsman's-knife makers were listed in the directories; and the total of table-knife manufacturers easily topped a hundred. Ironically, the War had fostered more individualism: it had weakened the biggest firms, which perhaps should have been the very ones to lead any restructuring of the industry, and boosted the profits of the medium- and small-sized producers. Since good profits could be earned on war contracts using the old technology and business organisation, there was little incentive to modernise. Concluded the *Sheffield Daily Telegraph* in its New Year trade review in 1919: 'when everything is weighed up, there has been little progress towards a new order of things'.

Once the War had ended, most of the trade's grand ideas about mechanisation and merger were forgotten in a post-war boom. The resumption of demand was confidently predicted by almost every industry in the country and the cutlers, too, looked forward to business as usual. However, it was soon clear that there would be no return to the golden age of the nineteenth century. Some of the big firms had been seriously damaged by the impact of the War. Their work's rolls were in decline: Dixon's fell from 1,000 to 850 during this period; Wostenholm's from 400 to 200; and Martin & Hall's from 750 to 500. This was partly the result of losses in the trenches, where Rodgers had lost 55 men, Walker & Hall 40, and Wostenholm 36. At Turner's, the top management was badly hit, when the two sons of Sir Albert Hobson lost their lives. When the firm became a limited company in 1918, the *Sheffield Daily Telegraph*, 2nd February 1918, stated that 'the flotation [was] the direct result of the heroic sacrifice of their lives for their country

of the sons of Alderman Hobson'. Moreover, in the inter-war period, the whole atmosphere of the knife industry had changed. This was partly due to technological factors; partly because of social changes; and also due to changing economic realities.

In the 1920s, many of the old-established Sheffield knife firms hankered for the days when customers demanded high-quality, hand-made products. Any wartime enthusiasm for mass-production methods had disappeared by the 1920s. W.C. Veall was quoted in one newspaper in 1926 as follows: 'I think it would be better to maintain Sheffield's high-grade quality than to go in for mass-production of low-grade articles'. This was astute: but once again the mistake was made of viewing mass-production as synonymous with poor quality.

There was still a considerable commitment to hand-forged crucible steel for the better qualities of pocket-knife and kitchen-knife. Several firms—John Wilson, Needham, Veall & Tyzack, Joseph Rodgers & Ibberson—were committed to the production of hand-forged cutlery. A few firms still used double-shear steel. For example, Southern & Richardson stated in 1928 that the manufacture of double-shear butchers'-knives was still an important part of the business. The trade catalogues of this era also show that many of the old firms were still producing the traditional patterns of pocket-knife. Butler's, for example, still displayed in its trade catalogues (one of which survives in Sheffield Library) Bowie knives and most types of multi-blades, such as smoker's-knives and fisherman's-knives. So, too, did Wostenholm, which still made much of its nineteenth-century heritage. A page illustrating several Wostenholm single-blade folding-knives, from a catalogue sent out to dealers in 1930, stated: 'The blades of these I*XL pocket-knives are forged from high-grade crucible steel, ground and whetted by hand by skilled workmen, many of whom are members of families that have worked for Wostenholm's for several generations'. However, the long term future of these steels was now in doubt. The electric arc and induction furnaces in the inter-war years dealt a mortal blow to the crucible process and after the Second World War the technology became extinct.

Hand-forging double-shear steel at Butler's factory between the wars. Foreign competitors, such as the Americans, had ceased hand-forging in the 19th century, but in Sheffield, makers still believed it gave the steel extra quality and they proudly advertised their blades as 'hand-forged'.

In the early 1920s, the commitment of the city's cutlers to defending their illustrious marks continued. In 1924, the Company of Cutlers succeeded in registering 'Sheffield' as a trade mark, the first time that a locality had done so. It showed that the industry's nineteenth-century obsession with trade-mark defence was as strong as ever. It also proved to be as big a waste of time as ever. Trade marking was to become less, not more important after the 1920s. It was natural when business turned sour in the black decades of the 1920s and 1930s, that the Company of Cutlers and the industry leaders would wish to capitalise on their traditional reputation and defend their name. What was less forgivable

was their Canute-like inability to recognise and adapt to new trends in the industry.

One of the most worrying trends was the fall in demand for many of the older styles of Sheffield knives and the introduction of completely new products. For example, as the motor car appeared on the scene, few wanted a sport's-knife with a hoofpick and a leather-borer. The market for many types of farmer's-knives, such as fleams, also fell victim to changing fashions and the rise of urbanisation. As industry became more mechanised, many trade-knives were no longer in such great demand. Pencil sharpeners meant at least one less use for the traditional Sheffield pen-knife. People were ceasing to carry fancy pocket-knives as an item of dress; and button-hooks were becoming a thing of the past. As the price of the best materials, such as pearl and stag, continued to rise, it was cost which dictated market trends. The consumer wanted cheapness and throw-away items. The safety-razor, marketed so successfully by Gillette, epitomised this change. Although many Sheffield razor makers (and some customers) retained their loyalty to the old cut-throat razor, by the 1920s Gillette had completely transformed the market. The Sheffield razor was another product that was condemned to commercial extinction.

Accelerating these trends was the continued spread of mechanisation. In America, even the pocket-knife was now machine-produced as firms such as Remington automated many of the old processes and began using interchangeable parts. The number of patterns was drastically reduced and the output was then advertised aggressively. The American cutlery tariff was again raised in the 1920s, thus virtually eliminating what was left of Sheffield cutlery exports to America.

Ironically, Sheffield's major innovation before the War—stainless steel—helped the spread of mechanisation. Once the ban on its use was lifted at the end of the War, Sheffield makers rapidly began making up lost ground in marketing the product. The city was undoubtedly the pioneer in making stainless steel cutlery, particularly table-knives, and for a brief period in the early 1920s it led the world. Millions of knives marked 'Firth Stainless' were soon in circulation. Stainless steel became a jewel in the crown for both the Sheffield cutlery and steel industries in the inter-war years. However, this development, which was the most important innovation in the cutlery industry since the advent of crucible steel, had profound implications. It destroyed jobs as well as creating them. Stainless steel could not be handled by the traditional methods. An air-hardening tool steel, it was a very hard material and difficult to forge and temper by the old rule-of-thumb methods. It was hard work grinding it, too, and grinders found that it clogged up their sandstone wheels. The product demanded mass-production and soon all stainless

Stainless table-knives made by Harrison Fisher in the 1920s. Like most stainless cutlery produced in Sheffield at this time, the blades are marked 'Firth-Stainless' (though some early stainless knives carry Brearley's name, too).

knives would be made in the same way: punched out of cold-rolled stainless strip and heat-treated and ground automatically, relying on the machining process to give the steel enough quality.

At first there was a celebrated debate as to whether stainless steel could cut as well as the older carbon varieties. Some decided it could not (it has been suggested that this was because older carbon-steel kitchen-knives were cleaned regularly with an abrasive, which maintained the edge.) Whatever the merits of this view, the introduction of stainless steel was not long delayed and by 1940, apart from certain types of butchers'-, trade- and pocket-knives, blades were increasingly made

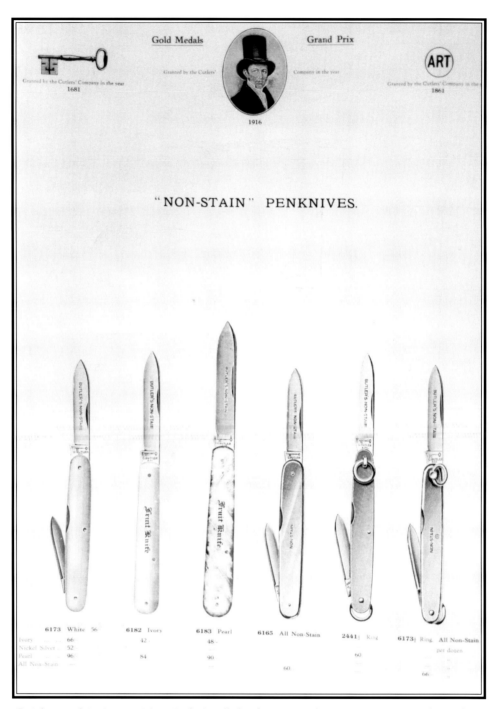

Stainless steel (or 'non-stain', as Butler's called it) began to make its appearance in pocket-cutlery during the 1920s, though pocket-knives continued to be made from carbon steel.

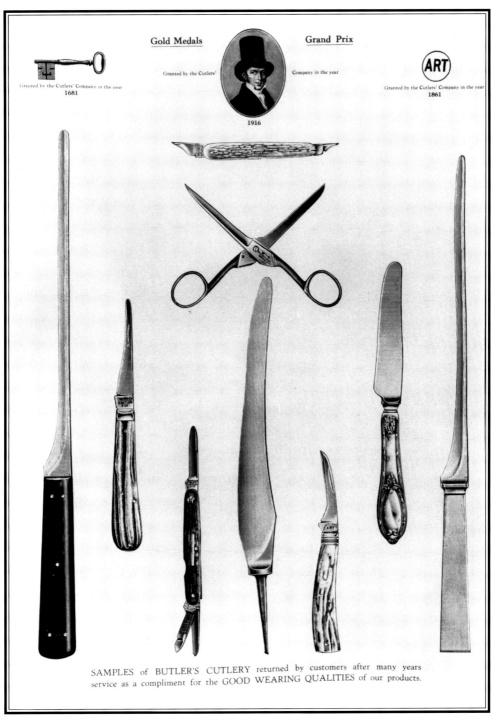

SAMPLES of BUTLER'S CUTLERY returned by customers after many years service as a compliment for the GOOD WEARING QUALITIES of our products.

In an increasingly throwaway era, Sheffield knifemakers doggedly made quality the prime consideration. George Butler, in a catalogue published in 1936, extolled the virtues of blades that were made to last.

Thos Firth became the leading manufacturer of stainless steel. This is the frontispiece of a little booklet (c. 1916) explaining some of the alloy's virtues for cutlery. Stainless steel was the biggest revolution in the cutlery trade since the introduction of crucible steel.

from stainless steel. Again this was something which hit the old-established firms hardest (at least, those which failed to adapt). An ancient name and mark were no longer the main criteria for joining the ranks of the city's cutlers. Some of the steelmakers tried their hand at cutlery manufacture. Soon it was realised that a complete knife could be made from stainless steel, totally dispensing with a traditional handle and all the costs of hafting. Naturally, many skilled jobs disappeared in the aftermath of the stainless revolution and so too did some products. The new alloy, for example, sounded the death knell of the silver fruit-knife.

The old-style Sheffield cutlery industry found itself in a downward spiral. The fact that business was so bad in the 1920s and early 1930s meant that unemployment and low wages were widespread, reducing the industry's attraction to new recruits, both as apprentices and managers. Tighter factory legislation also mean that many of the more antiquated workshops had to close.

Only a handful of attempts were made to break out of this downward trend and cater for the newly emerging mass market in knives: the firms concerned were Sheffield Steel Products, Sheffield Cutlery Manufacturers Ltd, and Darwins. The first of these companies was launched in 1918 and its history is covered in Part Two. In the mass production of knives, this company was a dismal failure. The second firm, Sheffield Manufacturers Ltd, was formed in 1919 by Needham, Veall & Tyzack. Perhaps hoping to build on the experience of the pocket-knife plant at Pond Street, Walter Tyzack had looked for other firms with which to co-operate and merge. After unsuccessfully trying to interest Wostenholm's in a joint-venture, Tyzack formed a consortium, which included Joseph Elliot (Hollis Croft), Lockwood Bros (Spital Hill), Nixon & Winterbottom (Pond Street), Southern & Richardson (Doncaster Street), and Thos Turner (Suffolk Road). These firms were under a holding company known as Sheffield Cutlery Manufacturers Ltd, which was capitalised at £350,000 (a good deal less than Sheffield Steel Products) and based at the Eye Witness Works. The company planned to:

...take full advantage of the phenomenal demand for Cutlery the world over. This can only be achieved by modernising the present factories or erecting new ones in order to co-ordinate the processes of manufacture and by the introduction of more modern plant and machinery with a view to mass production, coupled with improved conditions of labour and economy.

This company, too, was a disaster, due to shortages of orders and plain bad management. One director's report in 1928 remarked ruefully on how 'managers and deputy managers multiplied in the atmosphere of 1919 finance', and it took about eight years for the separate businesses to take on even a semblance of integration. The depression of the early 1930s killed off Sheffield Cutlery Manufacturers after a decade of losses, leaving Needham, Veall & Tyzack (which had taken over Southern & Richardson) and Joseph Elliot as survivors intent on going their own way.

Perhaps the most spectacular attempt (and failure) to launch a mass-market industry was made by Paul Kuehnrich (1871–1932). A German immigrant, Kuehnrich had arrived in Sheffield in 1888 and soon became one of the most talked-about industrialists in the city. He was not a cutler, but a steelmaker and metallurgist, who pioneered a variety of tool steels. His company, Darwin & Milner, made a fortune for Kuehnrich by 1918 and he decided to invest some of the profits in the mass production of cutlery. In 1924 he purchased Earl Fitzwilliam's Sheffield Simplex Motor Works in Tinsley and equipped it to manufacture safetyrazors on a huge scale. The fate of this venture (it rapidly went bankrupt) need not concern us here in a book about knives, but it should perhaps be mentioned that Kuehnrich also had grandiose plans to mass produce stainless cutlery. He hoped to utilise his patented alloys to make 'super-cutting' knives. In 1930 he founded the Universal Rustless Corporation to launch his 'Chrysteel' knives and holloware. Kuehnrich's idea was to produce all-steel knives. Factories were planned at Calver Mills in Derbyshire, though soon he took over an Attercliffe

Paul Kuehnrich (1871–1932) was a German-born Sheffield steelmaker. His plans to mass produce super-cutting stainless knives ended in failure in the Depression and he later shot himself.

factory, vacated by Dubied & Co., which he filled with knifemaking machinery. But the venture was still-born due to lack of finance and the chaotic state of Kuehnrich's business affairs. In 1932, this gifted entrepreneur—part genius, part hustler—shot himself at his mansion in Ecclesall.

The fate of these ventures reflected the difficult trading conditions for all the knifemaking firms. In 1924 the Government bowed to pressure from the cutlery industry for Safeguarding—in other words, tariff protection—and a $33^1/_3\%$ duty was slapped on foreign imports (mainly from Germany). In 1932, duties were increased to 50%, but this did little in the long run to improve the prosperity of the knife firms. Wostenholm's had a disastrous time in the 1920s, when it failed to break into new overseas markets and to modernise its factory. So, too, did Rodgers, which also had difficulty in acclimatising

to the demands of a new mass-production era. Its attempts to manufacture new lines, such as safety razors, did not prove successful. These firms did at least survive. But as the profiles in Part Two show, others did not.

In the 1920s and 1930s, the tide of Sheffield's fortunes in the cutlery trades very definitely began to turn. Nowhere is this more evident than in histories of the silver- and electroplate firms, which found their markets for hand-made luxury goods drastically reduced. In the 1920s, Maurice Baum and William Hutton's were the first to go bankrupt or be absorbed by other firms: then in the 1930s, John Batt; Fenton Bros; Martin, Hall; and John Round became casualties of the depression. Many other cutlery firms disappeared in this period, too, both large and small: Barnascone; Copley; James Deakin; Dickinson; Ellin; Lockwood; Turner; and Wheatley Bros were some of the more famous, but there were many smaller companies which quietly vanished. By the late 1930s, the Sheffield knife industry had a much slimmer look.

Employment in the cutlery industry had remained fairly static in the interwar years. Between 1918 and 1935 (except those years when severe unemployment hit the trades), the number of cutlers in the city seems to have hovered around the 10,000 mark. Unfortunately, official figures do not allow us to quantify exactly how many knifemakers were working in Sheffield between the wars, as the available data usually refers simply to how many people were active in 'cutlery' manufacture (and even these figures are difficult to interpret sometimes). Output had ceased to grow. Sheffield's share of world cutlery markets grew slowly in the 1930s, but this was offset by the decline in the luxury market and the fact that the demand for mass-produced cutlery was increasingly supplied by more efficient German and American producers (even Japan was making its appearance as an international competitor in shear- and scissor-making).

Nevertheless, the depression allowed some scope for growth. Although on balance, the number of Sheffield firms declined in this period, there were some new arrivals. The newcomers were not generally knifemakers, making those old Sheffield

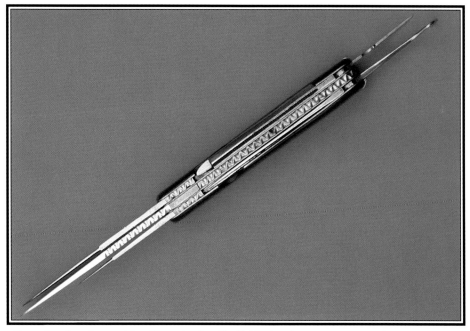

Exceptional craftsmanship still survived in Sheffield after the Great War. This fine tortoiseshell lobster knife was made in 1923 by John Slater at Ellin's Sylvester Works. It has a large silver master-blade, and eight other blades/tools, with a chased gilded back. However, the demand for this type of knife was to decline rapidly in the 1920s, as was the number of craftsmen.

staples, the pocket-knife and trade-knife: instead they usually targeted a broader customer base—the growing market for holloware and all types of household cutlery (including table-knives). Technological developments allowed the newcomers to manufacture a wide variety of stainless steel flatware, chromium-plated tableware, and sterling-silver plated holloware in hand-cases. Viners developed rapidly from its humble origins. In an unpublished company history, Ruben Viner wrote: 'Notwithstanding the general slump which followed the First War, the period up to 1930 was one of great expansion and growth for the firm and building followed building right up to the outbreak of World War II'. German in origin, the Viner family were the first immigrants to make a real mark in the Sheffield cutlery industry. In the 1930s, they were joined by two other German families—the Sippels and the Richartz. The Sippels came to England to demonstrate to English manufacturers how to machine-produce plated cutlery (particularly spoons and forks) and decided to stay. By 1939 their Sipelia Works was one of the most successful cutlery firms in Sheffield. Equally dramatic was the impact of the Richartz brothers, Stephan and Paul,

two Solingen immigrants who founded Richards Bros in 1932. This firm made pocket-knives, but it followed the same philosophy as the other 'German' Sheffield firms: its products were aimed at the mass market, with the emphasis on cheapness rather than top-quality. They all tried to cope with, what one reporter—in an account of Viners in the *Sheffield Daily Telegraph*, 29th December 1933—described as 'illimitable numbers'. Only one Sheffielder seems to have come close to matching the dynamism of these immigrants: that was Frank Cobb, whose Howard Works, also produced a wide range of plated goods. It, too, managed to expand in the depressed inter-war period.

The decline of the industry was therefore not a foregone conclusion. However, these firms were certainly the exceptions rather than the rule. On the eve of the Second World War, the basic structure of the cutlery industry in Sheffield was not much altered. There were still said to be some 500 little mesters in the trade, 500 outworkers and a thousand workers employed by them. The Sheffield directories in 1940 still listed nearly 200 manufacturers of cutlery in the city.

8

Boom and Bust, 1940–1990s

IN 1939, the Sheffield knife industry was faced with exactly the same challenge it had faced some twenty-five years earlier: how to change its output from normal peace-time work so that it could meet the demands of the war effort. The cutlery industry was still much overshadowed by the city's great steel industry: nevertheless, the knifemakers played an important part in supplying the Allied cause.

Providing details on the work of individual firms during World War II is difficult, since few records have survived and military contracts were secret. As in 1914, machines which were used for cutlery manufacture could, with a little adaptation, be switched to arms manufacture. Harrison Bros & Howson used exactly the same presses as it had in the First World War to produce again millions of steel helmets, together with quantities of sterilizing drums, and body armour-plates. Viners produced large quantities of steel helmets, smoke-bombs,

anti-tank shells, telephone boxes, forgings for Bofors guns, commando-knives, matchets, and rifle parts. Thos Turners's supplied the NAAFI with spoons, forks, and knives, and also manufactured rifle magazines, commando-knives, and army clasp-knives. Fighting-knives were obviously crucial to Britain's military campaigns. In 1943, W.G. Ibberson and his company were asked to make a British version of the German gravity-knife. This dual purpose survival tool and killing weapon had been designed for paratroopers. It could be opened with one hand, with the blade released by the force of gravity. It has been estimated that about 100,000 of these gravity-knives were made by Ibberson's; and perhaps another 30,000 by Joseph Rodgers (although intriguingly very few seem to have survived, leading one historian to suggest that they may still be locked away in some government store). Rodgers themselves designed special clasp-knives. Perhaps the most

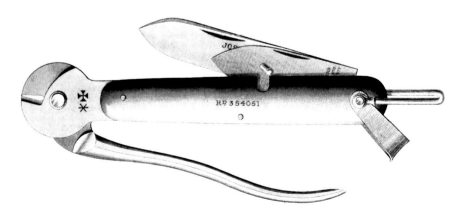

Rodgers' military-knives in the Second World War were based on its old Victorian patterns.

sought after by collectors is the rare Special Forces
and OSS clasp-knife. As much a tool as a knife, it
included wire-cutters, saw and screwdriver, and
was based on one of the firm's Victorian patterns.

However, assessing the overall impact of the
War on the Sheffield knife industry is difficult. As
with the First, the conflict brought disruptions as
well as increased orders. Predictably, the luxury
plate trades were hit by a fall in orders, supplies of
stainless steel and other materials were soon
restricted (Rodgers closed its holloware department permanently because of nickel shortages),
and several overseas markets were closed. At
Wostenholm's, nearly two-thirds of the work-force
either joined up or were engaged on other government work. Then in December 1940, the Washington
Works suffered a direct hit in an air raid, which
destroyed two boilers, a steam-engine and a 90-
foot chimney. Thos Turner's was severely damaged
and two direct hits resulted in the demolition of
almost all the old building. The top storey of
Viners was set ablaze by a stick of fire bombs. The
sparse data that has survived for a few companies
suggests that the war was not a particularly profitable time for the industry. For example, Joseph
Rodgers made a loss of £2,604 in 1939 and though
profits recovered, they only averaged about £6,000
a year between 1940 and 1942. Wostenholm's
average net profit was about £5,000 a year between
1939 and 1941—enough to pay a ten percent dividend. The War had probably helped bring these
firms back into profitability, but their performance
was hardly spectacular. High output and slim profit
margins were probably the main characteristics of
government orders.

At the end of the War, the Sheffield cutlery
industry, like the steel sector, began to count the
cost. Once more it was necessary to restore normal
production and markets, at a time when many of
the old firms were played out and greatly in need
of new investment. The post-war climate in a country which had virtually bankrupted itself to defeat
the Nazis was harsh. Recalls Ruben Viner:

    …owing to shortages of materials, excessive
    demand to make up for wartime shortages,

restrictions were still imposed as many materials
were difficult to obtain. It was a number of years
before stainless steel could be obtained here and,
in consequence, Scandinavian countries, where
this material was made, had some years' start in
this field. Utility pattern knives, spoons and
forks only were permitted to be made for quite a
time and the firm was hampered by the lack of
craftsmen due to the extended demobilisation
period. New plant and machinery, which was
essential as the original plant had been working
to the ground during the war, was very hard to
come by and, in any case, the period of the war
had meant a complete stoppage in any development of new ideas in the company's own field.

It is to the credit of the Sheffield cutlery industry that within three or four years several of these
problems were overcome. The industry, in fact,
began to enjoy a boom in the 1950s. This reflected
Britain's general economic performance, which
was also creditable at this time. The boom reflected
growth both at home and overseas, where European
countries were rebuilding their economies after the
war, and the old Empire trade was also reviving. In
fact, in the early 1950s Sheffield's export trade was
far better than before the War, despite problems in
some of the UK's best markets and the resurgence
of German competition. By the late 1950s, even
Sheffield's trade with America was showing promising signs of expansion, despite the bad memories
that many manufactures still had of this market.

At the old Victorian firms—Wostenholm;
Rodgers; Harrison Bros & Howson—trade began
to pick up again as they returned to their normal
rhythm. Sheffield's 'German' firms bounced back
particularly strongly after the war, since their business philosophy of catering for the mass market
was more in tune with the times. Richards became
the leading pocket-knife maker in the country in
the 1950s, when its workforce surpassed 500. Its
cheap, mass-produced knives (with blades blanked
out by machine and then hafted in plastic) would
have made the old-timers cringe. Such products,
however, made the owners of Richards a fortune.
Viners grew into the largest firm of all, employing
about 800 by 1965. The capital of the business
grew from £432,369 in 1953 to about £2.5 million

*Cutlery firms founded by German immigrants (such as Richards)
prospered in the 20th century, as their philosophy of cheapness was
more attuned to consumer demand. Richards (along with Viners) was
one of Sheffield's biggest cutlery companies by the 1960s.*

in 1974, with the Viner family still holding the controlling interest.

These successes had been achieved by an industry which still largely retained its Victorian outlook and structure. A study in 1957 by the economist Harry Townsend published some revealing data on the Sheffield cutlery industry. Knife-making was still important in the industry: over half the workers in the British cutlery industry were involved in the manufacture of fixed-handle knives (with safety-

and straight-razor blade makers accounting for about a quarter of workers). The sales value of the UK cutlery industry in 1951 was £16½ million, of which about a half was accounted for by safety razors and blades, a third by fixed-handle knives, and about six percent by spring-knives. These figures themselves give a striking illustration of the decline of one of Sheffield's mainstays—the pocket-knife.

UK cutlery manufacture was still highly localised in Sheffield and still conducted by small firms.

There were 700 cutlery firms in the UK at this time, some 650 of which were in Sheffield. The city employed about 10,000 workers, who supplied about ninety percent of the country's fixed-handle knife output.

Of these 700 firms in the UK:

Over 500 had under	11	workers
" 110 "	11–49	"
" 25 "	50–99	"
" 18 "	100–199	"
" 11 "	200+	"

Townsend was critical of the cutlery industry's faults—especially its reliance on the small family firm and the fact that output was unlikely to increase markedly in the immediate future—but, on the whole, he painted a sympathetic portrait of an industry that was a great survivor. Indeed, it was, but the position of the Sheffield knife industry was to prove highly vulnerable. Within a decade of Townsend's study—far sooner than he would have probably believed—that industry was under sustained threat and about to be eclipsed by its foreign competitors. It happened with frightening suddenness, but the seeds of decline could be seen even as the industry prospered in the 1950s.

John Price (of Arthur Price) describes the Sheffield situation as he saw it in the 1950s:

> There was an overall complacency: there was no knowledge of marketing, the industry was inward-looking, and consequently export markets began to fall away. In the late 1950s, imports began to arrive. The large complacent companies began tottering. Not surprisingly, the young lions of these family firms declined to go into the business. All this happened simultaneously. Many of the old families saw their firms as private piggy banks.

The small family firm was certainly a major weakness in the industry. It was a slow job for these firms to build up capital (or find external sources of finance) and the concentration of ownership in family hands made them vulnerable to death duties. Only two or three firms were big

enough to finance development work. Moreover, the owners tended to be highly conservative—not only in their dealings with their workers, but also amongst themselves. Despite organisations such as the Sheffield Cutlery Manufacturers' Association (which in 1947 had 191 member firms), there was a lack of co-operative endeavour in the trade, a legacy from the old days when all rivals were regarded with suspicion. Novel ideas were rarely shared, with a predictable and negative impact upon technical development. Substantial mechanisation was still absent at many firms, which preferred to concentrate on short runs of a few high-quality items, which were sold to a market which these firms never sought to influence. Consequently, Sheffield failed to break into the biggest sector in the cutlery trades—safety razors. This accounted for half the industry turnover in 1951, yet most of the industry was located in south-east England, not South Yorkshire.

Management in Sheffield cutlery was often amateur. Two economists, C.F. Carter and B.R. Williams, identified this as a major problem in the late 1950s. They firstly dismissed the idea that Sheffield craft workers were either resistant to change or heavily unionised (in the knife trade only about a fifth of the work force belonged to a union). They suggested instead that conservative managers damaged the industry far more. Again, this was partly due to the system of family succession in small firms, which often denied the company outside experience and bred a parochialism. Often foremen, who were usually close to the family boss, had no concept of modern management and technical practices. Training was often non-existent. Thus, wrote Carter and Williams, 'the past still seems to dominate the present. One can stand in a factory and easily envisage conditions 150 years ago, when a factory was little more than a gathering together of a number of craftsmen's workshops'. Many of these old factories were unfit for large-scale manufacture (in fact, some were unfit for any use).

A crucial weakness was in marketing, which had never been Sheffield's forte. John Price comments: 'My father believed that if a product was good people would buy it. There was a lack of awareness of marketing. Our sets of cutlery were simply put together: spoons and forks were made in Birmingham, the knives in Sheffield. Firms sold only to wholesalers up to the immediate post-war period'. In the late 1950s, the industry was still dominated by sales to wholesalers and retailers. Apart from Mappin & Webb, cutlery firms did not have their own retail outlets and since Sheffield Steel Products' abortive chain-stores venture in the 1920s, there had been no interest in this direction. (Similarly, no cutlery retailers had felt the need to acquire a manufacturing wing.) This bred an insular mentality. Most knife firms had no real sales force and modern marketing was almost unknown. According to Ruben Viner: 'We were the first firm that did any real marketing. Packaging, too. We made canteens that sold on attraction. But my father didn't believe advertising was worthwhile, but we eventually became the largest advertisers in the cutlery sector'. Even abroad (which accounted for half the industry's sales at this time), cutlery was sold mainly through agents, who secured orders for a commission but did not carry stocks or order on their own account. The fact that firms had no integration between their manufacturing and selling, led to a restricted outlet and narrow markets. This was why when Australia imposed duties on foreign cutlery imports in 1952, it proved so devastating to Sheffield. Some firms were revealed to be exporting eighty percent of their output there. When Sheffield's traditional overseas markets began to disappear, due mainly to the dismantling of the British Empire, the city was badly exposed to foreign competition.

Much of Sheffield's prosperity in the 1950s was due to the simple fact that in its home market it had traditionally faced little competition. This was especially true in the largest sector of the market—table-knives. In some ways, Sheffield's home market had always been sacrosanct. The Americans were too busy supplying their own vast internal market and the rest of the world to bother exporting knives to the UK; and anyway their products were often dearer. Germany had targeted the British market in the late nineteenth and early twentieth century with its cheap knives (and

razors), but two world wars had much muted its 'dumping' activities by the 1950s. Already, however, an unexpected threat was growing in the Far East.

Cutlery manufacture had suddenly become a favourite pastime for the Japanese. Before 1940, this country's production of cutlery, from its chief centre, Tsubame, had seemed insignificant, though exports of low-quality flatware had signalled Japan's arrival on the world cutlery scene. After the disruptions of the Second World War, cutlery was quickly re-established to dominate the economic base of Tsubame. Under their post-war reconstruction plan, the Americans gave the Japanese know-how and machinery; they also supplied them with patterns and finance. Crucially, they also gave them a market by allowing large quantities of Japanese cutlery into the United States. This not only hurt Sheffield exports to the USA, it also affected some of Sheffield's traditionally strong and favourite markets abroad, for when America imposed an import quota on Japan in 1959 it forced the Japanese to look elsewhere. Soon the UK market was targeted. With no cutlery tariffs and a relatively large market receptive to imported knives, Britain began to suck in foreign cutlery in unprecedented volumes.

Japan had several advantages. The first was lower labour costs at one-third of the Sheffield level. This was another Achilles heel of the Sheffield industry: in firms which employed under 200 workers, labour costs could represent 50-60 percent of the product price; for high-quality work, the labour cost could account for 90 percent. Japanese manufacturers had lower rates of tax, which gave them greater profits for expansion. Their stainless steel was half the UK price, and by copying foreign patterns they avoided development costs and design fees. Advertising and public relations were non-existent. The fact that table cutlery had now become the biggest sector of the industry world-wide only made matters worse for Sheffield. In table cutlery, the Japanese had picked a product that, as one British expert, Eric Williams, remarked:

...induces competition. Its near uniformity in size, shape, packaging, etc., means universal ease of manufacture, storage and transportation. Anyone can make it. Sheffield has even, over the years, sold traditional patterns to overseas producers. 'Parish' patterns, as they are called, can be made without let or hindrance by anyone who holds the dies or buys a set of them.

The competition did not end with Japan. As costs in that country rose, by the early 1960s Hong Kong and Taiwan stepped in and filled the gap; then within the next decade Korea began producing the cheapest cutlery with labour costs one-seventh of Sheffield's. Eric Williams noted in 1975 (in a description which might, if one thinks about it, have applied to nineteenth-century Sheffield): 'Those in the British table cutlery industry who have visited South Korea . . . can easily see why the product from that source is so cheap: slave wages, no worker-benefits or welfare of any sort, long hours and appalling conditions'. This allowed South Korea to put knives on the shelves of UK stores, many thousands of miles distant, cheaper than the local manufacturer could buy the basic raw materials.

Some manufacturers went to the Far East to see the situation at first hand. In 1964, John Price toured the cutlery factories in Japan and Hong Kong (Korea had not then started its cutlery industry) and was shocked by what he found. Appreciating that these factories could supply the world at impossibly low prices, he decided on his return to affect a major strategic re-direction of his company. He changed his company's name to Arthur Price of England and vowed that any product bearing that name would always be British. He decided to do what Far Eastern manufacturers could not do: launch a marketing campaign, with his own exclusive patterns aimed at British department stores, where the company began to establish its own shops.

Few Sheffield firms were as far-sighted: the industry's failure to plan ahead, its reluctance to invest and its feeble (or non-existent) marketing were no more apparent than in the face of Far Eastern competition. John Price recalls: 'I spoke at Mappin Hall to 400 cutlery directors about the Far

East trip. I said we all needed to get together. I've never had zero applause before. The reaction was: here's this little Brummie telling us how to run our businesses'. Some, though, felt that the decline could not be foreseen. According to Ruben Viner:

...this was partly due to the long boom. I often told my sons, you know nothing but boom times. These lasted from 1945 right up to Thatcher. Then there was a sudden large drop in demand. We were carrying large stocks (with inflation, stock was better than money). Most of our market was at home, but we had factories in Australia, Ireland and France. We put capital into these, but they were not showing much return. In France we had what we thought was a model set-up. We'd gone into Europe because it had not been a major market for Sheffield cutlery. The patterns there were different. But with the growth of Europe we thought we should be there. We thought by bringing in new technology we could supply Europe from France.

Viners reacted by importing cheap cutlery blanks from a subsidiary in Hong Kong, then stamping them with the Viners' mark. This practice, which was also followed by other manufacturers, was bitterly denounced in some quarters, especially by those committed to British goods. The importation of Far Eastern blanks—which had the effect of forcing Sheffield firms out of business, thereby increasing the reliance on imports—caused bitter controversy in Sheffield during the late 1970s, with the British Cutlery & Silverware Association (BCSA) and the Federation of British Cutlery Manufacturers (FBCM) at the forefront of attempts to resolve the matter. The arguments split the Sheffield cutlery industry at precisely the moment when it needed a united front in its pleas to the government for protection and quotas against the influx of imports.

While Sheffield manufacturers squabbled, imports soared. They gathered pace in the 1960s, and between 1966 and 1976 imports as a proportion of total cutlery sales in the UK more than doubled to 77.5 percent by value, and more than trebled to 88 percent in volume. By the late 1970s, the three big Far Eastern producers (South Korea, Japan and Hong Kong) accounted for over 90 percent of imports by volume and about 80 percent by value. The remainder came from high-value cutlery exporters such as France and Italy, some of which was Far Eastern in origin, too. By the 1980s, Britain's balance of trade in cutlery was strongly weighted in favour of imports.

This influx, combined with economic recessions in the 1970s and early 1980s, had a devastating impact on the Sheffield cutlery industry. It affected large and small firms alike. The industry had seen bad times before, but somehow the old firms had survived. This time they were not so lucky. Sippel's ceased trading in 1972. In the previous year, after a long and often troubled history, Wostenholm's was taken over by its rival Joseph Rodgers and the old Washington Works was demolished. In the mid-1970s, Rodgers-Wostenholm was in turn absorbed by Richards, but by 1983 this firm too, was bankrupt. Viners—the largest firm in the industry at that time with 530 workers and £12 million sales—went into liquidation almost simultaneously. The widespread use of stainless steel after the 1950s, combined with the rising cost of silver, dealt particularly harshly with the old silver-

and electroplate firms. In the early 1960s, Walker & Hall was sold and its great Electro Works demolished. James Dixon's died a slow death and by the end of the 1980s its large Cornish Place Works was largely derelict. Atkin Bros, Frank Cobb and Cooper Bros shared a similar fate.

In 1945, 800 Sheffield cutlery firms employed about 30,000; by the early 1990s, less than 2,000 had jobs in a cutlery sector of less than half a dozen firms.

Ironically, as the old firms faded away, the dwindling number of little mesters, which included men such as Ernest Mills, Eric Wragg, Stan Shaw, Graham Clayton and Rowland Swinden, became local celebrities. They allowed the city to brag with a clear conscience that it still made the best handmade Bowies and pocket-cutlery in the world. Even more ironic, was the fact that the old crafts suddenly became collectable. Americans, who a century before had done their best to throttle Sheffield's cutlery trade with their high tariffs, were now the biggest (and most efficient) scavengers of antique cutlery in Sheffield's crumbling factories.

Some little mesters, such as Stan Shaw, seen here assembling a hunting knife, survived as the cutlery industry collapsed around them, but they were very few in number.

By 1974 Wostenholm's Washington Works, looking far less impressive than it does in 19th-century engravings, was boarded-up. In 1978 it was demolished. (Sheffield Newspapers).

In the 1960s, Sheffield firms were hit by a decline in their traditional markets and by cheaper imports. In 1965, Walker & Hall's Electro Works was the first of the big factories to bite the dust.

Recession, imports and the decline for silverware hit firms such as Dixon the hardest. The Cornish Place Works was largely derelict at the end of the 1980s. It had employed 1,000 workers in its heyday.

Graham Clayton, at Kelham Island Industrial Museum, who is now almost the only maker of Bowie (and spring-) knives in the city.

George Watts, Sheffield's last knife-forger. When he died in 1985, an ancient trade became extinct in the city. (Sheffield Newspapers).

Rowland Swinden, knife-grinder, who in the later stages of his career partnered Graham Clayton at Kelham Island. He retired in 1995 after working at the grindstone for nearly fifty years—quite a record in an occupation that has never been described as either pleasant or easy.

9

Retrospect

TODAY'S VISITOR to Sheffield will initially find little evidence of its great knife industry. In the 1980s, Sheffield began discarding its old Steel City image like an old worn coat it was now ashamed to wear. Dirt and hard labour became unfashionable: shiny new sports stadia, ski-slopes and modern shopping malls became the order of the day. Sheffield became a city where no one got their hands dirty—at least, not unless they could help it. 'Industry' now meant banking, property, tourism and sport. For those lucky enough to have a job, it was a world of filofaxes, computer screens, air-conditioning, smart business suits and expense-account lunches.

The centre of gravity of the old cutlery industry—the area around Norfolk Street and Baker's Hill—became unrecognisable to nineteenth-century cutlers. The sites of Mappin's Queen's Cutlery Works and Rodgers' Norfolk Street Works were obliterated beneath motorways and new buildings. As a sign of the times, on the approximate site of Rodgers' factory stood the Crucible Theatre—though at least the spot was marked with a plaque.

Its cutting edge blunted, Sheffield became more anodyne and characterless. In the city centre one modern attraction encapsulated the change—Orchard Square shopping mall. Here in the middle of a recently opened open-air shopping arcade, all boutiques and piped Muzak, there is a clock tower. As each hour chimes, visitors are treated to the Disneyesque appearance of a Sheffield grinder and buffer girl—waxworks dummies that revolve to the huffings and puffings of taped grinding and polishing sounds.

A grinder and buffer in Orchard Square, a Sheffield shopping mall. This Disneyesque tableau is the closest most Sheffielders get to the old cutlery industry.

Yet amongst the motorways and glassy new office blocks Sheffield's cutlery past inevitably still lingered into the 1990s. The industry was far too big to be obliterated by a decade of hi-tech developments and silly waxworks. Within five minutes' walk of Orchard Square, the tourist who knows where to look can find decaying Victorian courtyards—real workshops, where Sheffield's little mesters produced their masterpieces of cutlery. Walking around the old cutlery area—Rockingham Street, Solly Street, Garden Street, Furnace Hill— one can see old factory frontages, courtyards, rows of workshop windows, and old forges. These old workshops are easily recognisable by their leaning walls and old brickwork, which was always of the cheapest and is now crumbling. Often they stand marooned in the middle of car parks or waste ground, awaiting the arrival of the demolition men. Windows are broken, or look as if they would fall out if they were opened too often.

Other relics of the industry are more substantial. At Neepsend, Dixon's Cornish Place Works and Walters' old Globe Works show something of the scale of the Victorian industry. Arundel Street, too, retains something of its nineteenth-century character: although many of the buildings are being renovated and transformed into desirable offices, several of the old factories—Slater's, Butcher's, and Elliot's—survive much as they were in the nineteenth century. Milton Street is another thoroughfare which has many old factories, such as the Eye Witness Works and the Beehive Works.

Sheffield is not, however, merely a museum for its old knife industry. In the 'de-industrialised' 1990s, when most of the city's workforce is employed in the service sector, Sheffield is still a knife city—if only a pale reflection of one. Remarkably, the little mesters have survived. Graham Clayton (at Kelham Island Industrial Museum) and Stan Shaw (at an old workshop in Garden Street)

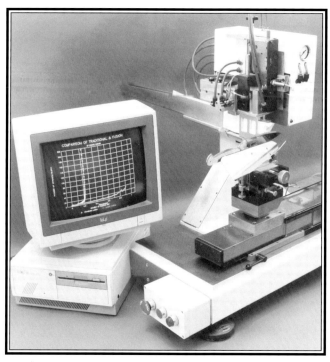

What would the 19th-century little mesters have thought of high-technology Sheffield knife-making in the 1990s? Computers and lasers are now part of the production line at Richardson Sheffield.

continue to produce superb pocket-knives and Bowies by the old Sheffield hand-methods. The demand for their custom-made pieces is, ironically, stronger than ever and both men have a problem in supplying the demand. Sheffield also still has a leading firm in the knife industry—Richardson Sheffield. Exploiting one of the few growth sectors in the market in recent years, for kitchen knives, Richardson Sheffield has established an international reputation for its 'Laser' knives. With the latest technology, vigorous marketing and a talented team of managers, Richardson Sheffield have succeeded in growing rapidly, whilst almost all their rivals have fallen by the wayside. In late 1995, as this book is completed, Richardson Sheffield is in the middle of an extensive advertising campaign for its 'Fusion' knife, which, with its indestructible edge of tungsten-carbide, the company hope will be as big a success as its Laser knife.

Richardson Sheffield's success points an accusing finger at the city's cutlery industry: after all, if it (and a few other firms, such as Arthur Price) have been successful, why has the industry as a whole caved in so meekly to foreign competition? This gives us an opportunity to review the historical development of the industry and examine the question as to whether the decline of the Sheffield knife industry has been inevitable.

Most people, if questioned about the decline of Sheffield cutlery, will usually blame cheap foreign imports. That straightforward reason contains a good deal of truth. It has obviously been impossible for much of the Sheffield knife industry to compete against countries with drastically lower labour costs. Nor, it might be argued, should Sheffield have tried to compete. Far better that the talents of its workers should be switched to higher-value, high-technology products, leaving mundane items such as knives to be produced abroad and then imported. In any case, the knife has become a far less important item in our everyday lives. Look at the trade advertisement for Unwin & Rodgers (reproduced on page 30): it is filled with objects we no longer use—fleams, Bowies, pistol-knives, pen-machines, pen-knives, erasers, and agricultural knives. Various social, economic and technological developments have made whole sectors of the knife industry redundant. We no longer sow and harvest our crops by hand, sharpen our pencils, or carry knives either as an item of dress or as a weapon. Quite simply, we no longer need to *cut* things as often as before and even when we do, the sharpness of the edge is often of secondary importance. Processed foods have reduced the need for sharp knives: in fact, plastic knives have proved quite adequate for many uses, such as in some sectors of the catering industry. The old Sheffield idea (which it once held very dear to its heart) that the chief selling point of a knife was its razor edge has simply faded away.

In this sense, the demise of much of the knife industry was unavoidable. So, too, it might be argued was the decline in the workforce. Not only do we not need so many varieties of knives, we no longer need so many people to produce them. Mechanisation has dramatically improved output and consigned to oblivion a huge number of skilled Sheffield trades. The impact of this mechanisation can be seen today in Sheffield itself. For example, at the Eye Witness Works of Harrison Fisher, where kitchen knives are made by mass production, the old forges and grinding wheels are long gone. Instead, machines rapidly punch out stainless kitchen-knife blades by the thousands; automatic grinding wheels soon shape them; another machine moulds plastic handles around the tang; and an automatic device wraps the knives in attractive packaging for the customer. It may be true that there are still tasks that the machine cannot do (Harrison Fisher still employ skilled workers to assemble its scissors, for example); and knives that a machine still cannot make (such as fine-quality pocket-knives, for which, anyway, there is now only a low-volume demand). Nevertheless, for most standardised knives, machine production has meant a cheaper, better-quality product than was available in the nineteenth century. Output has, of course, expanded, leading to the paradox that while the workforce and number of firms has declined, per capita output has increased.

Some might argue that the impact of mechanisation in reducing the number of jobs has been far

Modern knife technology at Harrison Fisher in 1995. This machine
stamps out kitchen-knife blades from stainless strip by the thousand,
yet needs only one operator.

from tragic in other respects. In forming a picture of the old Sheffield knife industry—usually from quaint old advertisements and Victorian prints—we are all inclined to be sentimental. We form a rosy picture of happy craftsmen labouring over those magnificent knives that have survived in the city's museums. The reality of nineteenth- and early twentieth-century knife manufacture was much grimmer. By modern standards, working conditions were dreadful: the work was hard, very poorly paid and based upon a highly divisive system that set

boss against worker, and cutler against cutler. The system lasted through the 1950s. Frank Hartley saw the industry at first hand after the last war and wrote in his book, *Where Sparrows Coughed* (1989):

> I hated the cutlery industry for its smug self-satisfaction of world fame that hid the often atrocious working conditions which produced the very source of that title. The grease and dust and fumes, the huge dangerous belts running from the main shaft high above you, driving the spindles which held the various stones or mops that you leaned over to do your work. It was a

dirty, repetitive and often dangerous job if you let your bored mind drift onto other things. I suppose that Sheffield…can count itself lucky to have access to the type of person who is willing to forego any talent that he or she may have lying dormant within them to do the tasks which result in those who employ them basking in the accolades which come their way.

The truth of that picture can be seen in the fact that many cutlers have not lamented the industry's passing (at least, the way in which it was once organised); they despised the job and refused to allow their sons to enter it.

However, had the industry been quicker to modernise, then it is also true that some of these problems might have been avoided. Certainly, it is an interesting fact that, whilst Sheffield's knife industry has declined, other countries—and not only Far Eastern ones—have done better. German firms, such as Henckels, and French knifemakers, such as Opinel, have been successful in competing against the Far East. In their leading lines, such as kitchen- and butchers'-knives, they have based their success on high-quality products and superior marketing. Similarly, Victorinox and Wenger in Switzerland have been highly successful with the 'Swiss Army Knife'—so much so, that in the twentieth century the term has become generic for almost any type of multi-blade utility-knife. For Sheffield, once the peerless maker of the multi-blade, this has added insult to injury, as its own pocket-knife trade has almost disappeared.

The success of these European makers points to an alternative viewpoint: that the decline of the Sheffield knife industry, while unavoidable to a large degree, was not inevitable to its present extent. Certainly, the performance of the Sheffield knife industry after its nineteenth-century heyday has been depressing. At the height of its Victorian eminence, the industry was somehow afflicted with the fatal and complacent notion, nurtured by its craft virtuosity and previous successes, that it had reached perfection in knife manufacture and that time would stand still. Sheffield believed that the world would forever want its top-quality, hand-forged knives; that machinery would forever remain in the shadow of the craft-worker; that

ancient names and trade marks would hold their value; and that overseas competition could be safely ignored. These views were shared by both the workforce *and* the bosses.

One can sympathise with this outlook: after all it was common in other sectors of British industry. Sheffield had worked hard to achieve its levels of skill and the reluctance to change tried-and-trusted methods to market cheaper products is understandable. Any attempts to mechanise the industry also ran into some severe structural problems. Changing the direction of the Sheffield cutlery industry was like trying to turn an ocean liner at right angles: centuries of traditions, workshop practices and company relationships needed to be altered. An industry which had grown up in a multitude of workshops could not be readily adapted to the factory era. Nor did Sheffield firms have some of the advantages of their overseas competitors. They did not have as large a home market as, say, the Germans, French or Americans. Whilst the British government has usually regarded the cutlery industry as too insignificant to merit support, in Europe, America and the Far East it has been a very different story. Both Germany and Japan, for example, benefited from American capital in the post-1945 reconstruction era.

Even when we allow for these factors, however, it is not easy to forgive the failure of the Sheffield industry to adapt after 1945. By then, the major weakness of the industry was its management. The unions were increasingly weak after the 1950s and there is little evidence that they impeded progress. A greater hindrance was the conservatism of the numerous small, family firms in Sheffield. These companies remained reluctant to invest in new technology and marketing, and responded to increased competition by minimising costs (especially of labour) and by allowing poor working conditions to continue. The Sheffield cutlery industry was cursed by a problem which has afflicted many other British industries: by failing to invest and tap the strengths of its workforce, the cutlery bosses ensured the survival of the Dickensian idea that their interests and that of their workers were somehow different. There was a lack of

A sight to make the old-timers turn in their graves. Swiss Army knives, by Victorinox, on sale in a Sheffield cutlery shop.

pulling together. The *Times*, 26th December 1901, had noted in its analysis of the crisis in British industry that 'the attempt to improve Sheffield industries by a resort to better methods of production will [have to] be accompanied by efforts to stimulate the zeal of the workmen, and to win them over to a keener sympathy and a greater community of interest with their employers'. Fifty or more years later this problem had still not been addressed. At heart, the industry remained hidebound and Victorian, its business leaders more concerned with the ceremonies of the Cutlers' Company than with modernising the industry. Only firms which have stood outside that culture in Sheffield, such as Richardson Sheffield, have prospered.

The cutlery bosses have ensured that what remains of Sheffield's knife industry is rich in ironies. It is a city which once raged against counterfeit marking, yet has happily imported knives and marked them as 'Sheffield'; in which the Master Cutler rarely has any connection with the cutlery industry; in which the university holds a chair in 'technological change', named after a cutlery manufacturer whose firm failed to adapt to technology; and in which the only dynamic firms since the war have been founded by the traditionally despised 'outsiders'. The latter is the cruellest irony of all: for it is a fact, and one which few Sheffielders appreciate, that the most successful British cutlery firms in the twentieth century have either been German (Sippel, Richards, Viner), or multinationals (Richardson Sheffield), or have operated from outside the city (Arthur Price).

The success of these firms shows that Sheffield businessmen should, despite the inevitable contraction of recent years, have made a better job of things. Largely due to them, the decline of the knife industry in Sheffield has been a depressing affair. It says something for the superb workmanship of the individual craftsmen in the industry's Victorian heyday that the image we still retain of Sheffield knives is one of quality and unsurpassed workmanship. That is an altogether more pleasing prospect and one on which a few surviving firms continue to build.

In 1986, the Queen opened a new wing at the Sheffield Assay Office, with Billy Ibberson in attendance. Since then, there has been less and less for Sheffield's traditional cutlers to celebrate.

Part Two

Sheffield Knifemakers

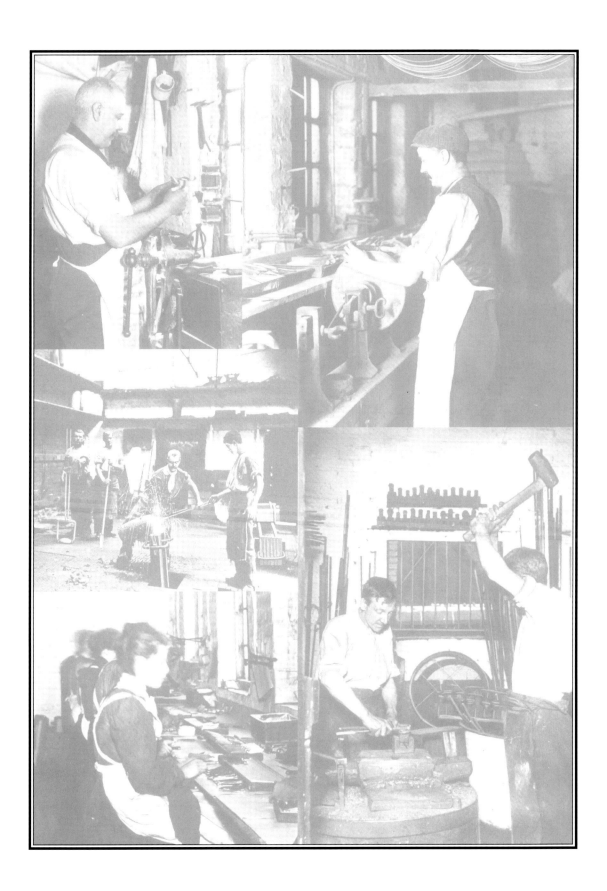

S O FAR WE HAVE EXAMINED the historical background of Sheffield knives, looked at the processes involved in knife manufacture, and also discussed styles and patterns. But what about the firms that made them?

As we have already stated, the market leaders—firms such as Rodgers and Wostenholm—were at the top of a giant pyramid. Beneath them many other cutlery firms and craftsmen plied their trade as knifemakers, some quite large firms in their own right, but many others no more than one-man businesses. There were hundreds of Sheffield knifemakers and any historian intent on describing their individual histories, products and trade marks faces an enormous task.

Not only is the sheer scale of the problem daunting—a glance at Sheffield trade directories will show that by the 1890s there were over 350 pen- and pocket-knifemakers alone—but profiling individual firms and marks is less straightforward than it might appear. The greatest problem is that we simply do not know enough about individual makers. Few cutlery businesses left much documentation, so that a line or two in a local directory is often all that survives—and even directories were far from complete and were often inaccurate. Newspaper obituaries can prove invaluable sources on key individuals, yet they too are often notoriously unreliable. Anyway, all of these published sources started too late to tell us much about the earliest years of the knife industry. The first really useful Sheffield directory was not published until 1787; and the town's major newspapers only began after the 1850s. The chances of finding detailed information on a Sheffield knifemaker before these dates are slim. Unfortunately, few Sheffield cutlery firms became large enough to merit a published company history.

To complicate matters further, the leading makers seldom made only one product and were rarely purely knifemakers. Silverplate firms, such as James Dixon and Walker & Hall, were clearly cutlery firms in the broadest sense of the term, but knifemaking was not their main activity. Should one include them? In this case, the answer is affirmative, since their production of table-knives and silver fruit-knives was significant. Also, many of the silver-platers were apprenticed as knifemakers (Sir John Bingham, Charles Belk, James Dixon, and C.H. Bingham were amongst those who took out their freedom from the Cutlers' Company for the making of knives). In other cases however, the answer is less clear cut. At the other end of the spectrum are toolmakers, who made products such as machine-knives and scythes: these I have been less inclined to include, especially since some of them have already been described in tool-collectors' publications. I have also excluded some of the steel firms: Samuel Osborn, Edgar Allen and Thos Ward, who stamped their names on cutlery products (such as razors and pocket-knives), but did not, as far as I can gather, usually produce them.

Another problem is that not every firm that was listed in trade directories actually *manufactured* knives: some were merchants and stockholders. Yet deciding how many firms engaged in these activities is often impossible. The fact that the term 'factory' in Sheffield was a rather loose one, with individual cutlers making knives on an 'outwork' basis even within a 'Works', also muddies the waters. Trade marks, too, were not always associated with a single manufacturer: they could be sold on to other makers, making it very difficult to be precise about when a firm was born and died. Manufacturers, of course, were always inclined to stretch the truth a little when describing their firm's foundation date: the older their business, the better it sounded.

Despite these problems, this chapter attempts to provide a history of over a hundred of the most prominent makers, which accounted for a large percentage of the town's output. Although this chapter is by no means exhaustive, there is a good chance that most of the knives surviving today in museums or as collectables will have been made by one of the following makers. Every effort has been made to cross-check details, so that the best information is presented on each firm (subject to the qualifications noted above).

Allen & Darwin

The two partners in this firm, C.J. Allen and Sidney Darwin, joined forces in 1887. The latter was the grandson of John Darwin, the owner of Elsecar Ironworks, and he worked for several firms before joining Allen. He was apprenticed to Walker & Hall, and afterwards had managerial posts with James Deakin & Sons, and Messrs Lee & Wigfull, as well as with a London silver firm.

Allen & Darwin specialised in silver and plated goods and were based at the Portland Works in Arundel Street. Directories show that they made silver fruit-knives, fish-carvers, and dessert-knives.

The partnership lasted until 1927. Sidney Darwin died in the following year, when the firm became simply styled as Allen's. Its last location, by 1957, appears to have been the Portland Works in Randall Street.

Allen & Son

This business was founded in about 1818. By 1870, it was conducted at the Granville Works in Granville Street. It made pen- and pocket-knives, and was particularly noted for its sport's-knives. Robert Allen, who died in 1898, managed the firm in the late nineteenth century. After his death, Allen & Son disappears from the directories after 1902 and it was bought by Joseph Elliot. Allen's used a masonic mark consisting of a picture of a set-square and dividers, below the name, 'John Barber'.

Joseph Allen & Sons

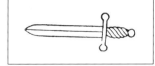

Allen's was said to have been founded in 1810. A Joseph Allen, presumably the owner of the business, was making razors in New Edward Street by the early 1860s. He later moved to Rockingham Street, then Solly Street, before occupying the Oak Works in New Edward Street. Allen's became one of the leading razor manufacturers in Sheffield in the nineteenth century, with a high reputation for its hollow-ground blades. By 1890, the Oak Works is said to have employed about one hundred workers. Its corporate mark on its razors was NON-XLL (an I*XL lookalike mark), which had been granted in 1838. (Unwin & Rodgers apparently used this mark prior to 1865.) It is not known whether Joseph Allen's mark was stamped on knives in the nineteenth century, but as the cut-throat razor business declined after the early 1900s, Allen's switched its attention to other types of cutlery. By 1893, Allen's had moved to the Eccesall Works at 245 Rockingham Street; and by 1913 its advertisements showed a number of other marks, above the registered name, 'Joseph Smith & Sons'. The marks included a man on a horse, the number 3415 (granted in 1810); a picture of two crossed fish; and a sword. Allen's also used the mark of Jonathan Crookes.

By the end of the First World War, Allen's was listed as a cutlery manufacturer as well as razor-maker. Henry Robert Hounam (d. 1925) is known to have been a partner in Allen's until 1921. It was last listed in the Sheffield directories in 1959.

John Askham & Son

John Askham was born in 1818 and served his apprenticeship in Broad Lane. At the beginning of the 1850s, he became a partner in the table cutlery business of Frost, Askham & Mosforth at the Broad Lane Works. Samuel Frost had been a cutler in Broad Lane since before 1828. Thomas Mosforth, who was born in about 1821, was the son of a table-knife forger. Local historian Mary Chesworth, who has located a billhead for the firm, writes that, 'the partnership …seems to have been of very short duration'. Frost died in 1853, aged sixty-three, and by 1855 Mosforth had disappeared from the local directories and electoral rolls.

By 1856, John Askham was operating the Broad Lane Works on his own account as a merchant and table-knife manufacturer. The only information we have on his firm, from the *Children's Employment Commission* (1865), is not very flattering: working conditions were described as cramped, neglected and untidy—though they were probably no different from many other factories.

Askham cultivated the market in America, where he resided for a time in New York (his five-year-old son had died in that city in 1850). He paid many further visits to the USA until at least 1884. His firm advertised products 'adapted…especially for the United States of America'. Askham's mark was a toboggan (name and picture).

A town councillor and prominent Congregationalist, John Askham died in Bournmouth on the 18th January 1894. The Broad Lane Works was then being managed by his son, Frank, who by 1914 had switched its interests to the manufacture of cardboard boxes. The company continued in Broad Lane until 1968.

Atkin Bros

Atkin Bros, the silversmiths, was established in 1824, trading as Atkin & Oxley until 1841, when Henry Atkin took over the business. Henry died in 1853 and three of his sons: Harry Wright Atkin, Edward Thomas Atkin and Frank Shaw Atkin, took over and formed Atkin Bros. They moved the business from its previous site in Howard Street to the Truro Works in Matilda Street. Harry Atkin (d. 1896) handled the London branch of the business, whilst Edward and Frank (d. 1901) ran the Sheffield factory. Edward Atkin, the last surviving brother, was considered an expert in judging art work in silver. When he died in 1907, the firm was probably amongst the top ten precious metals firms in Sheffield, employing nearly four hundred—a period when the firm was probably at its peak. It had various marks, some of which included the letters HA.

Descendants of the Atkin family continued to run the firm in the inter-war period. In 1925, the business became a limited liability company trading as Atkin Bros (Silversmiths) Ltd. It was acquired by C.J. Vander Ltd, a silversmithing firm of London and Sheffield, in 1958. The Truro Works was later abandoned and by the 1980s had fallen into decay. However, in the early 1990s it was renovated and became a residence for students.

Atkins' Truro Works in the 1990s.

Atkinson Bros

Atkinson was an old and dis-tinguished Sheffield family and one of the originators of this business was related to founder of the *Sheffield and Rotherham Independent* news-paper. The precise foundation date of this manu-factory is uncertain, but by 1876 it was located at the Milton Works in Milton Street. The founders were the brothers Edward Atkinson (1848–1904) and John F. Atkinson (1850–1914), who were the sons of William Atkinson. Edward's business career began with Ebenezer Parker & Sons at the Ecclesall Works, a business later taken over by Atkinson Bros.

Atkinson Bros was listed in directories as a merchant and manufacturer: besides razors, scissors and edge tools, it sold pen- and pocket-knives, and shoe- and butcher-knives. By 1880 it was one of the few Sheffield firms to advocate the use of machinery in the cutlery trades. It became a limited liability company in 1897, with Edward Atkinson and John Atkinson as co-managing directors. By then the firm was becoming increasingly involved with the

manufacture of silver- and electro-plate. John was the most prominent of the two brothers: he became Master Cutler in 1892, served on the Town Council in the 1880s, and was a leading local Conservative and freemason.

By 1910 the firm was located at the Milton and Britannia Works in Renton Street and Soho Street in Little Sheffield. It was active well into the twentieth century and was still listed in directories in 1985.

Atkinson Bros' corporate mark '3340' was granted in 1815; and it also used the well-known 'Bear In Mind' mark. Ebenezer Parker & Sons' mark—3709—granted in 1841, was also owned by the firm.

Lewis and Henry Barnascone

The Barnascones were an enterprising Swiss Catholic family, who established them-selves in Sheffield's cutlery industry in the early nine-teenth century. Lewis Barnascone made his mark first, opening a business as an optician and cutler in Waingate. By the 1850s, he was specialising in cutlery and advertising himself as a dealer in Sheffield and Birmingham hardware goods. By the early 1880s, Lewis Barnascone had moved his office to Mulberry Street and also had offices in High Street and in Rue de Braque, Paris. His mark was an insect (a grasshopper). His son, Charles, later took over the business, but died, aged forty-

five, in 1909 after apparently collapsing at the foot of the cliffs at Blackpool (while visiting on business).

Henry Barnascone, who was born in Switzerland in about 1825, first came to Sheffield to help his brother run Lewis Barnascone. By 1868 he set up his own business selling cutlery in Angel Street and then in the 1870s moved to York Street. His trade mark was PROLIFIC. Henry died in 1894, leaving the business to his son—(Charles) Henry Barnascone. C.H. Barnascone died in 1917, aged fifty-eight.

The businesses of Henry and Lewis Barnascone continued into the 1920s, but neither survived the depression of the early 1930s.

Edward Barnes & Sons

This maker first appears in Sheffield directories in 1833, when Edward Barnes was listed as a pen-knife and table-cutlery maker in Meadow Street. At the beginning of the 1840s, Barnes moved to Hammond Street, then in 1845 he was joined in the business by his sons (probably Isaac and Edward Jnr) and a move was made to Solly Street. Barnes was a prolific maker of knives for the American market before the Civil War, especially Bowie knives. Appropriately, his trade mark was composed of two letters: U * S. The Sheffield press reported that Edward Barnes (probably the cutlery manufacturer) died, aged eighty, on 16th October 1876 at Broad Lane. 'New York and San Francisco papers please copy', was the only other information in his obituary. In the early 1880s, Barnes' business was still operating, though it was now based at the Columbia Works on West Street. The range of products now included razors, desk-knives, erasers and buttonhooks. The firm had ceased business, though, by 1888.

George Barnsley

This business was launched in 1836 by George Barnsley, a Sheffielder of 'humble but respectable parents', who began making and selling files in Wheeldon Street, Brookhill. By 1849 the firm was located at Cornhill, but soon moved to another factory in Cornish Street, Neepsend, in about 1852. At the Cornish Works, Barnsley extended his product range to include steel, files and various kinds of tools. In particular, George Barnsley became noted in the UK and on the Continent for his tools for the leather and shoe trade. An exotic range of craftsmans' shoe-knives were made by Barnsley's for the clicker (foreman shoemaker) and leatherworker: these were used for hacking, paring, lining, breasting, and feathering. These knives were illustrated in one of the firm's trade catalogues and some of these illustrations are reproduced in R.A. Salaman's magisterial *Dictionary of Leather-Working Tools c. 1700–1950 and the Tools of Allied Trades* (1986). Barnsley had several corporate marks, the most frequently used being the letter 'A' next to a picture of a shoe.

George Barnsley had two sons, Arthur and George. The former died in 1889, aged thirty-eight, and so it was the eldest son, George, who became the leading influence on the business. The second George Barnsley was born in 1837 and joined his father's firm, when he was fourteen, as a traveller, journeying much of the year through England, Scotland and Ireland. In 1858 his father (who died in 1874, aged sixty-five) made him a partner, and henceforth the firm became known as George Barnsley & Sons.

George Barnsley Jnr was described as a 'typical representative of the manufacturing element in Sheffield, bluff and outspoken, with a hatred of concealment and double-dealing'. In his later life he became involved with civic affairs as a town councillor, alderman and JP, and became Master Cutler in 1883. He died on 8th June 1895.

The business survived into the 1990s, still producing shoe-knives and leather-workers' tools with a staff of about eight working from the factory in Cornish Street.

John Batt

John Batt founded his business in Arundel Street in 1845, later moving it to Cambridge Street in 1878. His company specialised in electroplated goods, amongst which were silver fruit-knives, butter-knives, dessert-knives, and fish-carvers. Batt died at his residence, Studely House, Oakhill, on 2nd November 1889, aged fifty-nine, and the business was taken over by his sons. They decided to relocate to the Park Works in Broad Street, which meant taking over the electroplate and Britannia business of George Cutts & Sons. According to the account of Batt's in *The Century's Progress* (1893), all the firm's products were made on the premises, by a staff of over one hundred. Australia and Canada were amongst the overseas markets.

Horace Batt handled the firm's London trade from an office and showroom at 157 Aldersgate Street. By 1913 the firm had moved to Sycamore Street and had become a limited company. It was last listed in a Sheffield directory in 1938.

Maurice Baum

Maurice Baum became a dealer in jewellery and fancy goods in Penistone Street in 1872, but by 1880 had begun cutlery manufacture in a four-storied building in Norfolk Street, known as the Albert Works. Essentially a silversmiths, Baum's also produced steel cutlery, and nickel-silver and Britannia metal goods. Like most of Sheffield's plated-goods manufactures, Baum's produced butter-knives, desserts, and fish-carvers. According to one business publication, in the 1880s and 1890s the company did a considerable business in table cutlery, and especially in meat-carvers mounted in silver and electroplate. It had also introduced a new metal, 'Silverine' (the name of which was often stamped on its goods), which was said to be notable for its whiteness. About 130 hands were said to be employed at the Albert Works in the early 1890s. The firm had an agency at 94 Hatton Garden, London.

By 1914, Baum's had moved to Nursery Street, but it did not long survive the war. It was last listed in Sheffield directories in 1921.

J. & J. Beal

An old-established business, Beal's appears to have begun life in an old road named Water Street and rose to prominence after the 1850s. In a directory of 1856, James Beal, a maker of scissors, shoe- and butchers'-knives, is listed at a yard in Silver Street (off Paradise Square). By the 1870s, it had moved into the Red Hill Works. According to *The Industries of Sheffield* (c. 1887), the factory covered an acre, with a frontage of nearly 140 feet, had three

large steam engines, and employed about 350 hands. Others worked for the firm at an additional workshop in Hollis Croft. Beal's described itself in an advertisement in *White's Hardware Trade Marks* (1892) as 'Manufacturers of Butchers', Bowie, Hunting, Table & Pocket Knives, in all Their Branches for Home and Colonial Markets'. It had several trade marks, the best known of which was a boar's head, above the word 'Endure'.

The firm was managed at around this time by Joseph Beal: later his sons, Joseph Ernest Beal (1850–1932) and Arnold J. Beal (1852–1926) were taken into partnership. J.E. Beal's obituarist in the *Sheffield Daily Telegraph* wrote: 'Time was when the firm did a large American and Continental business. But big tariffs hurt them, and latterly their chief trade has been in the home and Colonial markets'. Perhaps this explains why one collection of Beal knives, in Cutlers' Hall, were clearly designed with the Eastern and Colonial customer in mind (see Chapter 5).

Beal's was based in Corporation Street after the First World War and was active until the late 1950s.

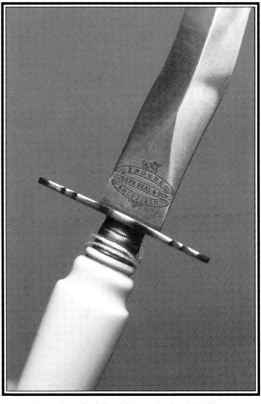

Ivory-handled Beal kris. (Cutlers' Hall).

Bingham & Ogden

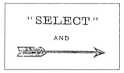

A pen- and pocket-knife manufacturer, this firm was founded in 1858. Four years later, it was listed in local directories at an address in Rockingham Street. The factory was known as the Select Works and the owners were a Mr Ogden and William Bingham. The latter, according to an obituarist, was a 'self-made' man. High-quality sport's-knives seem to have been a speciality and Weston Park Museum has a particularly fine example. The word SELECT and the picture of an arrow were the company's trade and corporate mark. Bingham retired in about 1893 and died in 1907. Bingham's son still operated the business, which by the First World War had moved to Arundel Street.

Bingham & Ogden was last listed in Eyre Street in 1938.

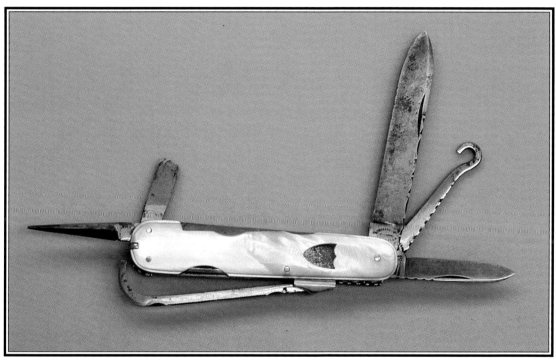

Bingham & Ogden 19th-century horseman's knife, hafted (unusually) with pearl scales.

Edwin Blyde

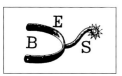

Blyde is a common name in the Sheffield cutlery trade and tracking the history of the various Blyde firms is difficult. This one was founded in 1854 (if its letterheads are to be believed). Certainly by 1876 Edwin Blyde & Co. were operating at 24 Bow Street (as sewing machine-makers and dealers) and at the Charleston Works in Rockingham Street (making cutlery, surgical instruments, plated goods and juvenile tool chests). The business transferred to Orange Street in 1896 and was bought in 1912 by the Trickett family. 'Cutlery and electroplate manufacturers' was how it described itself: its corporate mark was a picture of a spur.

It was still operating at Orange Street in 1974, but it later moved to premises in Little London Road, where in 1995 it still manufactures (under the Tricketts) cutlery and pewterware.

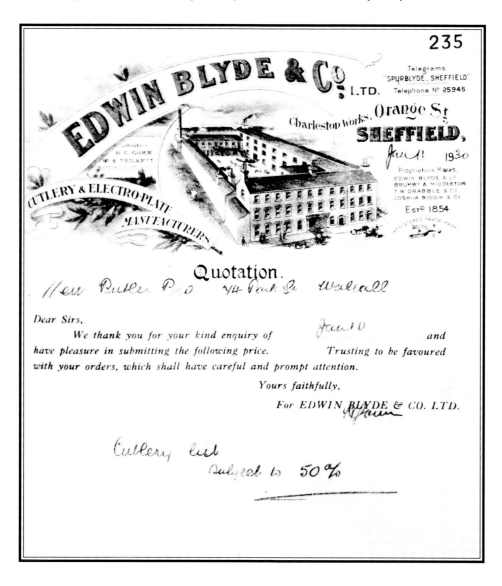

John Blyde

Founded in 1841 by John Blyde (d. 1899), in Burgess Street, this business had soon moved to the Clintock Works in Milton Street (the same address as J. Greenough)— possibly during the first year of its foundation. In directories in the 1880s, it was described as a 'Manufacturer of Fine Scissors, Pen-, Pocket-, and Table-Knives; Razors, Horse Scrapers, Clipping Scissors, Singeing Lamps'. One showpiece knife made by the firm in 1879, contained 23 working parts, some of which were forged from sovereigns and half sovereigns. The corporate mark was a picture of Saturn above the word GENIUS. In the twentieth century, the business was to switch almost entirely to hand-forged surgical scissors.

William Bocking

George Bocking founded this business in 1838. It was situated in the Ebor Works in Gell Street, a factory described as 'large and spacious' by one industrial journalist. This was rather an exaggeration, since the works was only a modest affair, employing probably no more than thirty or forty workers. But it did market a wide range of cutlery: fine table-knives, pocket-knives and 'every description of silver cutlery'. The latter was said to be Bocking's speciality. William Bocking (the founder's son and the owner of the firm by the 1890s) guaranteed every product, which was usually hand-made from the finest double-shear steel.

Its trade mark, granted in 1858, was the word "TRUE". In the twentieth century, Bocking's was still active in the inter-war years, but went out of business some time after 1945.

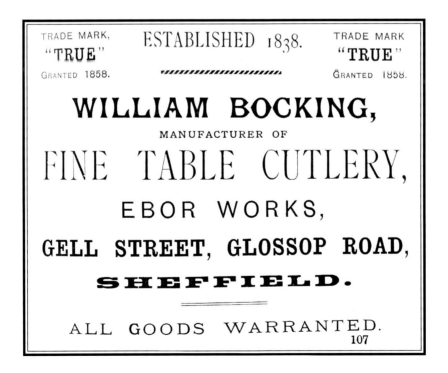

Brookes & Crookes

The origins of this firm can be traced to the activities of John Brookes, who was a maker of 'cutlery and pearl and polished steel articles' in Broomhall Street and later Mulberry Street. In 1858 he partnered Thomas Crookes in founding Brookes & Crookes, the two men acquiring a warehouse, workshops, engine-house, and grinding wheel behind a house on St Philip's Road. This was on the outskirts of the cutlery-making district, but not too far from the major cutlery firms in the town centre. The factory was named the Atlantic Works, previously the address of knifemaker, Thomas Wigfall.

In 1859 Brookes & Crookes appear in Melville & Co.'s *Commercial Directory of Sheffield* as 'manufacturers of spring-knives and dressing case instruments'. The firm was a latecomer to the Sheffield scene. Joseph Rodgers & Sons was by then well established and George Wostenholm was hitting his stride at the Washington Works. However, Brookes and Crookes experience meant that they soon made their mark. The timing was perfect: the cutlery trade was booming in the 1850s, particularly with America, as Sheffield's Bowie and hunting-knives found a ready sale.

Thomas Crookes (1825–1912) took over the business after Brookes retired early. Little is known of Crookes' early career, but he seems to have been a good salesman. In 1896 he was described as 'still hale and vigorous, and as energetic as ever in making his journeys through Ireland, Scotland, the north and south of England, London, Paris and Brussels'. He devoted himself completely to business, ignoring public affairs.

Crookes was soon joined in business by his two sons, Herbert (b. 1853) and Willis (b. 1895). By the turn of the century, the third generation was active in the firm in the persons of Herbert and Cyril, the latter in the commercial department. These men took over the business on the founder's death.

Even in its heyday, Brookes & Crookes never rated amongst the largest cutlery factories in Sheffield. In the nineteenth century, the number of hands probably never exceeded two hundred (whilst Rodgers eventually employed ten times that figure). However what Brookes & Crookes lacked in size, it made up for in quality, with its 'Bell' trade mark soon becoming a badge of excellence.

The firm's success brought it to the attention of a Victorian trade journal, *The Implement and Machinery Review*, whose reporters provided a detailed description of the Works in 1882. The journal warned that 'a stranger would, in looking for the Atlantic Works, seek in vain for a block of buildings with an imposing elevation, with extensive showrooms filled with magnificent and costly goods, or with anything in the shape of display. What he would find would be an admirably arranged establishment filled with an array of intelligent, respectable-looking workmen, industriously engaged in achieving the splendid results afterwards to be seen in the warehouse'. The report emphasised the output and variety of the spring-knife department:

Thomas Crookes (1825–1912).

Patent Triple-action Razor Guard.

BROOKES & CROOKES

ATLANTIC WORKS,

SHEFFIELD,

TRADE MARK.

Manufacturers of

FINE PEN KNIVES,

SPORTING KNIVES, TABLE KNIVES,

RAZORS, SCISSORS,

Dressing Case Fittings,

AND THE PATENT

CARTRIDGE EXTRACTING KNIFE,

With Graduating Extractor, to take any Size Cartridge.

1867, Paris International Exhibition—GOLD MEDAL AWARDED.
1878,   Do.   Do.   GOLD MEDAL RAPPEL Do.
1880, Brussels   Do.   GOLD MEDAL AWARDED.
1883-4, Calcutta   Do.   GOLD MEDAL AWARDED.

MORA'S PATENT LOCK GUARD.

[Brookes & Crookes'] policy has been to make themselves acquainted with what persons under special circumstances and in following special pursuits required in the shape of tools, and then it has been their endeavour to meet that want, always combining concentration and practical utility with the highest art and the most perfect workmanship. They have fraternised with the gardener, amateur and otherwise, and have ascertained from him what instruments he needed...As a result of such enquiries, the 'Florist' has been invented with pruners of steel and ivory, and curiously shaped blades for budding purposes; saw, magnifying glass, and so forth. They have consulted the sportsman as to what he felt in need of when following the hounds, or using the gun, or pursuing the 'gentle craft', and there has followed the 'Sportsman' replete with every instrument likely to be needed in the enjoyment of either or all of these national sports. The 'Cartridge knife' invented and patented by the firm, has been a marvellous success. Each knife has on the bolster or scales two extractors of different sizes, and by being placed there they are always ready for use without having to be opened. The 'Smoker' has not been forgotten; and for his special use and comfort has been designed a knife with stopper and fork, picker and striker, as well as many useful blades.

The quality of these knives soon won a string of awards for Brookes & Crookes. It soon distinguished itself at the International Exhibition in London in 1862. It alone of all the Sheffield firms appeared at the Paris Exhibition of 1867, where it was awarded the only cutlery gold medal. *The Art Journal* commented that 'Sheffield especially, and indeed Great Britain, owes much to Messrs Brookes & Crookes'. Nor did the firm neglect America: at the Philadelphia Centennial in 1876, a first-class prize was awarded to the firm. At Paris in 1878, where another gold medal came their way, a correspondent of the leading trade journal, *The Ironmonger* commented: 'Brookes & Crookes have a display which does them credit. Their goods are tastefully arranged, and razors, scissors and knives are of good material and workmanship; I believe that no Sheffield firm ever realised so good a position in so short a time'.

In the twentieth century, Brookes & Crookes experienced a fate common to Sheffield's top pocket-knife firms—a slow death. It was one of the last firms to employ skilled grinders, buffers and knifemakers, but after the Second World War the demand for their quality products fell drastically. In 1957 the Atlantic Works was closed, its assets auctioned and the factory soon demolished.

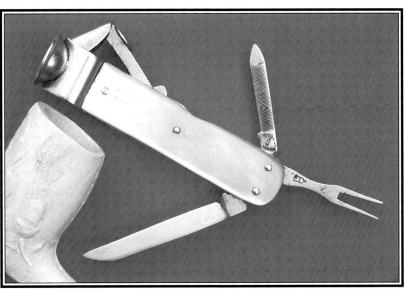

Brookes & Crookes' smoker's knife.
The trumpet-shape at the end is for cutting cigars.

Abram Brooksbank

Descended from a family involved in the leather trade, Abram Brooksbank was born in London on 27th February 1822. After apprenticeship to a London iron merchant, he came to Sheffield in 1847. When William Hoole's business in Malinda Street fell on hard times, Brooksbank bought it and the firm of Hoole & Brooksbank was formed. (William was related by marriage to Brooksbank, besides being the brother of H.E. Hoole of Green Lane Works fame.) When William Hoole died, Brooksbank took over the business, which was listed in 1849 as a merchants and manufacturers of steel, files, saws and cutlery. Table-knives and the more common sorts of folding cutlery, such as lambfoot-knives, were Brooksbank's specialties. His mark was a cannon (picture) and the word DEFIANCE.

At the end of the 1880s, when the firm sold and manufactured machine-knives, farriers'-knives and pen- and pocket-cutlery, Brooksbank took into partnership Mr Tregenza, one of his oldest travellers, and the firm took the title of Abram Brooks-bank & Co. Tregenza soon died and in the early 1890s, Brooks-bank was joined by his nephew, Bryant Turner.

It was said that Brooksbank's 'business aptitude was remarkable, and the firm soon acquired a capital reputation and an ever-increasing connection'. Brooksbank used this success to launch a municipal career in the 1870s: he became a member of the Town Council, served as mayor, alderman, and as a JP. Once described in the Council as an 'old fossil', it was said that at times 'his language was more direct than was altogether pleasant'.

Brooksbank died 1896. The business continued in Malinda Street until 1932, when it was taken over by the Eye Witness Works in Milton Street. Abram Brooksbank was still listed as a cutlery manufacturer in Milton Street until 1965.

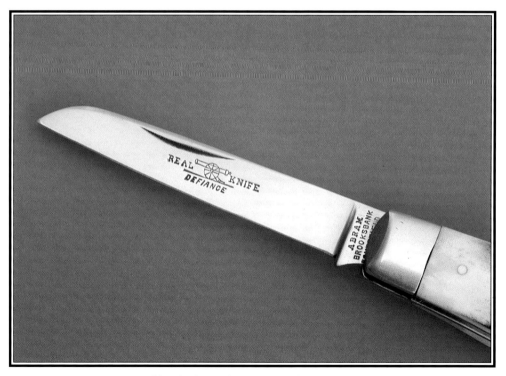

Lambfoot-knife, marked Brooksbank 'DEFIANCE'.

Robert Bunting & Sons

Sheffield directories list a Robert Bunting, pen- and pocket-knife maker, at Radford Street in 1825. By 1833 he had moved his business to Regent Street, where he began concentrating on knives for the American market. Bunting's products included 'Self-defence knives' in the 1830s, and by 1841 (when his son had joined the firm), besides table-, pen- and pocket-cutlery, he was manufacturing lock- and sneck-knives and dirks. Naturally,

Bunting made many Bowie knives, some of which have survived in the hands of American collectors. Local sources state that Robert Bunting died on 2nd July 1850, and the business passed to his son, Richard. It continued in operation at Regent Street through the 1860s, though by 1876 it was located at the Columbia Works in West Street. The business was no longer listed in trade directories by 1883.

James Burnand

Another 'anonymous' knife manufacturer, about whom we know frustratingly little, Burnand's was founded in 1850. The timing and the nature of the firm's output suggests that it was launched to exploit the American market. Its trade mark was a picture of an Indian brave above the words SELF DEFENCE; another mark guaranteed that its products were of the BEST STEEL for 'good cutting quality'.

By 1880, the firm was based at the Leicester Works in Leicester Street, where it manufactured Bowie, dagger, matchet, jungle- and hunting-knives. Butchers'-knives and steels, 'suitable for South America, River Plate, India, and other markets', were also made. A pattern book amongst the Wostenholm records in Sheffield Archives shows several fine drawings of Bowie and hunting knives made by Burnand, suggesting some kind of relationship between the two firms. Perhaps Wostenholm took over the firm when Burnand's ceased trading at the end of the 1920s.

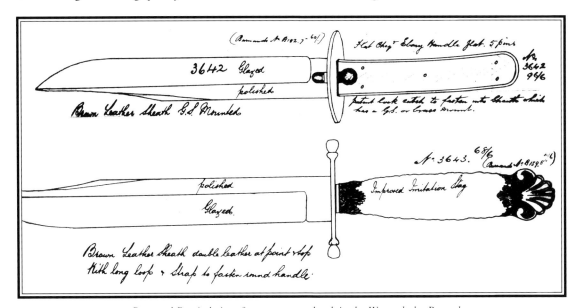

Burnand Bowie knives from a pattern-book in the Wostenholm Records.
(Sheffield Archives).

W. & S. Butcher cutlery labels, 1836, from Henry Fawcett's Scrapbook in Sheffield Library.

W. & S. Butcher

The Butcher brothers, William and Samuel, were one of the most enterprising partnerships in Sheffield in the early nineteenth century. They were not primarily knife-makers, since their widespread business interests included steelmaking, filemaking and edge-tool manufacture; but at their peak, the knives made by their firm won a very high reputation.

Both the brothers were born in Sheffield: William in about 1791 and Samuel in about 1797. They were the sons of James Butcher, a cutler in Charles Street. An establishment date of 1725 for the Butcher cutlery business is stated in later advertisements. Little is known of the brothers' early careers, though it would seem likely that apprenticeship to their father or another master would have been followed by them setting up on their own account.

By 1819 William and Samuel were partners and had a warehouse, workshop and yard at Eyre Lane. They turned their hand to a wide variety of steel goods, such as edge-tools, skates, saws, files, hoes and trowels. After 1822, the brothers began melting their own crucible steel for these products. Between the 1830s and 1850s, the Butchers' business expanded steadily, as they bought up steelmaking capacity, workshops, warehouses and steam grinding wheels in the Furnival Street, Eyre Lane area of the town. Butcher's 'Wheel', a large tenement-type factory, still stands in Arundel Street as a reminder of how big the business had become. At its height, the firm also expanded into the steel castings trade by occupying a steelworks and forge at the Philadelphia Works in Neepsend.

Many of the products made by W. & S. Butcher were destined for America; indeed, it was the New World which was largely responsible for the growth of the firm. Besides dealing in steel and tools, the firm sent large quantities of cut-throat razors to the USA, besides the best types of cutlery. These were usually stamped with the firm's name and its mark (an arrow and Maltese Cross). As one American explained: 'The fame of the brothers Butcher is as widespread as commerce itself, and

Entrance to Butcher's Wheel on Arundel Street.

many a boy even, will note on the blade of his pocket-knife the stamp of that firm, which never branded its name upon an article of which it had any cause to be ashamed…[so that]…it was entirely unnecessary for the purchaser to ask questions about the quality'.

Samuel appears to have acted as the firm's agent in the early years, but later it had a New York office headed by Robert Wade. Nothing is known about Wade, but he appears to have had a partnership with the Butchers', evidently to their mutual benefit. Wade's name was indelibly linked with that of the Butchers in the minds of US customers through the stamp 'Wade & Butcher'—a stamp which was on many (though not all) Butcher goods sold in America and Britain.

William and Samuel made the most of the American demand for Bowie knives before 1860 and became one of the most prolific makers. They marketed both folding and fixed-blade versions of the Bowie, adorning the knives with many Sheffield-style 'American' features: acid-etched slogans and eagles, horse-head pommels and ornate crossguards.

In the 1850s and 1860s, William Butcher emerged as one of the most important manufacturers in the cutlery and tool trades. His business employed about a thousand, placing it ahead of competitors such as Wostenholm (though, of course, Butcher's spread of products was far greater). He became Master Cutler in 1845 and played some part in local affairs as a Town Trustee and Town Collector.

The firm appears to have been highly dependent on the talents of William and Samuel and also on American orders. Neither could be guaranteed in the long-term. After the Civil War, the Americans had less need of Sheffield goods, once their own cutlery industry was established. The two brothers were also growing old. In December 1869 Samuel Butcher died, aged seventy-three; and within a year he was followed to his grave in Ecclesall Churchyard by William, who was seventy-nine.

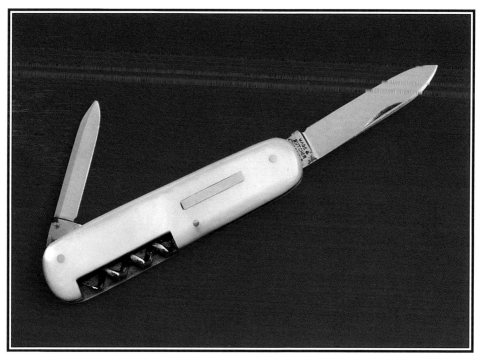

Pearl pocket-knife, marked Wade & Butcher.

With no heirs and no partners, the business suffered the most precipitous decline of any Sheffield manufacturer and it virtually disappeared overnight as a leading steel and tool manufacturer. The various steelworks were sold off piecemeal. The cutlery business in the Arundel Street and Eyre Lane area continued on its way as W. & S. Butcher, still using the Wade & Butcher mark. Charles Fosberry Butcher (c. 1842–1924), the son of Samuel, seems to have taken over the management.

The Americans in particular seem to have been attracted to the idea of using the mark. During the First World War, for example, Kastor Bros, a New York cutlery merchants, made a bid for Wade & Butcher as a way of penetrating the UK market. This enraged Wostenholm's, who pointed out that there was still 'magic' in the name. It is not known whether the bid went through, but certainly in 1921 the American firm, Durham-Duplex, bought the W. & S. Butcher company in Arundel Street as a vehicle for the manufacture of safety razors. It is also known that some of the first stainless hunting knives to hit the American market in the mid-1920s were marked Wade & Butcher (though it is unclear whether these were made in Sheffield or America).

W. & S. Butcher continued to make cutlery at 72 Arundel Street until 1959.

George Butler & Co.

According to *The Times Engineering Supplement* (1911): 'It is difficult to give the date of the foundation of the Butler firm, which is intimately woven with the history of the cutlery trade in Sheffield'. Certainly it had been active as cutlers in the town since the seventeenth century, when the name of 'Butler' was registered by the Company of Cutlers. The firm's well-known 'Key' mark was first registered in 1681 (and was acquired when Butler's took over Steer & Webster's Castle Hill Works); and their 'Art' mark was granted in 1861.

According to R.E. Leader, in *Remiscences of Old Sheffield* (1876), Butler's were the largest employers in the trade between 1810 and 1814. In the early nineteenth century, George Butler and James Butler ran the business, with the former becoming a leading figure in the trades. George Butler was the salesman and was described as an expert with the horse-reins, driving tandem through the North of England and elsewhere on the firm's business.

Butler's was then apparently taken over by William Henry Andrew and Albert George Andrew, relatives of the prosperous Andrews family of Furnace Hill and Westbar. Under their direction, in 1864 Butler's moved from its original location in Trinity Street to a larger works in Eyre Street, which had formerly been the location of the cutlers Corsan, Denton & Burdekin. (Eyre Street still exists, though only as a dual carriage-way which has obliterated all the old works.) Nineteenth-century descriptions and photographs of the factory, which was named Trinity Works, show that it was still one of the larger firms in Sheffield. The workforce was said to have been about four hundred in 1890. Noted one reporter: 'The manufacture of table- and pocket-knives, razors, scissors, electro-plate, fish carvers, fish-eaters, plated desserts, spoons and forks, etc., is carried on in the various stages at Trinity Works, which are amongst the largest of the kind in Sheffield. The buildings are four storeys, forming a square, and fitted with all modern improvements in machinery'. Amongst these was a large steam engine, supplying power for Butler's grinders and buffers. In the 1890s, the firm had a London office at 60 Holborn Viaduct (Rodgers were at 62).

In the late nineteenth century, the leading figure at the Trinity Works was Robert Belfitt (1842–1930). Born at Whittington, he began his career with Messrs Longden & Co., of the Phoenix Foundry, where he served his apprenticeship. He joined Butler's in 1870 and became its chairman until his death, when he left £29,635. He was Master Cutler in 1891.

Even allowing for the boosterish tone of the Victorian press, Butler's achieved an excellent reputation for its hand-forged, hand-ground cutlery both at home and in its major overseas markets in

FISHERMEN'S KNIVES. Hand Forged Blades.

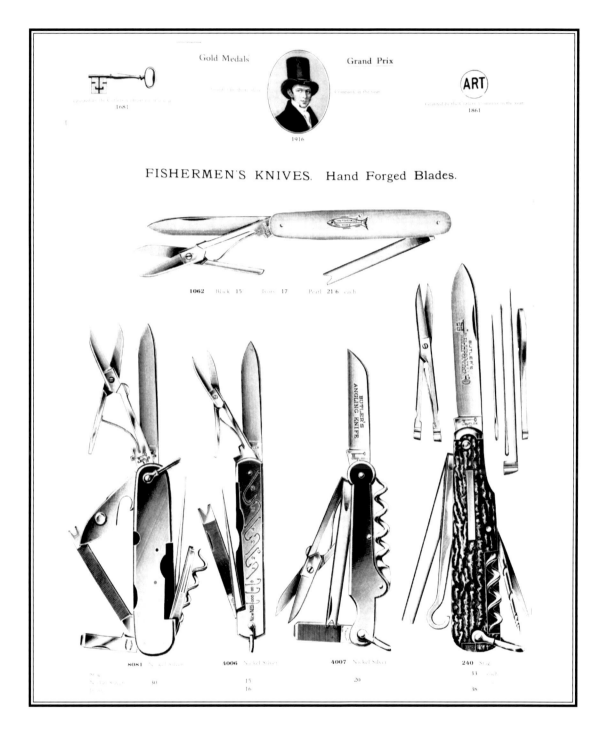

1062   Black 15   Ivory 17   Pearl 21 6 each

8081 Nickel Silver   **4006** Nickel Silver   **4007** Nickel Silver   **240** Stag

Australia and India. Its pocket-knives were first-class; and it seems to have enjoyed a particular reputation for its cut-throat razors. Butler's 'Keen' razor was described in the press as a 'distinctly special article': it was hollow-ground by the firm's own workmen. The trade name seems to have been derived from a line in Shakespeare's *Love's Labour's Lost*: 'Keen as is the razor's edge invisible'. Certainly the firm was fond of acid-etching this line on some of their 'Keen' razors. 'Cavendish' table cutlery was also a best-selling line, and the firm made high-quality carving knives. Sets of cutlery for special occasions were also produced, including presentation sets for the Royal Family, various dukes and archbishops. Butler's was a prize-medal winner at several exhibitions.

In the twentieth century, Butler's history mirrored the decline of the cutlery industry. In the 1920s, it was still producing a wide range of hand-forged pocket-knives and luxury table-knives, but it had difficulty in adapting to the mass-market era and eventually went into liquidation in 1952. The trademarks and goodwill were sold for £3,500. Butler's was reborn by Levington's in the 1950s, then sold in turn to a number of firms—Ingersoll, Heron, Coloroll—before finally being bought for £1 million by the French cutlery giant Guy Degrenne, who ran Butler's from a factory in Ecclesfield. Arthur Price of England bought Butler's in 1993, as a way of removing it as a source of competition. Price still uses Butler's name on table cutlery as a stand-alone brand in the market-place.

Thomas R. Cadman

BENGALL

The Cadmans were an old Derbyshire family, who had settled in Eckington, a hamlet several miles to the south of Sheffield. Originally they were farmers, but in the eighteenth century, the family was drawn into the cutlery industry. Luke Cadman (1727–1788) moved to Sheffield in 1740 and was apprenticed into the trade, becoming a freeman of the Cutlers' Company in 1748, when he was granted the mark BENGALL. Another line in the family was granted the mark, SENEGALL. Both trade marks were stamped on razors, for the Cadmans were razorsmiths.

Luke Cadman married Nancy Matthews in 1753 and had several children, two of whom joined the family business. These were Luke Jnr (1754–1816) and Peter (1764–1817). In the late eighteenth- and early nineteenth-century (when the BENGALL mark established an international reputation for quality), the Cadman business was located, in turn, at various addresses close to the town centre: Fargate, Surrey Street and Carver Street. Peter Cadman's marriage to Hannah Staniland in 1793 produced the line that was to run the firm in the nineteenth century. By 1839 Cadman's was located at Broomhall Street, with Alfred (Peter and Hannah's second son, born in 1802) as the owner. By 1841, Alfred had moved to Monmouth Street: then in 1845, Alfred's wife Mary was listed alone at that address (perhaps because Alfred had died). In the early 1870s, Thomas Radley Cadman (1833–1917) took over, by which time the firm had move to St Mary's Road (which was to be its address until 1938). By the First World War, the next generation was active in the firm through Edwin Cadman, the founder's great grandson. When the latter died in 1921, an obituarist stated: 'Although a successful businessman, Mr Cadman has for many years been the victim of a distressing malady [paralysis], which prevented him taking an active part in public affairs'.

The inter-war period was difficult for Cadman's, as it was for all the traditional razor makers. By 1933, the firm had diversified into safety-razor manufacture and also began the production of pocket-knives. At the outbreak of war, Cadman's had moved to Matilda Lane, which was still its address when the firm ceased business in the summer of 1965.

Henry Steel Carr & Son

Founded in 1872, by H.S. Carr, this firm was one of the many Sheffield table-knife manufacturers. By 1893 it was located at the Brunswick Works in Eldon Street. In the early 1900s, George Taylor Carr, H.S. Carr's eldest son, had joined as partner and was involved in perfecting the use of aluminium for the hafts of table knives and forks.

G.T. Carr died in 1909, when the business (now a limited company and with other sons in the management team) was based at the India Works in Clough Road. No trade mark for the firm has been traced and it seems to have gone out of business during the First World War.

Champion & Co.

By the late nineteenth century, Champion's, a small-scale family cutlery firm, was directed by the Walsh family, who were descendants of the founder. The business was established in 1791 and was eventually based in Broad Lane. It seems to have had an excellent reputation throughout the nineteenth century, exhibiting at the London International Exhibition in 1862. Its thirty or so workers specialised in scissors of superior quality, but Champion's also sold razors and penknives. These were marked with the letter 'C' in an oval.

Robert Laurie Walsh, took over the business from his father in 1925. After 1945, he developed the company into one of the largest European producers of scissors by introducing the kitchen scissor, which he advertised nationally under the name 'Kumficut'. He moved to larger premises in Petre Street and opened factories in Mexborough and Barnsley. After selling the business in the 1950s to Prestige, he began a successful second career in farming—though he later returned to manufacturing. Master Cutler in 1953, R.L. Walsh died on New Year's Day 1995, aged ninety-two.

John Clarke & Son

'Fine Cutlery Merchants' was how John Clarke liked itself to be known before the Great War. The firm was founded in 1848 by John Clarke and was based in Harvest Lane in Neepsend. The business expanded under the founder's son, Thomas, who took control in about 1873. The company acquired the business and trade marks of William

Rodgers, which had been founded in 1830. Wm. Rodgers' name and its catchy mark, 'I Cut My Way', was used prominently by Clarke's thereafter. The firm's own marks were 'Neva', granted in 1856; and EXPRESS. The 'Ring' mark was also used on Clarke's razors, which were an important line for the firm in the nineteenth century. Hollow-ground razors were a speciality and the firm also marketed one of the first safety razors—the Gem. Its showrooms also had a good selection of knives, including 'knives $5/_{16}$" long (perfect miniatures), to the most expensive sportsmen's-knives, gold and silver mounted, containing every article a sportsman can require'. Table-knives and carvers were another line. In the 1890s, it had agents in London, New York and Melbourne. By 1914, the firm had moved to nearby Mowbray Street, where its new factory was built on the banks of the River Don. It was to remain there well into the twentieth century as one of the last producers of hand-made pocket-knives: it also made large numbers of Bowie knives. Clarke's ceased making knives in about 1983.

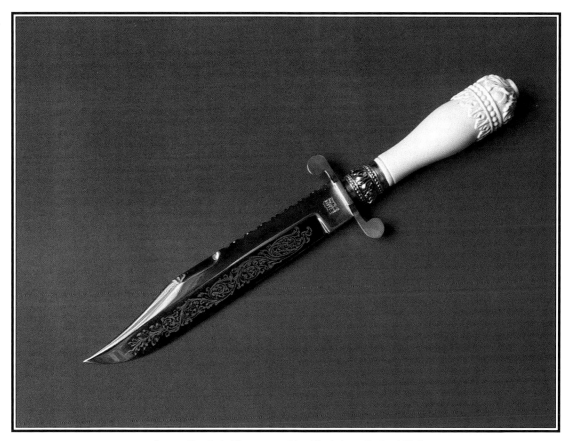

Ornate Bowie knife presented by Clarke's to Cutlers' Hall.

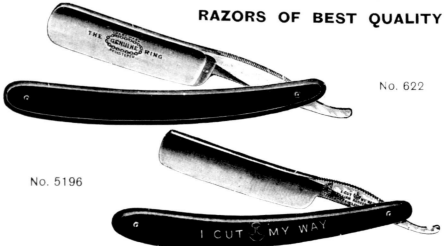

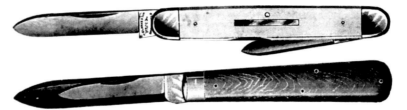

Graham Clayton

It is a modern irony that the same people who shun quality products and show little interest in Sheffield's traditional crafts will happily pay to see old-style Sheffield craftsmen in the artificial stage-setting of a museum. Kelham Island Industrial Museum provides a perfect example of this paradox. It is set in the heart of one of Sheffield's oldest manufacturing areas, where nearby can be seen the vast, decayed premises of nineteenth-century giants such as Dixon's, the silverplaters. Inside the Museum, alongside a host of fascinating exhibits on Sheffield's industrial past, can be found a series of workshops set in a mock cobbled street, where a home has been found for two little mesters—a grinder (Rowland Swinden) and a cutler.

The cutler is Graham Clayton. He makes spring-knives: in fact, in the 1990s he is one of only two men in England who can make them. He is also perfectly adept at making any type of fixed-blade knife.

Graham works for himself, producing Bowies, dirks, and pocket-knives for both English and (especially) American customers. An approachable and friendly man, he chats happily to visitors as he works at his bench. Unlike the old Sheffield cutlers, who, of course, are long since gone, Graham Clayton can be interviewed about his working methods and his life in knifemaking. When I talked to him he was filing to shape the crossguard of a folding dirk, a Sheffield favourite from the nineteenth century. Around him on the bench lay the usual paraphernalia of the cutler: pieces of stag, various blades and scales (handles) awaiting rivetting, a selection of files and hammers, and here and there a gleaming completed knife. Then as now, the cutler's workbench is typified by its clutter.

Graham's ancestors were not cutlers. His introduction to knifemaking came when he joined the Boys' Brigade and found that the captain was a surgical instrument maker. He gave Graham his first sight of this specialist trade and the youngster found himself fascinated by the exotic instruments. He thought to himself: 'That's not a bad little line—I'm interested in that'.

In about 1959, when he was fifteen, Graham began looking for a job, no easy matter when there was so much unemployment. However, when he mentioned his interest in surgical instruments at the youth employment bureau, they found a job on their cards for an apprentice spring-knife cutler at George Wostenholm & Son. Graham soon found himself at the entrance of the firm's great Washington Works on Wellington Street, though he was hardly aware at that time that he had been sent to one of the most famous names in Sheffield cutlery.

By the 1950s, the great days at Wostenholm's were over, but the firm was still busy and had its share of skilled cutlers. Graham's interview was brief and to the point. He was met at the factory gate by Bill 'Mac' McClaren, one of the firm's managers, who took him into a room filled with cutlers working at their benches. He introduced him to one of them, who turned to Graham and said: 'A' tha rart-'anded?'. A diminutive Graham replied in the affirmative, which satisfied his pipe-smoking questioner (who'd previously had an apprentice, whose left-handed stance at the vise had interfered with his own work), and so Graham got the job. Disconcertingly, when Graham stood at the leg-vise it was above his chin. It was arranged that this would be fixed with an appropriate stand and a delighted Graham looked forward to life as apprentice cutler.

It was Graham's first introduction to life in a noisy factory and he found it something of a shock after schooldays. 'The days were so long', he recalls, 'I couldn't believe how *long* the days were'. Take-home pay was £2 14s 1d for 52 hours (with Saturday working that was 56 hours):

> The man who apprenticed you paid your wages, though for the first six months the firm paid. It was piece work, so they made sure you soon started earning your money. They said: 'Tha'd better start earning ya' money, ya' kno'—only a month t' go an' 'ave got to start payin' your wages'.

It was busy and Graham enjoyed the work. At first he was given simple tasks, such as drilling the

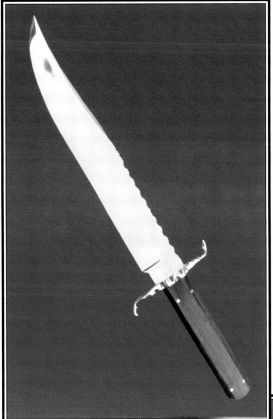

insides of knives. He became acquainted with all the old Sheffield patterns, such as stock-knives. The materials: drop-forged blades, inner scales, and handles, were all supplied by Wostenholm's first-class materials shop. Cutlers such as Graham had the complex task of assembling the parts.

Soon Graham was introduced to Fred James, the Bowie-knife man. For the first time Graham began working more with natural materials that were not machined, such as ivory, pearl and horn. The rate of production obviously slowed: 'instead of making 15–20 dozen knives per week, you might do half a dozen or less—but it was more satisfying. I got more into templates, hardening tangs and making boring plates'.

When he was about twenty-one, though he was still at Wostenholm's, Graham struck out more on his own. 'I went to Bill Mac and told him I wanted to work on my own, but I had to fight for my prices. Stock knives were the ridiculous price of 18s 6d a dozen, so I went to Bill and said I want these to be £1 a dozen. He replied: "Oh, I daren't". So I said, "right, I'll not do any more". Eventually, Bill did come back and I did make them for £1.

Clayton Bowie knife, with composite handle-grip.

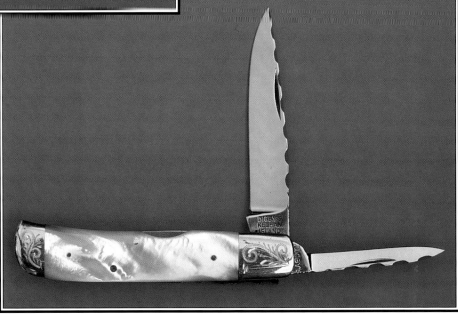

Workback Clayton pocket-knife, showing the skills that still survive in the 1990s.

That's how it was in the trade. If they could save a farthing they would do'.

In 1965 Graham married and determined to try and do better than the £12 a week he was earning at Wostenholm's (this was at a time when workers in other trades could earn £20 a week). So he wrote to Ibberson's, where he found a job that was far more congenial. With a good manager, George Hale, it was more forward-looking than Wostenholm's. 'Ibberson's was marvellous to work for', recalls Graham, 'it was a little family firm. So long as you did enough knives per week they were happy. The knives were all these little lobster patterns. So I got into making pearl pocket-knives'. Graham was now hourly paid—6s 6d per hour.

Ibberson's were however taken over. Graham was still in touch with Fred James, through the Wostenholm sick club, and perhaps inevitably he found himself back at the Washington Works. Eventually, he shared a workshop with Fred, making lock-knives and Bowies, especially for Australia and Canada. 'It was a big trade. Every day there were large packing cases full of knives ready for Australia, New Zealand and Canada'. But it did not last. Wostenholm's were about to be swallowed in a series of mergers that included Rodgers. 'It was a terrible pattern', reflects Graham, 'takeover, transfer of production, sale of site'. He saw what was coming and joined Slater's in Arundel Street. This enabled Graham to begin making Bowies and folding-knives (his main love) again, but by now he was thinking of going it alone.

In 1974 he made the break and began his own business. It got off the ground slowly, but surely. Some friends helped him exploit the growing knife collectors' market in the USA by displaying his Bowie knives and folders at some of the many knife fairs there. Graham himself visited America in 1978 and 1980 and participated in a number of knife shows. The result was a steady stream of orders. He found his own American agent, Trevor Digby, a Sheffielder who, conveniently for Graham, lived permanently in the US and could supply him with orders.

Sheffield's old nineteenth-century American trade, therefore, still finds its echo in Graham's order book. He continues the tradition of making Sheffield Bowies for the American market and has assumed Fred James's mantle as Sheffield's most prolific Bowie knife man. It is unusual for him not to have at least one or two completed, gleaming Bowie knives in his workshop. Some follow old nineteenth-century styles (though they are all stamped with his mark); they have coffin-handles, fileworked backs and ornate crossguards. Graham tries his own ideas out on others, using different handle materials such as laminates. Unlike the older Sheffield craftsmen, he is open to new ideas and more influenced by modern styles of folding-knives.

At Kelham Island Museum, through Graham's workshop windows, one can literally look into history and enjoy the sight of knives being made as in days of yore. At first glance, the work looks unspectacular. Most of the operations—the filing, drilling, marking and hammering—are done entirely by hand with the aid of a few simple tools. If one is patient, however, and tries to understand exactly what it is that the cutler is trying to do, then one's appreciation grows. The work is conducted with the skill of a watchmaker. Even though the process may take days, a small miracle occurs on Graham's bench. He does all the operations on a knife himself, gradually building up a pocket-knife with all its requisite parts: handle, shield, inner liners or scales, bolsters, springs, blades and tools; and then—hey, presto—the finished Sheffield knife, stamped with Graham's trade name (Digby's), or if one is lucky, his own name.

Frank Cobb

Frank Cobb founded his cutlery business in January 1903 in West Street, transferring it three years later to the Howard Works in Howard Street. Despite the difficult trading conditions in the 1920s and early 1930s, Cobb prospered. In about 1924 he purchased the old plate firm of Boardman, Glossop & Co. (established in 1833), which was located in the Clarence Works in Pond Street. By 1927, the firm's workforce (some 250) were reported to be busy at both factories. They made table-knives, especially in stainless steel, besides most types of plated goods. Cobb featured regularly in the New Year trade supplement of the *Sheffield Daily Telegraph* in the early 1930s, when the business expanded significantly. At some stage, Cobb also appears to have purchased the silver and electroplate firm of W.S. Savage & Co. in Pond Street (which had been founded by Walter Savage, who died in 1912). In 1933, when the Corporation needed the Pond site for a bus station, Cobb had to look for a new factory. He decided to buy Martin, Hall's Shrewsbury Works in Broad Street, which he renamed the Howard Works. He soon concentrated his operations there.

Frank Cobb died in 1957, aged seventy-nine, but his business continued. In 1983 Cobb's purchased the holloware business of Cooper Bros & Sons Ltd, incorporating it as part of the Frank Cobb Group of Companies. The Group was liquidated in 1986. A trade mark for the firm has not been traced.

Cooper Bros & Sons

John William Cooper founded this business in 1866. He was educated at Mr Bowling's school in Milk Street and served his apprenticeship at Hoole's Green Lane Works. He was partnered in his new enterprise (which was located in High Street) by his brother, Tom. After a move to Bridge Street in about 1886 the Coopers purchased premises in Arundel Street, which had belonged to Stevenson's Comb Works. The firm specialised in silversmithing and electroplate.

J.W. Cooper died in 1911, aged sixty-six, and was buried at Ecclesfield. His funeral was notable for, as one newspaper described it, a 'most painful' scene when the graveside service was interrupted while gravediggers widened his grave (as it had been dug too small to take his coffin).

In the twentieth century, the company was managed by the family owners until at least the 1950s (Joseph Cooper, a managing director, died in 1952, aged eighty). But in 1983 it was bought by Frank Cobb & Co. and was closed soon afterwards. Cooper's factory on Arundel Street, however, still stands and by the 1990s was the headquarters of Sheffield Science Park.

John Copley & Sons

An advertisement for this firm states that it was established in 1824. The founder was John Copley, who launched the business at Walkley. The firm remained there, though not at its original location: as trade expanded, Copley built the Richmond Works in Creswick Street. The company manufactured pen-, pocket- and pruning-knives, which were stamped XX on the blades. After John Copley's death in 1864, aged sixty-one, his son, also named John, became the senior partner. Under him, the firm became involved with the Indian and Eastern trade. John Copley Jnr died in 1903, when other members of the family took over. The business traded until the 1930s.

John Y. Cowlishaw

In January 1895, the Sheffield newspapers reported the death of John Yeomans Cowlishaw, which had occurred under the 'most distressing circumstances'. Suffering from depression since the death of his wife some fifteen months previously, on the morning of 23rd January Cowlishaw had shut himself in the lavatory of his home at Tapton Cliffe and then discharged a sporting gun at his head. He died instantly.

Aged sixty-five at his death, Cowlishaw had built up an enviable reputation as a knife manufacturer, specialising particularly in silver fruit-knives. He was a nephew of John Newton Mappin (1800–1883), the wealthy Sheffield brewer and art collector. However, Mappin's first job was designing pearl handles for silver fruit-knives under his father, Joseph Mappin. Later Cowlishaw joined him, when J.N. Mappin was working as a pearl cutter and dealer in Pepper Alley. In about 1854, when he was about twenty-four, Cowlishaw launched his own business in Norfolk Street as a silver fruit-knife maker and pearl cutter. He also continued to act as an agent for J.N. Mappin's brewery in Rotherham. When Mappin retired, Cowlishaw bought his silver and pearl business and combined it with his own. He moved first to Market Street, his address when his silver mark (JYC) was registered in 1854, then by 1862 to Baker's Hill. By 1876 he had moved to Arundel Street, though he continued to run his Sheffield Pearl Works in Baker's Hill. By the early 1880s, Arundel Street had become Cowlishaw's sole address as a pearl cutter and maker of silver fruit-knives.

An obituarist remarked: 'The concern has always been a prosperous one and Mr Cowlishaw has always enjoyed a high reputation for the quality of his manufactures'. That quality has been confirmed by twentieth-century collectors, who rate the knives Cowlishaw made in his heyday as outstanding.

Immaculate in execution and tastefully designed, Cowlishaw's silver fruit-knives represent the best that Sheffield makers could produce in the nineteenth century.

The business made Cowlishaw wealthy: in fact, it was said that he was 'rich beyond anything that he could possibly need'. (It was tragic, then, that in the depths of his depression he was to believe that he was poor and would end up in the workhouse.) He was also an influential businessman, serving on the boards of several leading companies, such as Mappin's Brewery, Newton, Chambers & Co. and the Sheffield & Hallamshire Bank. He also had investments in several leading Sheffield firms, such as Joseph Rodgers & Sons. Yet he was never prominent in public affairs or in politics, preferring to spend his time shooting, or indulging in his passion for art (which he shared with his close relative and friend, J.N. Mappin). When the latter bequeathed his art collection to the town, Cowlishaw became an influential member of the Mappin Art Gallery's committee. He not only loaned and gave pictures to the Museum (including one of J.N. Mappin himself), but also financed much of the elegant finish to the Museum and Weston Park.

On Cowlishaw's death (he was buried in the General Cemetery), the business in Arundel Street was taken over by one of his sons, John. The firm continued to make fine-quality silver fruit-knives up to the First World War—not quite such exceptional quality as those of the firm's early years, but high-quality nonetheless. When this trade was hit by the advent of stainless steel, somehow the later owners of the business adapted. John Y. Cowlishaw survived as a cutlery firm and after 1932 it was owned by a Mr Smith, who sold folding scissors and a folding knife-fork-spoon combination. The firm was still listed as a cutlers and silversmiths as late as 1974.

James Crawshaw

According to information in local directories, this cutler was active from about 1817 until 1850, selling a comprehensive range of knives and other cutlery. Crawshaw's entry in the 1833 directory, reads: 'jeweller, silversmith and cutler and dealer in fancy goods, 39 High Street, table, pocket, silver, dessert, fruit and improved pen knife and ultimatum razor, 61 Solly Street'. Crawshaw's premises had once been owned by Nowill & Kippax.

Crawshaw was Master Cutler in 1828, when a roving reporter, Sir Richard Phillips, described his products and shops:

> Very fine cutlery is manufactured by Mr. Crawshaw. I saw in his warehouse all those elegant patterns of penknives which, in the best of shops of London, Bath, etc., excite so much admiration. His lobster knives, with four or more blades on slit springs, with pearl and tortoise-shell handles, are the most perfect productions of British manufacture.

According to Phillips (as reported in Thomas Allen's, *A New and Complete History of the County of York*, 1831), Crawshaw made the best pocket-knives in Sheffield, which fetched in 'high mounting' (i.e. gold and silver) from two to five guineas. Moreover, Phillips credited Crawshaw as:

> ...the inventor of the patent tang and pen-nibbing knives; the lobster-knife, by which four blades open upon one spring; and of the quadrangular knife, the principle of which is adapted to any number of blades, and has been adopted for show knives with from one thousand to two thousand blades. To this gentleman the trade is indebted for what is called the lobster knife, consisting of a spring, which, instead of forming the back, as in the old method, is placed along the middle of the handle, and between the scales or sides of the handle, so that it works on each side, and hence admits of blades at each end, and even of any number of them. The mode of slitting the spring gave rise to many bladed knives in all their varieties. Mr Crawshaw took out no patent, but is a wholesale manufacturer, and the retail shop in his connexion, is Champion's, in High-street.

Little is known about Crawshaw, apart from the details in this account. A James Thomas Crawshaw, spring-knife maker, is listed at High Street and Tudor Street in the 1840s, but there is no entry in the directories after 1845. No obituary of Crawshaw has been traced, though examples of his fine work may survive in collectors' hands.

Creswick & Co.

Creswick is a distinctive local name and the family prided itself in being one of the oldest in the cutlery trade. Six Creswicks served as Master Cutler between 1630 and 1667.

This firm began in 1810, when it entered its first silver mark. In the following year, its Crossed Arrow (picture) mark was registered. The partners in the business were three brothers, Thomas (1788–1863), James (1789–1854) and Nathaniel (1793–1855), the sons of James Creswick, a file manufacturer and silverplater, and his wife Mary née Smith. Thomas and James ran the business first at Porter Street, but by the time Nathaniel joined

them in about 1817 it was located in Browne Street. By 1825, the business had settled at Paternoster Row and by the 1830s it also had a London address in the Strand. T. J. & N. Creswick became one of the most outstanding Sheffield Plate firms (whose products are well illustrated in Frederick Bradbury's study of the subject). Knife manufacture was not the firm's main line, but it is known to have made silver fruit-knives and dessert-knives. Presumably, it may also have made fish-carvers, butter-knives and other silver tableware.

Apparently, Elkington's electroplate process was offered to Creswick's, but they refused, leading to what one historian (C.C. Pilling, in a newspaper article) described as a 'downward slope'. This occurred roughly at the same time as the Creswicks were passing out of the business. By 1855, the firm had been renamed as Creswick & Co. and new partners (Nathaniel Irving, Charles Favell and Frederick Potter) took control; but in 1886, Creswick's works, by now located in Arundel Street, was closed. Charles Favell bought some of the best patterns and started his own business, while the Cross Arrow mark was later acquired by Wm Hutton.

Jonathan Crookes & Son

This firm is a good example of a knifemaker, whose trade mark proved more enduring than its manufacturing activities. The mark was a pistol and a heart, which was granted in 1780. Jonathan Crookes made it famous in the nineteenth century, though the details about him or about the early history of the firm are scanty. He appears in Sheffield trade directories in 1827 at Rockingham Lane. After briefly working in Bailey Lane, by 1839 Crookes was described as a maker of pen- and pocket-knives at 89 Eldon Street. Crookes made its name by making, according to one trade mark directory, 'superlatively finished Pen, Pocket, and Sporting Knives, Razors, etc'. It is not known when Crookes died, but an advertisement in 1888 in a Sheffield directory contains a very intriguing *nota bene*. It describes Crookes as: 'Inventor and Sole Maker of that unique and superb specimen of Cutlery, containing Eighteen Hundred and Twenty-one Blades, with different Instruments, value 200 guineas'. This could hardly be any other than Rodgers' Year Knife (see Chapter 5).

Before the First World War, the mark (and perhaps the business) was taken over by the razor makers Joseph Allen, which was based in Rockingham Street. In the 1950s, H.M. Slater acquired the Crookes' mark.

Deakin, Sons & Co.

This business was founded in 1868 by Joseph T. Deakin and three others, and first traded as Deakin, Ecroyd & Co. The leading member of the firm was a Sheffielder, who had spent his early career with Burys, the steelmakers. In 1872, after Ecroyd had retired, Deakin was joined by Ernest G. Reuss, an immigrant from Alsace who had come to Sheffield about thirty years previously. The partnership lasted until 1895, when Joseph Deakin took over the whole concern with the help of his two sons, Frank and Walter.

The firm's premises (which still stand) were on West Street and were known as Tiger Works—in deference to the firm's trade mark. It was not a manufacturing concern, however. On the ground floor of Tiger Works was a packing room, on the first floor were offices and a stockroom, and on the second were rooms for preparing and storing samples. Deakin's was a merchanting concern, which bought its products from other Sheffield makers.

Tiger Works concentrated on the Spanish and South American market. Deakin's South American trade was said to be equal to that of any other Sheffield concern and some claimed it was one of the first local firms to send a direct representative to that market. Naturally, the firm's products were oriented to the South American customer, with the emphasis on the cheaper grades of butchers'-knives, pocket-cutlery, dagger and spear-point knives, and razors.

Joseph Deakin died on 16th February 1898, aged fifty-nine (coincidentally, Ernest Reuss—who had taken over Hancock's Mazeppa Works—had died on 2nd February of the same year, aged fifty-five). The business apparently began to contract in the early twentieth century, since we know that Deakin's moved to 76 Arundel Street in about 1900, taking the Tiger name with them. By 1908 the Viner family had moved into the West Street building. Deakin's appear to have operated until the First World War, when the firm went out of business.

Tiger Works on West Street.

James Deakin & Sons

James Deakin, a Sheffielder born in 1822, founded this business in 1867. By 1886 the firm was known as James Deakin & Sons, signifying the arrival of the founder's sons: William Pitchford Deakin (c. 1847–1931), and John and Albert Deakin. The company operated at the Sidney Works in Matilda and Sidney Streets; it also opened offices and showrooms at 48 Holborn Viaduct, London, and in Glasgow and Belfast. The Sheffield Works was a four-storied affair around a quadrangle, which covered over half an acre of ground. It produced all types of silver and plated cutlery, including table- and pocket-knives—all stamped with the Deakin mark, a 'Bell'. Many of these products were sent overseas to Australia, South Africa, India and to the Continent. In 1894, the year after James Deakin retired, the firm took over the electroplate and silver firm of Shaw & Fisher (established in 1835). By now Deakin's workforce was said to be approaching about five hundred. In 1897 the firm was registered as a limited liability company.

William, John and Albert Deakin died between 1927 and 1937 and the company closed down in about 1940.

E.M. Dickinson

Edwin Dickinson appears to have begun his career as an agent for the merchant Alfred Field & Co on Westfield Terrace. By 1880, he had launched his own firm at the Murray Works on Cambridge Street. He manufactured pen-, pocket-, and sporting-knives, Bowies and daggers, and a range of trade-knives for butchers and farriers. The Murray Works changed its location several times: in 1888 it was in Division Street; in 1896 Rockingham Street; and in 1910 Arundel Street. Little is known about the founder, but Bernard Kaye (who died in 1929, aged sixty-one) was associated with Dickinson from about 1890 and became a director of the company.

After the First World War, Dickinson's added the manufacture of electroplate to its product-line, but at the end of the 1930s the Arundel Street factory ceased trading. Its marks—the words 'Invicta' and 'El Dorado', and a striking picture of a screw—were acquired by Needham, Veall & Tyzack at the Eye Witness Works in Milton Street.

TRADE MARKS

E.M.DICKINSON
SHEFFIELD

E.M.DICKINSON
SHEFFIELD

DICKINSON
SHEFFIELD

CAMBRIDGE & C°
SHEFFIELD

E. M. DICKINSON,
MANUFACTURER OF
PEN, POCKET, & SPORTING KNIVES,
TABLE & BUTCHERS' KNIVES,
SPEAR AND DAGGER KNIVES.
RAZORS, SCISSORS, &c.,
MURRAY WORKS, 51 to 57, DIVISION ST.
SHEFFIELD.

James Dixon & Sons

Undoubtedly the most impressive cutlery factory that still stands in Sheffield is that of James Dixon & Sons. In its Edwardian heyday, too, it was amongst the biggest cutlery firms, with perhaps only Walker & Hall and Joseph Rodgers surpassing it in size. Its factory was the Cornish Place Works on the banks of the River Don in Neepsend. Ball Street Bridge, which spans the Don, gives a superb view of this factory: the massive, blackened exterior and the grimy windows of the Cornish Place Works say more about what it was like to work in Sheffield's old cutlery industry than any words in a book.

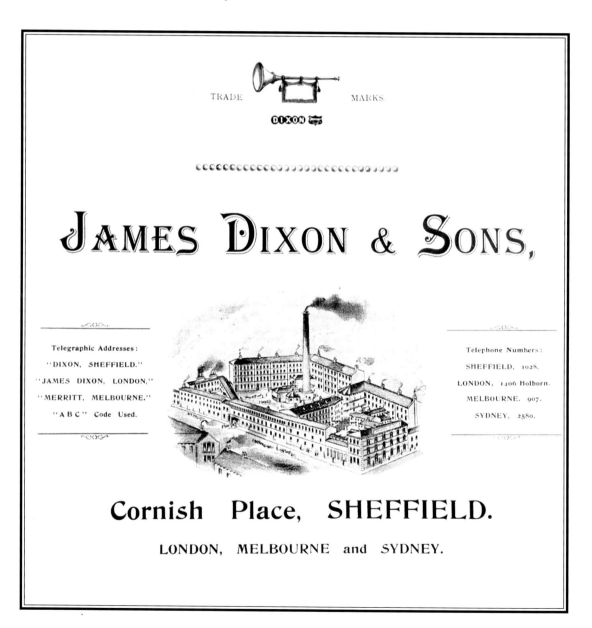

Big as it was, Dixon's was not primarily a knifemaker: its history was bound up with the development of pewter, Sheffield Plate, Britannia metal, electro-plate and silverware. Fancy dinner services and silver trays were the type of products for which Dixon's were most famous: these were aimed at the top end of the market, where cost was secondary to quality. But Dixon's did manufacture and market knives and so we have every reason to consider its history briefly in this book.

The business was begun in 1805 in premises in Silver Street by Dixon & Smith, makers of Britannia metal, pewterware and old Sheffield Plate. James Dixon (1776–1852), the founder, took over completely in about 1822. In that year he moved it to the Cornish Place site on the River Don, an area then in open countryside. By 1833 the name had changed to James Dixon & Sons, signifying the managerial input from the growing Dixon family. The founder had three sons, all of whom joined the business: William Frederick Dixon (1802–1871), James Willis Dixon (1813–1876), and Henry Isaac Dixon (1820–1912). William worked in the counting house, James looked after the American business in New York, and Henry was a traveller. James Dixon's son-in-law, William Fawcett, was also a partner. In the later nineteenth century, James Willis Dixon Jnr (1838–1917), who was born in New York, became the dominant individual at the company, which was the personification of the paternalistic Sheffield family firm. Another grandson of the founder, James Dixon (1851–1947), looked after the Continental business; he was Master Cutler in 1887.

According to Frederick Bradbury in his history of Sheffield Plate, 'no firm in Sheffield have ever made more goods of white [Britannia] metal'. This was the 'economy' version of Sheffield Plate, consisting of tin with an admixture of antimony and a little copper. But Dixon's were also masters at making Sheffield Plate; and then, when these products were superseded by the superior electroplate method from Birmingham, they readily adapted to that too. Dixon's also did a best-selling line in shooting accessories, especially powder flasks and gun implements, such as cartridge loaders.

The cutlery manufactured by Dixon's was wide-ranging: it included table-cutlery (including knives made from shear steel), pocket-knives, sport's-knives, and, naturally, silver fruit-knives. How much of this output was actually made in the Cornish Place Works is difficult to say. Probably much of it, with the exception of the silver fruit-knives (certainly a Dixon speciality), was manufactured outside the works, and then stamped with the firm's trade marks—a 'trumpet with banner' and the same in combination with the word 'Dixon'. The first corporate mark was granted to Dixon's in 1879, and the second, with the name added, in 1890.

The trade of the firm was truly global, beginning with the American market before the 1840s, then extending to the Colonies by the end of the century (with sizeable sales in the UK luxury market, too). The Cornish Place Works and its army of workers simply kept on growing. When the staff of Dixon's gathered in its courtyard in 1905 for a centenary photograph, flanked by Dixon's multi-storey workshops and its giant chimney, they numbered some nine-hundred (more than double the workforce of the 1840s).

Like the Sheffield silverplate industry, Dixon's reached its peak in 1914. But the First World War wrecked the market for luxury goods and demand never recovered in the difficult inter-war years (when Dixon's became a limited company and took over Hutton's). Although Dixon's survived into the 1950s as one of the larger cutlery producers, mass market goods in stainless steel sent the firm into sharp decline after the 1960s. By the 1980s, most of the Cornish Place Works was derelict and by the 1990s Dixon's had ceased production.

James Drabble

This firm was notable, like Nixon & Winterbottom, for its pioneering attempt to introduce machinery into the Sheffield cutlery trades. It first appears in the Sheffield directories in 1860 as a merchant and manufacturer of cutlery at the Orchard Works, Orchard Lane. It soon began specialising in table-knives and forks. By 1862 Drabble was creating an impression at the trade exhibitions, notably the London International Exhibition of 1862, where they displayed daggers, butchers'-, spear- and matchet-knives. The daggers had various mottoes inscribed upon them, such as 'Never Despair', 'A Sure Defence', 'Draw Me Not Without Occasion, Sheathe Me Not Without Honour'.

James Drabble & Co. applied machinery to the manufacture of these fixed-blade knives, the company stating in the *Sheffield Independent*, 28th May 1862, that:

…whilst other makers apply machinery only in part to the forging process, we have it complete: and in the hafting department we have every machine required in the various manipulations, which other manufacturers have not. Our object has been to put down machinery, so that we could compete with American and German manufacturers.

During the 1870s and 1880s, Drabble moved his business to Wellington Street and Trafalgar Street (where he occupied the Trafalgar Works). Drabble's, however, were not conspicuously successful and the firm proved short-lived. It disappeared from the directories after 1888. On 17th March 1908, the *Sheffield Daily Telegraph* noted the death of James Drabble, the merchant and cutlery manufacturer, aged eighty-six, who lived at 63 Clarkehouse Road. Apparently, he had spent the last thirty years of his working life as a traveller for the Nunnery Colliery.

Thomas Ellin & Co.

The founder of this business was Thomas Ellin (1771–1845), who was the eldest son of James Ellin (b. 1746), a husbandman, who disappeared soon after the death of his young wife in 1779. He left behind four young sons and was never seen again by his family. All four boys, left in the care of their grandfather, were apprenticed as cutlers. Thomas, the most successful, was apprenticed in 1785 and took out his freedom from the Company of Cutlers in 1792 (his name spelt as 'Hellen'). By 1797 he had become a partner with Joseph Oldale, whose daughter he married. The business, which made table-knives, was between the top of Eyre Street and Eyre Lane. According to the *Sheffield Daily Telegraph*: 'It is recorded that in his eagerness to get his goods on the market he had a field of unripe corn cut down so that the builders might start work without delay'. By the 1840s, the business address was Sylvester Gardens at the end of Arundel Street. It was said that Thomas Ellin was probably the first cutler to employ steam-power for his machinery, and the first to employ circular saws for the cutting of ivory, horn and bone.

In the nineteenth century, the business gradually expanded, eventually occupying a compact, three-storied block of buildings, known as the Sylvester Works. Besides making a wide range of cutlery (table-knives, shoe-, bread-, cooks'-, and spear-point knives), the firm also merchanted steel. By 1860, it had offices in Dublin and New York. Ellin became Master Cutler in 1833, a position also held by his son, also named Thomas, in 1841. Thomas Ellin Jnr had two sons, Arthur Robert and T.S. Ellin, but he died before they could take over the business. A.R. Ellin (1841–1908) eventually assumed control in about 1876, being partnered soon after by Joseph Merrill, the son of an ivory merchant. The product range was widened and included all kinds of table cutlery, pen- and pocket-knives, bowies, dirks, hunting-, palette-, butchers'-, and plumbers'-knives. Canada was a particularly

important overseas market. The firm's trade marks included a sailing ship ('Cutter') and Vulcan at his forge.

A.R. Ellin became Master Cutler in 1901—the first time a third member of the same family had filled that office. (T.R. Ellin, the owner of the Footprint tool works was a nephew).

Ellin's was last listed in 1933. The last member of the firm to have an interest in it, Arthur William Ellin, retired in 1934. The Sylvester Works still stands, though now the frontage is dominated by the name of Joseph Elliot & Sons, who took over the factory.

Ellin's Sylvester Works, later occupied by Elliot.

Joseph Elliot & Sons

Founded in 1795; by the late nineteenth century Elliot's was based at Hollis Croft. Little is known about the owners of the business, but the head of the firm at this time was James William Elliot, who died in 1904, aged sixty-two. Table-knives were an important line for Elliot's. In about 1902, the firm

bought the trade marks and business of Allen & Son, allowing Elliot's to rename its works in Hollis Croft as the Granville Works (Allen's old name from Granville Street). This remained the firm's address during the First World War, when it advertised most types of Sheffield knives: carving-knives, pocket-cutlery, and table- and plate-ware.

In the 1920s, the business became a limited company and moved to Sylvester Street. At this time, Elliot's became part of the Sheffield Cutlery Manufacturers Ltd, a grouping of firms led by Needham, Veall & Tyzack. Elliot's was brought into the combine to provide support for Lockwood's, but Sheffield Cutlery Manufacturers proved a financial disaster and did not survive the depression of the early 1930s.

But Elliot's did survive the inter-war period. J.G. Elliot assumed control of the business and it occupied the Sylvester Works of Thomas Ellin. Elliot's trade mark—two reversed letter 'C's, either side of a Maltese Cross—was granted in 1805. Besides acquiring Ellin's marks, Elliot's also bought the trade marks of other firms, such as James Barber, John Wigfall, John Wilson and Lockwood Bros.

A modest firm in the nineteenth century, Elliot's achieved greater prominence after 1945, as the decline of the other firms in the industry left it with fewer competitors. The chairman, J.G. Elliot, died in 1949, aged ninety-three, and left three sons—John, Hawksley and George. The latter was an army officer and never concerned himself with the business: John and Hawksley, however, travelled extensively for the firm. Hawksley's hunting-ground was Scotland, which he toured by train, as he had no car, even into his eighties. John covered Ireland, particularly the south of that country, where Elliot's had a good connection with their Barber mark for pen- and pocket-knives (and in the old days, razors). In Sheffield, the brothers relied upon Arthur Revitt, who had started in the firm's grinding shops, but later became a director and managed the factory.

In 1972, W.D. Slater (of Herbert M. Slater) and Jack Taylor, who together owned the cutlery materials manufacturer, J. Dewsnap Bowler Ltd, decided to buy Elliot's. By then, it was one of the last Sheffield firms to preserve the traditional knifemaking methods. Hand-forgers—such as Albert Craven—and grinders could still be seen at Elliot's in the 1970s and early 1980s and it still sold high-quality hunting- and pocket-knives. Jack Taylor retired in 1986 and Arthur Revitt left in about 1990, when he was over eighty. By then, cutlery production at the Sylvester Works had virtually ceased.

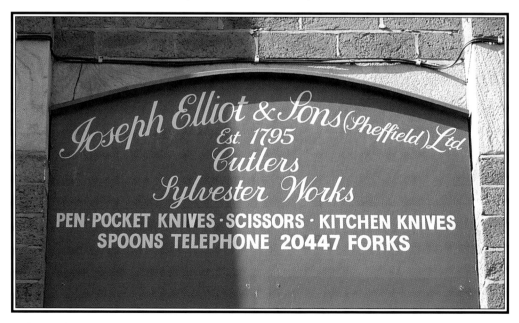

Elliot's side entrance with a description of its products. Most firms produced other cutlery besides knives.

Richard Elliott

Born in Sheffield in about 1805, Richard Elliott was the son of a barber in Scotland Street. His father died when he was about twelve years old and two years later Elliott began an apprenticeship to Henry Lee, a table-knife hafter, who worked for the cutlers John Eyre & Co. (founded, it seems, in 1810). Elliott worked his way up to become general manager and clerk in the warehouse of the firm, which eventually was known as Smith Bros. In 1837, however, his employer's business failed. Elliott, having saved up enough capital of his own, decided to take it over. He began with his own cutlery shop at the bottom of Coalpit Lane (Cambridge Street today). Elliott's operations were initially done by outworkers, but as trade expanded he was able to move to another factory in Fitzwilliam Street, where the cutlers worked on the premises. After occupying workshops in Chester Lane and Wellington Street, Elliott moved to more permanent premises in Arundel Street in 1860.

Elliott specialised in table cutlery, which he stamped with the word EXTRA. According to an obituarist, he:

> …got together a very nice connection, but made no effort to make it a large concern, preferring to have a moderate trade, and all the work done under his personal supervision, so as to maintain the reputation he enjoyed…His motto was 'quality'. He preferred to be content with earning a livelihood by doing the best possible work, even if it had to be sold at an inadequate price.

Richard Elliott died in Halifax in 1892, aged eighty-seven, having sold his business to John Sellers in Arundel Street, which continued using the name and mark.

Isaac Ellis & Sons

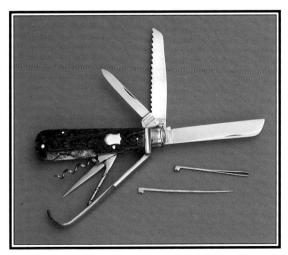

Trade advertisements claim that this firm was established in 1781, though the firm does not appear in directories until the nineteenth century. By 1839, an Isaac Ellis, table-knife manufacturer, was working at Hollis Croft (though by 1849 he had moved to Garden Street). By the mid-nineteenth century, this company was based in the Portland Works on West Street, though it later moved to Rockingham Street. Like many other firms, it appears to have mixed merchanting with manufacturing and offered for sale: table-, pen- and pocket-cutlery, besides scissors, razors and a wide range of plated goods. The firm exhibited at the Great Exhibition of 1851, where it won a prize medal. Its trade mark was PRIMUS, which first appears in advertisements in 1868.

In the early 1920s, the managing director of the firm was Robert Edward Wharam, who died on 21st March 1926, leaving £62,916 gross. Isaac Ellis & Sons was listed in Sheffield directories until 1932, when it was bought out by Edwin Blyde.

A sturdy Ellis horseman's knife, probably made in the early 20th century.

Isaac Eyre

This electroplate and cutlery business was founded in 1859 by James Townsend Henry in Howard Lane (though previously Henry appears to have been in partnership in South Street with Stacey & Horton, since at least 1856). By 1868 the firm occupied the Lincoln Works in Arundel Street, but in the following year Henry died. Isaac Eyre, the family trustee, then assumed control of the firm, which made fish-carvers, fish-eaters, dessert- and plated-goods generally. Table cutlery in the medium and best grades was also made. Isaac Eyre died on 14th September 1893, aged fifty-three, and his company ceased trading.

ISAAC EYRE,

(Successor to J. T. HENRY),

Lincoln Works, Arundel St., SHEFFIELD,

Electro-Plater and Gilder, Manufacturer of Nickel Silver and Electro-Plated Spoons, Forks, Fish Knives and Forks, Fish Carvers, Fish Eaters, Butter Knives, &c., &c.

Old Goods of every description Re-Plated and Repaired on the most reasonable terms.

Fenton Bros

According to Ivan Fallon's study of London silversmiths, this firm began its career as Hukin & Fenton of Cadman Lane, its mark being entered at the Sheffield Assay Office in 1856. However, within months John Frederick Fenton registered his own mark (JFF) at the same address. Fenton had worked previously for Hawksworth, Eyre & Co. in the Wicker, before starting his own small business. By 1860, he was listed as a silver- and electroplater at Norfolk Lane. A press report remarked: 'After several years of hard struggling and two dissolutions of partnership—and while the business was of but very limited proportions—he took into partnership his brother'. This brother, Frank Fenton, seems to have joined the firm by 1860. Fenton Bros opened a London showroom in about 1875 at 22 Bartletts Buildings. By then their Sheffield factory was the South Moor Works, at 66 Porter Street and Earl Street. Besides its silver marks Fenton Bros, by 1919, used two crossed knife-blades (without handles) as a trade mark.

In 1883, John F. Fenton died, aged sixty-three. Frank Fenton, who had retired to Jersey in about 1878, died in the following year at Leamington, aged fifty-two. Samuel Fenton, John's eldest son, was by then running the firm. At some time before 1888, Samuel took Alfred John Fenton into partnership. Samuel died in Sheffield in 1893, aged fifty-one. An obituarist stated: 'He was particularly well known and highly respected by a large circle of friends in the North of England and Scotland, where he had travelled for the last twenty years'.

In about 1896, the firm was registered as a limited liability company, with William Stainforth as managing director. Like many of the plate firms, Fenton Bros did not survive the depressed inter-war years and it ceased trading in about 1938.

Joseph Fenton & Sons

Another 'old and distinguished house', this firm was founded by Joseph Fenton in 1795 and for many years was situated in Scotland Street. The company mark, a Maltese Cross with the letters W W (one inverted above the other), was granted in 1796. In the early 1870s, the business moved to the Sykes Works on Matilda Street and Eyre Street. The contemporary trade press, in its customary deferential tones, describes Fenton's Works as 'commodious', 'well-appointed', with machinery of the 'most elaborate and effective character'. Apparently, the factory was amongst the larger of the cutlery firms in Sheffield, with about 300–400 workers in the early 1890s. A three-storied block of workshops, powered by a steam-engine, produced Fenton's specialities: table- and butchers'-knives, pocket-knives and files. Sportsman's knives, Bowies, dirks and other hunting-knives were displayed in the firm's showrooms. They traded throughout the UK, and also shipped overseas to Canada, Australia, New Zealand, Africa and China. Ireland seems to have been a particularly important market for the firm in the late nineteenth century. By the 1890s, Thomas Fenton directed the business.

In 1968, this company merged with Gregory Bros to become Gregory Fenton Ltd. By the 1990s the address of this firm was the Beehive Works in Milton Street.

William Greaves & Sons

When William Greaves built his Sheaf Works in 1823, it was the first inkling in Sheffield that great changes in the cutlery trade were on the way. The derelict main block of the Sheaf Works, which still stands in Maltravers Street near the Wicker, may seem nothing special to modern eyes, but it was the first large factory in the town. Sheffielders had seen nothing like it, when Greaves erected a £50,000 building in which 'one grand end was kept in view, namely that of centralizing on the spot all the various processes through which the iron must pass…until fashioned into razor, pen-knife or other article of use'. Contemporary accounts described how the firm converted and melted steel at one end of the factory; at the other tools and knives were despatched to destinations around the world. It was probably not quite so self-contained as these descriptions imply, but there was no doubting the novel size of the factory.

Greaves had been active since the late eighteenth century (its trade mark was registered in 1724), but it came into its own with the expansion of the American trade after 1815. By 1849 Greaves was describing itself as 'American merchants', selling table-knives, razors, files, edge-tools, railway springs and steel. Besides large quantities of table cutlery, the company made many Bowie knives for the American frontiersman.

In 1850 the Greaves' partnership was dissolved. The cutlery business was taken over by Benjamin James Eyre (the son of a grocer) and Frederick Ward; and the steel and tool activities were run by Thomas Turton & Sons. Both interests shared the Sheaf Works, with Turton's still owning the Greaves' marks. Eventually, the two sides of the business went their separate ways: Turton's stayed at the Sheaf Works and the firm was later bought by Frederick T. Mappin, who wished to broaden his interests outside cutlery. Meanwhile, B.J. Eyre & Co. moved to 116 Rockingham Street between 1863 and 1876. It does not seem to have prospered and in 1877 the Sheffield firm and B.J. Eyre's New

York house were bought by the New York merchanting house of Frederick Wiebusch. The latter therefore acquired Eyre's CHALLENGE trade mark, which had been in use since about 1867. Meanwhile, Wiebusch also invested in the Frary Cutlery Co. at Bridgeport, Connecticut. Sheffield newspapers reported that Wiebusch and Col. James D. Frary had decided to transfer 130 of the Sheffield workforce to Bridgeport. They duly arrived with their tools and some Sheffield water— everything, it would appear, apart from the 'Sheffield shop building and Sheffield air'.

Sheaf Works in about 1859.

John Greenough

This was another cutlery firm, whose reputation was out of all proportion to its size. Its workforce at its small Clintock Works on the corner of Milton Street and Bowdon Street, behind Wostenholm's Washington Works, cannot have been more than twenty or thirty (maybe less), yet its fine pen-, pocket-, desk-, and sportsman's-knives regularly carried away the prize medals at exhibitions. In 1879 (when it was based in Rockingham Street), the firm won the first prize in the Cutlers' Exhibition of 1879. A gold medal at the London International Exhibition in 1884 followed. Greenough's was founded in about 1867 and its mark was a Maltese Cross and the word VIENA. It disappeared from Sheffield directories in about 1926.

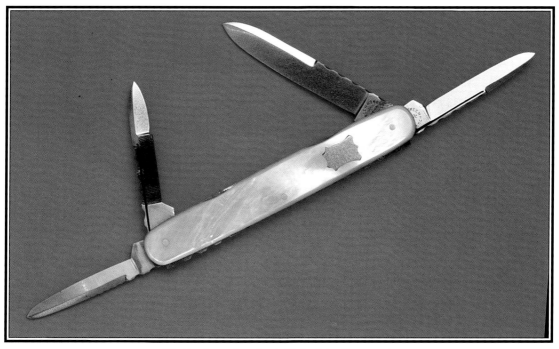

Workback pearl pocket-knife by John Greenough.

William Gregory & Sons

A self-made man of humble birth was how the founder of this firm was described. William Gregory, a Sheffielder, had learnt the art of forging and established his business in 1843. He appears in a Sheffield directory in 1865, situated in Peel Street, Broomhill, making table- and butchers'-knives. By the time he died in 1879 (when he had moved his business to the Westend Works in Bolsover Street) his goods had made his reputation. His son, Samuel Gregory, who had been born in Sheffield and educated privately, took over the business. After 1880, he was partnered by George Blagden Hawksworth (b. 1848), who was the son of a Sheffield bank manager, and who had worked for the cutlers, Steer & Webster. Samuel Gregory was the firm's traveller; Hawksworth managed the factory, which by then was at the Otto Works in Howard and Arundel Streets. In the mid-1890s, it employed 100–200 workers. Gregory's was well known for its butchers'-, grocers'- and farmers'-knives; it also sold ordinary cutlery and pocket-knives and tools. For the Victorian household, it also made 'Incorrodible' butter- and cheese-knives and 'Spanish Silver' butter-knives. These goods were also exported to Australia, Canada and the USA (where the firm had a resident agent). Its corporate mark was a crossed saw and cleaver, with the words 'All Right'; also a hammer, with the letters 'W G'. In about 1907, the business was taken over by John Petty & Sons.

Gregory Bros

This firm first appears in Sheffield directories in 1907 as a knife, spoon and fork manufacturer at the Exchange Works in Egerton Street. By 1916 it had moved to nearby Bishop Street and was concentrating on the manufacture of knives. Gregory Bros was to specialise in butchers'-, skinning- and sticking-knives. In about 1926 the business relocated to the Balmoral Works in Matilda Street and it remained there until the early 1960s when it transferred to the Sykes Works in Milton Street. In 1968 the firm took over Joseph Fenton, forming Gregory Fenton Ltd, which was based at the Beehive Works in Milton Street. The firm's trade mark was a picture of Beehive, which had once belonged to Slater. In 1995 the firm is still listed at the Beehive Works.

Gregory Fenton's entrance. The Beehive mark was acquired from Slater.

Samuel Hancock & Sons

This firm had one of the most striking of nineteenth-century trade marks—'Mazeppa', a man bound to a horse's back (a reference to the Russian nobleman, Ivan Mazeppa). Advertisements state that the mark was first used in 1787. The business probably began with Samuel Hancock, a grocer and razor manufacturer, who was listed in a Sheffield directory of 1841 at Peacroft. By 1849 Hancock had abandoned his grocery business and started making pen- and pocket-knives. In 1879 he was listed at the Mazeppa Works at 12 Sycamore Street; he then moved his factory to Button Lane in about 1883. A business review soon afterwards describes Hancock's main lines as follows: 'pen, pocket, sportsmen's, sailors', farriers', castrator, strike fire, spear, bowie, dagger, vine and Spanish lock knives, pen machines, butchers', curriers', cooks', bread and palette knives, spoon knives, picnic cases, razors, etc.'.

On 25th January 1889, the newspapers recorded the death of Samuel Hancock, aged fifty-six, a cutlery manufacturer, after 'a long and painful illness'. This may explain why the Mazeppa Works was moved to Bishop Street by 1893 and two years later it was sold to Ernest G. Reuss, who had earlier been involved with Deakin, Sons & Co. Reuss, who is known to have had a keen interest in the Spanish and South African markets, appears to have been responsible for the business moving to Charlotte Street, off West Street.

After Reuss died in 1898, the firm seems to have continued under its original name, though its history becomes difficult to track. On the eve of the First World War, Sheffield directories list a Samuel Hancock & Sons in Rockingham Street and a Samuel Hancock & Son at the Moorfields Works, Snow Lane. The Mazeppa mark was later used by the cutlers, Beeston & Co.

SAML. HANCOCK & SONS,

CORPORATE MARK,   'MAZEPPA.'

PEA CROFT WORKS, SHEFFIELD,

MERCHANTS, AND MANUFACTURERS OF

Fine Pen, Pocket, & Sportsmen's Knives

SAILORS', FARRIERS', CASTRATOR, STRIKEFIRE,

BOWIE, DAGGER, VINE, AND SPANISH LOCK KNIVES,

SPOON KNIVES, PICNIC CASES, PEN MACHINES, &c.

TABLE, BUTCHERS', CURRIERS', COOK, BREAD, & PALETTE KNIVES,

SPEAR KNIVES, RAZORS, &c.

N.B.—A LARGE STOCK ALWAYS ON HAND.

Hargreaves, Smith & Co.

The business was founded by William Hargreaves, who in a Sheffield directory of 1825 was described as a merchant at Brookhill. By 1841 William and Lydia Hargreaves (his wife, perhaps) had moved to 28 Eyre Lane, where the founder continued his merchanting activities and also made table-knives. After the 1850s, the firm also acted as agents for Swedish iron. At the Great Exhibition in 1851, the firm displayed a fine assortment of table-, carving- and bread-knives. *The Art Journal* remarked that all the 'handles are of fine ivory elaborately carved and mounted with silver ferrules, and the blades are of the highest polished steel'.

In 1864, by which time William Hargreaves was living at Cherrytree Hill, another individual was listed in local directories as a merchant working for the firm. This was Isaac Milner, a Quaker, who had been born in Sheffield on 18th September 1834. He was the son of Charles Milner, an ironmonger in Fargate. Isaac was educated at the Friends' Boarding School at Ackworth, and then made his way in the cutlery business for Hargreaves, Smith. Eventually, he became head of the company, presumably after the death in 1874 of William Hargreaves (who collapsed and died at the Sheffield Turkish Baths). Milner became a JP in 1893 and appears to have retired about two years later, when his old firm discontinued table-knife manufacture and switched to steel and edge tools (the name was still listed as late as 1959). Isaac Milner died on 6th August 1926, aged ninety-one, and left £47,656. The company had two marks registered for cutlery: the words, J. Smith & Co., and FRYERS.

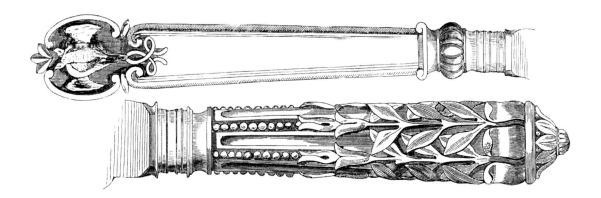

Harrison Bros & Howson

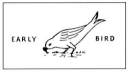

This company, which had its roots in the eighteenth century, became one of the biggest cutlery firms in Sheffield by 1900. It developed from a Norfolk Street cutlery business established in 1796 by Thomas Sansom under the style of Thomas Sansom & Sons. Thomas was later joined in business by his sons William and John, in 1826 and 1834, respectively. (Coincidentally, these were the years in which William and John Sansom became Master Cutler.) By the 1840s, George Howson, a cutler apprenticed in 1803, had become influential in the Sansom firm. He died in 1847, and it was about then that the style of Harrison Bros & Howson was adopted. The chief partners were William Howson (c. 1824–1884), George's son, who soon became a prominent traveller for the firm; and two brothers, James William Harrison (1816–1897) and Henry Harrison (c. 1825–1893). (The mother of the Harrisons had once been married to John Brocksopp, a Derbyshire ironmaster). According to one newspaper: 'The combination of these three men was a powerful one'. The business was initially run from 45 Norfolk Street, though by the early 1890s it was also operating from Shoreham Street. A contemporary business review, *The Industries of Sheffield* (c. 1887), had this to say:

> At their cutlery works three hundred men are in constant work. On the first floor of this building are the offices—large, handsome and well-appointed rooms; adjoining is a heavily stocked showroom, where ivory stock of every description is exhibited; near this is another showroom devoted to the display of butchers' and other knives, carvers and forks to match, and smaller knives of chaste design and wonderfully fine and careful finish. These goods are packed in hand-some plush cases, and from this room are despatched to various parts of the world, North America and Australia absorbing an immense quantity. Descending from these rooms into a large and spacious yard, we found about twenty forges in operation, two skilled artizans attending to each. At the side of this is the ivory-cutting shop, and underneath the yard are extensive and well-lighted cellars, which are utilized as warehouses for the Egyptian horns and African elephants tusks, which the firm import direct in immense quantities, and which are destined eventually to find their way to the dinner-table in the shape of knife handles. A great point of interest is found here in the powerful steam engine, by means of which the machinery throughout the factory is set in motion. Above the yard are seven shops for the seven different departments into which the manufacture of the products of the factory is divided. The goods turned out from this factory have gained a reputation for the excellence of their quality and the delicacy of their finish, and it is safe to predict that this reputation will be fully sustained in the future.

High-grade articles were clearly the order of the day, backed by a string of Royal Warrants from William IV, Queen Adelaide, Queen Victoria and King Edward VII. Silver- and electroplate items were added to the production of knives—a trend followed by all the leading cutlery makers in the late nineteenth century.

Harrison Bros & Howson expanded rapidly in the 1890s, when the firm had agencies in New York, at 66 West Broadway, and in San Francisco, on Sutter Street. This was achieved despite the American cutlery tariff. The company also had London showrooms at Holborn Viaduct. Henry Harrison became Master Cutler in 1862, but the Howson family became increasingly dominant in the business in the late nineteenth century. The senior partner was George Howson (1851–1930), the son of William, who after an education in France joined the business in 1867 and became partner in 1875 on the retirement of his father. Later George Howson had as his partners, Frank Harrison (the son of Henry Harrison, who retired in 1892) and John B. Wilkinson (1849–1919).

Harrison Bros & Howson's factory in the early 20th century.

George Howson became Master Cutler in 1893.

Following the purchase of William Webster's spoon and fork business in 1894, it was reported that Harrison Bros & Howson employed over 700 hands (double the number in the previous decade). Such was the expansion that the firm decided to move to another factory in Carver Street in 1900. The new building, bounded by West and Division Streets (but fronting Carver Street) was said to have been lit by more than a thousand windows! In 1902 Charles Ibbotson & Co., the pocket-knife makers of Melbourne Works, Cambridge Street (trade mark, 'Slash'), was acquired. By now the firm was amongst the top half dozen or so cutlery firms in the city, with a workforce of about 600 in 1911. However, although the firm obviously had high hopes for its new factory and employed the latest machinery, the company ran at a loss before 1907.

Above the main entrance to Harrison Bros & Howson's Works (which can still be seen on Carver Street) was the corporate trademark: a coronet with the word 'Alpha', granted in 1836. The firm also used the 'Stag's Head' mark of William Webster.

The firm declined steadily between the wars, when the Howson family was still in control. It was bought by Viners in 1959.

Main entrance of Harrison Bros & Howson's Alpha Works on Carver Street.
The main building still stands.

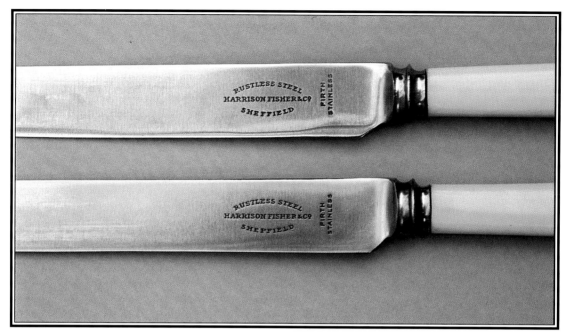

Harrison Fisher stainless table-knives, made in the 1920s.

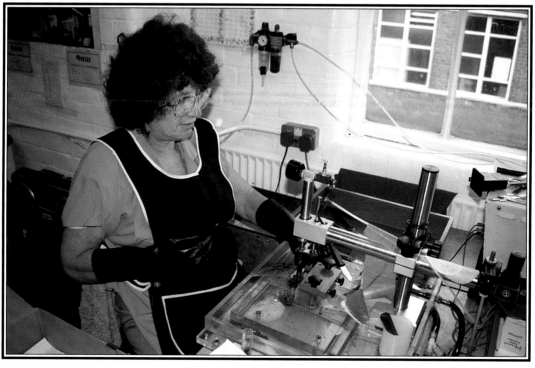

Etching kitchen-knives at the Eye Witness Works in the 1990s.

Harrison Fisher

This firm was founded in 1896 by Harrison Fisher, who was soon joined in partnership by his brother-in-law Samuel Lawton, whose previous experience of the trade had been with R.F. Mosely. The company specialised in high-quality products, particularly plated goods and table-knives, from its factory in Trafalgar Street. The company prospered, but in 1907 tragedy struck and the founder died leaving a widow and two young children. For several years, the firm continued under the surviving partner, until Harrison Fisher's widow married Samuel Marsden Inman, who then joined the firm. He served as joint managing-director under Samuel Lawton's chairmanship, until the latter's retirement in 1936. Roger Inman, the youngest son of Samuel, joined the firm in 1931, and after the War became joint managing-director.

Various small acquisitions contributed to growth: Thomas Frost & Co., A. Milnes & Co., John Sanderson & Sons, Dawes & Ball Ltd, and Walton Bros. But the major development was the friendly takeover of Taylor's Eye Witness Works (formerly Needham Veall & Tyzack) in 1975. Subsequently, Harrison Fisher's Trafalgar Street premises were sold to Sheffield Corporation for redevelopment (though most of the old Harrison Fisher factory still stands). Taylor's Milton Street Works was then enlarged to house both companies. The merger, which was achieved without redundancies, was successful and led to a period of steady growth.

In 1995 Harrison Fisher, which employs a workforce of about two hundred, is probably the only contemporary example of the type of cutlery firm which flourished in nineteenth-century Sheffield—one which produces a comprehensive range of knives. It is also still family-owned, with Roger Inman as chairman and joint managing director, Alastair Fisher Harrison in charge of sales and marketing, and Christopher Inman running the factory operation.

According to Roger Inman:

Despite all the problems of recession and competition from the Pacific Rim and other low-wage countries, there remains genuine demand for high-quality Sheffield cutlery providing it is well-designed, well-presented and produced by modern methods so that it can be sold at reasonable prices. The Harrison Fisher Group remains a leading player in this field. The product ranges now include, as well as table cutlery and flatware, pocket-knives (including Eye Witness and Saynor brands), trade-knives, scissors; and there is a special emphasis on kitchen-knives. Although quantity-wise, the Group is not the largest producer of kitchen knives in the UK, informed opinion accepts that Harrison Fisher/Taylor's Eye Witness make kitchen-knives of better quality than any other Sheffield producer and fully equal to the world's best.

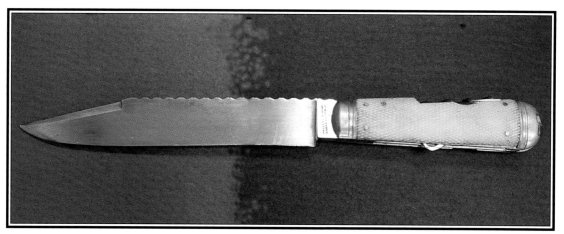

Large 19th-century Joseph Haywood Bowie, with blades and tools in the checked ivory handle. (Weston Park Museum).

Joseph Haywood & Co.

Born in Sheffield in about 1822, Joseph Haywood was apprenticed to Robert Sorby & Co., Carver Street. Aged twenty-one, he succeeded to the cutlery business carried on by his uncle, George Willis Hinchcliffe, and by his mother. The Works were then at the top of Victoria Street, off Portobello. Later the business was moved to Holly Street and then to Garden Street.

In about 1880 the workshops were moved yet again to a much larger factory—the Glamorgan Works in Little Pond Street. Pocket-, sport's- and budding-knives were the staple lines of business, though the firm also made table-cutlery and plated dessert-ware and also did business as a 'general merchant' in cutlery, partly through a London office at 56 Holborn Viaduct. Its corporate mark was a kettle.

According to one reporter: 'Mr Haywood was a successful manufacturer and splendid man of business. The qualities which make up the latter he largely inherited from his mother, who in his early career was in the habit of attending to the works while he was travelling for orders'. Joseph Haywood died in 1888. In 1902 the Glamorgan Works was sold to Needham, Veall & Tyzack, and Haywood's trade marks were sold to Thos Turner for £660.

George Hides & Son

EXCELSIOR

One of the oldest cutlery firms in Sheffield, Hides was established in Hollis Croft in 1790 by Robert Hides—though the family had apparently been involved in the cutlery business as early as 1609. One member of the family, William Hides, had been Master Cutler in 1750. Robert Hides ran the business for about thirty years, and he then passed it on to his son, George Hides, who spent some fifty years in the enterprise. George seems to have died in 1887 and his son, William F. Hides, took over the business in the 1890s, bringing a seventh generation into the firm. As one contemporary remarked, this was 'an example of hereditary connection unparalleled in the annals of the trade'.

The Hollis Works occupied a modest red-brick building at the bottom of Hollis Croft. It was typical of the smaller cutlery works, covering 600 square yards, with a frontage of about fifty yards or so, a gateway entrance to a small central courtyard, and three or four storeys of workshops. The firm produced the better qualities of table- and spring-cutlery, razors, palette-, putty- and oyster-knives. Butchers' steels and knives were amongst Hides' major specialities and in these products and in its

table cutlery the firm was renowned for using best shear steel. The corporate mark was EXCELSIOR. The firm sold a wide range of pocket-knives, such as its 'cycle-knife' introduced in the 1890s to tap the new craze for cycling: $1\frac{1}{2}$ ounces in weight, it included a tyre wrench.

Overseas trade was important to Hides, especially in the Colonies. Its trade with South Africa was said to be increasing towards the turn of the century and this may have been important in the expansion of the firm. It employed about fifty hands in the late 1880s, but by 1900 this had increased to nearly a hundred.

George Hides seems to have ceased business towards the end of the First World War.

Francis Howard

This manufacturer, who specialised in electroplated cutlery, is first listed in local directories in 1868, when he was working at Wm Batt & Sons in Mulberry Street. By 1876, Howard was working on his own account at the West End Works in West Street. He then moved his operations to Division Street, where he occupied the Aberdeen Works, which was built in 1883 (the three-storied building still stands on Trafalgar Street). Much of the trade was done in Scotland, with Francis Howard himself doing much of the travelling for orders. He sold plated fish-servers and eaters, dessert- and butter-knives, besides spoons and forks. Howard died in 1905, aged sixty-eight. The business continues to make sterling silver flatware at the Aberdeen Works in the 1990s. The company trademark is an archery target (with an arrow in the bullseye), with the words WELL DONE.

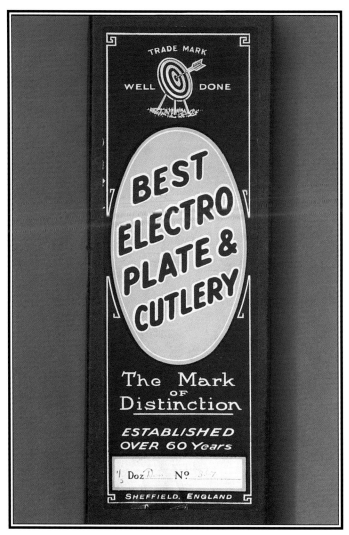

Howard table-knife box from the 1920s.

W.R. Humphreys & Co.

Born in the north of Ireland in about 1856, W.R. Humphreys was apprenticed in the ironmongery trade before becoming a traveller for a cutlery firm. By 1880 he had launched his own cutlery business in Eyre Street. In about 1900 he took over the business of John Wragg, based in the Advance Works in Denby Street. Humphreys renamed his Denby Street business, the Haddon Works. Trade catalogues show that the firm manufactured (or marketed) a wide range of knives, including most types of table-knives and pocket-knives. Humphreys died in 1911, leaving a widow but no children. However, T.R.H. Graham (c. 1873–1932), Humphrey's nephew, joined the firm as a young man and became managing director until a year before his death. Charles Hinchcliffe (d. 1932) is also known to have been associated with the firm for many years after the founder's death. The firm's trade mark was a lamp with the word "RADIANT".

One of the last chairmen at the company was Frank W. Blaydes, who died in 1954, aged ninty-two. Humphreys manufactured cutlery at the Haddon Works until the 1960s, when it moved to the Portland Works in Randall Street. It was last listed at Matilda Street in 1970.

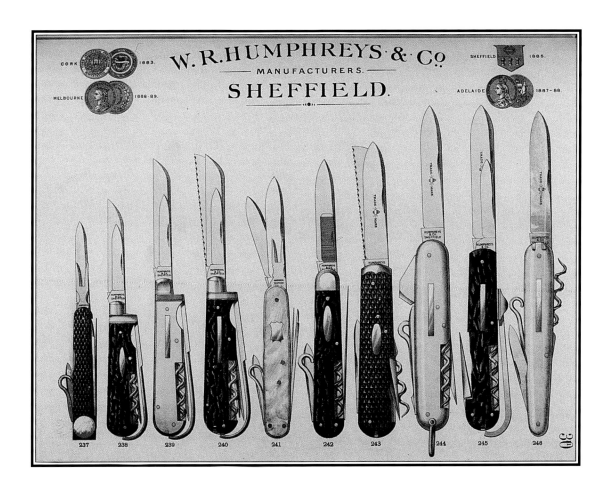

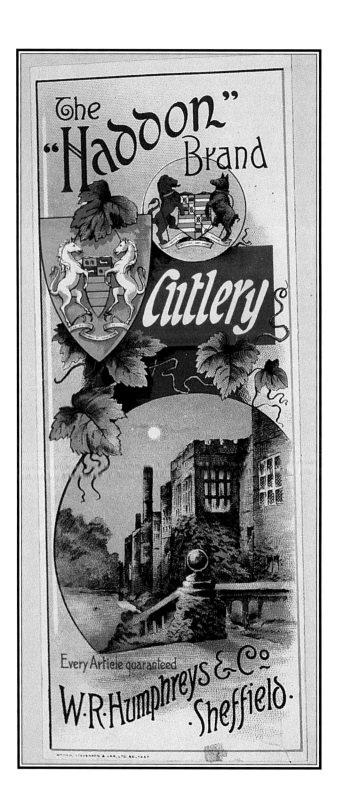

M. Hunter & Son Cutlery & Plate.

SHOOTING AND FISHING KNIVES.
KNIFE CHAINS FOR THESE, 4/6 & 8/- PER DOZEN.

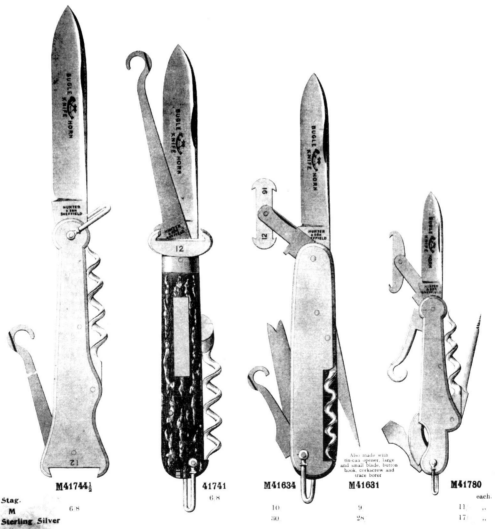

Also made with
tin-can opener, large
and small blade, button
hook, corkscrew and
trace borer

	M41744½	41741	M41634	M41631	M41780
		6.8			each.
Stag.	6.8		10	9	11 ,,
M					
Sterling Silver		30		28	17 ,,

Key to Handles. No Letter—Stag. A—Black. B—Bone. C—Cocowood. D—Chequered Black.
F—Ivory. G—Tortoise Shell. H—Pearl. M—Nickel.
———— ONLY THE HANDLES PRICED ARE KEPT IN STOCK.
IF REQUIRED THESE KNIVES WILL BE MOUNTED ON ATTRACTIVE SALF CARDS, FREE OF CHARGE.

Michael Hunter & Son

The Hunter family were closely connected with the cutlery trade and three of its members became Masters Cutler within fifty years in the late nineteenth century. The Hunters liked naming their sons Michael.

One Michael Hunter, who was the father of the noted Hallamshire antiquarian, Joseph Hunter (1783–1861), was born in Ecclesfield, the son of a prosperous factor or 'hard-wareman' (also named Michael). One report states that he started a small business in West Street in 1760; another account dates the firm from 1780, when it began as Hunter & Twigg (a firm listed in 1787 as a knifemaker in Back Lane). Either way, the real expansion of the firm began with the second Michael Hunter (1800–1886), who became Master Cutler in 1852. According to one report, the latter waged war unceasingly on the unions: he was the first to apply circular saws in the cutting of knife handles (a claim also made for Ellin), and the first to use machines to forge knife blades. 'I would', he once said, 'rather make the best goods at 5% profit, than an inferior kind at a greater gain.' In the late nineteenth century, the third Michael Hunter (1821–1896) then built up the business, which was located at the Talbot Works, fronting Savile Street. Its corporate marks were the 'Bugle', granted in 1860; 'Bison', with the Spanish word 'Fuerte' (meaning strong); and 'Llama'. The firm made (or at least marketed) a wide range of cutlery: table-, and butchers'-knives, spear-knives, razors, pen- and pocket-knives, and sportsmen's-, gardeners'- and hay-knives. Articles as diverse as skates, files, edge tools, and electro-plated and Britannia metal goods were also stocked. As its trade marks indicated, business was world-wide, with agencies in Australia, Cape Town, Montreal, Hamburg, and many South American towns.

Michael Hunter mixed business with a wide range of public duties—mayor, alderman, JP, the Master Cutlership (1860), and work for the Unitarian church. His son, Michael Joseph Hunter (1856–1928), was educated at University College School, London, before joining the family firm as an apprentice at the age of seventeen. In 1883 he was made a partner and took over after his father's death, making the firm a limited liability company in 1897, with himself as chairman and Thomas T. Hardy (d. 1910) as managing director. The Master Cutlership followed in 1903. He married the second daughter of the late Henry Harrison, the noted Sheffield cutler: and his son was named, inevitably, Michael.

In the first decade of the twentieth century, Hunter's absorbed the businesses of Parkin & Marshall and Slack & Grinold. Then Hunter's itself, which had by now moved to Reed Street, was absorbed by Needham, Veall & Tyzack, sometime before about 1911. Hunter's marks were later acquired by Slater's.

William Hutton & Sons

The Huttons were manufacturing silversmiths in Birmingham soon after the start of the nineteenth century. A member of the family, William Carr Hutton (1803–1865), moved to Sheffield in 1832 and began the manufacture of silver- and British-Plate products. (The latter were made from copper, zinc and nickel—an alloy sometimes known as German- or nickel-silver.) Until the 1850s, the business occupied various workshops in Eyre Street, Pinstone Street, South Street (The Moor), Surrey Street, and High Street. The business prospered. In 1843, Hutton's became the second Sheffield licensee (after John Harrison) of Elkington's electroplate process.

William C. Hutton had five sons, the youngest of whom, Herbert Hutton (1843–1904), joined the business in 1864 and became the dominant figure in the Sheffield factory in the late nineteenth century. (The other family members ran the firm's offices and branches in Birmingham, London and overseas.) Under Herbert, the business expanded into a large factory in West Street in 1885.

In 1893 the firm became a limited company, the same year it took over Rupert Favell & Co., a London silversmiths. Then in 1902 Hutton acquired the Sheffield silversmithing firm of Creswick & Co., based in Arundel Street. A decade later, Hutton's appears to have reached its peak, one newspaper reporting that the business employed over nine hundred (a far cry from the days in South Street when it had only about a dozen employees).

In its early days, much of Hutton's output consisted of forks and spoons, a product line that was considerably extended by the end of the nineteenth century, when a wide range of luxury silverware was marketed. Like most of the silver firms, Hutton's was not primarily a knifemaker, but it did manufacture plated table-knives, including butter- and dessert-knives, fruit-knives and fish-slicers.

The firm's heyday did not long survive the death of its most dynamic member. After 1904, as one family member put it, 'the business lacked the leadership and drive of Herbert Hutton', and there were also conflicts within the family. The firm entered the First World War with its future uncertain.

In 1914 some of the Hutton family joined James Dixon & Sons, Walker & Hall and Barker Bros in starting the Sheffield Flatware Co. to manufacture spoons and forks by a new process. The machinery was soon turned over to war work. In the 1920s, the Hutton factory in West Street was closed and the trade and goodwill were transferred to James Dixon & Sons. Cutlery products carrying the Hutton mark (three crossed arrows, which was originally owned by Creswick's) continued to be made.

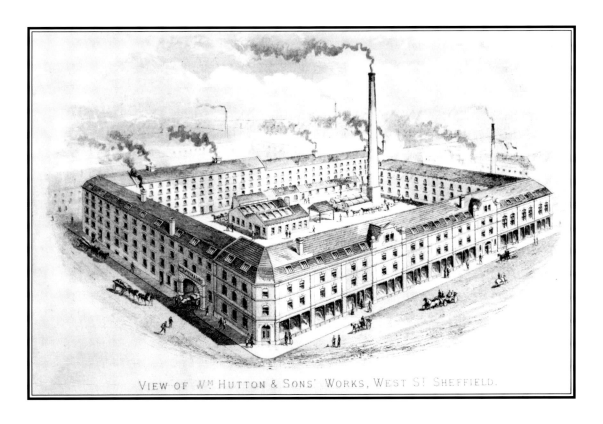

VIEW OF Wᴹ HUTTON & SONS' WORKS, WEST Sᵗ SHEFFIELD.

George Ibberson & Co.

When the Ibberson family first started making cutlery is unknown. It seems that the business was founded in 1700 by Joseph Ibberson, but apparently the Ibbersons had long before been producing cutlery in a small way. In the records of the Cutlers' Company, the first mention of an Ibberson is in 1666 (the year of the Great Fire of London), when William, son of George, was granted the freedom by which he became an accredited maker with his own mark. The firm first came into prominence in 1759, when Joseph Ibberson, son of the founder, was installed as Master Cutler; and in 1791 William, the son of Robert Ibberson, was granted the trade number 717 by the Cutlers' Company—these numbers being the forerunners of modern trade marks.

The actual place at which the business was located was known as Gibraltar. From 1805 to 1842 we find Ibberson's located in Mary Street; from 1842 to 1861 in Exchange Gateway; and from 1861 to 1911 at the Central Works in West Street. In 1911 it moved to the address with which most people associate the firm: Rockingham Street.

Management changed hands over the years, but always an Ibberson was appointed as head: William (1700), Joseph (1716), George (1723), Joseph (1753), John (1765), Charles and Henry (1782–3), William (1800), Joseph (1840), George (1860), Wilson & Ibberson (1875), and George Ibberson (1885). In the 1890s, the business was taken over by Joseph William Ibberson (1865–1954), who had joined his father in 1883. A Wesleyan, it was said that Joseph was 'the soul of affability in private life, and one of the easiest men to talk to in Sheffield'.

Ibberson's made the usual run of cutlery: table-, pen- and pocket-knives, carvers, trade-knives and razors; but it was particularly noted for its high-quality pen-, pocket- and sport's-knives made in pearl, tortoise-shell and ivory. These were invariably made from hand-forged crucible steel. The author has a vivid recollection of being shown by the firm's twentieth-century boss, Billy Ibberson (1902–1988)—the son of J.W. Ibberson—an old company sample roll. Unfurled, it was stuffed with pearl pocket-knives—lobsters, smoker's-knives, and many other multi-blades. This was 'bread and butter' output to Ibberson's nineteenth-century craftsmen. These knives were stamped with Ibberson's most famous mark—the Violin—which was acquired in the 1880s along with the cutlery business and goodwill of J.C. Skinner. Later trade marks were the 'Strad' and the musical motif and words 'Double Sharp'.

J.W. Ibberson has a place in steelmaking as well as cutlery history, since he helped produce some of the first stainless steel knife blades in 1914.

Ibberson's was very much a typical Sheffield cutlery firm: typical in its ancient lineage, typical in its modest size and typical, too, in its consistently high quality (at least in its heyday). On the backs of such modest businesses, the reputation of Sheffield knives was built. Unfortunately, the

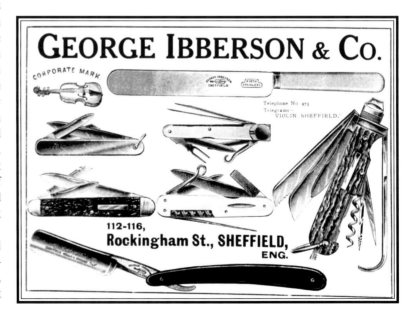

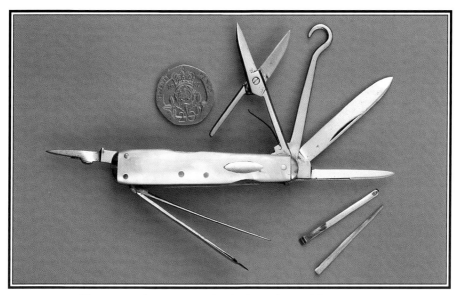

Ibberson pearl manicure pocket-knife, made in a lobster pattern.

business also typified the decline of the industry. In the inter-war period the company managed to survive the depression by—as one journal, *The Ironmonger*, put it in May 1937—'a remarkable blending of old methods and new. Ibberson's have modified some of the old craftsmen's methods in order that they may produce cutlery of medium price; but never has this modification been allowed to bring Violin cutlery anywhere near shoddiness'. For Ibberson's this meant, on the one hand, retaining the old cutlery crafts (albeit at low wage rates) by building up a skilled workforce, with men such as Ted Swinden (forger), Bill Thackray (hardener and temperer and marker of blades), and Ted Osborne (pocket-knife maker). On the other, the firm tried to introduce new machine-made products, such as the safety-razor.

The company's spiritual home however, remained the nineteenth century. Ibberson's was a friendly place to work, but very conservative, especially under Billy Ibberson, the dominant personality in the firm after 1945. A raconteur, Ibberson became a familiar figure on the Sheffield scene at institutions such as Cutlers' Hall (where he served as Master Cutler in 1954) and at various social functions, where his jolly figure, cigarette holder and lapel flower made him instantly recognisable. But his

business did not fare well in the industry crisis of the 1970s, failing both to retain its traditional craftsmen and to break into new markets for knives. In the 1980s, Ibberson's was taken over by British Syphon Industries and the Ibberson family withdrew from the cutlery trade. A company using the Ibberson mark still makes pocket-knives from a factory in Garden Street.

Ted Swinden, the forger at Ibberson's, in 1939.

Fred James

When he died in 1986, Fred James was Sheffield's best known Bowie knife maker. Sheffield born and bred, his grandfather had worked as a grinder at Burgon & Ball, the sheep-shear makers; whilst his father had a specialist job grinding the guards for carver forks at a workshop in Lambert Street. On his mother's side, the family were involved in the pocket-knife trade as forgers.

Not surprisingly, when he left school at fourteen in about 1935, Fred James went straight into the cutlery trade at Christopher Johnson's Portobello Works. He was apprenticed as a pen- and pocket-knife materials maker, furnishing the cutlers with all the parts—blades, bolsters, scales and springs. His apprenticeship was interrupted by Army service, but after the war James returned to his old job at Johnson's and worked there until it was taken over by Wostenholm's in 1956. This meant a move to the Washington Works, where James took charge of the materials department of about eight workers. At around this time, he began working on

specialist jobs, such as ivory-tipped forceps and Bowie knives. He recalled:

> There was a Maharajah of India who used to send for knives, three knives every year, big game-hunting knives, beautiful things. He would have a safari for his friends, you know, shooting tigers, leopards—whatever they were shooting. We used to have to make these three ivory-handled hunting knives, beautiful things. I loved making them.

Although he was not trained as a cutler, Fred James acquired many of the skills of the old Sheffield Bowie-knife makers—and this was made easier by his situation in the Washington Works where many etching plates, die-stamps, and spare knife-parts had survived from the great I*XL era in the nineteenth century. Wostenholm's also still attracted orders from American customers for the company's most famous knife. The result was that Fred James began to acquire a reputation as a Bowie-knife maker.

Fred James Bowie knife.

In 1971, when Wostenholm & Rodgers merged, Fred James decided to start his own business making knives. He rented a backyard workshop on Broomspring Lane, working for a time with a hafter named Herbert (Sandy) Lowe. His blades were usually forged by George Watts, ground by Rowland Swinden, and then acid-etched by Doris Walsh. James would then assemble and finish them in the traditional manner.

Big Bowie knives were his speciality, though he also made daggers and other styles of knives (though not spring knives). The Bowies were often acid-etched with Wostenholm's nineteenth-century American mottoes and surmounted by horse's head and half-horse/half alligator pommels. James often preferred to stamp these knives I∗XL (or with other Wostenholm stampings), rather than use his own mark or that of 'James & Lowe'. Perhaps inevitably, James' I∗XL Bowies began changing hands for high prices in the USA in the early 1970s (up to $1500). Although his Bowies are too big and heavy to pass as original I∗XL knives to experienced eyes (most are made of modern steel, too), they hoodwinked many American museums and collectors. Disappointment followed when their owners discovered their true provenance and value.

Fred James' reputation in America is therefore somewhat controversial, though the knives stamped with his own mark are still valued highly.

Christopher Johnson & Co.

Christopher Johnson started his cutlery business in Howard Street in 1836. In the 1840s and 1850s, he moved it to Gell Street and then to Rockingham Street. In 1859 he moved to Portobello, where his Western Works (a name which signalled the importance for the firm of the trade from the south-western counties of England) produced table- and pocket-knives. Nine years later, a partner, John Marshall, joined the business, and the title of '& Co.' was added to the founder's name.

The range and quality of Johnson's products were first class. Sheffield City Library's Local Studies collection has more trade catalogues and manuscript letter-books for this firm than it has for more well known makers. These show a characteristically wide spread of cutlery products: everything from table-knives to hunting-knives. A Johnson sample book, probably pre-dating the First World War, has photographs of sportsman's-knives and farmers'-knives. Hafted in buffalo, ivory and stag, the quality of these knives is self-evident.

Johnson's aimed its goods increasingly at the overseas market. In 1880 it won a gold medal at the Melbourne Exhibition and followed this up by appointing an agent in Australia, J.W. Bunby, who developed a flourishing trade in the 1880s and 1890s for Johnson's table cutlery and pocket-knives. In about 1884 the firm also sold plated-ware, and steel and files. Johnson's trade mark, a flag enclosing its initials, was also well known in South Africa, where the firm won a gold medal at the Kimberley Exhibition in 1892. At the turn of the century, Johnson's were hard-pressed to satisfy the demand from these export markets.

After 1945, the decline of overseas markets hit the Western Works hard. In about 1956 it was bought by Wostenholm's and Johnson's factory was closed.

CHRISTOPHER JOHNSON & CO., MANUFACTURERS, WESTERN WORKS, SHEFFIELD.

SPORTSMEN'S KNIVES.—ENGRAVED FULL SIZE.

TRADE C.J. MARK

6644
48/ each.
4½ in. Stag Horn Handle,
German Silver Shoulders,
10 articles. Lock Blade.

6659
45/ each.
4¾ in. Diamond Cut Ivory
Handle, 8 articles, Lock Blade.

6642
40/ each.
4¾ in. Stag Horn Handle,
11 articles, Lock Blade.

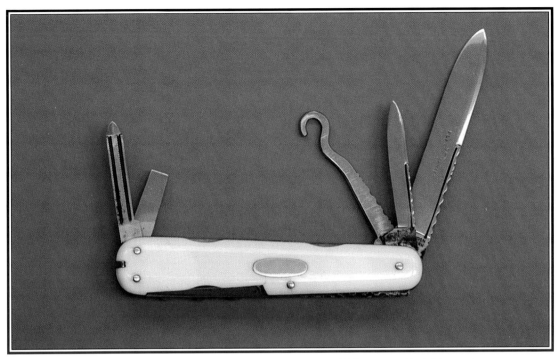

Christopher Johnson workback ivory sport's-knife, c. 1900. (Weston Park Museum).

A.J. Jordan

This was one of the few nineteenth-century Sheffield cutlery houses that was run by an immigrant. Andrew J. Jordan was an American, born in Baltimore in about 1846, who established a cutlery business in St Louis in 1871. A merchant, he decided that he would only deal in top-quality goods, a decision that led him to look across the Atlantic. Noted an obituarist: 'His trade was almost entirely in America, but it was in Sheffield that he established his factory, as he wished to deal only in first-class Sheffield goods'. In 1885 he started his own works in the town, first at 20 Radford Street, and then in a more substantial building in Baker's Hill. Jordan named his factory the East India Works. By the end of the 1880s, he employed about 120 skilled workers, who were kept busy making and shipping orders to his St Louis showrooms at 612 Washington Avenue and 613 St Charles Street. By the turn of the century, Jordan had moved his operations to a larger factory

in Furnival Street. He also acted as agent for an early American version of the safety razor, the 'Star', made by Kampfe Bros; and also had cutlery made in Germany.

Unusually for an American, Jordan 'specialised in hand-made goods and would not deal in machine-made articles'. His speciality was kitchen- and butcher-knives, which he described in his catalogues as 'The Best on Earth'. Bernard Levine, an American antique-cutlery dealer and historian, comments:

> Although his was an era of grossly exaggerated advertising claims, this claim, as far as I can tell, was true. All Jordan kitchen and butcher knives have 'seasoned Persian boxwood handles'. This costly wood is a light golden color, takes a high polish and wears almost like iron. Many of his handle and blades shapes are original and distinctive. Jordan kitchen knives are light in weight, and they do not have bolsters. For his blades Jordan used a special formula of double

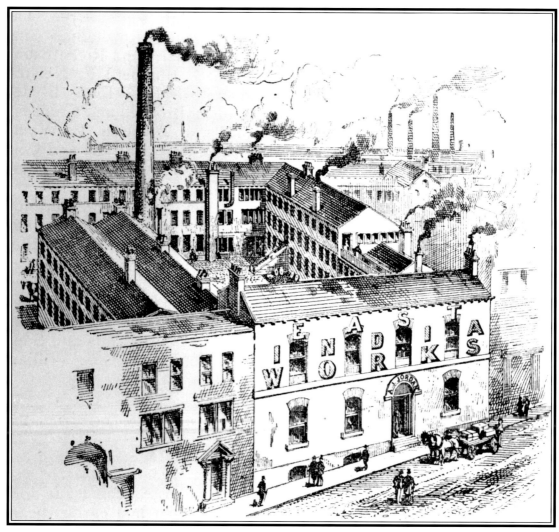

A.J. Jordan's East India Works, Furnival Street.

shear steel. Jordan acknowledged that cast steel was superior to shear steel, but he asserted that his shear steel was better than any other steel, and his knives seem to prove this point.

Jordan's knives were stamped AAA1 out on the blade and were sold in the American West. Another trade mark was 'Old Faithful'. According to one historian, much of the firm's business was done with Indian tribes, mainly the Gros Ventre, Blood, Blackfoot and River Crow Indians.

Jordan, who lived in Sheffield at various times, residing for a period at Clarkson Street, left the city for the last time in 1920. He died in St Louis in 1929, his Sheffield firm still in operation as a maker of razors; but it did not survive his passing.

S. & J. Kitchin

According to J.B. Himsworth, the Kitchin family probably settled in Sheffield from north Nottinghamshire in about 1737. The founder of this firm was probably Samuel Kitchin (sometimes spelled as Kitchen), who was listed in Sheffield directories in the mid-1850s as a cutlery manufacturer of Hollis Croft. Table- and butchers'-knives seem to have been his main output at this time. By 1868, Samuel had been joined by John Kitchin (perhaps his son) at the Soho Works in Summerfield Street. The product-line was soon extended to include, besides table cutlery, most types of Bowie and hunting-knives, matchets, daggers, palette-, shoe-, saladero-knives, and pocket-knives and razors. The company mark was a snake, with the letters XCD.

Little is known about the owners of the company, but in the early twentieth century Thomas Edward Kitchin was the senior partner. He died, aged fifty, in 1917. After the end of the First World War, Kitchin's were amongst a delegation of Sheffield cutlery manufacturers which travelled to Solingen to inspect mass-production techniques there.

By 1939 Kitchin's had moved to a factory in Heeley, at Broadfield and Saxon Road. The company did a large trade in the 1950s in matchets for African tribesmen. By the mid-1960s the firm had abandoned cutlery manufacture (apart from machine-knives) and was making agricultural machine parts in Chesterfield. The Kitchen family sold out in 1987 and in 1995 operate a ground steel stock business in Dronfield. The original Kitchen firm is still in business at Chesterfield.

Lockwood Bros

The exact foundation date of this business is unknown, but it is recorded that in 1767 John Lockwood of Ecclesfield registered his first trade mark and began making files. His son, William, moved to Sheffield in 1798 and occupied premises at 74 Arundel Street. William's four sons: William, John, Joseph and Charles, succeeded him. The manufacture of other tools began and by 1850 Lockwood's had expanded by taking over the marks and business of tool manufacturers John Sorby & Sons, which had been established in 1780 and operated at Spital Hill. By the late nineteenth century, Lockwood Bros began selling cutlery, too. Under George F. Lockwood (1850–1919), who was the son of John Lockwood and a great-grandson of the founder, the firm became a well known tool and cutlery firm. When he became Master Cutler in 1886, aged thirty-six, G.F. Lockwood was one of the youngest holders of the office. By 1893 the firm had moved to the Sorby factory at Spital Hill, overlooking the Wicker and the big steel firms in the Don Valley.

Lockwood's nineteenth-century trade catalogues show, besides a large selection of tools, a wide range of knives. These included all types of pocket-cutlery, with the emphasis on complicated sportman's patterns, and hunting- and skinning-knives. The firm's trade mark included the letters C:X and usually a running ostrich with the words 'Real Knife' and PAMPA on the blade—perhaps an indication that the South American market was once particularly important to Lockwood's. Knives stamped the 'Bushman's Friend' conjure up perhaps an intrepid Australian colonist or explorer heading into the interior. It is not known how many of these knives were actually made by Lockwood's.

In 1919 the firm became part of Sheffield Cutlery Manufacturers Ltd, a grouping of cutlery firms led by Needham, Veall & Tyzack. Lockwood's, which had been losing money for years, did no better allied with firms such as Joseph Elliot. By the early 1930s, after a decade of losses, Lockwood's had moved to Sylvester Street, but by 1933 the name had disappeared from local directories. Its marks were acquired by Elliot.

LOCKWOOD BROTHERS LIMITED, SHEFFIELD.

Made in Oak, Walnut, and Mahogany.
Domed Top, Quadrant Hinges, Patent Mitres,
Celluloid Racks, Flush Brass Handles at ends,
Lined Silk Velvet.

PATENT MITRES.

Patent Brass Mitres are fitted in this Cabinet,
which will stand all Climates.

PATENT RACKS.

Patent Celluloid Racks are fitted in this
Cabinet, or Cloth Racks if preferred.

136.

Contents:

12 Table Knives.
12 Dessert Knives.
12 Table Forks.
12 Dessert Forks.
12 Table Spoons.
12 Dessert Spoons.
12 Tea Spoons.
 6 Egg Spoons.
 4 Salt Spoons.
 2 Mustard Spoons.
 1 pair Sugar Tongs.
 2 Sauce Ladles.
 1 Soup Ladle.
 1 Gravy Spoon.
 4 Knife Rests.
 1 pair Meat Carvers.
 1 pair Game Carvers.
 1 Steel.

110 pieces.

				£	s	d
136A	Contains 074 Celluloid Cutlery, and B quality Medium Size Old English Silver Plated Spoons and Forks		...	£19	3	0
136B	„ 069 „ „ B „ Full „ „ „ „		...	20	6	0
136C	„ 564 Medium Size Ivory Cutlery, and A quality Medium Size Old English Silver Plated Spoons and Forks		...	20	6	0
136D	Contains 564 Full Size Ivory Cutlery, and A quality Full Size Old English Silver Plated Spoons and Forks		...	27	8	0
				28	16	0

If Cloth Lined Cabinet, 24/- less.

Estimates given for the above assortments in any others of our patterns.

The patterns mentioned above will be found on pages 224, 228, 244 to 247.

Long, Hawksley

By the late nineteenth century, this firm was based at the Hallamshire Works in Rockingham Street. One publication, *The Century's Progress* (1893) stated that its history dated back 'upwards of a century'. In the nineteenth century, it came into the possession of Henry Godfrey Long, who was probably the H.G. Long, 'merchant', who is known to have died in 1853. The firm continued under a number of titles. Various partners—such as Wragg, Gregory and Marples—passed through the business. By the early 1870s, the firm was styled Long, Hawksley & Co., and operated as merchants and manufacturers of cutlery and tools. Its knife output included, in the words of the above publication: 'table and dessert knives and carvers, butchers' and cooks' knives, Long's celebrated farriers' knives, pen and pocket knives in great variety, pruning and budding knives'. This was aside from a wide range of razors, plated-goods and edge-tools. The corporate mark, granted in 1833, was a shield enclosing two crossed daggers. In 1911 the firm became a limited company, and was styled H.G. Long & Co. Ltd. By 1913, it had moved from Rockingham Street into the New Hallamshire Works in Boston Street.

By 1924, H.G. Long was listed at Bridge Street, then between 1941 and 1959 at the Ecclesall Works in Rockingham Street. The mark was eventually taken over by Slater.

John McClory & Sons

The foundation date of this business is unknown but *Pawson & Brailsford's Illustrated Guide to Sheffield and Neighbourhood* (1862) has an illustrated advertisement for John McClory, a cutlery and tool merchants in Waingate, Sheffield. By 1884, John McClory & Sons was based in the Eldon Works in Eldon Street, close to Wostenholm's Washington Works. It was listed, like many other firms, as a table- and pocket-cutlery manufacturer and general merchant. What was unusual about McClory's was that it did not aim its goods at the top end of the market. As a reporter in *The Industries of Sheffield: Business Review* (c. 1887) remarked:

> A few years ago, partly owing to the apathy of the older firms, who in a great measure confined themselves to the manufacture of the more expensive classes of cutlery, the enormous trade in cheap and middle-class goods seemed likely to fall into the hands of our German rivals. Messrs McClory & Sons, rightly thinking that if an article as cheap and attractive as the German one, while combining the substantial merit of Sheffield-made goods, could be placed on the market, an enormous trade must result, acted on this idea and turned their attention to the manufacture of low-priced cutlery on a gigantic scale, and while not unmindful of durability and solid utility in all their manufactures, they gave special attention to the sending out of their goods in such a manner, that not only would the attention of such as required a knife be attracted, but even the careless gazer in shop windows would be induced to buy by the attractiveness of the designs and moderation of price. The result of this policy has far exceeded their expectations.

McClory's evidently did not have quite the glorious history before it, that this extract would suggest. By the 1890s, it was operating from the Continental Works in Milton Street, but it certainly did not grow dramatically and for many years before 1914 it disappeared from the Sheffield trades directories. The stainless era after the First World War proved more congenial to the firm and it was one of the first makers of mass-produced stainless knives. Its trade mark was 'Scotia' and a thistle. After the Second World War, the Continental Works was moved to Herries Road. It ceased business in the 1980s.

Maleham & Yeomans

This firm made its appearance in the Sheffield directories in 1876, with its advertisement for its steel, tool and 'Superior Table Cutlery', which it manufactured at the Burgess Works in Burgess Street. By the end of the 1870s, Maleham & Yeomans had moved to Bowdon Street, near to Wostenholm's Washington Works. The product-line of the two companies was very similar: like Wostenholm, Maleham & Yeomans, though it seems to have dabbled in steel merchanting in the 1880s, increasingly concentrated on fine-quality pocket-cutlery

and razors. A salesman's catalogue for Maleham & Yeomans has survived, apparently dating from before the First World War. Smokers'-knives, sport's-knives and the various types of pruning- and pen-knives are featured in its pages. The tangs are stamped with the firm's mark—a Maltese Cross and complicated group of symbols, one of which resembles a V—granted in 1780.

The firm continued to trade from Bowdon Street until about the mid-1960s, when it moved to Pond Hill after a takeover by Rodgers. It was last listed at that address in 1970.

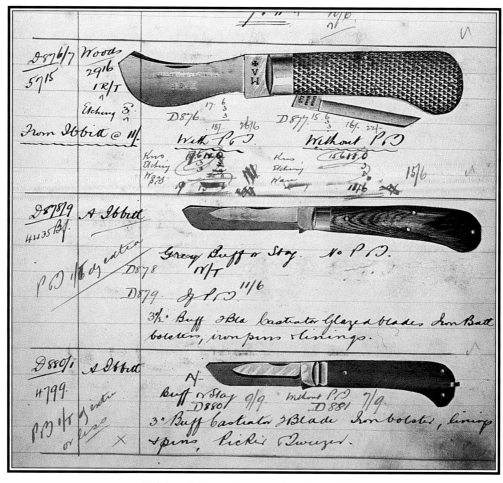

Maleham & Yeoman's pattern book, pre-1914.

Mappin Brothers/Mappin & Webb

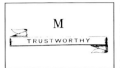

Mappin & Webb is a house-hold name on our high streets as a maker of high-class jewellery and silver-ware. After several changes of ownership, the business is presently owned by the London luxury-goods dealer, Asprey & Co. Few people, however, are aware that its roots lay in Sheffield as a knifemaker.

Mappin is a Sheffield name, dating from at least the end of the sixteenth century. By 1800, one branch of the family had entered the cutlery business and a descendant, Joseph Mappin, had become an engraver and was recorded as working at Fargate in Sheffield. Joseph had two sons: John Newton Mappin and Joseph Mappin. The first made a fortune in the brewing industry and later bequeathed his collection of paintings and the Mappin Art Gallery to the town. The other son started his own business in Norfolk Street and Mulberry Street in 1810, trading with another partner in the 1820s as 'Arundel & Mappin', manufacturers of pen-knives, spring-, sporting- and table-knives and razors. The company's corporate mark was the Sun, granted in 1810.

Joseph Mappin had married Mary, the daughter of Thomas Thorpe, a Bedfordshire land agent and surveyor. On 16th May 1821, their first son, Frederick Thorpe Mappin, was born. After an education at Wright's School in Sheffield, Frederick—like many young apprentices—joined the family firm. He did so at the early age of fourteen, as his father's partner, Arundel, had retired through illness. This early experience was to be vital, for Frederick's father died in 1841, while still in his early 'forties, leaving his son in charge of both the firm and of three younger brothers (Edward, Joseph Charles, and John Newton) who were soon to be introduced to it.

Fortunately, Frederick Mappin proved an immensely able and energetic businessman. Later in life, he would recall the Sheffield of his youth as an 'old-fashioned place, with narrow streets, and

Sir Frederick Mappin (1821–1910).

poor spirit…a little bit of a place, of no consequence, and no trade'. He did much to change that himself, by fully exploiting marketing opportunities both at home and abroad. In 1845 he purchased a London shop to bypass London factors, the success of which led to the acquisition of a London warehouse in 1856, allowing the firm to tap the wealthy metropolitan market. Frederick personally built up the firm's overseas trade by travelling in Europe and America, and agencies were also set up in Canada and Australia.

In 1845, Mappin's absorbed the cutlers William Sampson & Sons and six years later further expansion led to the opening of the Queen's Cutlery Works in the heart of Sheffield's knife-making district. Bounded by Baker's Hill, Flat Street and Little Pond Street, it rubbed shoulders with Rodgers' Norfolk Street Works. (On the site of the old works today stands the Central Post Office.) Mappin's Queen's Works was amongst the largest cutlery establishments in Sheffield, and there are reports of the firm employing about five hundred at this time, which would have placed it not far behind the industry leaders, Rodgers and Wostenholm. Like them, Mappin's Works was more a collection of workshops than a factory. Contemporary maps show that the grandly-titled Queen's Works was a hodge-podge of buildings around a couple of courtyards, where several hundred workmen produced Mappin's famous lines in knives, razors and plated wares. The firm, which was renamed Mappin Brothers in 1851, became particularly well-known for its sportsman's knives.

When the youngest brother, J. Newton Mappin (1835–1913), became a partner, however, disputes arose amongst the family members. (In view of later developments, one wonders whether the arguments were over the future direction of the business, as to whether it should be a knifemaker or a silver- and plated-wares firm.) Frederick left the cutlery firm in 1859 and took his talents elsewhere: he became a senior partner in Thos Turton & Sons, the steelmakers of Sheaf Works fame, and then embarked upon a highly successful career as a Sheffield industrialist and politician. Sir Frederick (he was knighted in 1886) was one of the few Sheffield businessmen to become a Member of Parliament and when he died in 1910 he left nearly £1 million—an unprecedented fortune for a Sheffield manufacturer. Meanwhile, his brother Newton had launched his own electroplating and cutlery business, which by 1868 was known as Mappin & Webb.

Mappin Bros continued to operate under the two remaining brothers, Edward and Joseph Charles. Already, the firm had apparently lost its dynamism, as the trade journal, *The Ironmonger*, highlighted in 1863 that Mappin Bros now only employed about two hundred. Nevertheless, the firm was still producing fine-quality products, especially sport's-knives.

From the 1860s, however, the course seems to have been steadily downhill, due mainly to poor management. By the end of the 1880s, the Mappins had either died or retired from the business and it was taken over by a Belfast jeweller. In 1899 Mappin Bros was bought by the London firm, Goldsmiths & Silversmiths Co.

Ironically, Newton Mappin's business was thriving. If he had left Mappin Bros to prove a point, then by the turn of the century he had certainly succeeded. Mappin & Webb occupied a large building within walking distance of Mappin Bros further along Norfolk Street and directly opposite St Paul's Churchyard. The main entrance, supported by granite columns, was flanked on either side by showroom windows stuffed with the firm's productions. The vestibule was laid with mosaics of black and white marble, and mural decorations and furnishings of American walnut embellished the wide staircase that led up to the main offices. Inside the factory, silversmiths and platers laboured over the firm's main lines: up-market silverware and electroplate salvers, dish covers, entrée dishes, carvers, dinner- and dessert-knives, even some pocket-cutlery. These products, stamped with the corporate mark—M and TRUSTWORTHY—demonstrated that typically Mappin concern for the artistic and tasteful in cutlery design ('tasteful', that is, according to their Victorian standards). A limited liability company, with Royal Warrants and agencies around the world, the 'Royal Cutlery and Plate Works' of Mappin & Webb made the Queen's Works seem very much the poor relation.

In 1903, Newton Mappin had the satisfaction of buying Mappin Bros from the Goldsmiths & Silversmiths Co. The Baker's Hill factory was vacated and soon demolished and the workforce of the two concerns was combined (it had reached six hundred by 1909). Mappin & Webb's speciality had always been plated ware, and after the First World War the manufacture of knives as a main line was slowly discontinued. This decision secured the firm's long-term future and explains why it is still one of the few Sheffield 'names' still with us at the end of the twentieth century, but it was at the cost of the product that had launched the business—the knife.

Mappin & Webb's Royal Cutlery & Silver Plate Works, c. 1914.

Marsh Bros

Even in Sheffield, where ancient names and marks were so common that they were almost taken for granted, not many firms could trace their history back to the seventeenth century. Marsh Bros could. It was founded in 1631 by an old line of Sheffield cutlers.

Between 1780 and 1815 the firm traded at Park Hill, with a James Marsh building up the business. It was known as James Marsh & Co., or Marsh & Shepherd and specialised in making knives from bars of Sheffield steel. Pen- and pocket-knives, pruning-knives and table-knives were amongst the earliest specialities. The company had several marks: its stamped cutlery and tools with a mark granted in 1716 featuring a Maltese Cross and the letter 'y'.

By 1819 the firm was prospering, capital was £10,000, and it was well-positioned to benefit from the upswing in trade caused by the burgeoning American demand. It now operated at Castle Hill, but as trade grew in 1822 it moved to Porter Street, and then in 1828 to the Ponds Works. This was an area close to Baker's Hill, notable for its streams, millponds, dams and goits (which now provides the site for the modern Ponds Forge sports centre). When Marsh & Shepherd arrived they found a typical courtyard-style factory, with house and garden, warehouse, counting-house, forge, old water-wheels, crucible steel furnace, rolling-mill, grindstones and engine-house. All that was lacking to launch a self-contained business was a set of converting furnaces for blister steel. In the 1830s the firm erected those, too, at nearby Navigation Works.

Capital rose from £28,000 in 1828 to £58,000 in 1837, as the firm began to market a wide range of products—steel, saws, files, and many different types of edge-tools. As the firm's historian, Sidney Pollard, writes: 'To maintain the high quality of these varied goods must, by itself, be ranked as a major achievement of the partners, who had made their way up in the world from small masters of spring-knife cutlery in one generation'. The firm appears to have made (or commissioned from outworkers) almost every type of knife. Pocket-knives and razors were still important lines for the firm, especially for the American market which dominated the business in the 1840s and 1850s. The firm (which became Marsh Bros in the late 1840s) had permanent representatives in Philadelphia and New York, and these were often Marsh family members. In the heyday of the American trade, Marsh Bros also had connections in New Orleans and Boston. Despite problems with financial fluctuations and unpaid bills, the American trade was a major factor in the firm's expansion. By 1862 it employed about 250.

However, the decline in the cutlery business after the 1880s (caused partly by high American tariffs on Sheffield goods) caused Marsh Bros to ponder the future direction of its business. In the 1890s, knife production (apart from razors) was abandoned and Marsh Bros decided to concentrate its energies on making special tool steels, combining this with the making of tools for the engineering trades. It survived as an independent and successful steel and toolmaker until the 1960s, but its illustrious career as a knifemaker was over.

Theophilus Marsh (1826–1881),
who handled the firm's business in America.

Martin, Hall & Co.

This business, which was one of the largest of the city's silver- and electroplate firms by the 1890s, developed from the firm of Henry Wilkinson of Low Street. The business was built up by John Roberts (b. 1798), a silversmith and plater, who was Wilkinson's son-in-law. Roberts' marriage did not produce a son: instead, he virtually adopted Ebenezer Hall (1820–1911), who was the son of a lead miner in the village of Middleton-by-Wirksworth, near Matlock and Cromford. Hall became an apprentice in 1836 and later joined Roberts in partnership in 1847. The business became Roberts & Hall, with John Roberts contributing £2,750 capital and Hall £100. The firm then appears to have moved into premises which Henry Wilkinson had occupied—Shrewsbury Works, 53 Broad Street. In 1852 Roberts & Hall merged with Martin & Naylor (the successors to Hatfield & Sons), and Richard Martin of the latter firm joined them in partnership. The firm was now known as Martin, Hall & Co.

Roberts retired in the mid-1850s. In 1866 the firm became a limited liability company, with an authorised capital of £150,000, of which £100,000 was called up in five years. Richard Martin and Ebenezer Hall were joint-managing directors, with Bernard Wake as chairman. (Wake, it might be noted, was also chairman of Wostenholm's in 1875.) Martin seems to have controlled the London business of the firm; Hall the Sheffield operations. The firm prospered in the first eleven years after its incorporation as a limited company, paying dividends which averaged 15 percent a year—though at the end of the 1870s, a difficult period seems to have followed, which spurred Hall to seek new markets in Australia in 1879.

When Wake died in 1891, Hall took over. Generally, the firm seems to have expanded steadily under his chairmanship: the workforce was approaching 400–500 by the turn of the century, and before 1914 it may have reached 750. The main site was the Shrewsbury Works in Broad Street, and by 1905 the company also had a plant in Ludgate Hill, Birmingham, for light silver goods and ornamental products. A London showroom at Holborn Circus, a warehouse in Glasgow, and an agent in Sydney, Australia, distributed the firm's products. Knives were not the firm's staple line: nevertheless, it made silver-plated knives of every description for table and household use. The company had a number of marks, including MARTINOID, MARTINIUM and MARTIN (the latter below the picture of a bird).

Hall eventually retired in about 1904, after sixty-four years in the business, and the firm was then run by a board of directors. Hall left £194,632 gross.

Martin, Hall was hit by the decline of the silver- and plated-goods market in the First World War and it never recovered its position in the 1920s. It went into liquidation in 1933 and the Shrewsbury Works was then occupied by Frank Cobb.

David Mellor

David Mellor was born in Sheffield in 1930. He studied silversmithing at Sheffield College of Art, the Royal College of Art and the British School at Rome, before returning to Sheffield in 1954 to set up his own workshop and design office. He developed a considerable reputation for his silversmithing, producing custom-made commission pieces for various organisations and private clients. One of the most spectacular pieces was the large bowl commissioned by the Cutlers' Company to commemorate the 200th Anniversary of the Sheffield Assay Office.

As a designer, however, Mellor's primary interest has been in cutlery (particularly flatware). His first appointment as a design consultant was with Walker & Hall, for whom he developed the 'Pride' silverplate design with white xylonite handles (Mellor had originally conceived this while still a student at the Royal College of Art). A string of popular designs followed: 'Campden', one the first modern stainless designs; 'Symbol', an attempt to mass produce high-quality cutlery by precision engineering; 'Embassy', commissioned by the government for use in British embassies; and 'Thrift', designed for the opposite end of the spectrum—government canteens.

In 1969 David Mellor opened his own London shop, and then in 1973 he set up his own cutlery manufacturing organisation at Broom Hall, a renovated historic building in Sheffield (now Grade II* listed). Mellor wanted an organisation that was relatively small scale—somewhere between a small factory and a large workshop—which would allow artistic freedom for the designer, yet achieve a high standard of production. By the 1990s, a new factory and shop, the Round Building, had been opened at Hathersage in Derbyshire.

Mellor's reputation is now international. He has regularly won Design Centre Awards and examples of his work can be seen at the Victoria and Albert Museum and the Museum of Modern Art in New York.

Ernest Mills

As the Sheffield cutlery industry contracted in the 1960s and 1970s, the remaining pocket-knife cutlers—Stan Shaw, Eric Wragg and Graham Clayton—were left to eke out a living in obscure workshops around the city. In the early 1980s, the oldest working cutler in the city, Ernest Mills, could be found in a basement workshop at Gillott's pearl-cutting factory in Union Lane, still making pocket-knives by the traditional methods his father had taught him.

He was born in Sheffield in 1900 and his cutlery lineage was impeccable: his father, Willis Mills, was a spring-knife cutler at Thos Turner's; his grandfather had made knives at Brookes & Crookes. Ernest joined his father as an apprentice in 1914. In 1921, a matter of months before the end of his seven-year apprenticeship, father and son lost their jobs during a slack period of trade and decided to go-it-alone at a small workshop in Napier Street (later they moved to Egerton Street). Ernest recalled that his 'first wage was five shillings a week—and they were long weeks: nine hours on Mondays; eleven hours on Tuesdays, Wednesdays and Thursdays; twelve hours on Fridays; and seven hours on pay-day, Saturdays; and sometimes we had to put in overtime if we were behind with a job'.

The Second World War broke up the partnership and after his father died in 1947, Ernest worked on his own. From about 1950 his base was his rented workshop at Gillott's. From there he made knives that went around the world, though few were marked with his name. Instead, they carried the marks of the cutlery merchants and firms with whom he dealt: Mappin & Webb (London), Landells (Glasgow), Clement (London) and Dunhill (London). These firms demanded top quality multi-blade knives, such as smokers'-knives and champagne-knives, made in silver and ivory. Mills once said: 'I particularly liked making complicated knives—champagne and lobsters and anything like that…They were mostly made for the upper end, these country houses, Chatsworth House, those sorts of people. The customers we had were very good'.

As the number of little mesters dwindled in the 1970s, Ernest Mills became a minor celebrity and he was often interviewed about his working life. Like many cutlers, however, a lifetime in the trade had embittered him and not all his recollections were fond ones. His 'story' was one of low wages, undercutting and increasingly shoddy goods. When interviewed by Clare Jenkins and Steve McClarence for their book, *On the Knife Edge*, Mills recalled:

Undercutting went on all the time. Unless you were in a reasonable firm that kept the wages at a reasonable level, no matter where you went there was always somebody ready to undercut you by a penny or tuppence a dozen. And if you wanted an increase, there was a row. They'd perhaps pay you for the first couple of weeks, then all of a sudden that knife would go off you and to someone who could make it cheaper. So we were competing against each other...It made us very bitter. Oh, yes. We hated one another like poison.

On a happier note, Ernest Mills always said he liked making knives, especially the finer qualities worked in silver and gold. The job must have had some attraction for him since he carried on working at Gillott's until his retirement in 1985. He had made knives for about seventy years. Ernest Mills died in 1992.

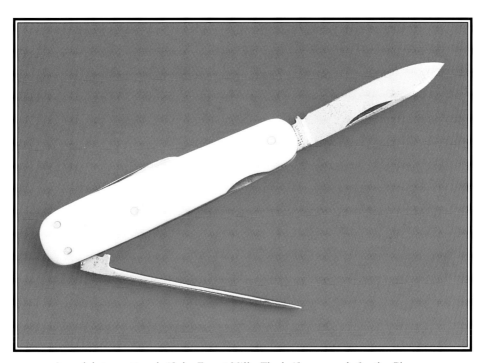

Ivory lobster-pattern knife by Ernest Mills. The knife was made for the Glasgow retailer Landell's and is so marked.

John Milner

Established in 1848, the history of this firm is obscure. John Milner Snr, the 'much respected' seventy-four year-old cutlery manufacturer, who died in Sheffield in 1863, was probably the first proprietor. His son, probably also named John, seems to have taken over. The concern was based at the Trafalgar Works in Trafalgar Street and its trade, according to one report, consisted of 'exclusively the best pen- and pocket-knives, and surgical and anatomical instruments of every description'. The corporate mark INTRINSIC was granted in 1848. In about 1890, Walter Asquith—who had been a partner in the business for about twelve years and associated with it for over twenty—became the sole owner. By 1905 he had moved the firm to the Orient Works in Matilda Street.

J. Milner & Co. was still manufacturing cutlery in the inter-war period and by 1940 was located in Arundel Street: it seems to have ceased trading at the end of the 1960s.

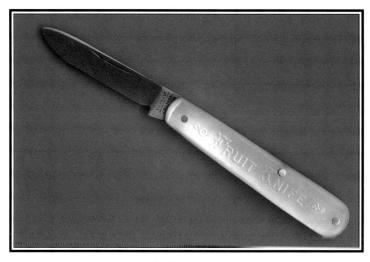

J. Milner fruit-knife, with a stainless blade.

William Morton & Sons

This firm was first listed in directories in 1876 at the Old Rockingham Works, 175 Rockingham Street, as a maker of table-, pen-, pocket-, and sport's-knives, and razors and scissors. The founder of the business, William Morton, was the youngest son of George Morton, of Cheapside, London. The date he launched the business is unknown, though a William Morton was listed as a spring-knife maker at Darnall in 1868 and trade advertisements state that the Morton's Old Rockingham Works was 'the successor to Anthony Rotherham'.

William Morton, who lived at Grenoside, died on 31st May 1889, aged fifty-six, and was buried at Ecclesall churchyard. He had at least two sons, who took over the Rockingham Street business. One of them, also named William, died in 1932. The other brother, George, then took over and, like many cutlery managers, did all the travelling, whilst his manager, named Gibbins, looked after the factory. George Morton, who was also a partner in Ragg's (the razor firm) died during the Second World War and his widow ran the business for a time. The firm closed in about 1971.

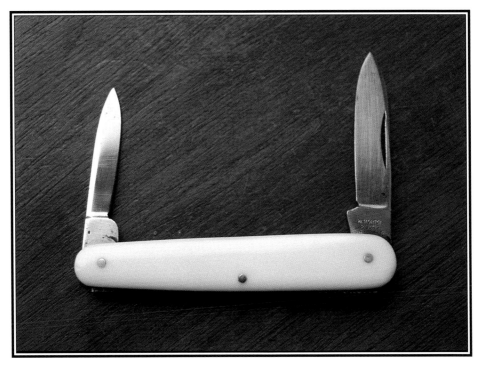

Ivory Morton pocket-knife, made in a sleeveboard pattern.

R.F. Mosley & Co.

Robert Fead Mosley was born in Hatton Garden, London, in 1841, the eldest son of Cornelius Mosley, a wholesale stationer and pen manufacturer. A Mosley of Hatton Garden (probably Cornelius) exhibited cutlery at the London Exhibition of 1862 and probably many of these items were made in Sheffield. Perhaps this led to his son's links with the town, as Robert Mosely arrived in Sheffield in 1856. He was apprenticed to the scissor manufacturer, George Oates. After the latter's death, Mosley began his own cutlery business in Brookhill. In 1878 he occupied the Portland Works in Randall Street and remained chairman until his death in 1921.

The Portland Works covered about three-quarters of an acre on the usual Sheffield plan: two- and three-stories of offices and workshops around a central courtyard. The firm was described in the trade press as 'General Cutlery Manufacturers'. According to one report: 'A valuable feature of their business, and one which has been made a speciality by them, is the manufacture of case goods on an exceedingly artistic and extensive scale. These cases are fitted up with satin and velvet linings, etc., for the reception of cutlery of the best and highly finished kinds, also for silver dessert and table spoons, forks, fish knives, etc., mounted in pearl, ivory, silver, metal, and other choice mountings'.

R.F. Mosley and his company have a special place in knife history, because it was to this firm that Harry Brearley turned in the summer of 1914, when he wished to make a trial with his new rustless steel. The manager of Mosley's, Ernest Stuart, helped Brearley forge a dozen or so knife blades from the new material—a milestone in cutlery history. Consequently, Mosley's were the first firm to predict a future for stainless steel and the first to order supplies of the revolutionary alloy. They marked their knives 'Rustnorstain', the only mark the firm appear to have used.

Mosley occupied the Portland Works until 1968.

Needham Bros

Needham was a common name in the Sheffield cutlery trades in the nineteenth century. This firm was founded in 1851 by Joseph Needham, a cutler who was Sheffield born and bred, and who was listed in directories in the following year as a spring-knife maker at Garden Street. He commenced business with his brother Edwin, who died in 1854. By 1856, Joseph's enterprise, now known as Needham Bros, was based in the Hanover Works in Milton Street. By the early 1860s, William Needham had joined Joseph in the business. (Interestingly, a directory published in 1862, shows another Needham Bros operated briefly at the Cavendish Works. It was owned by William, Henry and Charles Needham.)

By 1868, Needham Bros was based at the Commercial Works in Baker's Hill and manufactured pen-, pocket- and sport's-knives. The firm's knives, which were stamped with the trade mark "REPEAT", were made to a high standard and are consequently highly-rated by collectors. The firm's sport's-knives were imported into the USA in the late nineteenth century through the New York agency of Wiebusch.

In 1897 Needham Bros became a limited company, with Joseph Needham at its head. Besides running his own factory, Joseph was chairman of the Old Albion Brewery Co. and a director of a number of other concerns, such as the Atlas Rolling Co. It was said that he was 'singularly gentle in disposition, generous and kindly disposed [and] was incapable of making an enemy'. He died in 1898, aged sixty-eight.

Needham Bros continued in business, but little is known of the men who operated it: however, E.G. Needham, the forty-two year-old son of Francis Needham, was chairman when he died on 14th December 1916. The business had moved to Matilda Street in about 1903. It remained there until Needham Bros went out of business after the Second World War. Its "REPEAT" mark was later acquired by Slater.

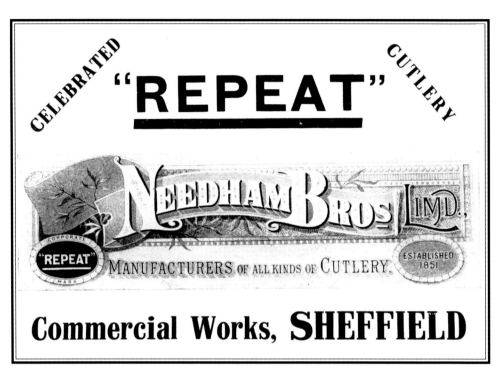

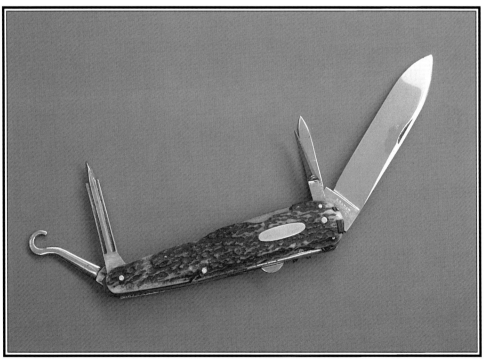

Fine late 19th-century sport's-knife by Needham Bros. Hafted in genuine stag,
it has a locking master blade.

Needham, Veall & Tyzack

This business is said to have begun in about 1820 when John Taylor opened a small workshop in St Philip's Road. He was granted the striking 'Eye Witness' corporate mark in 1838. (The inspiration for the choice of 'Eye Witness' is believed to be a Shakespearean line in *King Henry IV*: 'no eye hath seen better'.) Taylor specialised in pen-, pocket- and sport's-knives.

Also located in St Philip's Road was a cutler and shopkeeper, Thomas Brown Needham, who by 1856 had taken over Taylor's business. Needham manufactured knives at the Exchange Works in Headford Street during the 1860s, but by 1876 he had joined forces with James Veall (d. 1906) at a factory in Milton Street. Veall was a Sheffielder, who had been apprenticed to H.G. Long & Co. Another new partner, Walter Tyzack (1857–1925), who was a descendant of the scythemaking Tyzacks of Abbeydale fame, joined the business in 1879 and henceforth it was styled, Needham, Veall & Tyzack.

Together these men began to expand the business. The firm's growth seems to have been particularly marked in the 1890s, when the business was reorganised. In 1897 Needham, Veall & Tyzack became a limited liability company, with a capital of £60,000, and with Walter Tyzack, James Veall and William C. Veall (d. 1941) as directors. Another director of the firm, Edwin Needham, was a cutlery manufacturer and merchant, living in Birmingham. At about the same time, the company purchased Nixon & Winterbottom, and formed it into another limited company capitalised at £20,000. Needham, Veall & Tyzack's purchase of this firm, one of the pioneers of machine-produced cutlery in Sheffield, would have been a logical step for the company if it wished to mass produce cutlery. We know that the first chairman of the firm, Walter Tyzack, was particularly sensitive to the threat of German competition and was committed to following their example in mechanising many of the cutlery processes.

A detailed description of the manufacturing processes and products at the firm's Eye Witness Works in Milton Street can be found in a Victorian tour of the town, entitled *Sheffield and Rotherham (Illustrated), Up-to-Date* (1897). It stated that:

> The leading features of Messrs Needham, Veall & Tyzack's manufactures in these departments are pen and pocket knives in an infinite variety of useful and elegant shapes, table knives, butchers' knives, carvers, scissors, pruning shears, and razors of the finest make in hollow and plain ground, for which latter goods in particular their reputation is speedily becoming world-wide. Some idea of the range of patterns kept in these various goods may be derived from the fact that in pen and pocket knives alone the firm possess over two thousand separate designs, most of which are made in four or five separate coverings.

In 1902 the firm also bought the cutlery business of Joseph Haywood & Co., based at the Glamorgan Works in Pond Street. This was acquired for the sake of the factory site, since Haywood's trade marks and goodwill were immediately sold to Thos Turner. By 1911 the operations of Nixon & Winterbottom had been moved to the Glamorgan Works (where it joined another firm purchased at about this time—Michael Hunter & Co.).

Needham, Veall & Tyzack also expanded into the market for plated-goods. It introduced the manufacture of spoons and forks, fish-eating knives, plated desserts, fish-carvers and tea- and coffee-services. The Nimrod Works in Eldon Street (formerly owned by Bartram, the powder flask maker) was occupied to deal with these products. Showrooms were also opened to demonstrate Needham, Veall & Tyzack's tastefulness in these matters, and 'well got-up' catalogues were issued to customers. But 'Eye Witness' knives remained the firm's best known line and both hand-forged and machine-made knives were produced.

According to an obituary of James Veall, the company employed about thirty or so workers in the 1870s, a number which had reached nearly a

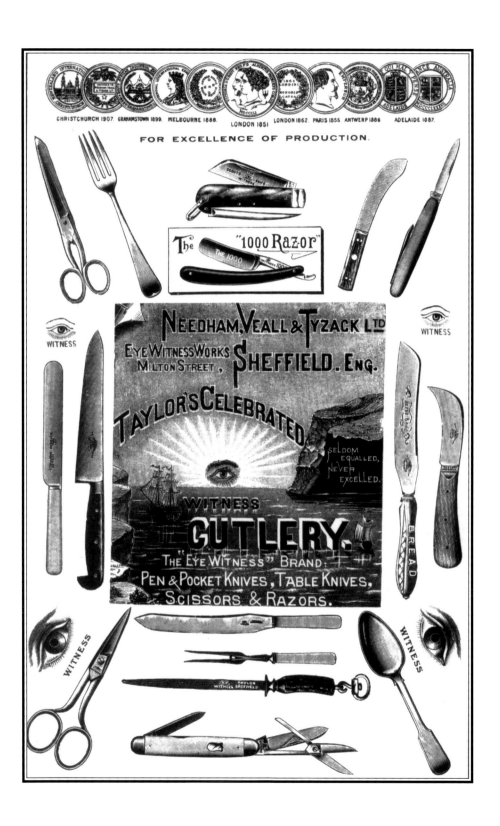

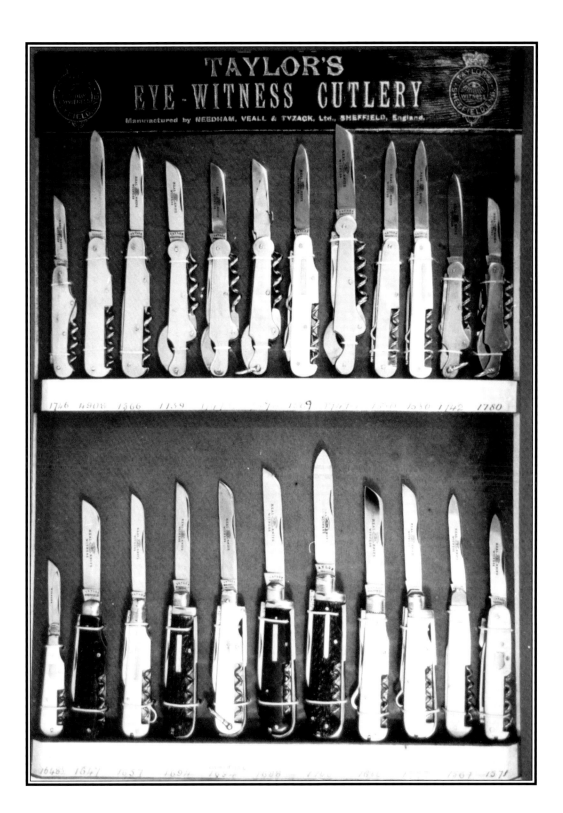

thousand by 1906. However, if this figure was accurate (and it seems rather high), this was undoubtedly a peak and the number of workers at the firm may have fallen to less than half that total by the end of the First World War. After 1918, Needham, Veall & Tyzack suffered the fate of many other Sheffield makers: they were hit by the fall in the demand for high-quality pocket-knives and razors. This factor (alongside bad management) crippled Needham, Veall & Tyzack's attempt after 1919 to merge several firms—including Joseph Elliot, Lockwood Bros, Nixon & Winterbottom, Southern & Richardson, and Thos Turner—into a larger whole. In the aftermath, Needham, Veall & Tyzack took over Southern & Richardson.

Nevertheless, the company did survive and after the Second World War it began to take over other Sheffield marks. It acquired Saynor, Cooke & Ridal in 1948; and also 'Wheat Sheaf' (Wheatley) and XL ALL (Parkin & Marshall). In 1965 the firm was styled as Taylor's Eye Witness. Ten years later, it was absorbed by Harrison Fisher & Co.

Taylor's Eye Witness Works in Milton Street, occupied in the 1990s by Harrison Fisher.

Francis Newton & Sons

Francis Newton was born in about 1776, the son of a well-known grocer. He launched his cutlery business in 1838, manufacturing (or selling) table cutlery, pen- and pocket-knives, sportsman's knives, razors and various tools, such as saws and files. He also advertised blister, shear and cast steel, though the firm may not have manufactured these products at its factory—the Portobello Works, in the street of the same name. According to R.E. Leader, in his history of the Sheffield Banking Co. (of which Newton was a director), Francis Newton, who was Master Cutler in 1844, was 'a gentleman of sedate mien who, from the style of dress he affected, might well have been thought to be a clergyman, rather than a cutlery manufacturer and merchant'. Elsewhere, Leader describes Newton's 'tenacious cleaving to a tail coat with velvet collar...[with] a neckcloth, adorned with a pin whose design was an eagle's claw clasping a large emerald'. Besides the Portobello Works, Newton also operated the Roscoe Wheel in the Rivelin Valley. He lived in a house called Broombank, at the corner of Clarkehouse Lane and Park Lane. He died on 21st July 1864, aged sixty-eight, when the business passed to his sons (the firm's name being amended accordingly).

In 1884 the Newtons took over the steel, tool and cutlery business of Joseph & Robert Dodge Ltd at the Continental Works in Bridge Street. This acquisition was then moved to their premises at the Portobello Works. A trade review in 1897 stated:

> The front portion of the building is occupied as general and private offices, stock warehouses, and packing and despatch departments; in the rear of which are the works, comprising ranges of premises of varying height appropriated to the various industrial branches. These include grinding shops, smiths' forges, with a full equipment of machinery and appliances for forwarding the work of production on the most efficient labour-saving methods. Motive force is supplied by steam power, and about four hundred hands are employed in the various departments.

The firm's products were impressed with the corporate marks, PREMIER, the figure of a swan with the word 'Try', and 'Juste Judicato' (the latter having been J. & R. Dodge's mark). Newton's sold to the home market and on the Continent, particularly to Dutch and German customers.

The firm proved a survivor and it was still listed in directories at the end of the 1980s.

Francis Newton (c. 1796–1864).

John Newton & Co.

Established in 1861, this firm was the successor to Arthur Lee & Son and was based in Arundel Lane. The name of this company's works—Manhattan—suggests an involvement with the American trade and this is borne out by other evidence. The firm was a merchant and manufacturer of table- and pocket-cutlery, Bowie knives and razors. These were sold in America through the New York cutlery-importing business of H. Boker (a house founded by German immigrants). Meanwhile, Newton's in Sheffield imported certain American goods, such as R. Heinisch's American shears, scissors and trimmers. About fifty workers were based at Newton's in the 1880s. The works had moved to Lambert Street by 1900. Newton's trademark was a distinctive picture of a frog and the words 'Manhattan Cutlery Co., Sheffield'.

After 1926 the firm was no longer listed.

Nixon & Winterbottom

Joseph Nixon and Jabez Winterbottom founded this firm in 1864 as a spring-knife maker, based in Pinstone Street. By 1876 they had moved into the Pyramid Works in Broomhall Street and had extended its product-range. Nixon & Winterbottom manufactured special articles—table cutlery, Bowie-knives, spear- and camp-knives—for the South American and other foreign markets. In the late nineteenth century, table-knives seem to have been the company's main line. Nixon & Winterbottom had been one of the first firms to introduce machinery for the mass-production of such cutlery. The firm's advertisements in Sheffield directories in the 1870s announced cutlery made by 'patent machinery' on the 'interchangeable' system. This was no doubt an attempt to emulate the Americans, one of whom had this to say (in the *Sheffield Independent*, 13th October 1873) after a visit to the Pyramid Works:

Visiting the works of Nixon and Winterbottom, we found only Mr Nixon, a man whose enterprise would do credit to New England. He assured us that machinery might be used to advantage in Sheffield with English mechanics. In their manufactory they employ cutting presses, gang drills, shapers for knife handles, etc. In fact, they seem to be awake to the importance of mechanical improvements, and believe that they manufacture as good cutlery as those using only hand-power.

In about 1897, Needham, Veall & Tyzack bought the firm and around the turn of the century moved Nixon & Winterbottom's operations to the Glamorgan Works of Joseph Haywood (which Needham, Veall & Tyzack had also bought). The latter continued to use the Nixon & Winterbottom name and its mark—NW and a picture of pyramids.

P 475   P 476   P 225   P 240   P 238   P 241

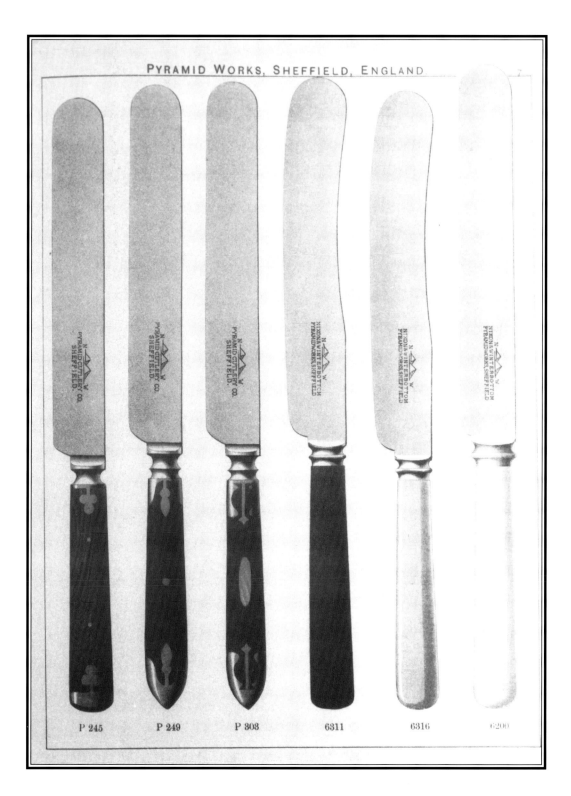

P 245   P 249   P 303   6311   6316   6200

John Nowill & Sons

Nowill's was a quintessential Sheffield knifemaker. The family who operated it were ancient, prolific, often long-lived, and successful—though in a typically unostentatious way.

The earliest record of this business is in the books of the Cutlers' Company on 27th April 1700, when a corporate mark, the letter 'D' and a star, was granted to Thomas Nowill, 'Maker of Knives'. Thomas Nowill's great-grandson, Thomas II, who became Master Cutler in 1788, founded the business of Nowill & Kippax at 37 High Street. Later, another Thomas, cousin of Thomas II, founded Hague & Nowill at 7 Meadow Street. The partnership lasted from 1786 to 1797, when Thomas took over the business.

Thomas Nowill & Co. combined cutlery manufacture with victualling—not an unusual combination in the early days of the industry, when firms often had their own retail grocery and liquor stores. The historian Peter Garlick has described the cutlery side of the business in detail. The range of Nowill's products, according to Garlick, was 'wide but unexceptional', chiefly comprising all types of pen- and pocket-knives, with all manner of hafting materials—ebony, pearl, buffalo and other horn—pike-knives, knives containing tweezers and corkscrews, sportsman's- and lobster-knives, forks, nail-files, toothpicks, fruit-knives, and plated cutlery. But silver blades are recorded from the earliest days and it is interesting to note that Joseph Hunter's *Hallamshire* (1875) refers to a knife made by Nowill & Co. having 'a reputation within the living memory of cutlers which has not been surpassed'. These products were usually sold to the firm's major customers—merchants in Sheffield, Birmingham and London. The firm's workforce varied between about ten and thirty before 1815.

In 1825 Thomas Nowill retired and left the business to his sons, William and John. An 1828 *Directory* has 'William and John Nowill, manufacturers of silver fruit and dessert knives, fancy, pen and pocket and desk knives, also nails, files, button hooks, stilletoes, etc, 7 Meadow Street'. In 1836 Thomas Nowill died aged seventy-eight, and soon afterwards the two brothers went their separate ways: William set up in Rockingham Street; John in Scotland Street. It was the latter

Nowill trade mark on semi-finished blade.

who lived on in the firm's name. Nowill's reputation was maintained: it acquired a further trade mark in 1842—crossed keys—and won a prize medal at the Great Exhibition of 1851.

In the late nineteenth century, the business was operated by a family team consisting of John's four sons: John, Henry, Arthur and Thomas. When the latter died in 1892, Arthur was aged sixty-nine, Henry, seventy-three and John, seventy-four. The team retired in 1893 and another generation took over. The senior partner was John's son, Charles Richard Nowill (1850–1910). Educated at Milk Street and Boulogne-sur-Mer, he joined the Works and became a partner in 1878. Frank Nowill, Ernest Nowill (d. 1926) and Bradley Nowill were also active in the business before the First World War. Nowill's had a London office; and its overseas business included countries in the Near East and it had agents in Constantinople, Athens and Egypt.

John Nowill & Sons remained in Scotland Street until 1949, when, after being bought by F.E. & J.R. Hopkinson Ltd, it was relocated to 87 London Road. At that date, Esmond Nowill, a descendant of the founder, still retained an interest in the business as a manager. Trade-knives and Bowies continued to be made at Nowill's into the 1960s, but slowly the firm wound down. Nowill's is still listed in Sheffield in 1995, but it is some time since it made knives.

Louis Osbaldiston & Co.

This firm first appears in Sheffield directories in 1865, when it was listed as a merchant and manu-facturer of saws, files, edge-tools, machine-knives, loom and legging springs, and busks. The address was Glasgow Place, 1 Porter Street, Moor Head. By 1876 the business had moved to Eldon Street; and then sometime in the early 1880s it relocated to Arundel Street, when it was also advertising cutlery. Pen- and pocket-knives and table-knives were some of the items Osbaldiston sold, though whether these were actually made at its premises—the Challenge Works (a building which still stands)—is unknown.

The trade mark was HYDRA. The owner of the firm was Lewis Henry Osbaldiston, who always did his own travelling. He died, aged sixty-five, on a train to London on 11th November 1901. The business continued to operate, but in 1910 it moved to the Bath Works in Bath Street. It was listed there in directories until 1940.

Osbaldiston's Challenge Works in Arundel Street.

Edward Osborne

One of the tragedies of the Sheffield knife industry was that it was peopled by so many skilled and dedicated cutlers, whose names are now completely effaced—each one a 'mute inglorious Milton'. Occasionally, however, we are allowed a glimpse of the lives of the knifemakers who made it all possible.

Let us briefly look at Edward Osborne. In some ways he was an unremarkable man, yet he was an exemplar of the craftsman on whom the reputation of the Sheffield cutlery bosses depended. He was born in Sheffield on 25th April 1893, the son of a cutler, whose family had long been involved with the cutlery trades. He left school at the age of twelve and, with a break in his career for Army service in the First World War, he was to make knives for some fifty-four years.

He was at the skilled end of the cutlery trade—making the finest qualities of pocket-knives, for firms such as Wostenholm. Later in his career he worked for many years for George Ibberson's, becoming their top-man between the wars and into the 1950s.

It was Ted Osborne who designed many of the Ibberson patterns, building on the experience of past cutlers, but supplying his own original ideas to create something new. The forerunner of Ibberson's 'Prince George' knives was made by Ted as a 'special' in the 1930s for presentation to the Duke of Kent (George, the son of King George V). He also made an Ibberson fisherman's-knife in response to a challenge from a foreign customer. Even for a man as skilled as Ted it took hours of work on the prototype, which is not surprising when one considers that it is an 8-piece knife with two blades, disgorger, scissors, spike, corkscrew, can-opener and a strange-looking pair of tweezers that are used for fly-dressing.

An example of Ted's expertise and the character of Ibberson's forgers and grinders occurred when French cutlers made an exhibition-knife, which fitted inside a plum stone. Sheffield's honour was felt to be at stake and Ted and his fellow-workers made a fully-working folding knife which fitted inside a cherry stone!

His son, Harold, recalls Ted Osborne's working habits and his skills:

There was in the back room a kitchen range and one of my earliest memories is of my mother collecting empty Rowntree's 'Elect' cocoa tins and Coleman's mustard tins (the oblong sort). Every night Dad would put blades and springs he had brought home into these tins and then put them under the back boiler in the kitchen fire. At bedtime all the embers would be piled round them, the damper drawn fully out so that the fire glowed a cherry red. In the morning one of my jobs was to recover these tins for Dad, who would empty them and look at the contents and like as not say 'Aye them's champion' and take them off to work, or if he was not satisfied, they would get another dose of the fire the next night.

Dad's knowledge of steel was a source of wonder to me. He could pick up a blade, a spring, a scale or any other part of a pocket-knife, run

Ted Osborne (1893–1975) using his parser at Ibberson's. His apprentice Stan Shaw is in the background.

his finger over it then touch it against a grinding wheel running at full pelt and from the colour of the sparks and the way those sparks wrapped themselves round the wheel he could tell 'that'll be all reight', or 'thar'll never do owt wi' that'.

Yet these skills barely earned a living for Ted Osborne in the days of piece rates and low wages. 'Heaven above knows how my parents managed to feed and clothe my sister and myself', recalls Ted's son. On occasion, even buying winter clothes was beyond the pocket of a cutler working nearly 50 hours a week.

Nor did the prodigious skills of the cutler command other less tangible compensations, such as respect for their craftsmanship or any social status. On the day Ted Osborne retired—his elbow joint worn out from the constant filing of knives, and his thumb like leather from a lifetime of touching blades to test their sharpness—the boss called him into the office and presented him with a bottle of whisky (not the most appropriate gift for a Methodist!). The company then forgot about him; and, needless to say, there was no company pension. Little wonder that Ted Osborne was adamant that no one in his family was to follow him into the trade.

In the opening page of a scrapbook he started in his happy retirement (he died on 3rd January 1975), Ted Osborne wrote: 'in my younger days the wages were poor. Men took a great interest in their work and some very fine workmen emerged of which I hope, after looking through this book, I think without boasting I may be one of them'. Indeed, he was. Not only are his Ibberson knives still in use (some lucky owners will find that they are stamped inside the liner 'EO' and sometimes dated), but his skills and patterns were transferred, at no little personal cost to himself, to Stan Shaw—the success of whom would have surely pleased him.

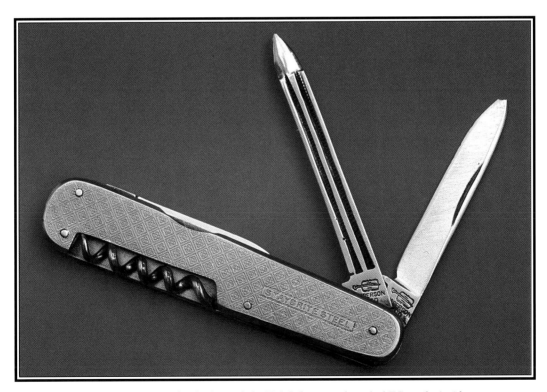

Stainless Ibberson pocket-knife, made by Ted Osborne and marked EO on the inside.

James Oxley

 This firm began knife manufacture in the early 1820s. In 1825, a John Oxley is listed in a directory as a maker of shoe- and butchers'-knives at Hollis Croft. By 1841, John had been joined by George Oxley (perhaps the former's son). In 1852 another son had perhaps arrived on the scene, since the firm was listed as George and James Oxley, located at 56 Garden Street. James had assumed control of the business by 1868, when he was listed as a maker of cook's- and palette-knives at Garden Street, with a 'depot for inventions of domestic utility' in Devonshire Street. He also advertised a patent bread-slicer. The trade mark—a butchers'-knife crossed with a sharpening iron (and the letters 'JO')—was appropriate. According to one business review in about 1884, James Oxley:

> …manufactures table knives and forks; knives and tools for shoe-makers, and curriers; butchers', bread and cooks' knives; butchers' knives and steels; table, pen, pocket, palette, putty, and hacking, plumbers', farriers', pruning, oyster, potato, mincing, basket makers' and other knives and tools, not forgetting the Patent Bread Cutter.

Before the First World War, James Oxley's was still based in Garden Street, though the factory was renamed as the Toronto Works. The firm was an enduring presence in Garden Street until it moved to Cornish Street and the Globe Works in about 1970. It had ceased business by 1980.

Parkin & Marshall

The founders of this business were Messrs Smith & Moorhouse, who began it in 1770 in Furnival Street. They were succeeded by William Parkin, who in 1846 took William Marshall into partnership. The latter died in 1852, leaving Parkin in sole charge. In 1855 he expanded the business, which was known as the Telegraph Works, by taking over John Brown's old Atlas Works in Furnival Street for the manufacture of steel and files.

In 1870 Parkin added the manufacture of machine knives to the firm's staple items: table cutlery and pocket-knives. Parkin & Marshall also had a growing reputation for its electroplate products. The corporate mark was XL·ALL, which had been granted in 1789. The words 'Sharp Edge' was another corporate mark used by the firm. William Parkin died on 19th January 1873, aged forty-nine, leaving his two sons, William and Bernard, in control. The firm seems to have been amongst the top twenty or so cutlery firms in the 1890s, when it relocated to Sylvester Street, but it soon seems to have passed its peak. The business was bought by Michael Hunter's sometime before 1910 and it did not long survive the First World War as an independent cutlery manufacturer.

John Petty & Sons

John Petty first appears in Sheffield directories as a shopkeeper at 58 Garden Street, but by the late 1860s he had decided to branch out into cutlery. By 1868 he was advertising himself as a maker of farriers'- and oyster-knives. Trade-knives would always be an important part of the Petty line. Soon John Petty had his own factory, known as Perth Works, a compact building of several floors, standing towards the top end of Garden Street as the road wound its way up and over the hill towards Solly Street. Its corporate mark was a barrel, granted in 1791. Although the firm was always one of the smaller Sheffield works and probably only employed forty or so hands in the late nineteenth century, it slowly expanded to take in other works. By 1907 it had incorporated William Gregory & Sons, the maker of butchers'- and trade-knives; and also Joseph Mills of Scotland Street (whose mark was a judge's head). Petty's could now offer a complete range of knives: best-quality butchers'- and trade-knives; 'Green River' knives; pocket- and sportsman's-knives. Even after the First World War, much of

Petty's factory in Garden Street, shortly before its demolition.

Petty's output was hand-forged, as befits a firm sited in Garden Street—a location well-known for its forges. Little is known about the family who ran the firm: but John Thomas Petty (1848–1931) was associated with the business for many years.

Petty's remained in business until 1986, when it finally closed its doors. The Perth Works was bought by property developers, who immediately demolished it.

Arthur Price of England

In the 1990s, Arthur Price is almost the last successful firm in the cutlery industry. It is not a Sheffield-based firm, however; nor is it primarily a knifemaker (it mainly manufactures plated holloware, such as forks and spoons, and giftware); but it still produces knives from a factory in Sheffield and so its history is worthy of inclusion.

The company was formed in 1902 in Birmingham by Arthur Price, a thirty-seven year-old from a local metalworking family which had roots in the Boulton and Watt era. The capital of the concern was about £1,000 and it employed only about twenty workers. It concentrated on making high-grade nickel-silver pieces for South America and Cuba; and silver pieces on 12 percent nickel-silver for Russia.

Arthur Price had a family of two girls and two boys (Arthur Jnr and Frederick). The latter joined the business, which after the First World War began to open up the home market. The company has claimed it was the first to chromium-plate spoons and forks (1927); the first to make stainless steel flatware (1928); and the first to sell sterling-silver plated gift cutlery in hand-cases (1930). It also believes it was the largest customer of the Birmingham Assay Office in pre-war years. The first Arthur Price was also an innovator: the first to grind and glaze fork prongs by machine; and the first to discard hand-swung presses and drop stamps in favour of friction screw-presses.

Arthur Price died in 1936; Arthur Price Jnr in 1942. This left Frederick to deal with the impact of the war, when normal commercial business was disrupted and the firm was turned over to munitions work. In 1946 he bought a rolling mill (Parkfield Rollings Mills) to roll ingots and in 1948 built a new knife factory in Sheffield, at Petre Street in Brightside. Both ventures lost money, but the post-war boom meant he had a full order-book with 70 percent of production sent overseas.

Frederick's only son, John Price (the only male member of the third generation), joined the business in 1949, when he was twenty. He learned the business on the shop floor in Birmingham and Sheffield, studying accountancy, design and toolmaking in his spare time. By 1951 he was running the operation in Sheffield, which he turned round. He recalls:

> The post-war years in Sheffield were difficult. Everyone was working flat out, but they were hampered by raw material shortages and lack of labour. The great cutlery names were still intact and, with their full order-books (up to two years), were still operating as in pre-war times. Then in 1951 Australia put up barriers to imports with its duties. Within a matter of weeks, Sheffield was on a *two-week* order book.

As a response, between 1958 and 1968, Price set up separately—as a 'hobby' company—a firm that concentrated on major cutlery promotions, using products such as Weetabix and Maxwell House coffee as a vehicle. This taught him about marketing; but the turning point was in 1964. Although he had trebled the size of the company, he had not changed it radically. At that point, he decided to make a three-week tour of Hong Kong and Japan, then the only two countries producing cutlery in the Far East (though they had the capacity to make for the whole world). Price was in for a shock: 'I went into all the factories there, so I could see *exactly* what was happening. It was quite a staggering experience. I became fully aware of the Far Eastern threat and of the importance of marketing'.

On his return, he immediately changed the company name to Arthur Price of England and decided that there would be no place for low-cost table cutlery. He abandoned it over a period of time—part of a plan he had evolved flying back over the Pacific. He decided the firm would be a *British* company, which would sell directly to retail outlets, and not wholesalers who depressed manufacturing.

While new technologies were introduced, Price set about claiming a strong home market (whilst the other cutlery firms were collapsing around him). He decided to do this by using the chinaware companies—Wedgwood, Doulton—as a model. Price asked: why should not cutlery be sold from shops within shops? He widened his range with special patterns and giftware to get 'concessions' in shops, following this up with the same approach as the china firms. In 1977 he was granted his first Royal Warrant; then followed this up in 1988 with a Royal Warrant from the Prince of Wales. Price built up one hundred 'shops', which accounted for 40 percent of company sales. As he puts it: 'I started this network because I wanted to express the company on the High Street as I did in my own showroom'. It also insulated the company from central buyers, who were able to play one firm off against another.

Price's strategy has proved successful and has taken the company into the 1990s as a thriving concern. In 1995 it employed over four hundred at its separate companies. Holloware is made in Birmingham; cutlery in Sheffield (at a new factory in Handsworth); and these products are distributed from its headquarters in Lichfield. The company is still family-owned (though now John Price's sons run the business) and still produces mostly British products. (It does import cutlery, but this accounts for only five percent of its trade at the lower end of the market). Interestingly, it also uses the George Butler brand, which it bought from the French firm Guy Degrenne in 1993. In the words of John Price: 'I've done what the Japanese and Koreans can't do—put together a marketing programme. We've identified a brand—we offer a service and a greater range than any other (3,000 lines). Our concessionary shops produce a higher square foot return than any other business except cosmetics'.

John & William Ragg

Corporate Marks.

"NAPOLEON."
"PARAGON."
"PLANTAGENET."

When *Quality of Sheffield*, the journal of the Sheffield Chamber of Commerce, ran an article, in March 1957, on firms that had existed for a century or more, Ragg's qualified easily. Its business was founded in 1831 by John Ragg and William Ragg in Johnson Street, Sheffield: however, Richard Ragg, a knifemaker and ancestor, was working at Ecclesfield in 1601. By the late nineteenth century, the firm was operating in Nursery Street, specialising in razors and scissors, for which it had a high repute. However, it also made 'pen-knives in every variety'. From 1907, it was located at the Nursery Works, Eldon Street, and broadened its product-range to include other types of knives. Its trade marks were NAPOLEON (accompanied by a striking picture of the Frenchman on a rearing horse), PARAGON and PLANTAGENET.

In 1956 Ragg's moved to Nursery Works, Little London Road, and Norton Hammer, Sheffield. The firm continues making professional knives, surgical scalpels and tuning forks in the 1990s as Granton Ragg Ltd.

Rawson Bros

Based at the Globe Cutlery Works in Carver Street, Rawson Bros was founded in 1870. Little is known about the origins of the firm, though the leading light was Frederick Percy Rawson (1843–1909), who was born at Hill Foot in Sheffield. He was the son of Samuel Rawson, a builder. The Rawsons were an old-established Hallamshire family and a John Rawson had been the second Master Cutler in 1625.

Rawson Bros manufactured pen-, pocket- and sport's-knives, besides table- and butchers'-knives. Scissors, razors, files, saws and electroplated goods were also part of the firm's output. Its corporate mark was a bird and outstretched wings. The 'Globe' name signified the wide-ranging nature of its trade, with its customers as far afield as India, China and Australia. Percy Rawson was said to have been the first Sheffield manufacturer to open out direct trade with the Far East, having visited India and Ceylon in the mid-1880s. He was also involved with trade-marking problems and visited Germany in 1890 to assess their alleged counterfeiting of Sheffield marks. However, it was mostly for his public activities that Rawson was known in Sheffield. Commented one newspaper: 'Considerable as were his position and influence in the business world, political and temperance work may be said to have been the main interest of his life'. He was said to have made many enemies in his life, and one local historian (J.H. Stainton) wondered how many political fights he had hatched in his upstairs warehouse in Carver Street. Added Stainton: 'A flash of the native wit which always characterised the Sheffielder gave him a curious nickname and he became known as "Rawcy Person", a nickname which tickled the groundlings at any rate'. Unfortunately, local writers were singularly uninformative about the details of his business life.

James Kinder, who had joined the firm as an office boy in 1875, took over the business in 1911. He died in 1953, aged ninety-two. Rawson Bros was located at Carver Street until 1963; it then moved to Bath Street and Penistone Road by 1973, and was no longer listed in directories by 1980.

Thomas Raynes

This business, based at the Permanent Scissor Works in Eyre Street, was launched by Thomas Raynes in 1874. As the title of the factory indicates, Raynes's main product-line was scissors, which were 'warranted free from soft blades and to cut'. The company had its own forging hearths on the ground floor of the works, with the finishing shops, offices and packing sections above. In the 1890s, Raynes was also described as a manufacturer of table-, pocket- and sportsman's-knives—cutlery which was perhaps supplied by outworkers. The firm's market seems to have been mainly in England, Scotland and Ireland. Its trade mark, if it used one, has not been traced.

Thos Raynes was active well into the twentieth century and by 1936 it had become a limited company. Table-knives were amongst its products at this time. During the Second World War and its aftermath, the firm relocated to Arundel Street, then Eyre Lane, which was its address when it finally closed its doors in 1960.

Thomas Renshaw & Son

The founder of this firm, Thomas Renshaw, was born in about 1815. Little is known about his company, though one contemporary description of the firm suggests that it was a typical Sheffield cutlery business: a four-storied building around a square, with showrooms, offices and warehouse; 'improved machinery and appliances'; and a management characterised by 'honourable methods, energy and enterprise'. It was founded in about 1840 and occupied the Stand Works in Corporation Street, where about a hundred hands were employed by the early 1890s. The trade mark was the word STAND. Table- and pocket-cutlery (in pearl, tortoiseshell, ivory and horn) were the main lines, alongside scissors and razors. Thomas Renshaw died in 1893, aged seventy-seven, leaving two sons (one of whom, William, was manager of the Stand Works). Renshaw's was no longer listed in local directories after 1900.

Richards

Richards was arguably the only twentieth-century Sheffield firm to make money from what had once been the cutlery industry's staple—the manufacture of pocket-knives. Significantly, the company was not founded by Sheffielders.

The Richards' story began in that rival German centre of cutlery production, Solingen, where in about 1900 a family named Richartz launched the factory of Gebruder, Richartz and Soehne. They made pocket-knives and straight razors, sporting a lamppost logo, which were aimed at the low-quality end of the market.

In 1932 one of the family, Stephan Richartz, came to Sheffield to try to repeat the formula. He bought a small cutlery factory in Broomhall Street and was soon joined by a German colleague and engineer, Wilhelm Muller. The company was registered as Richards Bros & Sons (with a trade mark of a tent, as well as the lamppost) and it began growing rapidly. The staff at first was less than ten, but by 1934 this had increased to 134, and by 1938 it was 400. In 1937, Stephan's brother, Paul, had joined him in the management of the business and in the following year the trio judiciously decided to become naturalised (though this did not prevent Paul from being briefly interned).

Richards seems to have benefited from war work, switching its output to spanners and other military products, but its factories in Broomhall Street and Soho Street were damaged in the blitz.

Richards' pocket-knives were cheaply-made and aimed at the mass market.

In 1945 the owners decided to build a new factory on a redeveloped site bounded by Moore Street, Charter Row and Fitzwilliam Gate. According to cutlery historian Jim Taylor: 'When completed, the building comprised no less than 153,600 square feet and was easily the largest, most modern and best-equipped cutlery factory in Sheffield, possibly the world'.

Pocket-knives, kitchen-knives and scissors were the company's main lines, which it decided to mass produce. For example, a die-casting plant was installed for making scissor parts in their thousands. Quality was a secondary consideration and many of the firm's pocket-knives would have been regarded with contempt by the old nineteenth-century masters. Cheaply blanked-out from sheet steel, and featuring celluloid handles, which were often garishly decorated, Richards' pocket-knives were a world away from nineteenth-century Sheffield products. Yet these cut-price knives sold in their thousands (even millions) to a public who now cared more about price than craftsmanship.

In the 1950s and 1960s, Richards' growth was rapid. By 1960 it employed about 800, making it the largest cutlery factory in Sheffield alongside

Viners (though we may note that Richards undoubtedly had a higher output of traditional knives than Viners). Richards had swallowed some 60 percent of the country's pocket-knife market; and it also made about 40 percent of the UK's scissors.

Paul Richartz died in 1961, aged seventy-three, and his brother took over for a time until his retirement a few years later. By the mid-1960s, Wilhelm Muller was the chairman of the company (now known simply as Richards). He bought the Rodgers-Wostenholm group in 1975 and then sold Richards to an American firm, Imperial Knife. Muller retired a rich man. The American owners of Richards were unable to repeat his success, especially in the face of the growing importation of Far Eastern and European cutlery. After losing heavily, in 1982 Imperial sold out to a group of businessmen who operated a firm called Western Knives. This consortium rapidly became insolvent and in 1983 Richards closed. The Moore Street factory was demolished in 1985.

Pocket-knife assembly at Richards in 1976. (Sheffield Newspapers).

Richard Richardson

This was one of the oldest firms engaged in the Britannia metal and electroplate trades, having been founded in 1796. It was also, according to one report, one of the pioneering firms in this branch of the trade. By the 1880s, the firm was based at the Cornwall Works in Norfolk Street, and also had a London office at Ely Place, Holborn. By 1893 the Cornwall Works had been moved to Scotland Street. The firm made a wide range of luxury goods: silver fruit-knives, carvers and dessert-knives were amongst its specialities, marked with a company shield enclosing two co-joined 'R's (one reversed).

In 1932 Richardson's was taken over by E.H. Parkin, which had a works in Brookhill.

Richardson Sheffield

This company, famous for its Laser Knives, is that rare Sheffield phenomenon since the 1960s—a successful world-class knifemaker. It now caters for the modern mass market in kitchen- and butchers'-knives, though its more distant roots were in the Victorian era.

The originator of the business was Westall Richardson, a man variously described in local directories as an agent, broker and gentleman. His start as a knifemaker does not appear to have occurred until about 1879, when he began table-knife manufacture at the Cavendish Works, Cavendish Street. By the 1890s, Richardson had moved his operations to Brookhill and Sarah Street.

The business was incorporated as Westall Richardson in 1929 at the Cavendish Works in Brookhill, operating as a typical family cutlery business. In 1956, Regent, an American cutlery firm, bought a half-share in Richardson, intending to use it as a source for knife blades. It needed substantial investment in machinery to bring the firm up to scratch, something which launched Richardson on its road to success and also led the American interests to acquire the remaining shareholding by 1960. In 1986 the Americans sold the business to McPherson's Ltd, the leading Australian manufacturer of kitchen-knives and cutlery, which had diverse interests in publishing and engineering.

Under both American and Australian ownership, Richardson—which was based at the Regent Cutlery Works—had an important element of continuity in the presence of Bryan Upton, who had joined the company in 1959 and was managing director after 1966 (becoming chairman of Richardson Sheffield in 1988). Under his direction, the company made two key decisions: in 1966 it began making complete kitchen-knives; and in 1979–80 it introduced its well-known Laser knife. Underlying these decisions was a policy of concentrating on increasing the efficiency of its manufacturing operations through process innovation and cost saving. Upton and his engineers began building their own automated machines, then applied flow-production ideas and eventually computers to reduce their costs further. Meanwhile, they abandoned one of the time-honoured traditions in Sheffield cutlery—piecework—in favour of hourly wages, which cut supervision, yet allowed greater control of the manufacturing system.

Improved manufacturing techniques then paved the way for Richardson Sheffield's major breakthrough in product development—the Laser knife. This was a mixture of clever technology—the Laser knife was designed never to need sharpening, due to its optimum angle of edge and minute serrations—and even better marketing. The success of this product appears to have owed as much to the inspired linking of the high-technology word 'Laser' with the Richardson Sheffield brand, as to any radical innovation in cutting. Most customers are actually unsure of why the knives are so named, many believing that they are somehow sharpened by laser (actually the beam only checks the angle of edge). No matter. Richardson Sheffield used the Laser knife to expand its sales and marketing operations. With a good product, an unprecedented 25-year guarantee and an evocative brand name, it set out to capture a large share of the kitchen-knife market by paying careful attention to all the things that Sheffield firms had so often neglected: styling and packaging, custom-labelling for large department stores, and speed of delivery.

Upton stated in an interview to *The Guardian* (19th July 1986) that he had four basic ground rules for success:

> One is leadership by example. The managing director is no better or no worse than any other member of the company. I get involved in every aspect of the business. I worked my way up through the company. I know it inside out. Typically, you don't find that in British industry. The second is to answer letters the same day. The third is to provide samples the same day. The

fourth is to make use of Telex…[which]…is of crucial importance today.

> That's how to get ahead—being able to deliver a good value-for-money product, on time or ahead of schedule. British industry has never learnt that lesson. It rested on its laurels—on its assumed quality.

The results of Upton's policies were dramatic. In the early 1970s, the company's turnover had been £¹/₂ million; by 1987 it was over £12 million; and by 1993 it had reached nearly £20 million. The return on capital had been consistently good, rising to about 25 percent in the early 1980s after the introduction of the Laser knife (with all the profits being reinvested in the business—an unusual policy in a Sheffield cutlery firm). In the 1980s, the firm had also bought Elford Plastics Ltd, in order to secure supplies for knife handles, and also purchased one of the nine Sabatier professional

knife manufacturers. By 1993 Richardson Sheffield had won 55 percent of the UK market in kitchen-knives and about 9 percent of the market in Europe, where it had sales offices in Germany, Italy and Scandinavia. In 1995, the firm (which employed about 400) launched a new Fusion-edge knife, which contained tungsten-carbide. The company's advertisements claimed: 'It's a knife you will never, ever, ever, ever, have to sharpen in your entire life'. The company was linked with materials research at Sheffield Hallam University and at Sheffield University through a £1 million government-sponsored project. This was a remarkable performance in an industry which had seen output and employment shrink.

Even though Richardson Sheffield import some of its knives—and this trend could increase to the point where it is no longer, strictly speaking, a local manufacturer of knives—for the moment Sheffield's traditional presence in the department stores and shops around the country has been preserved.

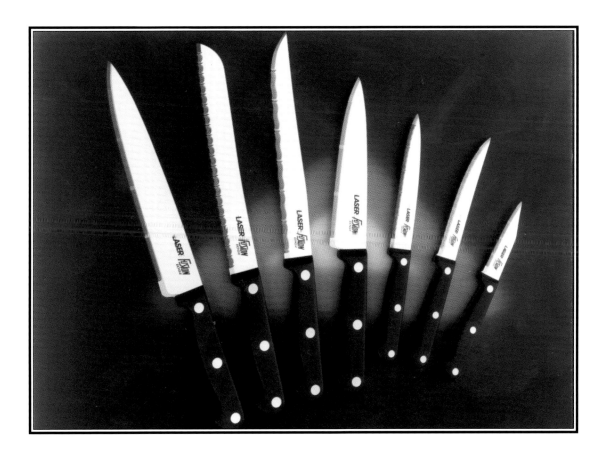

Roberts & Belk

This silversmithing firm was founded in 1809 as Furniss, Poles & Turner in Furnival Street. It changed hands a number of times, becoming Roberts & Slater in 1845 and Roberts & Briggs in 1859. By 1864, Samuel Roberts (1809–1885) had entered into partnership with Charles Belk (1840–1904), a Sheffielder who was descended from a family well known in Pontefract. Orphaned in his infancy, Belk was apprenticed to Francis Newton & Sons. When Roberts retired in July 1879, Belk took over the business, which made silver, electroplate and table cutlery at the Furnival Works. 'Mr Belk abhors shoddy', commented one reporter, 'He abominates the cheapness associated with inferior quality and poor workmanship, and will have none of it'. He was a prominent member of the Company of Cutlers and was 'for ever diving into its records, and dragging from an almost forgotten past much that was of genuine interest, especially to those identified with the old industries of Hallamshire'. Belk was Master Cutler in 1885, when the principal guest was Lord Randolph Churchill. He was regarded as an authority on Sheffield trade matters and attended foreign conventions on trade marking. 'He was something more than a successful manufacturer', noted an obituarist, 'in fact he had all the cultivated tastes of a successful English gentleman'.

Roberts & Belk used various silver marks: SRCB, CB and R&B, over the years. These were registered in Sheffield and London, where the firm had an office since about 1882.

In 1901 the firm became a limited liability company with Charles Belk and his son, William Patrick Belk (1872–1963), as directors. Still based in Furnival Street in the 1950s, W.P. Belk eventually sold the firm to C.J. Vander, a London silversmiths, in 1961. Hugh Norton Lister (d. 1967) became manager of the company. The firm is still listed in Sheffield directories in 1995.

Joseph Rodgers & Sons

Rodgers had an unsurpassed reputation for knife manufacture in the nineteenth century. It was said that 'the history of the firm was to a large extent the history of the cutlery trade in Sheffield'. No one quite knows when Rodgers began, but one local historian had heard it stated 'that originally they came from Stannington', the district of Barlow-knife fame; whilst an old indenture of apprenticeship mentions the family at 'Brightside Byerley'. Certainly Rodgers were working cutlers before 1724. At that date, a house, workshop and land were 'lett' to a John Rodgers, for a yearly rental of seven guineas, at Holy (or Hawley) Croft, a small street close to the present Cathedral. By 1730 Hawley Croft was becoming too cramped for the increasing trade, and so workshops were also occupied in Sycamore Street (a road which no longer exists, but which once ran from the present Central Library down to the main Post Office). Rodgers' famous mark—the Star and Maltese Cross—was confirmed to Joseph Rodgers by the

Company of Cutlers in 1764. Sketchley's *Sheffield Directory* (1774) lists 'Joseph and Maurice Rogers [sic], penknife and razor makers, Holy Croft'. After John Rodgers' death in 1775, the business gradually extended from the Sycamore Street premises to occupy a nearby block of buildings at an address Rodgers were to make world-famous— No. 6 Norfolk Street.

Originally, Rodgers' trade seems to have been confined to pen- and pocket-knives. In this trade it quickly established a reputation both for quality and innovation in design. Weston Park Museum has a fine collection of early Rodgers' penknives, which gives some idea of the unusual types of knives the firm marketed. They made library knives which consisted of an ivory pen-knife with a pen-blade at one end. Others had a pen-knife and small box for snuff or for wafers (the small discs of flour and gum used to seal envelopes). More elaborate types had a wafer seal at the base, a perpetual calendar, and a compartment for pen blades which screwed into the top when used.

After 1800, as the reputation of Rodgers' productions grew, new lines were begun. In that year, the manufacture of table cutlery commenced, and a few years later the production of scissors was added. Through all these early years, the firm always had a family member at the helm. The bosses in 1730 were Maurice and Joseph Rodgers, sons of the Joseph Rodgers in Hawley Croft. By the opening year of the nineteenth century, the head of the firm was Joseph Rodgers, who died in 1821, aged seventy-nine, and who left four sons in the business—John, Joseph, Maurice (d. 1827) and George (d. 1842). Joseph was blind for the forty years preceding his death in 1867 and took little part in the business, so that the management rested in the capable hands of John Rodgers (1779–1859). Under his direction, the firm began expanding rapidly in the early years of the nine-teenth century. In the *General Sheffield Directory* (1817) they appear as 'merchants, factors, table- and pocket-knife, and razor manufacturers'.

This no doubt reflected Sheffield's own rapid expansion, but it also owed much to John Rodgers. R.E. Leader, in his history of the Sheffield Banking

Co. (of which John Rodgers became a director) had this to say about him:

> Unobtrusive in manner, he shrunk from public affairs, convinced that he best discharged his duty by enhancing the name of his native town for the excellence of its staple manufacture by steadfastly refusing to stamp on his good any name but his own, and by realizing the obligations of an employer.

John Rodgers certainly had a particular flair for marketing. His letters give an insight into the life of a travelling cutlery salesman at that time. A letter, dated 18th February 1819, contains a large order for cutlery from a Manchester house: John Rodgers advises his safe arrival 'without any rain the whole journey. The little horse performed his journey wonderfully. He is perfectly steady and safe and very willing to work'. In Bradford on 26th

John Rodgers (1779–1859).

Some of the earliest Rodgers' pocket-knives were made with the 'running dog' motif.

Joseph Rodgers' cutlery label.

March 1819 he writes: 'I arrived here to breakfast. I expect to reach Halifax this evening; am sorry to hear Brother George is still indisposed and unable to attend business. This has prevented me visiting various houses. Write and say if you are much inconvenienced without me for a few weeks longer. I shall visit Huddersfield and then try some new towns such as Otley, Knaresborough, Hull, Leeds'. Besides these orders taken 'on the road', Rodgers sold to wholesalers and other firms.

In 1821 Stuart Wortley (then Member of Parliament for Yorkshire and later Lord Wharncliffe) presented John Rodgers to the Prince Regent at Carlton House. The knifemaker presented to the Prince a minute specimen of cutlery with 57 blades, which occupied only an inch when closed. A Sheffield worthy later wrote:

> A ludicrous incident occurred at this interview, which Mr Rodgers himself used to relate. The miniature knife of many blades fell, in the act of presentation, amongst the thick pile of the carpet, and could not at the time be recovered. But the Prince took the accident with great good-humour, and gave substantial proof of his satisfaction by a liberal order for more useful articles.

He also conferred upon Rodgers a Royal Warrant, which gave the firm a further boost towards the production of the finest cutlery.

Rodgers' knives are particularly sought after by modern collectors. The reasons: not only was this firm's output and range greater than any other Sheffield firm (particularly of pocket- and hunting-knives), but also its quality was that much better, even in a town which prided itself on quality. Why was it better? Simply, it seems, because Rodgers' decided that things should be that way. A brief 'house' history, published in 1911, contained Rodgers' manifesto:

> The principle on which the manufacture of cutlery is carried on by this firm is—quality first, and with this in view it is evident that their competition with other firms as to price comes second; it is the object of the firm to produce the finest quality of article both as regards material and workmanship, at a reasonable price, so that

anyone who purchases one of this firm's productions bearing not only the name, but also the trademark, a star and Maltese cross, can depend on the fact that he or she has obtained an article which can be relied upon, and if properly used will give complete satisfaction.

Rodgers was not shy about announcing to the world that it made only the best. Shortly after the meeting with the Prince Regent, John Rodgers decided to open a cutlery showroom for his firm's products in Norfolk Street. In a town where the bulk of the trade was in the hands of the little mesters, who did not bother to display their goods, and where such establishments were consequently unknown, the founding of the showroom proved to be a marketing masterstroke. In fact, it was the first such showroom in the world. It caused a sensation, disrupting the Norfolk Street thoroughfare, as visitors came to gape at Rodgers' knives. As one local writer remarked, it was not appreciated at first that it was a *salesroom*, not an exhibition. Local curiosity soon abated, but the showroom remained a tourist attraction, especially for foreign visitors, who often recorded their impressions. Wrote one of them in about 1825: 'Our next call was at the splendid establishment of Rogers [sic] & Sons   The showroom of their manufactory is brilliant. All their articles are highly burnished, kept perfectly clean, and arranged so as to produce the finest effect'.

Rodgers' display knives in particular attracted attention. Of course, other Sheffield cutlers made such pieces, but none made exhibition knives quite as magnificent as those of Joseph Rodgers. Sir Richard Phillips, a noted writer and publisher, described these products of Sheffield skill in his *Personal Tour* (1829). In the Rodgers' showroom Phillips stood in awed admiration before the Year Knife, which was displayed in 1822. Phillips also described masterpieces of miniaturisation, counterparts of the Royal Presentation knife:

> A knife containing seventy-five blades, not a mere curiosity, but a package of instruments of real utility, in the compass of a knife of four inches long, three inches high, and one and a quarter inches broad. It is valued at fifty guineas;

A miniature knife enfolding seventy-five articles, which weigh but seven pennyweights, exquisitely wrought, and valued at fifty guineas; A common quill, containing twenty-four dozen of scissors, perfect in form and made of polished steel.

Such brilliant marketing was extended to America, which became one of the main sources of the firm's business. It had been active there since 1800, when John Rodgers visited Birmingham and, as he later recalled, was 'more than usually fortunate on that particular day, in opening a connection with some respectable houses in the American Trade, which considerably promoted our success in that quarter of the globe'. In 1902, the American ambassador, J.H. Choate, speaking in Sheffield, said: 'Half a century ago the American boy thought he was in luck if he carried in his pocket a knife on which was stamped the name of Joseph Rodgers & Sons, Sheffield. They knew that they had got the best that could be had the world over'. Buffalo Bill, in his duel with Sitting Bull, relied on a Rodgers' Bowie knife given to him by General Custer. Or at least, so Rodgers said: and who are we to question them?

Fuelled by the American demand, Rodgers' expansion was inexorable. By the time it came to unveil its Norfolk Knife at the Great Exhibition, Rodgers was easily the largest cutlery factory in Sheffield. Its premises had steadily expanded to take in the whole of the block of buildings bounded by Norfolk Street, Flat Street, Milk Street and Sycamore Street. By 1860 the firm also had a London office. Scattered evidence suggests that the number of workmen had grown from about 300 in 1820s, to 520 in 1840, and still it kept rising. In 1862 new showrooms were built on an even grander scale than the original: frequented by kings, princes, dukes, maharajahs and American generals, these showrooms remained an important item on any 'Grand Tour' of northern England.

Various sons and grandsons directed the business, with the help of two other partners, Atkins and Nelstrop, who had joined in the 1840s. As John and Joseph Rodgers had no children, the former took into partnership in 1850 some of his nephews, including a man named Robert Newbold, who had married into the family.

Rodgers continued to catch the eye at the exhibitions. These were the remarks of the *Sheffield Independent's* 'practical correspondent' at the Great International Exhibition in June 1862:

> I would direct particular attention to the daggers, or hunting knives exhibited by [Rodgers]. There are many other exhibitors who show daggers, bowie knives, etc, which I must say are comparatively failures. Those of Messrs Rodgers are by far the best specimens in the British section. They are all within the limits of utility, and the grinding of the blades is beyond all praise. Some of them, with very little ornament, are almost the perfection of finish. I cannot particularise them, but there is one dagger well worthy of notice from its appropriate guard. It consists of two stags' heads and horns filed out of steel and chased. The handle of this dagger is of stag horn, and the whole is a consistent piece of design and good workmanship. There is one serpentine dagger (or, as they are sometimes called, flaming swords), which is superior to any other of that class in the British section.

By 1870, Rodgers employed 1,200 workmen. In the last week of 1870 Rodgers was reported to be sending upwards of ten tons of finished cutlery to the USA, which accounted for one-seventh of all Sheffield's American trade; and its travellers were active throughout the Southern American states. The firm also had offices and warehouses in Cullum Street and Fenchurch Street, London; and also in New York, Montreal, Toronto, and New Orleans. Calcutta, Bombay and Havana also at various times had a Rodgers' office. In 1871 a member of the Rodgers' family, Joseph, and Robert Newbold decided to organise the business into a limited company with a capital of £130,000. The vendors became the first managing directors, so that the Rodgers' business remained 'private' and retained its exclusive character. Joseph retired some years later, leaving Newbold as the sole managing director, though he was helped by several members of the Rodgers family.

Rodgers was now the largest cutlery factory in the world—the 'Knife of Kings and the King of Knives', was one popular slogan. In 1882 the firm

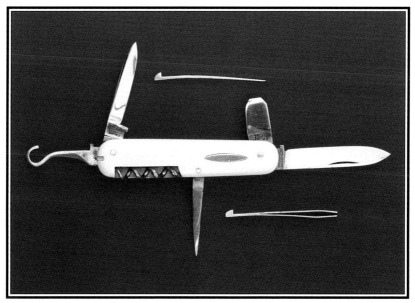

Fine Rodgers' combination knife, with picker and tweezers concealed beneath the ivory scales. It was probably made before 1914.

Delicate Rodgers' tortoishell pen-knife. The company aimed at quality above all other considerations.

P. 1857.   P. 1858.   P 1859.   P. 1860.

Pen- and pocket-knives	1,600,000
Razors	500,000
Table-knives, butchers'-knives, etc.	1,450,000
Carvers (pairs)	35,000
Scissors	144,000

Fifteen tons of ivory were used each year.

built a factory in Pond Hill for the manufacture of pocket-knives, and three years later Rodgers added the manufacture of silver- and electroplate. In 1889 a showroom was opened in London at 60 Holborn Viaduct for the display of silver and electroplate. Still the Sheffield premises proved too small, and in 1889 a plot of land in River Lane and Pond Hill, opposite the pocket-knife factory (and close to the site of the modern bus station), was acquired. On a portion of this site was erected a factory for the manufacture of table cutlery, and this was considerably extended in 1905, when the silver and electroplate department was removed to the new premises from Pond Hill. In 1907 the Sheaf Island Works of Messrs Wm. Jackson & Co. was purchased, bringing the total ground covered by Rodgers' works to about five acres.

According to one report, between 1901 and 1907 Rodgers' average annual output was as follows:

Some idea of Rodgers' product-line can be gathered from surviving catalogues. One of them, published during the reign of King Edward VII (1901–10), has 128 folio pages, packed with every type of knife imaginable. 'Manufacturers of Every Description of Cutlery and Silver and Plated Goods' announced the title page, and the firm was not joking. Rodgers clearly aimed at being a 'Universal Provider'. It was an era when modern 'buzz' words such as rationalisation and standardisation were unknown and it was seen as a virtue to offer the customer as wide a range of goods as possible, sometimes even without thought to the cost. There are over sixty pages of pocket-knives alone; and many pages contained illustrations of over a dozen different types. Still in regular production were Rodgers' magnificent daggers and Bowie knives, each a tribute to the cutlers' art. Complicated horseman's-knives in ivory and stag were depicted, too, besides more mundane knives, such as pruners, carvers and ordinary pen-knives.

The quality was as good as ever, since throughout the nineteenth century Rodgers backed up its workmanship by always using only the best materials. In an age less sensitive to conservation, its ivory cellar in Norfolk Street, crammed with giant tusks bought at the quarterly sales in London, Liverpool and Antwerp, was one of the hidden sights of town. Four or five men were constantly employed in sawing this ivory. Rodgers' appetite for stag was no less marked: deer horns and antlers filled another cellar. Pearl came from the Philippines, and was cut from the finest Manila shells, whose fire and lustre were regarded as unequalled. Boxwood, beech, rosewood and ebony were also used.

None knew better than Rodgers that 'the foundation of good cutlery is the quality of the steel employed'. In about 1890 they began manufacturing their own shear steel at a water-powered forge in Leppings Lane, Wadsley Bridge, a small hamlet about four or five miles north-west of Sheffield. Later the operation was transferred to nearby Middlewood Forge. In 1894 Rodgers began melting crucible steel at the River Lane Works. Quite why they felt obliged to begin steel manufacture themselves is uncertain: perhaps it reflected problems in obtaining steel of the correct tempers (Rodgers would have been very fussy about such matters and we know that other cutlers had supply problems as the crucible steelmakers became more involved with the engineering industries). Or perhaps producing their own steel was cheaper. Either way, Rodgers now had complete control over all their manufacturing processes. Any collector lucky enough to own an Edwardian Rodgers' knife has the extra satisfaction of knowing that it contains Rodgers' steel, too.

This close attention to detail does much to explain Rodgers' success. The firm was immortalised in the pages of Herman Melville's *Moby Dick* (1851), where in the 'Counterpane' the author describes Ishmael's reaction to the sight of Queequeg shaving with a harpoon: 'Thinks I, Queequeg, this is using Rogers' [sic] best cutlery with a vengeance'.

As Rodgers were fond of pointing out, not without a touch of patronising arrogance, their great name and mark had spread even into the 'uncivilised' corners of the world. 'Stories are constantly told by travellers', remarked the firm, 'of incidents in stores in South Africa, India, and other places, of the persistency of the natives in their demand for a Rodgers' knife; this name is probably the only English word they know'. A writer, John Keane, in his book *Six Months in Mecca* (1881), related the pride of an Arab chief in the possession of a Rodgers' carving knife, as the Meccan pointed out the mystic characters which signified that the knife was first-class, 'the word [Rodgers] having been generally adopted as a synonym for good steel'. In Persia, India and Ceylon, the name entered into the language as an

adjective expressing superb quality. The Singhalese used the term 'Rujjus' in this sense, and applied it to other articles besides cutlery. According to one report, in Bombay in the late nineteenth century a sign appeared as follows: 'Tea, coffee, soda, lemonade, ice cream, all Rojers' best things, poodings, and custer, can be had here'. Inevitably, the famous mark was much imitated and involved the firm in a great deal of trouble and expense in defending it. But this was only to be expected, when producing 'Rodgers' Best Cutlery'.

Despite this problem and increasing foreign competition, particularly from Germany and America, Rodgers' performed reasonably well in the decade or two before the First World War: between 1906 and 1913 the annual dividend to its shareholders (mostly the Rodgers' clan and their close friends) was never less than $12\frac{1}{2}$ percent. There are however other indications, such as in its employment rolls, that the company had passed its peak:

1830	300	1890	2000
1840	520	1897	1800
1862	1000	1911	1600
1872	1200	1914	1500

By 1914, Rodgers had lost its No. 1 position as the largest employer in the cutlery trades to Walker & Hall.

Worse was to follow in the First World War, when the company was hit by the falling demand for high-quality pocket-knives, the impact of Army conscription, and the loss of 55 of its men in the trenches. It was hardly the best preparation for the depressed inter-war years, when Rodgers had to come to terms with the advent of stainless steel, the need for increasing mechanisation and a further decline in the high-quality sector of the cutlery trade.

In 1929 the company minute book recorded an historic event: Rodgers had sold the Norfolk Street site for £52,500. This was a prelude to consolidating its operations in its three remaining sites. The pocket-knife business was concentrated in the Pond Hill Works. (Rodgers had bought the assets of the silver-plate firm, John Round, and transferred that business to the Pond Hill Works, too.) In the Sheaf Island Works the firm manufactured scissors and also had its forge and laboratories. In the River Lane Works, the manufacture of table-cutlery and trade-knives was conducted.

Despite this attempt at rationalisation, and despite much talk of merging with Needham, Veall & Tyzack and Wostenholm, these were dismal years for Joseph Rodgers. Like Wostenholm's, it barely kept its head above water in the depression, and often recorded losses. Attempts to break into new markets, such as safety-razor manufacture, were failures. In 1937, there was a shareholders' revolt, with much criticism of the Rodgers' management. The company struggled on and returned to profitability in the Second World War; but due to the wartime shortage of nickel, the holloware business was closed down and was never re-opened. By this time, the Rodgers' family's involvement with the business was fading.

In the 1960s, Rodgers' pocket-knife business was hit by growing German and Swiss imports, while its table cutlery faced fierce Far Eastern competition. Events at the company began to move to a swift close. In 1966 the Sheaf Island Works and the River Lane Works were relinquished, leaving only the Pond Hill Works still in production. By 1967 Rodgers had only about a hundred workers; it was no longer a quoted company, but had over a hundred shareholders. In 1968 it was taken over by Archford Investments, a London financial group, and they began a more thoroughgoing rationalisation, which involved the closure of the antiquated Pond Hill Works. In 1971, Rodgers bought its old rival, Wostenholm. But this combined group did not survive long, as in 1975 it was taken over by Richards.

This was more or less the end of the story for Joseph Rodgers: though, in the time-honoured fashion, the trade marks were soon bought by other firms. Egginton Bros, Sheffield, now own the famous Star and Maltese Cross, though needless to say, the pocket-knives they adorn are a pale imitation of those from Rodgers' heyday.

For Rodgers was once simply the best: the greatest of Sheffield's knifemakers. The sheer quality of its knives, its Royal Warrants, its catalogues and trade marks, and the spread of its name around the globe summon up a lost world when Britannia ruled the waves, most of the map was coloured Empire red, and the foreigner knew his place. Ah, if only time stood still!

A Rodgers' grinder showing his skills on a giant hunting-knife, c. 1907.

John Round & Son

A leading manufacturer in the plated goods and holloware branches of the cutlery trade, this company was not primarily a knife manufacturer—in fact, its factory in Tudor Street was known as the 'Spoon & Fork Works'. However, it also marketed the better qualities of table-knives and silver fruit-knives. The business was founded in 1847 by John Round (c. 1809–1877), a metal worker who had been employed by the electro-platers William Hutton's. With a capital of £200, he established the business in Tudor Street at a house with a workshop attached, but these premises were soon expanded. Having taken his son, Edwin, into the partnership, he renamed the firm, John Round & Son. It seems to have been one of the leaders in the plated goods sector and by 1862 the workforce was said to be about two hundred. Turnover grew from about £40,000 in 1866 to £56,000 in 1869. The firm had an agency in Montreal, Canada, and offices in London.

However the business seems to have expanded too rapidly and in 1870 it went into liquidation. The creditors were however repaid and in July 1874 the business was converted into a limited liability company, with Henry Pawson, Joseph Gamble and J.W. Barber as directors. In 1886, Round's absorbed an Eyre Lane electroplate manufacturer, Ridge, Allcard & Co. of Lion Works.

Forty years after its founding, a business writer credited Round's as 'one of the pioneering and fostering firms of this [plated-goods] industry'. By then the workforce had increased to 250. Its mark and slogan was 'All the World Round'.

In 1932 the assets of John Round were purchased by Joseph Rodgers for £5,000 and its business was transferred to Rodgers' Pond Hill Works. The Tudor Works was vacated. Photographs show it as a rather dingy four-storied building on the left of Tudor Street, as the road ran down to Arundel Street. (The site is now an open recreational area, Tudor Square, in front of the Crucible Theatre.)

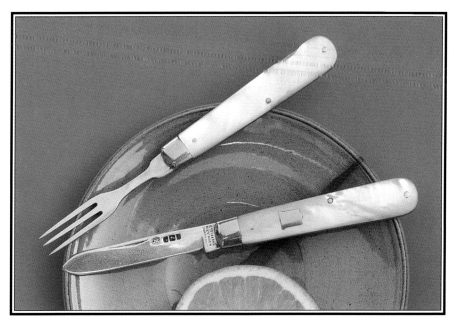

Silver fruit-knife and fork made by John Round in 1899. A simple patented mechanism
allows the two halves to fit together when not in use.

Sanderson Bros (Naylor & Sanderson)

Sanderson Bros were amongst the leading tool steelmakers in Sheffield in the nineteenth century: however, in its early days the company also had a high reputation for its cutlery.

In the late eighteenth century, when the business was founded, it was known as Naylor & Sanderson. The firm's historian, Bernard Callan, has described how the original concern had two sides: cutlery and crucible steelmaking. Thomas Sanderson (1775–1836) purchased his 'freedom' as a knife-maker from the Cutlers' Co. in 1802, his registra-tion number being 2558 (though he registered no specific mark). George Naylor (1769–1841) also took out his freedom at that time, registering a mark with symbols (though it is not known if this mark was ever used by Naylor & Sanderson). Probably Sanderson and Naylor were trading in knives before 1802, since we know that George Naylor's apprenticeship to his father (also named George Naylor) had been completed in about 1790.

Bernard Callan believes that George Naylor II went into partnership with Thomas Sanderson sometime before 1800. Their premises were in Carver Street Lane, with access from Carver Street through a passage between other buildings into a yard behind the Naylor & Sanderson workshops. The business prospered and it was reinforced in 1802 with capital from two more Sanderson brothers, John (1777–1852) and James (d. 1853). A filemaker, Daniel Bramall of the White House, Bramall Lane, also contributed capital.

According to R.E. Leader's, *Reminiscences of Old Sheffield* (1875), Sandersons 'got up more table-knives than anyone else in the town'. In particular, the business thrived on the American demand for cutlery, so much so that the firm protested to a Parliamentary Committee in 1812 about the disruptions to the US trade caused by the war with France. According to George Naylor, the firm had been engaged in the American trade for about six years and sent about five-sixths of its manufactures there. Not surprisingly, the names of

Naylor and Sanderson (together and separately) are two of the commonest on surviving examples of American table-knives (and forks) in the late eighteenth- and early nineteenth century.

Perhaps stimulated by this demand, the steelmaking side of the business, based in West Street by 1814, expanded steadily and after 1829 (when the firm was reorganised as Sanderson Bros) it soon entirely superseded the manufacture of cutlery. (Interestingly, Sanderson's mirror image firm, Wilson, Hawksworth & Moss followed exactly the same path from cutlery to steel, eventually transforming itself into Kayser, Ellison & Co. It was this firm which eventually merged with Sanderson's. As Sanderson Kayser, the firm has survived to the present day as a tool steelmaker.)

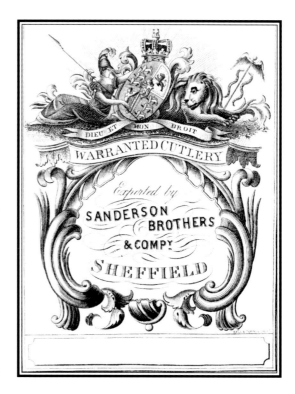

Saynor, Cooke & Ridal

The Saynors were an old-established family in the cutlery trade. R.E. Leader, in his *Reminiscences of Old Sheffield* (1876), provides some information on their early history. The original Saynors were Samuel and John, who were factors and manufacturers, conducting their main business with London in all kinds of knives, swords, shoe buckles, skates, scissors and razors. According to Leader, the Saynor factory in Bank Street employed more hands than any other firm prior to 1810. The business passed to Samuel Saynor, of Scargill Croft, who manufactured sport's-knives, scissors and pen-machine knives. The mark he struck included the word 'Rainbow'. Later Samuel, during a voyage from London to Hull, was incapacitated for life by a drunken sailor falling on him from a hammock. The business was taken over by his son.

A branch of the Saynor family operated a cutlery business in Edward Street after the 1820s (one source stating that the business was launched in 1738). A Samuel Saynor is listed as a table-, pen- and pocket-knife maker in Edward Street in 1833 and 1841. (There was also a Thomas Saynor, pen-machine maker, located in Westbar in 1844; and a William Saynor, making table cutlery in Duke Street and Eyre Lane at the same date.) The Edward Street business had become Saynor & Cooke by 1852 and was already secure in its chosen niche of the cutlery market: the manufacture of pruning-, budding- and grafting-knives. A Sheffield journalist noted Saynor & Cooke's display at the London International Exhibition in 1862. 'This firm', he wrote, 'have long been noted for that branch of cutlery, which has reference to horticultural uses. This is their speciality, and it will be expected that they would produce good things. Such is the case. Their display of these articles is excellent'.

In the 1880s, Saynor, Cooke, & Ridal (the latter having joined the firm by 1876) were based at the Paxton Works in Edward Street.

Besides the RAINBOW mark, the firm also used a picture of a penny-farthing bicycle, and the words OBTAIN and SAYNOR. Saynor's trade marks were taken over by Needham, Veall & Tyzack in 1948 and henceforth its address was Milton Street. A range of Saynor pruning knives is still made by Harrison Fisher (the owners of Needham, Veall & Tyzack).

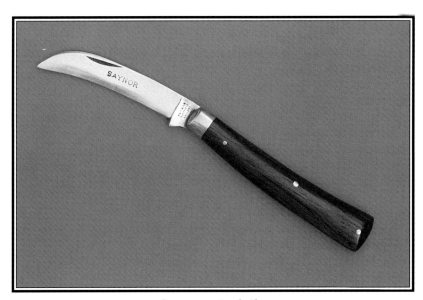

Saynor pruning-knife.

W. Saynor

DEPEND

This firm had much in common with Saynor, Cooke & Ridal—especially since both made horticultural knives—though the exact relationship between the two firms is unclear. W. Saynor's was established in 1865 and appears to have developed from the table-knife business of Joshua Saynor in Jessop Street. By 1868 William Saynor was running the firm at the same address. William Saynor's appear in the Sheffield directories in the 1880s and 1890s at Cambridge Street, Howard Street and Charles Street. By 1903

W. Saynor had moved to 29 Eyre Street and the factory was soon named the Carlton Works. By 1910 the firm had become a limited company, producing pruning- and budding-knives, and table-, pocket- and butchers'-knives. Trade marks included the words DEPEND and PIONEER. In 1912 the Carlton Works relocated to Sidney Street, where it remained until after the Second World War. By 1953 Saynor's Carlton Works was based at Furnace Hill. This factory was closed in 1958 and the firm moved to Milton Street—the same address as Saynor, Cooke & Ridal.

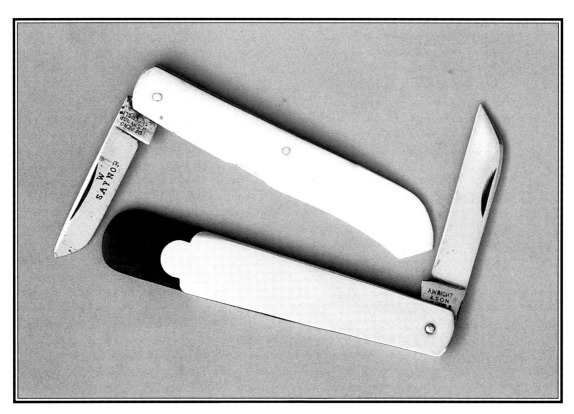

Budding-knives. The upper one is by W. Saynor and is hafted in ivory.

John Sellers & Son

Sellers was amongst a small group of cutlery firms (Brookes & Crookes and Harrison Bros & Howson are other examples) which, despite the American duties on Sheffield imports, managed to sell knives in the USA in the 1880s and 1890s on the basis of high quality.

The firm was established in Sheffield in 1820 by John Sellers, whose grandsons, John Sellers and William B. Sellers, were running it by the 1890s. The oldest part of the business was said to have been the manufacture of steel and copper plates for engravers, besides the tools needed by such craftsmen. Sellers' output included transfer plates, steel dies, monogram dies, photographers' steel plates, and patent etching ground.

Sellers' Works were at 151 Arundel Street, where about a hundred hands manufactured (or distributed) fine table-cutlery, pen- and pocket-knives, sportsmen's-knives, and hollow-ground razors. Silver- and electroplated ware was another speciality, besides nickel-silver spoons. In America, between 1881 and 1891, Sellers had a New York office at 17 Day Street. William B. Sellers directed these import offices, which flourished for a time, despite the high US cutlery tariff. Besides knives, American bank-note printers were good customers for the firm's engraving plates.

The corporate mark of Sellers, granted in 1838, was a dagger entwined with the letter S. In 1890, Sellers strengthened the cutlery side of the business by buying the Arundel Street table-knife firm of Richard Elliott. Henceforth, 'Richard Elliott. Extra' became the mark on Sellers' table knives.

Sellers' remained at 151 Arundel Street in the twentieth century, but appears to have dropped cutlery manufacture by the 1950s (though it still made engraving plates). It ceased business completely in 1975.

Stan Shaw

In the 1990s, Stan Shaw is the most experienced knifemaker in Sheffield—though it might be argued that there is now little competition. On the other hand, his range of skills and the quality of his knives, show that as a 'little mester' he would stand comparison with any of Sheffield's best from its golden age.

He works near the top of Garden Street, that famous old cutlery road that winds its way steeply up a hill, not far from the city centre. An affable and talkative man, Stan Shaw is pleased to lay aside his rivetting hammer and parser to chat about his life as a knifemaker.

He recalls how he started in the trade: 'It was 1941—wartime. I was a young lad looking for a job, so I simply walked into the Sheffield cutlers George Ibberson's, in Rockingham Street, and asked for work'. As he points out, his family did not come from a Sheffield cutlery background, though it seems that one of his distant ancestors was a file cutter. So, to that extent, it was in his blood. He lived on the outskirts of Sheffield at Worral, a small village not known for cutlery. Wadsley, another village nearby, had been famous for knifemaking in the past, but never in Stan's day, and anyway the 'Wadsley Jacks' (as the cutlers from there were known) had the reputation for cheapness and low-quality. The big local industry was refractories (the materials used in lining furnaces and making crucibles) and his father mined ganister, an unhealthy job that killed him prematurely. He was brought up by his mother in a large family, though he spent nearly ten years of his childhood in hospital with a tuberculous hip.

He admits that it was not the best start for a cutler. Moreover, when he started at Ibberson's he had never handled tools nor seen the inside of a cutlery factory. He had hardly ever visited Sheffield either, but on one of his first visits there he had seen pocket-knives on sale in the market, and it was that more than anything that gave him the idea of becoming a cutler. 'One day I just decided to go into Sheffield on my own, I was fourteen then, and look for work. That's how I ended up knocking on Ibberson's door. You had to go out and find a job for yourself in those days'.

At Ibberson's he was lucky enough to start on top work under the Osborne brothers, Ibberson's premier craftsmen. In particular, it was Ted Osborne who introduced Stan to the crafts. Soon he was making the type of knives for which Ibberson's were particularly noted: multi-blade pocket-knives, such as lobsters and smokers'-knives—all made with the best materials, such as pearl, tortoiseshell and ivory. Ibberson's had their own grinders and forgers and they were very skilled men. All Ibberson's pocket-knife blades and springs were hand-ground and hand-forged; only stainless table-cutlery was produced by machine.

Stan recalls:

> The whole business of making pocket-knives fascinated me. It wasn't long before I was pestering the older hands at Ibberson's to show me how they did their jobs, too. I learned all about forging, grinding and preparing the hafting materials simply by watching the old craftsmen and asking them how things were done. I was a real pest! I was a little bit different in that respect, because usually Sheffield cutlers were happy making one kind of knife all day long. There was a lot of conservatism. I couldn't be like that. I needed to know how everything was done.

This stood Stan in good stead since, when the industry began to collapse in the early 1980s, he was forced to go it alone. He left Ibberson's after twenty years following a disagreement over wages: as he puts it, 'I got fed up asking for a rise'. He then worked for a number of famous 'names'—John Watts, George Wostenholm, John Clarke, even back again for a time at Ibberson's—but by the 1980s it was all getting very unsettled. The invasion of cheap foreign imports was ruining the pocket-knife trade and when Clarke's shut in the early 1980s there were no firms left to employ him. The dole at that time was an awful prospect for someone who had worked all his life, so he set up on his own. It was sink or swim. Fortunately, the work (much to his surprise) has never stopped rolling in.

Eleven-piece pearl exhibition knife made by Stan Shaw in the early 1990s.

The change in status was also considerable:

Cutlers were never valued much in the old days: in fact you felt a bit ashamed to say you were a cutler, since it was regarded as very lowly. Now I can suit myself and also have the satisfaction of dealing direct with customers. With being virtually the only mester, I never have to fight for orders or even go out looking for them. People come to me—which suits me fine, because I can concentrate on what I do best.

Stan Shaw's main problem in the 1990s is that he only has one pair of hands, since he has to make all the parts for each knife. He has to do everything, because no forgers, grinders, scissor-makers and so on are left. His earlier experience with Ibberson's has proved invaluable in that respect. He hafts, grinds and assembles all his knives himself. The work is harder, but the satisfaction is greater, both for himself and the customer. Scissors, files, punches, shields, shackles, handles, scales, bolsters—the list is endless; but each part is made by Stan on his wheels and dollies with only hacksaws, files and a few other traditional tools such as his parser. The only job he hands over to others is the occasional engraving on the bolsters—usually given to Peter De Vine, an engraver who once worked for James Dixon's—and the case making for exhibition knives.

Stan still uses only traditional materials. He works mostly in pearl (occasionally abalone), stag, buffalo horn, ivory and wood (such as cocobolo). Knives with silver and gold are made to special request. In 1986 he even made a knife in *platinum* for the Queen. Tortoiseshell he once worked with regularly, but it is now more or less unobtainable.

The blades of Stan's knives are usually made from stainless steel. As he explains: 'it makes the job harder having to work with it, because it's so hard, but most customers expect stainless steel. A few collectors, though, still ask for carbon steel and I'm happy to oblige'. He still uses Sheffield stainless steel, which he buys from a stockist at Attercliffe, but interestingly, Stan still makes blades from old hand-forged Sheffield carbon steel. He has boxes of old hand-forged Sheffield

blade blanks, usually with the manufacturer's name and mark stamped in them. For example, he has many blades with 'lambfoot' stamped in them. Some date from the nineteenth century. He grinds them up himself—taking care to leave the original marks intact—and then makes the scales, bolsters, handles and springs. Naturally, this saves him a lot of time, as it avoids cutting out the blade and the customer has the chance to buy a real hand-forged blade at a bargain price.

Of course, Stan does his own hardening and tempering, relying on the skill of hand and eye to judge the correct temperatures. Since he has no hearth in his Garden Street workshop—he had to relinquish the last one when property developers forced him out of a previous workshop—he has his forge in his workshop at home. He always hardens and tempers his blades and springs the day before in batches (a dozen or so at once to save time) and then does all the other jobs the next day in Garden Street.

Stan Shaw is particularly renowned for his exhibition knives, which are now much in demand by collectors. Stan makes several showpiece knives, most of them designed by himself. The largest is his Hallamshire Knife, which weighs several pounds, has 15 blades and is about nine inches long when closed. He designed it in Deepcar about twenty years ago in his workshop at the bottom of his garden. All the blades are different and it has pearl scales. Remarks Stan: 'It's a nerve-racking experience putting one together'.

All his knives are stamped with the name 'Stan Shaw' on the tang; and he also has his own silver mark ('SS') from the Assay Office. He has no trade mark, but admits that if he did register one he might be tempted to use the word 'Deepcut'—a reference to his home town. Of course, most of the knives he has made over the years do not carry his name at all: they carry the Ibberson mark, or perhaps Slater, Wostenholm or Clarke.

A striking feature of Stan Shaw's career is his sustained capacity for hard work, a legacy perhaps from a generation who took hard, steady work as a simple fact of life. He 'retired' in 1992, yet he regularly puts in a week's work that would shame many younger people. Asked how many knives he has made, Stan laughs, and replies:

> I have absolutely no idea. It must be thousands, though. At one stage when I started up on my own, I was making a couple of dozen knives a week for the shops in Sheffield. They were only simple knives such as sleeveboards, but it gives you some idea of the number I have turned out. As I've said, it must be many thousands. I've been making pocket-knives as a full-time job for over fifty years. And in the early days it was a six-day, 48-hour week.

Surprisingly, he never seems to get bored with knifemaking. In fact, he never tires of discussing the subject and his enthusiasm is still easily fired by the thought of a new knife he has not yet tried to make. Unlike many of his generation, the experience of working so long in the Sheffield cutlery industry has not embittered him. Occasionally, he becomes annoyed at his recollections of the idiocies and slights of the old cutlery bosses and managers, but usually it is a passing feeling. Neither of his two sons have followed him into the trade, but that is not because of Stan's wishes. Actually, he would love to train an apprentice and pass on his skills, but he explains the problems involved:

I could have taken on an apprentice myself, in fact some of the old bosses had the cheek to suggest as much, but it would have really slowed me up. With expensive materials like pearl, I would have had to watch them like a hawk all the time. It would have been impossible for me to get anything done, and I had enough problems at that time coping with setting up my own business. Nowadays the problem is that no youngsters appear to be interested in making pocket-knives. Perhaps it looks too much like hard work, when you can earn a fortune in front of a computer screen. My own lads are not a bit interested. You have to have a certain personality and aptitude for this job.

I'd be happy to work with an apprentice now, though it would probably need some sort of subsidy from the City Council, because I could not pay them enough. But the Council are broke, so I can't see that happening. Anyway the City has never shown any interest in the little mesters; as far as they are concerned, we don't exist.

Perhaps that is why Stan Shaw's knives are in such great demand (at present he has enough orders for several years), because it has been realised that when he (and Graham Clayton) do retire it will no longer be possible to buy a hand-made Sheffield knife. Long may they continue.

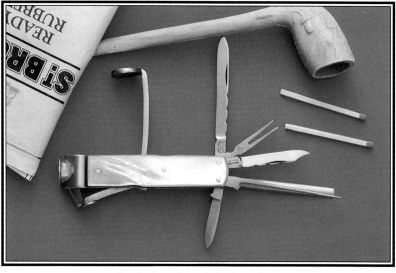

Smoker's knife made by Stan Shaw.

Sheffield Steel Products

After the First World War, as the market for mass-produced goods increased and new technologies such as stainless steel appeared, it was no longer necessary to have a long-established 'name' or traditional skills in knifemaking. Even in Sheffield, new companies were launched which were designed expressly to cater for the demand for mass-produced cutlery.

The most prominent of these companies was Sheffield Steel Products Ltd, which was a consortium of ten firms—amongst them: W.K. & Peace, Boswell Hatfield and Moses Eadon—which in 1918 took over a National Projectile Factory at Templeborough. The intention was to mass produce cutlery and tools.

Most of the constituent firms of Sheffield Steel Products were toolmakers, rather than knifemakers, though the company did have some cutlery expertise. One of its directors, William B. Hatfield (who had directed Boswell Hatfield), had once been a manager for twenty-five years at Joseph Rodgers. He had visited the USA twice and, according to his obituary in the *Sheffield Daily Telegraph* (12th December 1929), 'as a result [he] was the first to introduce into Sheffield machinery for the mechanical production of cutlery on a mass scale'.

The history of Sheffield Steel Products is obscured by the lack of any surviving business records or information. For example, it is not known how wide-ranging was its line of knives, though the company certainly manufactured table-knives. However, its cutlery products, which were sometimes marked DURALITE, were certainly low-cost. As one worker there recalled: 'This firm was quite big and produced in quantities for the lower end of the cutlery market. In other words, rubbish'.

It is also clear that Sheffield Steel Products was not a great success and it soon became deflected from its original intention to sell vast quantities of cheap knives. It was, in fact, a typical post-war boom flotation, its capital rising from £1 million to £2.4 million in only two years. It expanded by acquiring Oxley Bros foundry in Mowbray Street and also launched a multiple-shop chain around the country to sell its cutlery and tools. By 1924, seventeen firms were involved, some outside Sheffield. But in that year the stores scheme collapsed (probably through bad management) and a re-organisation followed. With government funding, the company began extending its product-range by manufacturing two-wheeled trailers. By 1929 (when its paid-up capital had plummeted to £53,000) the output was even more diverse and included automatic scales, bacon slicers, vending machines, and safety razors. In the early 1930s, when the depression hit its standard lines of cutlery, files and other tools, the company began manufacturing magnets, forgings and stampings for the motor trade.

Sheffield Steel Products survived the difficult 1930s, but after the Second World War it sank into obscurity. It had ceased trading by the 1960s.

B. & J. Sippel

The Sippels came from Germany in 1931 to assist English manufacturers mechanise plated spoon and fork production. They were first based in London, but two years later they opened their own works in Arundel Street in Sheffield. By 1939 the Sippels (by now naturalised) had relocated their firm to Cadman Street, where the Sipelia Works was said to have the largest press plant for forks and spoons in the country. The workforce had grown from about 75 in 1933 to 400 by 1939. The firm stamped its goods, SIPELIA.

Benno Sippel died in November 1946, but the firm continued to prosper after the War. By the early 1960s, under the management of Kenneth Collin, Sippel's had become the biggest manufacturer of spoons and forks in Europe. With a workforce of about 500, it was amongst the five largest cutlery firms in the city. It was not primarily a knifemaker, but it did produce knives as part of its cutlery range. Besides ordinary tableware, it was reported in the 1960s to be making a special knife for the American market for picking up peas, and a special Canadian knife for opening clams.

Sippel's, hindered by a management which was prone to taking far too many orders at unrenumerative prices, did not long survive the post-war boom. It went out of business in 1972.

Herbert M. Slater

This cutlery business was founded by Warrington Slater in 1858. Known as Slater Bros, it was based at the Beehive Works in Fitzwilliam Street. It manufactured pen- and pocket-knives, table-cutlery, Bowies and dirks, many of which were shipped to South American markets. It appears that the firm's 'Beehive' trade mark was bought from John Hinchcliffe—probably the well-known maker of Bowies and dirks—at about this time. In a later memoir, Slater wrote: 'For about thirty-nine or forty years, we struggled hard, made a great deal of money, had large families, a good deal of expense attending their education and very considerable affliction through it all, but, right up to 1896 there was every prospect of both Slater Bros and myself becoming rich'. Alas, Warrington Slater over-reached himself and in 1901, after some disastrous and well-publicised property speculations, he was declared bankrupt. He died in 1907.

His son, Herbert Slater (b. 1863), bought up the stock of the business and re-established it in the Venture Works—a compact, three-storied factory at 105 Arundel Street. The firm was incorporated in January 1931. Before the First World War and later, Herbert Slater picked up where the old business left off, producing most types of cutlery, but especially pocket-knives and razors. This time the family firm was far more successful and was to prove, under Herbert's son and grandson—Warrington Percy Slater (1897–1983) and Warrington Denis Slater (1923–1994)—one of the survivors of the Sheffield cutlery trade in the twentieth century.

In the inter-war period, it made pocket-knife materials—such as blade blanks, springs and liners—for many of the leading firms, such as Rodgers and Wostenholm. After 1945, it had a policy of acquiring many old businesses and their marks. These included Jonathan Crookes & Son (with its noted heart and pistol trade mark); John Milner's INTRINSIC mark; M. Hunter & Son of Reed Street; Needham Bros REPEAT mark; H.G. Long's 'Cross Dagger' mark; Westby; and the CURRENT mark of Albert Oates. By the end of the 1980s, however, knife production had ceased at the Venture Works. It had, in fact, been many years since Slater's own workers made the premium pocket-knives it sold (these were invariably made by outworkers such as Stan Shaw and Graham Clayton and then stamped with Slater marks). By the early 1990s, Denis Slater had sold the business and retired.

Slater's Venture Works, Arundel Street.

Southern & Richardson

 According to this firm's brief company history, *A Century of Progress, 1828–1928*, the enterprise was originally known as Wilson & Southern and was founded in 1828 at a small factory known as the Wheeldon Works. It seems that Wilson managed the Works, while Francis Southern (c. 1799–1877) was the traveller. A promising trade began with Mediterranean countries. When Wilson retired in 1847, Samuel Richardson (1812–1887) became a partner.

In 1851, Southern & Richardson moved to a new location at the Don Cutlery Works in Doncaster Street, Shalesmoor. Samuel Gray Richardson (b. 1851), the second son of Samuel, joined the firm in 1867, two years before Francis Southern retired. On his father's death in 1887, S.G. Richardson became the sole owner. He became Master Cutler two years later.

The business seems to have reached its peak in the 1880s and 1890s. Its output included: table-, pen- and pocket-knives; butchers'-, farriers'-, and Bowie knives; and razors and scissors. The corporate mark, granted in 1880, was a bird's nest containing three eggs: hence the slogan, 'Nest Cutlery'. Little is known about the company's operations, apart from bland comments in the trade press, but by the late 1880s its workforce may have reached two hundred, placing the firm amongst the top twenty cutlery manufacturers in the town.

In 1912, S.G. Richardson took Harold Willey into partnership; and the business was then registered as a limited liability company. In 1919 Southern & Richardson joined the Sheffield Cutlery Manufacturers Ltd, a merger of firms led by Needham, Veall & Tyzack. Under the charge of Willey and another director, Henry E. Brant, Southern & Richardson moved to more modern premises in Thomas Street and Milton Street (where Needham, Veall & Tyzack were located). Besides pocket- and table-knives, the firm also manufactured safety-razors (stamped 'Shaveesi'), scissors, electroplate and holloware. But Sheffield Cutlery Manufacturers performed dismally in the 1920s. S.G. Richardson retired in 1928, to Lower Guiting, near Cheltenham, and died there on 16th May 1934. The company and its name survived as part of Needham, Veall & Tyzack. Southern & Richardson was no longer listed in Sheffield directories after 1975.

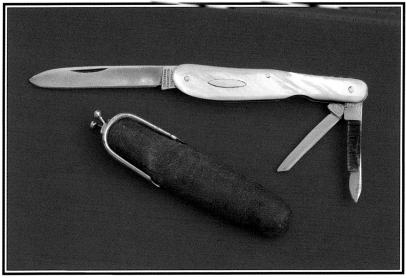

Pearl whittler by Southern & Richardson.

William Thomas Staniforth

It would be unusual to have a listing of Sheffield cutlery firms without at least one Staniforth: not only is it a quintessential Sheffield surname, but the Staniforths had been involved in the cutlery trades since at least the sixteenth century. This Staniforth business was founded in 1849. William Thomas Staniforth was listed as a spring-knife maker in Norfolk Street in 1852. Ten years later he had moved to Brown Street; then in 1876 his address was at the Eldon Works, Eldon Street. By 1884 the business operated from the Ascend Cutlery Works in Arundel Lane. Little is known about this firm, except that it made high-quality pen- and pocket-knives. It was particularly noted for its fine sportsman's-knives: but it also made table-knives, razors, scissors and operated as a general cutlery merchants. Its first corporate mark, open wings above the word ASCEND, was granted in 1852. Another trade mark was registered in 1884: it featured a two-blade pocket-knife, with the words VALUE RECEIVED. Sheffield newspapers recorded the death of seventy year-old William Thomas Staniforth on 6th September 1890 at his home in Fieldhead Road, Sheffield. 'American papers please copy', instructed his obituary, signifying Staniforth's involvement with the American trade. The business did not long survive him and it ceased trading on the eve of the First World War.

Edwin Terry

 This business was founded in 1864 by Edwin Terry and in its early days operated from West Hill Lane, Devonshire Street. In about 1889, Terry bought the premises of James Dodsworth at the Reliance Works in Bolsover Street (a road alongside the present University of Sheffield). Trade knives of various types were Terry's speciality: palette-, putty-, hacking-, gilders'-, farriers'-, and plumbers'-knives.

Plumbers' shavehooks and graining combs were also made. The trade mark was the encircled word OPTIME. The United Kingdom, the Continent and increasingly the Colonies, were the firm's major markets in the late nineteenth century. Terry's remained at Bolsover Street in the inter-war years; by the 1950s, it appears to have abandoned cutlery manufacture for the hand-tool trade.

Thomas Tillotson & Co.

The Tillotson family were one of the most important members of Sheffield's cutlery fraternity. Thomas Tillotson had been Master Cutler in 1789; John Tillotson in 1810; and George Tillotson in 1817. Originally, the cutlery business was located in Lambert Street (or Croft), but by the early 1820s it was operating from premises in Coalpit Lane, where John Tillotson & Son were making table-knives and scissors. Until 1845, a number of Tillotsons, including Thomas and John Jnr, ran the business at this address. It was also listed as a merchants. Many of the Bowie knives that have survived in American collections were made by Tillotson; and many of the books that have been written on this knife have at least one illustration of a Tillotson Bowie. The firm was located at Columbia Place by 1852, but it seems to have gone out of business in 1863.

Thomas Turner & Co.

 By the end of the nineteenth century, Turner's was one of the most important cutlery firms in Sheffield, though its exact ranking as a knifemaker is clouded by the fact that it also made steel and tools.

The business was founded in 1802 by Thomas Turner and its 'Encore' trade mark was granted three years later. By the 1820s it was listed in Sheffield directories at Norfolk Street. When Turner died, the business was taken over by his eldest son, also named Thomas, who had been born in Sheffield on 10th January 1829. He was later helped by his brothers, Benjamin and William. Like Marsh Bros, the company mixed steel and tool manufacture with knifemaking, and also operated as a general trader: *White's Sheffield Directory* (1837) lists: 'Turner, Thos & Co., merchts, steel refiners, and cutlery, saw, file, and edge tool manfrs, Suffolk Works'.

Also like Marsh Bros, Turner's exploited the American market. Cutlery historian Bernard Levine has described how Thomas Turner made a concerted effort to woo the American customer: 'Turner's early folding knives made for America were big and stout and plain. Yet even though they had no fancy decoration, every one of his early pocket-knives that I have seen was embellished with a veritable essay to tell potential American customers how good the Turner knife he was examining would prove to be'. 'Warranted Really Good'; 'Made Expressly for America'; and 'Alabama Hunting Knife' were some of the slogans stamped on Turner's blades—and there were several others. Leaving nothing to chance, sometimes Turner stamped several slogans on each knife!

Thomas Turner Jnr became Master Cutler in 1871 and retired in 1893, when he sold the business. He had made a considerable fortune and when he died on 18th March 1916 he left £55,169

THOMAS TURNER & COMPANY'S

"SUFFOLK KNIFE,"

Warranted Secure Handle,

SUFFOLK WORKS,

SHEFFIELD.

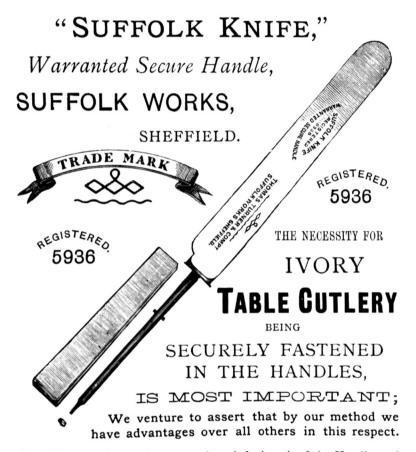

TRADE MARK

REGISTERED.
5936

REGISTERED.
5936

THE NECESSITY FOR

IVORY

TABLE CUTLERY

BEING

SECURELY FASTENED IN THE HANDLES,

IS MOST IMPORTANT;

We venture to assert that by our method we have advantages over all others in this respect.

The TANG being made strong the *whole length* of the Handle, and **A CROSS PIN,** (*as shown in the sketch*) being inserted into a small Groove, and turned into a Cavity Inside the Handle, (made for its reception) forms an **INTERNAL LOCK:** an OVAL RIVET, fastened upon the *Square Tang* of the *Head* **PREVENTS** the possibility of the Blade TURNING ROUND in the Handle, or becoming Loose in any way.

27

gross. Turner's was bought by (Sir) Albert Hobson (1861–1923), the second son of Alderman John Hobson (d. 1889), scissor maker of Arundel Street, and his wife Thryza. A childhood accident meant that Hobson was unable to walk without sticks, but he still made a success of running his father's business, Joseph Hobson & Sons (which had been in the family upwards of 120 years). In 1889 he sold the business to Joseph Rodgers, joined their board, and also became a director of the steelmakers, Jessop's.

In 1893, with brother Wilfred, Albert Hobson bought Thos Turner, which then employed about three hundred. He began a policy of expansion, adding Wingfield, Rowbotham & Co. to the business in 1898. In 1902 the trade marks and goodwill of Joseph Haywood, the pocket-knife cutlers, were acquired.

Turner's Suffolk Works, located next to the Midland Station on Porter Brook and the River Sheaf, was now one of the biggest cutlery factories in Sheffield, employing about a thousand. The firm's centenary year was 1902, the same year that Albert Hobson became Master Cutler, and the company decided to publish an anniversary pamphlet. Titled significantly, *Handicrafts that Survive*, the slim volume was an unashamed celebration of the old crafts (which neglected to mention that many of the processes in the Suffolk Works were now being mechanised). Nevertheless, it drew attention to the many traditional knives still

made there: top-quality pocket-knives, spear-points and Jack-Tar knives for the Admiralty. Customer service was still the order of the day:

> One of the most interesting departments of these works is the pen-knife hospital, established for the convenience of the numerous customers of the company who send in through the retail trade old pen-knives to be repaired. From the delapidated condition of some of the knives undergoing treatment in the hospital, it must be assumed that only sentiment can have induced the owners to ask for them to be repaired, as in many cases the repairs cost more than a new knife. A classic case of repair was that of a five-bladed knife, which was sent in requiring five new blades and a new spring and scales, the only parts of it still good being the brass divisions on the inside, the value of which was perhaps 2d.

Turner's became a limited liability company in 1918, partly because Hobson's two sons had been tragically killed in the war and were therefore unable to inherit the business. The share capital was £50,000 and the prospectus described a company that covered a site of 4,507 square yards: 'The business includes departments manufacturing crucible cast steel, files, saws, cutlery and electroplate'. In the following year, it became part of Sheffield Cutlery Manufacturers Ltd, an amalgamation led by Needham, Veall & Tyzack. But Turner's did not survive the depression and in 1932 the bankrupt business was bought by Viners,

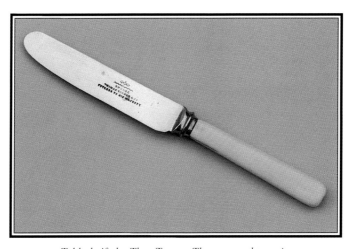

*Table-knife by Thos Turner. The patented tang is
visible through the ivory handle.*

Unwin & Rodgers

For those interested in Sheffield cutlery Americana, this firm holds a distinctive place. It was first established in about 1833 in Charles Street as a manufacturer of pen-knives and lancets. By the end of the 1830s, the product line had widened, with the emphasis very much on 'Self-Defence Knives'—in other words, the type of knives beloved by the American frontiersman, such as lock- and sneck-knives, daggers, dirks, and sportsman's-knives. The firm also advertised 'Indian Hunting' knives, though whether these were for hunting Indians, or for Indians hunting, was not made clear! In 1839, by which time its business had moved to Burgess Street, Unwin & Rodgers advertised its most distinctive product—its Life and Property Preserver, or pistol-knife. This weapon was said to be capable of killing a victim at 50 yards.

By 1849 Unwin & Rodgers had occupied the Rockingham Works in the street of the same name and the firm's range of products had been extended considerably. Table-knives, agricultural-knives (such as fleams), pen-knives, razors, scissors, gadget-knives are all displayed in a fine trade advertisement that the company ran in the Sheffield directories in the early 1850s. American-style Bowies and dirks remained a leading line. The advert points out that the firm won a prize medal at the Great Exhibition in 1851.

In 1865 Unwin & Rodgers took over the Globe Works of John Walters & Co. According to evidence published in the *Children's Employment Commission* (1865), the firm employed about 150 at its main works and about another hundred in other parts of the town. The Globe Works remained the firm's address throughout the nineteenth century, though it is evident that Unwin & Rodgers did not occupy the whole of the Globe Works—the workshops at the rear of the factory were divided between a number of small manufacturers. For a brief period between 1875 and 1883, Unwin & Rodgers adopted limited liability status, with a capital of £40,000.

Unwin & Rodgers' first trade mark seems to have been NON*XLL—but after 1865 it adopted Walter's mark SUPERLATIVE; NON*XLL was later used by the razor maker, Joseph Allen.

Unwin & Rodgers disappeared from the Sheffield directories after 1910.

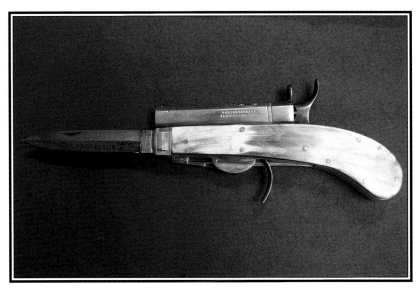

Unwin & Rodgers' pistol-knife. (Weston Park Museum).

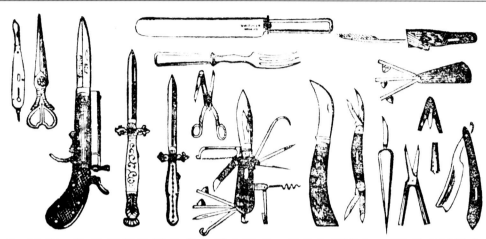

THE BREECH-LOADING PISTOL KNIVES,

INVENTED AND MANUFACTURED BY

UNWIN & RODGERS,

ROCKINGHAM WORKS,

124, ROCKINGHAM STREET, SHEFFIELD,

MANUFACTURERS OF

Table Knives and Forks; Shoe, Butcher, and Cook Knives; Spear, Dagger, and Bowie Knives; Pen, Pocket, and Strike-fire Knives; Lock Knives; Sailors', Gardeners' and Sportsmen's Knives; Farriers' Knives; Razors, Scissors, Lancets, Fleams, and all kinds of Cutlery. Plated Dessert Knives, Forks, Spoons, &c., in great variety.

FROM TWENTY TO THIRTY THOUSAND DOZENS GENERALLY IN STOCK.

CORPORATE MARK, NON * XLL.

Prize Medals of the Exhibitions of 1851 and 1862 were awarded to Unwin and Rodgers

Viners

This firm grew from humble beginnings to become the largest cutlery factory in Sheffield after the Second World War. Its specialities were household plated holloware and flatware, including all types of table-knives.

The founders were a large Jewish family (originally named Viener), who came to England from Germany in the late nineteenth century. By the turn of the century, they were travelling salesman and peddlers throughout the UK. Ruben Viner, who eventually became the dominant individual in the business, was the son of Adolph Viner (d. 1953) and was born in Newcastle-upon-Tyne in 1907. Amongst the products they sold was cutlery, which led to contacts with Sheffield firms.

In about 1900, the Viner family, which included the father and five brothers, settled in Sheffield. In 1908, they occupied the Tiger Works in West Street, where the oldest brother, Willie, became the driving force. Recalled Ruben: 'As was not unusual in those days, they lived on the premises. This was most useful and probably considered essential as it enabled them not only to put in a full day's work, but a full night as well, to the great delight of Mr Willie, who appeared to enjoy this immensely'.

By 1910 the members of the firm were listed in local directories as:

Viener, Adolphe	silversmith	378 Glossop Road
Viener, Emile	electroplate	378 Glossop Road
Viener, W. & E.	electroplate manufacturers	West Street
Viener, William	electroplate	378 Glossop Road

Two years later, the family moved to the Broomspring Works in Bath Street, where about 60–70 workers produced plated holloware. Viners became probably the first firm to produce this in such large quantities. The company's progress was briefly interrupted in 1914, when the brothers were briefly interned: but they were quickly released and contributed to the war effort by turning to the production of helmets.

Resourceful and hard-working, Viners were one of the few Sheffield cutlery firms to expand in the depressed inter-war period. In 1923, Plata Reuss was bought, which traded with South America. Then in the following year the business was incorporated as a private limited company, A. & E. Viener Ltd (it became Viners in 1925). Willie had left to go into retailing, while Ruben Viner had joined the business.

The company diversified into spoons and forks, especially in 35% nickel-silver, which it produced by a kind of consolidated 'little mester'-type operation. According to one trade journal:

> The company really developed and extended its activities by taking over a number of small companies engaged in the manufacture of different products, employing the ex-owners as managers, for whom they provided space, power, plant and machinery, as was the custom in those days. The managers had carte blanche to engage and remunerate anybody in the way that they wished, Viners guaranteeing to take the output produced at an agreed rate. The managers then paid out the workforce and kept the balance for themselves.

Amongst the failing firms taken over at this time was Thos Turner, which was absorbed in 1932. Two years later Ruben Viner became its manager and he ran it separately for the next twenty years. In about 1934 Viners became a public company, with the issue of £135,000 preference shares, with all the voting ordinary shares held by the Viner family. The workforce was then over a thousand. By the end of the 1930s, Viners had taken over the responsibility for all the staff on its premises, signifying its marked growth.

The company began making silver products at this time, as demand grew from places such as London. Profits increased steadily, despite the depression, from £31,296 in 1929, to £38,008 in 1940, and to £76,703 in 1946. The workforce, meanwhile, increased to about 1,250 at the end of the Second World War—a peak figure for the firm. In 1949, over seventy percent of the business was in stainless-, silver- and electroplated-holloware (often sold in canteens and cases); while a quarter of the trade was in other cutlery.

In the 1950s and 1960s, the pace at Viners began to quicken. In 1953, Thos Turner was taken over completely; and in 1959 Harrison Bros & Howson was acquired. By 1965 Viners employed 800, making it easily the largest cutlery factory in Sheffield. It was relatively progressive in its marketing and was one of the first Sheffield firms to hire designers and consultants to develop and advertise a brand image for the mass market. Ordinary shares in the business had been offered to the public in 1948, but the firm was still controlled by the Viner family, led by Ruben.

Ruben and his team began to reorganise the company, which until the late 1950s had been run as virtually a collection of separate workshops, on a more unified production-line basis. Manufacturing processes were simplified, the product-line drastically reduced (sterling silver tableware, for example, was gradually abandoned because it was selling too slowly) and cheaper styles of stainless cutlery were vigorously promoted. The impact of these changes at Viners was dramatic. In 1953, its turnover was £419,830; by 1974 it was over £7 million. Meanwhile, profits had jumped from about £65,000 to nearly £750,000.

In the middle of this boom, in about 1968, the board made a major strategic decision to embark upon a massive five-year expansion plan. Expensive capital equipment was installed (such as a computer-controlled electroplating plant) and

factories were acquired in Ireland, Australia and France. The new plant expanded production enormously, the assumption being that with a large enough marketing effort Viners could sell its productive capacity rather than simply make to meet a demand. Ironically, profits and market growth peaked at about the time Viners' investment plans were reaching fruition. After £1.2 million of investment in machinery between 1971 and 1976, internally-generated funds were not flowing strongly enough to finance the increase in working capital which accompanied higher output. Viners also proved highly vulnerable to the tide of Far Eastern cutlery imports, which by 1977 had a stranglehold of something like ninety percent of the UK demand for stainless steel flatware. Viners' reaction had been: 'If you can't beat 'em, join 'em', and the firm caused controversy in the city by importing its own Far Eastern cutlery to stamp as 'Sheffield made'. It was soon evident that profit margins on these pseudo-Viners' products were too thin to support the company. Crippled with interest charges on its loans, it was this development which toppled Viners over the edge. In 1980 Ruben Viner, who had been chairman since 1966, retired and only two years later his company went into receivership.

The Viners' name was then bought by a London cutlery distributor and it is now stamped on Korean imports.

Walker & Hall

In the world of the little mester, Walker & Hall was a giant; in fact, even amongst its big brothers in the cutlery trade, this firm was something out of the ordinary. If the contemporary reports are to be believed, Walker & Hall was easily the biggest employer in the cutlery trades before the First World War.

There are two accounts of the firm's birth. One is the Walker & Hall version as told prior to the First World War, which argues that the company began in about 1845 when George Walker, a working cutler, helped 'perfect' the process of electroplating with an Attercliffe surgeon, John

Wright. From this discovery, it is inferred, stemmed the whole electroplate industry of Britain. However, we should note that almost everyone else favours another version, which credits the Birmingham manufacturer, Elkington, with doing most to develop the electroplate process. This version argues that Walker & Hall's claims, made in the late nineteenth century, that they had developed electroplating are, to put it mildly, economical with the truth.

A less fanciful story from the historical records runs as follows: the firm was established in about 1845 by George Walker, a table-knife forger, who

Walker & Hall's factory and workforce in about 1918 (compared, inset, with the original premises).

had learned electroplate technology in Birmingham at the prompting of the first Sheffield licensee of the process, John Harrison. Walker used his new-found experience to take out a licence for himself and his partners, William Robson and Samuel Coulson. The firm was named Walker & Co. Following Robson's retirement in 1848, Henry Hall of Worcester joined the partnership, the firm becoming Walker, Coulson & Hall, electroplaters and gilders. When Coulson retired in 1853, the firm was renamed Walker & Hall and was located at the Electro Works in Howard Street.

In 1852, John E. Bingham (1839–1915), the nephew of Henry Hall, joined the firm and became partner. When Henry Hall retired in 1873, J.E. Bingham assumed sole control of the firm, bringing his brother, Charles H. Bingham (1848–1900), into the firm as partner. The Binghams became the

dominant influence in the business before the First World War. Indeed, they were 'men of mark' in Victorian and Edwardian Sheffield itself. *Sheffield and District Who's Who* (1905) described the business and public activity of Sir John Bingham (he was knighted in 1884) as 'of so comprehensive a character as to touch almost every department of local life'. He was often in the news with his forthright views on smoke abatement, tariff reform, and the dangers of granite setts (having once been thrown on his head, when his horse slipped on them). Observed one journalist: 'He is a man of strong antipathies. The mention of granite to him is worse than waving a red flag before a bull'. A Conservative, a zealous Protestant and prominent freemason, Bingham was twice Master Cutler in 1881 and 1884 (his brother held the office in 1894).

Like Dixon's, Walker & Hall's main line was in plated goods: the fancy entrée dishes, soup tureens, meat and venison dishes, tea trays, presentation plates and prize cups, beloved by the Victorian and Edwardian luxury market. The firm was though, increasingly making steel table cutlery, including knives of the best qualities. The firm had its own forging shop for producing double shear steel. One giant carving set made by Walker & Hall is in the possession of Cutlers' Hall. Perhaps the set was designed to show how well it could produce table cutlery, besides plated goods. Certainly the carving set is eye-catching: the ivory-hafted carving knife is nearly three-feet long (the blade itself some two-feet), while the matching fork (also in ivory) is over two feet long. All the firm's products, whether large or small, were stamped with the 'Flag' trade mark, a banner bearing the letters W & H, which was first registered in 1861.

W & H flags crowned Walker & Hall's Electro Works and being made of metal they always 'flew'! The works was a landmark in the city centre. One writer noted in 1893: 'the firm have in their employ nearly 1,000 workpeople, and their huge establishment, the result of many and frequent enlargements, is now one of the sights of Sheffield, particularly at night time, when its

hundreds of close-set windows, emitting a ray of light from within, present a very brilliant and striking scene indeed'.

The quarter century before the outbreak of the War in 1914 was evidently a time of steady expansion for the company. In 1892 Walker & Hall bought the manufacturing silversmiths, Henry Wilkinson & Co., in Norfolk Street. In the years immediately before the First World War the workforce is said to have hit the 2,000 mark, a veritable army, and a far cry from the score or so who started the business. Col. Sir John Bingham organised his staff like an army, too. According to local historian Martin Olive, the works was organised on semi-military lines, rank was strictly observed and staff and workpeople were forbidden to fraternise. Ambitious male employees, though, had use of the rifle range, as Sir John was a keen Volunteer and an early advocate of national service.

Walker & Hall combined with Mappin & Webb and Elkington to form British Silverware Ltd in 1963. Two years later the old Sheffield factory was demolished. However, due to industrial action, British Silverware was closed down in 1971 and Walker & Hall was revived as a retail firm, but only under the control of the Mappin & Webb group.

Walker & Hall trade mark on a large exhibition carving-knife. (Cutlers' Hall).

John Walters & Co.

Little is known of the early history of this firm, except that it first appears in Sheffield directories in 1841 as a maker of table- and dessert-knives and forks, and palette-knives. It was located in Burgess Street, close to the town centre. By 1846 it had moved to Carver Street, and had begun selling goods in German silver. In 1852 (the year after it won a prize medal at the Great Exhibition) it moved again: this time to the Globe Works, a large factory in Neepsend, which had been built in 1824 to house the steel business of William Ibbotson. By 1862, however, Ibbotson's had vacated the Globe Works and John Walters had taken over the whole factory. The company advertised its activities at the Globe Works as 'Manufacturers of Every Description of Table and Spring Cutlery', but they also traded as steel and tool merchants. In *Pawson and Brailsford's Illustrated Guide to Sheffield and Neighbourhood* (1862), Walters are described as being 'amongst the largest manufacturers of table knives . . . who send out goods not merely to the United Kingdom, but to America, the Continent, etc.' Its trade mark was a winged horse and the word SUPERLATIVE.

Walters' move into the Globe Works coincided with the heyday of the American trade, which the firm exploited. Cutlers' Hall has several fine Bowie knives made by Walters. One is a particularly large example (shown on page 28), with handle and blade measuring about twenty inches. The blade has a large clip, a sturdy steel crossguard and ornate stamped nickel-silver handle, while the ricasso carries the stamp, 'J. Walters & Co., Globe Works, Sheffield'. Particularly interesting are the numerous trade marks that run along the length of the blade: a liberty cap, a lion, a kneeling Indian with a bow and arrow, a buffalo (enclosing the mark XLNT), running hounds (over the words 'Best Quality'), a horseman (above the motto 'Rough & Ready'), and an American eagle surmounting the scrolled words, 'Hunting Knife' and 'California Knife'. Perhaps the knife was made as an exhibition piece: if not, if would have made a formidable weapon.

Another fine 16-inch Bowie knife made by Walters at the Globe Works has a horsehead pommel and ornate ferrule and crossguard (besides tortoiseshell scales and an acid-etched blade). A slightly smaller (14-inch spear-point Bowie with a false edge has attractive shielded grey buffalo horn scales: but its most notable feature is a handle mount featuring the renowned 'half-horse, half-alligator' motif. This folklore beast symbolized the 'Hunters of Kentucky' in an American song of the same name dating from the war of 1812.

Walters' pre-eminence and its occupancy of the Globe Works proved short-lived. For reasons unknown, the factory was occupied by Unwin & Rodgers in 1865, and Walters disappeared.

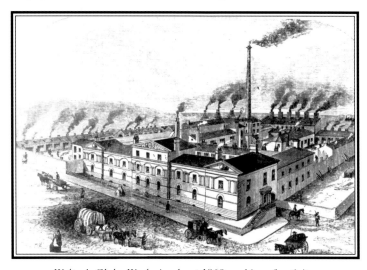

Walter's Globe Works in about 1860—a hive of activity.

The Globe Works in the 1990s—largely derelict,

John Watts

Most businesses are conservative, but occasionally, like some individuals, they can be eccentric. Watts was certainly in the latter category and always seems to have been something of an oddball. It had the most unusual early history of any Sheffield cutlery manufacturer. It was founded in 1765 in Lambert Street by Michael Shaw as a clog-clasp and dog collar maker. In 1790 it was taken over by John Shaw, who ran it until 1800, when Joseph Wilson became the owner. In 1830 the business was taken over by Bates and Watts; and in 1853, John Watts took control. As late as 1888, the firm was still described in directories as a clog-clasp manufacturer in Lambert Street, but John Watts died in 1895 and his son, John Robert Watts (1859–1939), became proprietor.

By then, the firm had emerged as a fully-fledged cutlery manufacturer, selling pen- and pocket-knives and razors, besides graining combs, skates clasps, stampers and piercers. J.R. Watts had a reputation as an innovator and he was one of the pioneers of the safety razor in the 1890s: his carbon steel wedge-blade razor with a guard beat Gillette by over a decade. John Watts was also said to have been a pioneer in many other articles, such as automatic razor-blade stropping machines and trouser presses. Indeed, although the firm remained well known for its knives until well after the Second World War, especially its gadget knives, it was notable for the range of products it made: clog-clasps, cloggers'-knives, toe-plates, abrasive-wheel dressers and cutters, ice skates, can openers, surgical scapels, wardrobe fittings and trousers-presses. It used the B4*ANY mark, formerly used by the merchants Frederick Ward & Co. The company was still listed at Lambert Street in 1995.

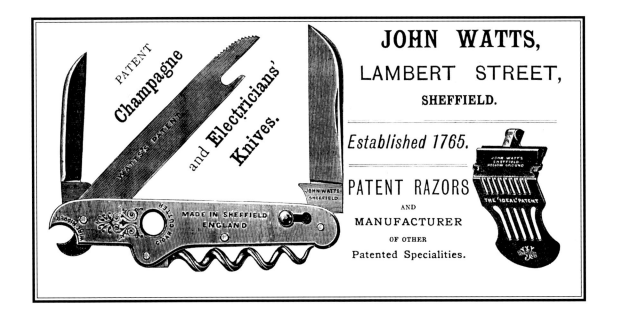

Joseph Westby

The founder of this business began his career with an apprenticeship at Brookes & Crookes in St Philip's Road. He was listed as a maker of knives in his own right at the Atlantic Works between 1876 and 1888. By 1893 he had set up on his account, the directories listing 'Westby Jsph., Levick & Co., Trippett Lane'. By 1913 Westby was listed at the Times Buildings in Bow Street, as well as at Trippett Lane. The firm manufactured pen- and pocket-knives. After the war, Westby moved to the Central Works at West Street and became one of the first firms to introduce stainless steel cutlery. He died in 1929, aged seventy-five. The firm moved to Furnival Street during the Second World War: it had ceased trading by 1965. I have not been able to trace a trade mark for this firm.

Wheatley Bros

This firm was a successful latecomer to the Victorian Sheffield cutlery scene, having been established in 1878 at the Eclipse Works, New George Street, by William Thomas Wheatley (1846–1912) and his brother, Sam V. Wheatley (d. 1887). They were the sons of John Rimmington Wheatley, who had founded a successful business for manufacturing mineral waters and cordials. By 1893, the Eclipse Works was situated in Boston Street, off the London Road, in Little Sheffield. By the turn of the century, about two hundred workers were employed there in the manufacture of a wide range of cutlery, scissors, razors and electroplate. Like many other plated wares firms, Wheatley Bros benefited from the consumer boom for luxury goods. It was a leading supplier to hotel proprietors of table cutlery, tea services, entrée dishes, electroplate on best nickel-silver, toast racks, spoons and forks. It also made (or merchanted) steel products, such as saws, files and joiners' tools. However, it also made traditional pocket-knives and hollow-ground razors, which it sold in competition with the Americans and Germans. W.T. Wheatley was a keen proponent of trade mark defence and supported the idea of a national trade mark for British manufacturers. Wheatley Bros' own mark was a wheatsheaf. On W.T. Wheatley's death in 1912, the firm became a limited liability company under his son William Ernest Wheatley (d. 1931). Before the First World War, the business was re-located to the Wheat Sheaf Works in John Street. In 1936 Wheatley Bros appears to have ceased trading and its marks were acquired by Needham, Veall & Tyzack's Eye Witness Works in Milton Street.

John Wigfall & Son

BONA FIDE.

Established in 1843; by the 1850s this business was located at 35 Howard Street and manufactured table-knives. The product-range expanded and by the end of the 1870s—when the firm occupied the Auckland Works in Eldon Street—shoe-, bread-, glaziers'-, farriers'-, table- and butchers'- knives were sold. In the 1880s, the company was also listed as a maker of electroplated goods. In March 1905, John Sidney Wigfall, who was presumably the son of the founder, was knocked down by a lorry outside North Shields railway station. He died a few days later on 30th March 1905, aged about fifty. Within six years the firm had gone out of business, though the trade mark— BONA FIDE—was acquired by Joseph Elliot.

John Wilson

This firm gave its own description of its place within the scheme of things: 'THE OLDEST AND FOREMOST FIRM IN THE WORLD specialising in the Manufacture of Butchers' and Provision Dealers' Cutlery'. It was founded in 1750 by Thomas Wilson, who was succeeded in the business by his son, John (d. 1849). The latter had four sons: John, William, Samuel and Thomas, with the last-named as partner between 1851 and 1897.

The business, according to R.E. Leader's *Reminiscences of Old Sheffield* (1876), seems to have started at Ran Moor or Hallam, then moved to Cross Smithfield in about 1750. According to Leader, Thomas Wilson was one of the most enterprising of the town's knifemakers:

> ...who first saw the possibility of dispensing with factors and of opening up connections of his own without the intervention of the middle-man. Determining to offer his knives—shoemakers' and butchers'—for sale himself, he packed up his goods and took them on his back into Lancashire. Whenever he sold any knives, he told the purchasers he should come again at a fixed period of time, and if the article did not suit he would return with the money. On his next journey he had no complaints, but so much greater demand that some of the retail shops would have purchased the whole of his stock, but he kept to his promise to the others. He readily sold all he had taken, and soon returned home to manufacture more goods with which to complete his journey.

By the early nineteenth century, the Wilson business was based in Sycamore Street and had one of the best-known marks in the cutlery industry—peppercorns and a diamond. According to a Sheffield newspaper in 1849, John Wilson 'was as well known to the town as the old church', and that 'he struck four peppercorns upon his wares as the old church strikes twelve'. In their marking the 'J' looks like an 'I', leading to the firm occasionally being referred to as I. Wilson.

Butchers'-, skinning-, farriers'-, flaying- and shoe-knives were amongst Wilson's chief products, all invariably hand-forged. It also made American-style 'Green-River' knives. Wilson's knives had a particularly high reputation in the nineteenth century, when its knives sold at a premium on the American frontier. Consequently, it was one of those firms with the biggest headache over the counterfeiting of its marks.

Thomas Wilson died in 1905. It is not known whether any more members of the family continued the business, but it remained in Sycamore Street after its sale to Frederick Ridgway in 1903.

The trade mark and name were later acquired by Elliot's of Sylvester Street.

Wilson, Hawksworth & Moss

This was one of the first firms to establish a reputation in America in the early nineteenth century. It was founded in 1825 by John Wilson and John Wilson Hawksworth, who manufactured cutlery and razors and also traded as general factors. John Wilson (d. 1848) had a works in Sycamore Street and the new firm rented from him a portion of these premises. His speciality was butchers'-knives, for which the firm had an excellent reputation.

The company's American representative after 1829 was Joshua Moss, who was so successful that he was offered a partnership in 1832, the firm's name being changed accordingly. In 1836, as trade expanded, the business was moved to Arundel Lane. Beeley Wood Works was also rented from Wilson for the manufacture of steel. There the firm not only made its own steel, it also forged it under water-powered tilt hammers and took on outside work.

Steelmaking brought even more orders from America, where Joseph Ellison was appointed in 1846 as representative (the firm's name being changed again). By the 1850s, when it built a new steelworks in the Don Valley, the firm was moving out of knifemaking—a trend hastened by the introduction of punitive American cutlery tariffs during the Civil War. In the early 1870s, under the direction of another new partner, Charles W. Kayser, knife manufacture was abandoned and the company, eventually known as Kayser, Ellison, launched itself on a career as one of Sheffield's leading special steelmakers.

Its trade marks in the 1880s were a padlock (picture) and the words MANUFACTURING UNION COMPANY.

Wingfield, Rowbotham & Co.

In its day, this was an important Sheffield cutlery firm. It was established in the late eighteenth century and by 1825 appears in Sheffield directories as Wade, Wingfield & Rowbotham. (This may have been the Robert Wade, who partnered William and Samuel Butcher.) By the late nineteenth century it was located in Tenter Street, in what one trade journalist described as 'old-fashioned two- and three-storied buildings', covering an acre. Two to three hundred hands found work there in 1890, producing saws, files and scissors, besides table- and pocket-knives. Wingfield, Rowbotham seems to have been unusual in that, like Rodgers and Turner's, it had the facility to convert and refine its own steel. Its products were destined for the UK and export markets, especially Australia, where it had an agent in Sydney. The trademark was the letter 'S' above crossed clay pipes; "AIGO" was also stamped on some of the firm's goods. Although it built up a successful business, this seems to have been dissipated in the 1890s through bad management. The cutlers, Christopher Johnson, stated in 1898: 'it is no secret they have been losing heavily for years, and we fear the late proprietors have little left of the large fortune their father left them. So much for underselling and low prices'. In that year, the business was bought by Thos Turner.

CORPORATE MARKS.

WADE, WINGFIELD,
&
ROWBOTHAM.

"AIGO."

WINGFIELD, ROWBOTHAM & CO.,

82, Tenter Street,

SHEFFIELD, ENGLAND.

STEEL CONVERTERS & REFINERS,

MANUFACTURERS OF EVERY DESCRIPTION OF

CAST, SHEAR, MINING, BLISTER & SPRING

STEEL.

TABLE AND SPRING CUTLERY.

RAZORS AND SCISSORS,

FILES, SAWS & MACHINE KNIVES,

Solid Cast Steel Engineers' Hammers & Mill Bills,

AND

GENERAL MERCHANTS.

10, GEORGE STREET,
EDINBURGH.

51, MITCHELL STREET
GLASGOW.

LONDON OFFICE:—

321, HIGH HOLBORN, W.C

George Wostenholm & Son

If Joseph Rodgers was the 'King' of nineteenth-century Sheffield cutlery, then the heir-apparent or brash pretender was 'Georgie' Wostenholm. This knifemaker was not much less ancient than Joseph Rodgers—Wolstenholme was an old Saxon name—but its rise was far more meteoric.

Rodgers was well established as a leading maker by the time Wostenholm's emerged as a serious challenger. The story began in the eighteenth century when a George Wolstenholme (b. 1717) was apprenticed as a cutler in Stannington. By 1745 he had set up his own business, which was later run by his son, Henry, who was one of the first cutlers to make spring-knives. The second George Wolstenholme (b. 1755), Henry's son, was the next recruit to the business and he partnered his father until the latter's death in 1803. George Wolstenholme then moved to Sheffield, first to Garden Street and then to Broad Lane. The next move was to the rear of the future site of Rockingham Works, which was built as the enterprise prospered. The Rockingham Works, constructed in 1815 and using steam power, was well timed to prosper from the marked expansion of the Sheffield knife trade at the end of the Napoleonic war.

The stage was set for the appearance of the most remarkable of the Georges in the family. George Wostenholm (the name was apparently shortened to facilitate its inclusion on knives) was born, on 31st January 1800, in Sheffield, and entered the industry by the classic route—apprenticeship to his father. In the early 1820s, his father brought him into the business, which was described in a Sheffield directory as 'George Wolstenholme & Son, manufacturers of table knives, and forks, pen, pocket, and sportsman's knives, and general dealers in cutlery, 78 Rockingham Street'. George Wostenholm was admitted as a freeman of the Cutlers' Company in 1826 and was granted the trademark he was to make world-famous—I*XL—

an old mark originally granted to one W.A. Smith in 1787.

So far, so good: but Wostenholm's was still only one firm amongst many and it was almost anonymous against the backdrop of the cutlery industry. Two things took the firm into a higher orbit: one was the personality of George Wostenholm, the other was the American trade.

Surviving photos of George Wostenholm show a stocky, thick-set man, with balding head and determined gaze. His whole personality seems to radiate energy, which exactly fits the first-hand

George Wostenholm (1800–1876).

descriptions we have of him. 'Enterprise', 'devotion to business', and 'unconquerable energy' were the adjectives that slipped most readily from the lips of his contemporaries. According to one observer, Wostenholm's 'whole thought and ideas—apart from realising a fortune—seemed to be centred in achieving in his cutlery the legend of his trade mark, I∗XL'. He was not only a practical cutler, well versed in the 'mysteries' of the trade, but a brilliant salesman, who cut his teeth, like John Rodgers, with some arduous business trips around England. There were also some less printable adjectives used about 'Georgie' by his employees, for undoubtedly he could be a ruthless and autocratic taskmaster. An excitable workaholic, he had a volcanic temperament which he did not hesitate to vent on subordinates. He used the 'bounty system' to bind men to him by advancing loans of £5 or £10 to be paid by installments; and enforced the rule of 'fourteen to the dozen' knives. But if he did not spare his workers, Wostenholm did not spare himself, either.

His ambition needed far more than the national stage, and, like many Sheffielders, it was in America that he found scope for his prodigious energies. A man of vision, he seems to have immediately recognised the importance of the USA to Sheffield's trade. In 1830 the two Wostenholms, father and son, launched a brief partnership with Sheffield salesman William Stenton. The latter began opening up the American market, largely as a reaction to a period of depression in 1830 which saw a surplus of stock build up in the works. George Wostenholm, who was to take control of the firm on the death of his father at the end of 1833, picked up on this lead and set out for America himself. We cannot be sure of the year, but it was probably 1831. He was to make about thirty visits to the country—no mean achievement when crossing the Atlantic could take weeks and was often hazardous. A New York office was opened and the I∗XL mark was also established on the distant West Coast. On his American visits, it was reported that Wostenholm thought nothing of travelling as far west as San Francisco merely to defend his name in a trade-mark court case.

Consequently, said one Sheffield newspaper: 'Probably no Sheffield face was so well known as his in America, and none of our people could vie more successfully than he with the business enthusiasm and push of the keenest New Yorker'.

For Wostenholm, America was the ideal market, as an expanding frontier meant an enormous demand for pocket-knives, ranch-knives and weapons. In fact, the firm's trade soon became almost exclusively American and, unlike Rodgers, George Wostenholm made almost no attempt to nurture other markets. This may have been short-sighted in the long-term, but it seemed beyond reproach at the time, as Wostenholm's business rocketed. His imagination fired by all things American, Wostenholm began thinking big. In 1848 he bought a tenement factory, which had been owned by a firm named Oakes, Tompkin & Co., and renamed it appropriately the Washington Works. Fronting Wellington Street and bounded by Bowdon and Eldon Street, the Washington Works was regarded as something new in Sheffield. Wrote one local historian:

> In previous generations, cutlery works in Sheffield had been virtually unknown, save those of very small character; the town had been hemmed round by the factories owned and run by the 'little mesters', but it was the American zeal for big things which inspired the acquisition of the big place in Wellington Street. When it was built, it was regarded as an unnecessary extravagance, and Sheffielders of small vision wagged their heads solemnly and waited for the crash, which never came.

Washington Works was not a factory in the modern sense and it still retained its tenement character—indeed that was partly why Wostenholm had bought it—but some benefit was derived from bringing so many workers and manufacturing processes under one roof. Despite his autocracy, Wostenholm earned the loyalty of his workforce as the orders from America rolled into the Washington Works. Although the US market was volatile and the firm was at the mercy of its financial panics, business grew steadily. By the mid-1850s, between 600 and 700 workers were

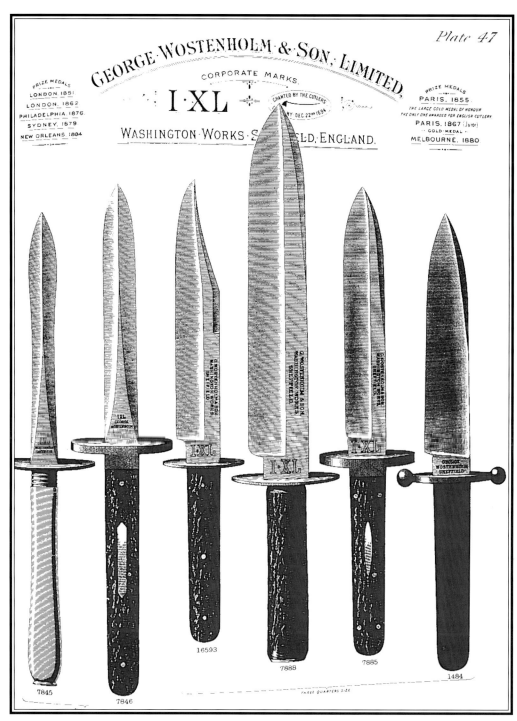

*1*XL Bowie-knives from a late 19th-century
Wostenholm catalogue.*

employed there, which shows how dramatically business had boomed. From almost nowhere, the firm was now breathing down the neck of Joseph Rodgers.

The products that poured out of the Washington Works during this golden age were heavily influenced by the American market. Examining the firm's records (many of which happily were rescued when the Washington Works closed and are now in Sheffield Archives), we can see that production was dominated by two lines: knives and razors. Wostenholm's could not hope to compete with Rodgers's spread of cutlery, so there were several lines that do not appear in Wostenholm catalogues—notably, silver- and electroplate and table cutlery. Instead, Wostenholm concentrated his energies on pocket-knives (the firm was said by the 1860s to be the largest maker of spring-knives in the town), ranch-knives (such as stock-knives and complicated horseman's pieces), hunting- and self-defence knives, and trade-knives. In other words, exactly the type of knives that would sell best in the USA.

It was not long before Wostenholm took a close look at the Bowie knife market. Surprisingly perhaps, given his early transatlantic journeys,

Wostenholm does not seem to have shipped many Bowie knives to the USA before 1848. Wostenholm Bowies marked 'Rockingham Works' exist, but they are rare. With the production facilities of the Washington Works at his disposal, however, he soon changed his mind and in the 1850s the firm became the most prolific maker of Bowie knives. An oft-repeated (but probably apocryphal) tale is that I✲XL Bowies were found on James Bowie's body at the Alamo. More certain is the fact that the firm's Bowies were all top-quality. They were made by its highly skilled forgers, grinders and polishers, ensuring that I✲XL Bowies, like many of those made in Sheffield in this era, are notable for using only the best materials. Alongside the I✲XL stamp, the blades are often decorated with acid-etchings that pander to American tastes and patriotic sentiments. These include eagles, General Zachary Taylor mounted on his horse 'Old Whitey', and slogans such as: 'AMERICANS ask for nothing but what is RIGHT and submit to nothing that is WRONG'. As American collectors have noted, quality was never sacrificed regardless of demand.

The same was true of the firm's spring-knives. Some of Wostenholm's pattern books have survived

Washington Works in about 1860.

from the 1850s and 1860s, and they show something of the care which the firm's cutlers lavished on its pocket-knives. Pearl and ivory scales, silver shields, milled linings, exquisitely filed blade-backs and springs, and pieces which bristle with useful tools—nothing appears to have been too much trouble! But then Georgie could be a difficult man to please.

As one of Wostenholm's managers said: 'The great leading aim of [his] ambition was 'quality', and a firm determination never to play second fiddle'. One of the firm's cutlers, Henry Coward (who was trained as a spring-knife cutler at the Works, before becoming a renowned and knighted musician), has left us with a vivid description of how that extra quality was achieved. Wrote Coward later:

> I used to marvel at the way he struck the blades on a tiny anvil to find out any defect. I thought, at the time, he was foolish to run such risks of breaking the blades. It was part of his plan, for above all he would have sound blades in every knife he sold . . . 'Drilling' was the term used to denote that critical examination of every knife which was a custom peculiar to Wostenholm's. While it was a good means of securing a high standard of work, and not unreasonable when carried out fairly, it could be, and often was, made a means of petty tyranny in the hands of the under-managers…When 'His Majesty' [G.W.] was in genial mood, as he could be, there was a rush to get the work examined, but when the 'Little Devil' was on the throne no one went unless forced.

Drilling had the desired effect, however, and soon the I✻XL stamp vied with Rodgers' star and Maltese cross as a badge of quality. Like Rodgers, too, Wostenholm made its share of superb exhibition pieces. At the Great Exhibition in 1851 Wostenholm displayed a set of ornate sheath knives, including a large dagger commissioned from the well-known artist Alfred Stevens. The firm grew accustomed to carrying off the prize medals at exhibitions in America, France and Australia. Many of the firm's exhibition pieces still survive, though sadly very few are owned by English museums and collectors.

In the 1850s and early 1860s, George Wostenholm was at the height of his powers. He would ride into work each day on horseback, with such regularity that people would set their watches by him. So busy was he, that even at church he would sometimes be seen reading business letters. He also declined various public offices to further pursue his business interests, including that of Master Cutler (though he eventually agreed to serve in 1856). He was, however, a JP and had a few interests outside his firm, one of which was the chairmanship of Truswell's Brewery. The only thing that seems to have really interested Wostenholm outside the Washington Works was property development and land speculation. As early as 1835, he began buying up land around Cherry Tree Hill at Nether Edge and decided to build himself a house there and a suburb. Naturally, given Wostenholm's standing in the community and his wealth, it could be no ordinary pile. With the help of a leading architect and landscape gardener, Wostenholm built the Kenwood Estate, at the centre of which was a large stone mansion, 'Kenwood'.

At Kenwood, George Wostenholm lived in some style with his wives (he was married three times) and several servants. This was Wostenholm's 'kingdom', which was modelled, so it is said, along the lines of the country estates he had seen in upstate New York. Not only did Wostenholm landscape the grounds of Kenwood, he also influenced the layout of the surrounding roads, one of which was named appropriately Washington Road. While he may not have surpassed John Rodgers in the business of making cutlery, Wostenholm definitely has had the last laugh from beyond the grave. While John Rodgers' Abbeydale House has fallen into decay, Kenwood still retains something of the splendour its creator intended. Walking around the pleasant, leafy roads of Kenwood and the beautiful grounds of the house (which are now owned by a hotel), is a fine way of appreciating the unprecedented wealth and social standing of its first owner.

George Wostenholm was active until the end, though he sold out to his business associates in

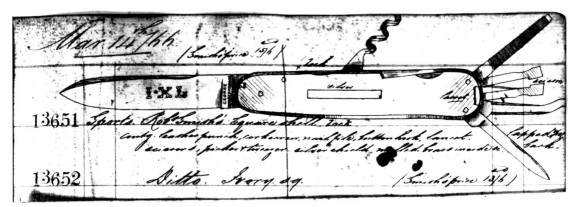

Wostenholm pattern book, with an I*XL *knife drawn in 1866. (Sheffield Archives).*

1875, when Wostenholm's became a limited liability company with a paid-up capital of £43,400 and over 500 workers. Perhaps this was Wostenholm's recognition that, after a period of ill-health, the end was not far away. He died at Kenwood in the following year on 18th August 1876. Local obituarists were not entirely uncritical. The *Sheffield Independent* stated: '[Wostenholm] was as most of us are, a mixture of good and evil, of weakness and strength'. But everyone paid tribute to his single-minded determination and business acumen, and his dogged battle against illness. There is a characteristic story of him on his death bed asking to examine a set of Wostenholm knives. As one obituarist remarked: 'It would certainly have conduced more to his comfort and might probably have prolonged his days if he had in his late years devoted less thought and time to business; but it was not in the nature of Mr Wostenholm to do so'. Wostenholm left a fortune of £250,000—an astonishing sum for the time and far larger than any cutlery manufacturer until that date.

Like many great men, his death marked the end of an era, though in retrospect we may appreciate that the cracks were beginning to appear in the I*XL empire before 1876. The American trade began to contract after the Civil War and so too, it appears, did the size of Wostenholm's workforce. One official report stated in 1865 that the number of workers at the Washington Works was only 300–400, a significant fall from the 1850s. Even

George Wostenholm would have known that America was no longer the country he had first visited in the 1830s—the place where the Sheffield manufacturer had simply to arrive with his sample case and return loaded up with orders. The 'heroic' age of the American frontiersman was passing: the Indians had been banished to the reservations, the buffalo were gone, and cowboys and gamblers settled their differences with a revolver, not a knife. The Bowie knife was passing into history and folklore. Moreover, the Americans were no longer content simply to import Sheffield knives, wonderful though these were. They had begun to manufacture their own and began using machinery to give them a competitive edge. To protect American industry, 'Brother Jonathan' left nothing to chance. Hefty tariffs were placed on imported Sheffield knives, pricing most of them out of the market. Thus as George Wostenholm was laid to rest in All Saints Parish Churchyard, in Ecclesall, the problems for his successors were only beginning.

After Wostenholm's death, the company made steady progress for the first decade or so after 1876, and good profits were made. But the American Tariff of 1890 raised the duties on Wostenholm's US imports to unprecedented heights and caused a crisis at the company. Its directors were most reluctant to abandon such a profitable market, however, and did all they could to resurrect the trade—alas, unsuccessfully.

Meanwhile, they attempted to break into new markets, such as Australia, confident that 'goods of the quality and style such as we produce, could and would make their way very rapidly, and hold it firmly, in any market where they are introduced with ability and energy. Such has never failed to be the invariable rule of the past'. Such complacency did not bode well and Wostenholm's efforts in Australia, a market the Sheffield directors never seem to have visited, were largely a failure, too. These Colonial markets, less prosperous than America, demanded more mundane knives than Wostenholm's were often prepared to supply, and were already thick with competitors.

Like Rodgers, Wostenholm's had passed its peak in the decade before the First World War. Its workforce of 700–800 in 1890 had fallen to about 650 in 1900 and 400 by the outbreak of the War. Further contraction occurred between 1914 and 1918, when Wostenholm's quality pocket-knife trade was severely disrupted and the firm was also hit by rising costs of raw materials and wages. Wostenholm's workforce halved in the war to about 200, and some 36 men never returned from the trenches. Unable to compete effectively, even at the high-quality end of the market, the famous

Washington Works was looking increasingly dated.

Fortunately, in 1922 the overall management of the company passed to Frank Colver (1873–1954), a relatively dynamic director, who was keen to push Wostenholm's towards a more modern and mechanised future. Despite some bitter opposition from Wostenholm's old-guard, Colver overhauled the antiquated administration at the Washington Works and installed American machines for making pocket-knives.

Colver's initiatives in the immediate post-war era were partly successful, but they did not go far enough to change Wostenholm's conservative outlook. It unfortunately fell between two stools: committed to producing its traditional spring-knives, it proved unable to maintain the quality in the face of the declining number of craftsmen and changes in demand. As one director stated in 1925: 'our old reputation will no longer secure us the trade we want. The market now is competitive and to make goods above the ordinary, means a very small trade because of the price and the difficulties to persuade a shopkeeper to speculate'. On the other hand, it was unable to embrace fully the idea of machine production, which its directors felt was akin to renouncing the firm's heritage. Certainly,

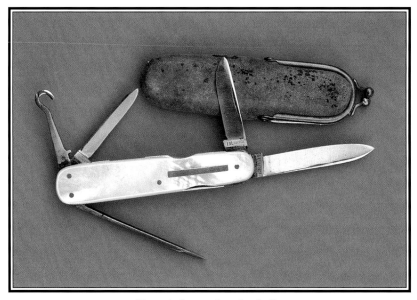

Wostenholm pearl pocket-knife.

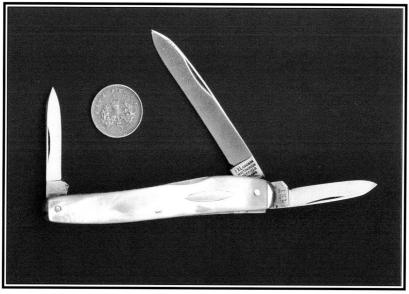

Wostenholm 3-blade pocket-knife, with delicate bolsters to protect the pearl.

the depression did not help, either, and for most of the 1920s and 1930s Wostenholm's struggled to make a profit or pay dividends. In fact, in the mid-1920s the firm almost went under and only survived after an appeal to the shareholders.

After the Second World War, when part of the Washington Works was destroyed by a German bomb, Wostenholm's was poorly positioned to make the most of the economic upturn in the late 1950s and early 1960s. Competition was also growing from the Far East, which was eventually to drive Wostenholm's out of business. In 1971 it was bought by Joseph Rodgers and, while the Washington Works was demolished, the new company (Rodgers-Wostenholm) moved to Guernsey Road. In 1975 this joint-firm was bought by Richards, which in turn was bought by the American firm, Imperial Knife, in 1977. The business never made money for its American owners, however, and by 1983 the Richards-Rodgers-Wostenholm group of companies was bankrupt. The I*XL mark is now owned by Egginton Bros, Sheffield, who continue to use it on pocket-knives, which have little in common with old Wostenholm knives apart from the mark.

It was a sad end for a company that had once hit the heights and had done so much to enhance Sheffield's reputation as a cutlery centre. Rodgers may have been the dominant Sheffield cutlery firm in the nineteenth century, but it was George Wostenholm who was arguably the most dynamic and successful individual Sheffield knifemaker. If Rodgers summon up images of the great days of the Empire, Wostenholm's name and I*XL are forever linked with the frontier era of the American Wild West.

Stock-knife made in the late 1970s after the merger of Wostenholm with an American company.

Eric Wragg

After the 1960s, Eric M. Wragg (1920–1994) was almost the only high-class maker of Bowie and sport's-knives in Sheffield. He was born in Edale, Derbyshire, the son of William Henry Wragg and his wife, Jessie, née Marshall. The family was steeped in the cutlery trade and Eric was the last of four generations of knifemakers. In 1871, his father had established his business of W.H. Wragg in the Horn Works in Cambridge Street. Eric recalled: 'My father was a good cutler and my grandfather was a very proud man, they would both work for honour and not for money. We were always short'. However, W.H. Wragg made knives of the highest class: sport's-knives, folding hunting-knives and Bowie knives. A trade card for the firm shows that he was the patentee and manufacturer of the 'Explorer's Knife and Tool Roll' and the 'Emigrant's Knife and Tool Roll'.

Eric was educated in Sheffield at Lydgate Lane School, in Crookes, and at the age of eleven or twelve began to come down to the workshop with his father. However the 1930s were bad times for the spring-knife trade and Eric's father had to take on part-time work, such as playing the piano every night in pubs, to earn a living. Eric's mother died when he was fourteen (at about the time he left school) and then at the age of eighteen, in 1938, he joined the Royal Artillery.

His career as a knifemaker did not begin in earnest until 1946, when he was demobbed and joined his father at 100 Rockingham Street, where they rented a workshop from William Morton & Sons. They operated as little mesters making knives for local shops and firms (such as Elliot, Petty, Taylor's Eye Witness, and Morton), London retailers (such as Clements and Selfridge) and American customers. He took over the business on the death of his father in 1955.

Like his father, Eric specialised in the best classes of sport's- and hunting-knives. These included such old nineteenth-century favourites as the folding Bowie, a very difficult knife to make technically. He also made scout's-knives, lock-knives and stencil-knives. Eric was also skilled enough to make a knife from a customer's specification.

Eric Wragg.

He married in 1943 and he and his wife, Edith, had one son, named John, who did not follow him into the trade. In the late 1950s, Eric moved to a workshop in West Street and continued his knifemaking, though by now it was becoming increasingly difficult to earn a living as a little mester. The demand from private clients for custom-made knives was not yet strong enough to support him fully and finding the materials (springs, blades and scales) was becoming even more difficult as the industry declined around him.

Between 1965 and 1983, he therefore became a part-time telephonist, but continued to make knives part-time from mid-morning to late afternoon. He did so, explains his son, because 'he enjoyed the job very much—in fact, he loved it. That is why he continued making knives part-time until his retirement in 1985'. A cheerful and outgoing man, he also regularly lectured about the cutlery trade to women's groups, to businessmen and to schoolchildren.

John Wragg & Son

 Wragg was a common name in the Sheffield cutlery trade, though this John Wragg made his fortune in other ways. He came to Sheffield from his native Derbyshire in 1835, aged twenty-two, and by the 1840s had built up a highly successful business in Bath Street importing and selling eggs. 'Wragg's Pickled Eggs' became a household word in Sheffield.

John Wragg's eldest son, Thomas (d. 1919), took over the business on his father's death in about 1887. However, his youngest son, Joseph, seems to have decided to branch out into cutlery manufacture and (perhaps with his father's backing, or with his own money from the egg business) took over the Advance Works in Denby Street (formerly New Thomas Street), Little Sheffield. The business was launched as John Wragg & Son, with Joseph apparently running the firm. The contemporary trade press gives the impression that the Wraggs built the Advance Works, but this was inaccurate. A trade advertisement in a Sheffield directory in 1876 shows quite clearly that the factory was owned (and probably built) by Edwin Blaydes & Co. Wraggs appear to have taken it over in the late 1870s or early 1880s and then expanded it. By the 1890s, the factory was a relatively large three-storied affair having a frontage of 126 feet. Two gateways led into the Advance Works, which had two courtyards and three rows of workshops to the rear of the main block. The firm's corporate mark (originally Blaydes')—two knife blades crossed—was stamped on the firm's wide-ranging product-line: table- and butcher-knives, pocket-cutlery, razors, and camp- and dagger-knives. The firm's *Illustrated Catalogue* was said to feature about a thousand illustrations of the company's cutlery items. Wragg's also supplied other cutlery houses with finished goods and raw materials, such as scales, forks and blades. A wide export trade was done with the Americas, Germany, France, Austria, Denmark, Switzerland and Bohemia.

Despite the eulogies in the trade press, Wragg's never seems to have realised its potential. Perhaps Joseph Wragg was over-ambitious or simply a bad manager. By the early 1890s, workshops at the Advance Works were already being rented to separate businesses. Then, in about 1900, the Advance Works was sold to W.R. Humphreys, and Wragg's name disappeared from the cutlery sections of the Sheffield trade directories (though the egg importing business flourished as a family firm until at least the 1950s). Joseph Wragg died in 1904, aged fifty-one.

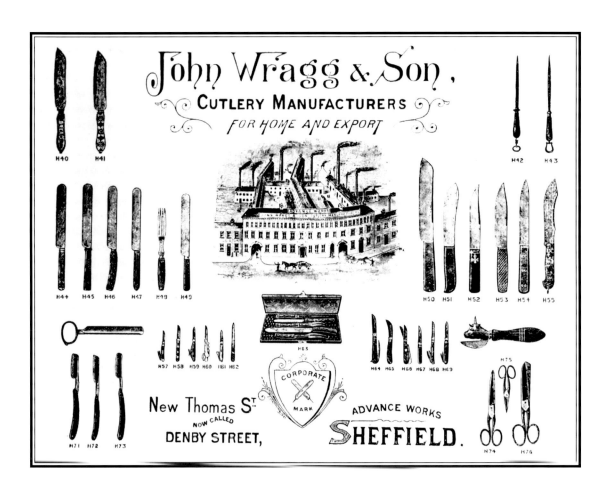

A Note on Identifying and Dating Sheffield Knives

WITH THE EXCEPTION of silver-bladed knives, there is no simple way of assessing the age or provenance of a knife. Historians and collectors examining old Sheffield knives will usually evaluate them by a number of criteria: the type of steel, handle material, markings, trade mark, quality and style. None of these yardsticks alone is enough to give all the answers. Yet together, they may provide that indefinable something called 'feel', which, while not as good as an exact date and identity, will often give a reasonable idea about when and where a knife was made.

In pondering some of these variables, the collector or historian will have in mind some of the historical events already described in Part One. They will know, for example, that stainless steel was discovered in 1913 and that not until after the First World War was the commercial production of stainless cutlery fully underway (and, that even then, carbon steel was still widely used for pocket-knife blades). They will know that the 1920s and 1930s were the last decades when shear steel was used for knives. They will be aware that pen-machines and pen-knives (for cutting quills) were essentially Victorian products, and not widely made outside that era. Likewise, big horseman's-knives soon became obsolete after the 1920s. Our knowledgeable collector/historian will also be able to evaluate some of the stylistic and functional elements in a knife. Even the nail mark in a Sheffield knife may provide helpful information (a 'long-pull', or French nailmark, for example, in which the mark runs in a straight line along part of the blade, denotes a knife that was probably made in the late nineteenth century). Similarly, even the shape of the 'kick' may help roughly to date the knife: a narrow, square kick was very typical of knives produced up to the 1850s.

Perhaps the most useful single piece of information that will be seen on a knife will be the maker's name, usually stamped on the tang. Almost all knives carry a maker's name of some description (though I have seen some splendid anonymous Sheffield knives, even exhibition pieces, which are unstamped, perhaps because cutlers made them in their own time). Usually, the city's knives are stamped 'Sheffield', too. 'England' was also sometimes stamped on knives for export, especially those sent to America after the McKinley Tariff Act of 1890, which required a country-of-origin mark on all foreign knives.

The maker's name is invaluable because it can provide an entrée to the historical sources. Sheffield directories have been published from the late eighteenth century up to 1974 and (at their most detailed) these give alphabetical company listings, classifications of trades, besides advertisements and information on trade marks. With a little research, the life dates of a company or cutler and a location can be traced. Naturally, there are drawbacks to using this source. Directories were not published every year, they are incomplete and the information was often out of date. Nevertheless, they can provide priceless leads and were used extensively for this book. Directory-based information can allow knife-makers to be tracked in the Census (though a lack of time prevented me utilising this source); or it can be combined with other information, such as newspaper obituaries.

Whatever the name on the tang, some of the characteristics of the Sheffield cutlery industry should be borne in mind. A 'maker's' name may not always be quite what it seems. Some 'manufacturers' were actually merchants, though they tended to give the impression in directories that they were fully-fledged makers. Again, makers not only made for themselves, but for each other, so that a maker's name does not always mean that the knife was made in a specific factory (nor would all the processes on a knife be executed in one factory or by a single maker). Rodgers are said to have made knives for many other firms, when times were busy—even Wostenholm! Many of the leading special steelmakers, who did not make cutlery at all, had their own branded knives made locally. For example, in the 1920s the giant local engineering firm, Thos Ward, advertised a range of table cutlery and pocket-knives, stamped 'Wardonia'. These were almost certainly 'contract' goods made for Ward's by local cutlery firms.

Sometimes, a name on a knife tang does not match with any Sheffield information. Assuming that the knife was made in Sheffield (and by the late nineteenth century, almost every knife in the country was made there), this may simply mean that it was made for a retailer in London or Birmingham. Sheffield firms made large quantities of knives for retailers all over the country, especially in London, and were quite happy to stamp the buyer's name and mark on them. Some of the early nineteenth-century Bowie knives carry London retailers' names and addresses, though the knives could not have been made anywhere but Sheffield. Similarly, any English nineteenth-century multi-blade or horseman's-knife was almost certainly made in Sheffield, whatever the mark states. The Victorian knives in many London distributor's catalogues, such as those for the Army & Navy Stores and for A.M. Silber, show Sheffield-made (though not Sheffield-marked) knives.

Trade marks can provide another clue to dating and identification, and here Sheffield has been fortunate: the Company of Cutlers, which regulated the industry and always controlled marks, has kept

a continuous run of registers from 1624. These records are currently being analysed and computerised in a joint project by Sheffield University and the Cutlers' Company. A preliminary report on the project's findings is to be published by Joan Unwin in a forthcoming history of the Company. The earliest marks, up to 1791, are recorded in the Company's so-called Great Mark Book, which has about 6,600 cutlers' marks. After 1791, a change in the registration procedures meant that numbers were used for a time (beginning at No. 91), until 1814 (when No. 3,694 was reached).

At first, marks were used purely to identify a craftsman's work; but gradually, the idea developed that marks might convey information to the purchaser, even that they might have a commercial value in their own right as a 'trade mark'. Because of Sheffield's close identification with quality and as it was almost impossible for a consumer to assess the quality of steel by any practicable methods (other than by extended use), Sheffield became perhaps the most committed user (and defender) of trade marks in the world. The town became, as one journalist remarked, 'the very metropolis and headquarters of trade marks'.

After 1814, when the relaxation of the Company of Cutlers' laws meant that anyone could claim a mark, the heyday of corporate marks began. As one Wostenholm director expressed it:

> Many people who cannot read English buy our goods, Chinese for instance . . . and I have heard say those on the Pacific Coast will not buy a knife unless these strange marks I*XL are on the side of the blade. You will see, therefore, when dealing with foreign markets, how important it is to have a very distinctive mark—we must presuppose in the purchaser not only ignorance of quality, dense ignorance even, but also ignorance of the English language.

As the cutlery trade expanded in the nineteenth century, marks reached an unprecedented level of refinement and artistic invention. An interesting article could be written on the development and iconography of Sheffield marks, but here we can only discuss their importance in knife identification.

The best way of tracing manufacturers' trade marks is from the records of the Company of Cutlers. This is not a source that is available to most, so it is fortunate that several published listings are available. W.C. Leng's *List* (c. 1880) was the first; but the most comprehensive nineteenth-century compilation was *White's Hardware Trade Marks* (1892). These listings were supplemented by published Cutlers' Company *Registers* (edited by Whitham and Vickers/Sykes, 1919, 1953). In addition, the Sheffield trades directories often included information on Sheffield marks. Modern collectors' guides, such as Goins (1986) and Levine (1993) are useful, too.

Unfortunately, although most firms had a mark (and in compiling the profiles in Part Two, I only found one or two firms which appear to have never registered a mark), they did not always use them. This was especially so on pocket-knives. Some-times the blades or tools may have been too small for stamping or etching; perhaps it was cheaper to dispense with marking altogether; and one also suspects that sometimes firms simply did not bother with the mark, once they had registered it. A firm's commitment to its mark seems to have varied with its size and reputation. For example, Joseph Rodgers and Wostenholm always seem to have used their mark on their knives. Smaller firms evidently did not. So, simply because a knife does not carry a maker's trade mark does not mean it is not genuine.

However, a famous mark also brought its own problems, since it could be counterfeited. The stamping of Rodgers' star and Maltese Cross on 'false wares' was a major headache for the firm in the nineteenth century, as was the illicit use of I*XL for Wostenholm. Fraudsters (which were often the hated Germans) would use either a counterfeit

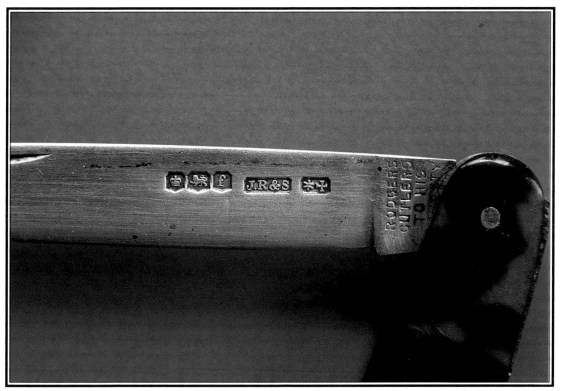

Hallmarks on this Joseph Rodgers' silver fruit-knife allow the precise dating of this knife to 1923.

mark or a similar-sounding Sheffield company name—such as Rogers or J. Wostenholm. Look-alike marks were another favourite subterfuge, no more so than with the world-famous I*XL. The number of manufacturers who paid George Wostenholm a back-handed homage by registering a look-alike mark is its own comment on the spread of this Sheffield firm's reputation. Amongst the imitation marks were:

NON-XLL	Joseph Allen, Sheffield
XLNT	Walter's Globe Works, and later Kastor, N.Y., and other makers
XXL	J.W. Billings, Sheffield
XL ALL	Parkin & Marshall, Sheffield
UN-X-LD	Northfield Knife Co, Connecticut
XLCR	W. Bingham, Cleveland, Ohio

Naturally, this type of mimicry and outright counterfeiting can fool the unwary collector, who must also be aware of another pitfall. Trade marks sometimes kindled such intense brand loyalty that they endured long after the original firm had departed. As should be apparent from Part Two, when firms became bankrupt the trade marks were often bought and sold like any other asset. As the Sheffield knife industry declined, several firms Elliot, Taylor's Eye Witness and Slater are good examples—clung onto old marks like life-jackets. By the 1950s, Elliot's had over 30 registered marks. Sometimes a well-known mark would only be sold once or twice and its history will therefore be easy to follow. However, the trail can be more complex. For example, the DEFIANCE trade mark, with its picture of a cannon, was made famous by Abram Brooksbank. I have however, also seen the same mark used by the razor maker, Charles Pitts; George Wilkin, the scissor manufacturer; and John Bedford, the steelmaker. Only the most dedicated researcher (and this historian is not amongst them) can hope to solve these riddles, if then.

Fortunately in modern times, the counterfeiting of antique Sheffield knives themselves has not been a major problem for collectors. Almost no

makers are left now with the skill to make, for example, a nineteenth-century multi-blade, and even if they could it would be economically more worthwhile for them to make knives stamped with their own name. Sheffield Bowie knives, however, have been counterfeited and some American collectors have been stung in recent years (though, in terms of how much value Americans have had out of Sheffield over the years, they are probably well ahead collectively). The repair of old knives, with new blades and parts, is another grey area, which the collector can only counter by common sense and scepticism.

With silver knives, we are on safer ground. The blades (or outer scales) on these knives are usually hallmarked, with a place code (for Sheffield, it was a crown), a date stamp, and a maker's mark, amongst others. In identifying marks the reader can refer to published listings of silver hallmarks, such as *Miller's* (1994) and *Fallon* (1992), though there are several other handbooks and guides.

One final marking may prove helpful: the Royal imprimatur, indicating that the firm had secured a Royal Warrant for its products. The number of Sheffield firms allowed to use these marks was very small: Joseph Rodgers; Harrison Bros & Howson; and Mappin & Webb. In these cases the Royal initials around a crown and the words 'His Majesty', or 'Her Majesty' may date a knife. The markings were:

G	(crown)	R	Georgian, up to 1830
W	(crown)	R	William IV, 1830–1837
V	(crown)	R	Victoria, 1837–1901
E	(crown)	R	Edward VII, 1901–1910
G	(crown)	R	George V and VI, 1910–1952

'Royal' markings, too, it should be noted, could be used spuriously. This leads to a final suggestion, which may already be apparent: when looking at any antique, judge it on its merits, as well as on its name and mark.

Places to Visit

IT USED TO BE SAID, quite accurately, that Sheffield was one of the worst places in the country to buy cutlery—the main reason being that so many people worked in the industry that they could usually get their cutlery through the trade. It might also be argued that Sheffield has never been one of the best places to actually see old Sheffield knives on display.

It is not that Sheffield does not have fine cutlery in its collections—the places listed below have some of the best Sheffield knives ever made—but taken as a whole, the city has done a poor job of preserving its cutlery past (just as the industry has performed dismally in publicising itself). Not until 1982 did Sheffield open a major industrial museum: this was well over a century after a local man, William Smith, had urged the creation of a permanent display for Sheffield's unique skills. Sheffield Museum has acquired a large collection of knives (and other artefacts) over the years, but its actual display has always been relatively small and low-key. In the early 1990s, in a surprising decision, the Museum's cutlery exhibit was partly dismantled in an economy drive.

In nearly twenty years, I cannot recall a single major cutlery exhibition (or publication) sponsored by the City. At present, the City's Museums have only one curator for industrial history. Quite why that should be so, when the City has poured millions into costly fiascoes such as the World Student Games, perhaps only Sheffield City Council and its taxpayers can explain.

Cutlers' Hall has an impressive display of knives, but overall its collection does not do justice to a body that has been headed for centuries by the leaders in the cutlery trade. Put simply, the former Masters Cutler never saw knives as something which should be systematically collected or preserved (maybe they saw too much of them at work). Whatever the reason, it must be counted as a loss to the city that, while private collectors (mostly American) have steadily stripped the industry of many of the best of Sheffield's knives, no one at the Company of Cutlers (at least until recently, under Master Cutler Raymond Douglas' stewardship) had the initiative to build up the cutlery collection into something greater. The Company's tastes have always tended in the direction of fancy silverware, where it has found benefactors.

Significantly, it was left to a private collector (Ken Hawley) to provide the impetus for the first real knife exhibition for many years in Sheffield in 1995. He has been one of the few Sheffielders to stem the inexorable flow of old Sheffield cutlery and tools to collectors across the Atlantic. Now that Sheffield Museum has at last (in October 1995) reopened its cutlery galleries and now that the Cutlers' Hall has found a new awareness of its undoubted potential as a repository of the city's knifemaking past, perhaps Sheffield will at last begin to do justice to the skills of its former generations.

Notwithstanding, all the places listed overleaf are worth a visit.

Abbeydale Industrial Hamlet:
A restored eighteenth-century scythe and steel works in a rural setting. Although it did not make knives, Abbeydale (which was owned by a family named the Tyzacks) provides a marvellous insight into the Sheffield trades. Besides a water wheel and grinding shops, not the least of the attractions is the world's only surviving crucible steel furnace.
Abbeydale Road South, Sheffield S7 2QW.
Tel: (0114) 236 7731.

All Saints Parish Church:
For those whose tastes run to the funerary, this graveyard is a cutlers' Necropolis. Many of the most famous names in Sheffield cutlery are buried here: Wostenholm, Rodgers, Mappin, to name only a few.
Ecclesall, Sheffield.

Assay Office:
Excellent library and some fine Sheffield silver-ware, including knives. Visits by appointment.
PO Box 187, 137 Potobello Street,
Sheffield S1 4DS.
Tel: (0114) 275 5111

Company of Cutlers in Hallamshire:
Small, but select collection of knives, which includes the Rodgers' Norfolk Knife. Visits by appointment.
Cutlers' Hall, Church Street, Sheffield S1 1HG.
Tel: (0114) 272 8456.

Kelham Island Industrial Museum:
Covers all aspects of the Sheffield trades, with displays of knives and a restored cutler's workshop. Little mester Graham Clayton (virtually the last in the trade) shows visitors how knives are still made by the traditional Sheffield methods. The old industrial area

surrounding the Museum is fascinating, with many old factories to be seen, such as James Dixon's Cornish Place Works.
Alma Street, Sheffield S3 8RY.
Tel: (0114) 272 2106.

Ruskin Gallery:
Occasionally hosts exhibits relevant to Sheffield cutlery, especially from the Hawley Trust Collection.
101 Norfolk Street, Sheffield S1 2JE.
Tel: (0114) 273 5299.

Sheffield City Library:
The Local Studies Department has an outstanding collection of books, articles, trade catalogues, directories and photographs on Sheffield cutlery.
Surrey Street, Sheffield S1 1XZ.
Tel: (0114) 273 4712.

Sheffield City Museum:
Contains the city's largest collection of Sheffield knives, with a good display of Joseph Rodgers' knives.
Weston Park, Sheffield S10 2TP.
Tel: (0114) 276 8588

Shepherd Wheel:
An early water-powered grinding wheel (dating from the late sixteenth century) on the Porter Brook. It is thought to have been used primarily for the grinding of table- and other domestic-knives as well as pen- and pocket-knives.
Whiteley Woods, Sheffield S11.
Tel: (0114) 236 7731.

Victoria and Albert Museum:
Some Sheffield knives, mainly pre-1800.
Cromwell Road, South Kensington,
London SW7 2RL.
Tel: (0171) 938 8500.

Sources

THE BEST WAY OF LEARNING about old Sheffield knives is to look at them and handle them, but even the best artefacts mean nothing without further information on the historical context. This often needs to be sought in manuscript and printed sources.

What sources did I use for this book? Undoubtedly, the best materials for reconstructing the past are the business records of the firms themselves—their letters, minute books, accounts, billheads and pattern books. Unfortunately, only for a minority of firms do such records survive. This is partly due to the fact that many records have been destroyed over the years. Company takeovers, neglect and the fact that many businessmen have not thought their records worth preserving, have all taken their toll. Moreover, many Sheffield cutlery firms were quite small, often no more than one-man businesses, which often meant that detailed accounting and managerial records were sparse in the first place.

However, in some cases we have been lucky. Sheffield City Library Archives contain some very useful collections of business records on the cutlery industry. Easily the most important is the George Wostenholm collection, which is probably the largest group of cutlery manuscripts for one firm in the world. Although few records pre-date George Wostenholm's death in 1876, thereafter the company's minute books, letters and printed ephemera tell the Wostenholm story in great detail. Particularly illuminating are the company secretary's copybooks, which document the firm's attempts to come to terms with the loss of the American trade.

Another important collection relates to Marsh Bros, which was an important cutlery manufacturer in the early nineteenth century. Again, the company letters give an insight into the importance of the American trade in nineteenth-century Sheffield. Unfortunately, the records for other Sheffield knifemakers, such as Joseph Rodgers & Sons, are not as voluminous (in the latter case, only a handful of letters and a couple of minute books have survived). Some records have survived for Christopher Johnson & Co. (such as its nineteenth-century Australian letters), and for Needham, Veall & Tyzack. Sheffield Library has published a listing of some of these records: *Catalogue of Business and Industrial Records* (Sheffield, 1977), but a more recent guide is published by HMSO: *Records of British Business and Industry, 1760–1914: Metal Processing and Engineering* (1994).

Fortunately, business records can be supplemented by information from printed sources. Sheffield City Library Local Studies Department has a huge collection of articles, journals, obituaries, and books relating to the Sheffield cutlery trade. Particularly useful for this book were several nineteenth-century trade catalogues for makers such as Christopher Johnson, Michael Hunter and Needham, Veall & Tyzack. Also useful was the Local Studies' card catalogue, which, along with Sylvia Pybus' published bibliography, gave a rapid entrée into the Library's holdings. Another powerful research tool was Peter Harvey's unpublished 'Sheffield Obituary', which enabled many nineteenth-century cutlers to be traced. For this book, Harvey's listing was simply invaluable and one can only admire the patience in compiling it. Local newspapers, particularly the *Sheffield Independent* and the *Sheffield Daily Telegraph*, provided a rich source of information in other ways. Until about 1930, the press covered the cutlery industry in great detail in its advert-isements, company reports, and profiles of leading cutlers. The only obstacle to utilising newspapers as a source was, as ever, time and patience; but there are some more accessible accounts listed in the following bibliography.

A page from Kelly's Directory of Sheffield (1922)

Further Reading

Unpublished theses and reports

Garlick, P., 'The Sheffield Cutlery and Allied Trades and Their Markets in the 18th and 19th Centuries' (Sheffield University MA, 1951). A very useful study that deserves publication (though an incomplete summary did appear in the *International Cutler*, 1951–3, before that journal ceased publication).

—'Letters from Hobart, 1835–41'. Typescript in Sheffield City Library Local Studies, concerning immigrant letters and the Ellin family.

Grant, R.M. 'The Richardson Sheffield Story: A British Winner', London Business School, Case Series No. 2 (Feb. 1988). The story of a rare post–war success story.

Grant, R.M., and S. Downing, 'The UK Cutlery Industry 1974–1982: A Study of Structural Adjustment, Business Strategies and Firm Performance', unpublished London Business School Study, May 1985.

Handley, J., 'The Grand Old Man of Abbeydale: Ebenezer Hall JP', typescript in Sheffield City Library Local Studies.

Harrison, M., 'Cadman Families With Others' (1994), typescript in Sheffield City Library Local Studies.

Harvey, P., 'Sheffield Obituary', typescript in Sheffield City Library Local Studies.

Hutton, R.S. 'Notes on the History of William Hutton & Sons: Sheffield and Birmingham Silversmiths and Platers' (1956), typescript in Sheffield City Library Local Studies.

Lacey-Hatton, J., 'Ebenezer Hall JP', typescript in Sheffield City Library Local Studies.

Ledbetter, R.M., 'Sheffield's Industrial History from about 1700, with Special Reference to the Abbeydale Works' (Sheffield University MA, 1971).

Speirs, W.B., 'Billy Ibberson Cutlery Research Project', unpublished Sheffield University Management School study, 17th Dec. 1993. Business analyst's view of the contemporary industry, blunted by the cutlery firms' secrecy and the author's surprising agreement that 'the current state of the industry is not one which should be made public'.

Taylor, S., 'Tradition and Change: The Sheffield Cutlery Trades 1870–1914' (Sheffield University PhD, 1988). Superb scholarly treatment, rich in detail, and sadly unpublished.

Books

Abels, R., *Classic Bowie Knives* (New York: Robert Abels, Inc., 1967).

Adams, W., J.B. Voyles, and T. Moss, *The Antique Bowie Knife Book* (Conyers, Georgia, 1990). Limited edition coffee-table book, containing photographs of many fine Sheffield Bowie knives.

Allen, T., *A New and Complete History of the County of Yorkshire* (3 vols., London, 1831).

Answer, V., *Sheffield's Traditional Craftsmen* (Sheffield, 1980). Profiles and interviews the little mesters. A pioneering, yet little-known book, in which the author displays a real feel for the subject.

Baylis, D. (ed.), *Industrial History of South Yorkshire* (Sheffield, 1995).

Bexfield, H., *A Short History of Sheffield Cutlery and the House of Wostenholm* (Sheffield, 1945). Dated and uncritical history by a Wostenholm director. Interesting, nevertheless.

Booth, G., *Diamonds in Brown Paper: The Colourful Lives and Hard Times of Sheffield's Famous Buffer Lasses* (Sheffield, 1988). Brief, but useful illustrated account.

Bradbury, F., *History of Old Sheffield Plate* (London, 1912). Unsurpassed study and a 'Bible' for hall marks, some of which can be found on table-cutlery and silver fruit-knives.

Carter, C.F., and B.R. Williams, *Industry and Technical Progress* (Oxford, 1957). Includes a case-study of Sheffield cutlery.

The Century's Progress (London, 1893). Period-piece, filled with fascinating company vignettes.

Chesworth, M., *Bought Of: Nineteenth Century Sheffield Through Its Billheads and Related Documents* (Sheffield, 1984).

Colbeck, M., *Made in Yorkshire: Second to None* (Huddersfield, 1992). Features little mesters Graham Clayton and Rowland Swinden.

Coward, H., *Reminiscences of Henry Coward* (1919). Evocative portrait of George Wostenholm and life in the Washington Works.

Creswick, T., *Engravings of All the Pressed Horn Handles and Scales Manufactured in Sheffield up to the Fifteenth Day of November, 1811* (Sheffield, 1811).

Crossley, D., N. Cass, N. Flavell, and C. Turner, (eds), *Water Power on the Sheffield Rivers* (Sheffield, 1989). Reference book, written by industrial archaeologists.

Dixon, James & Sons Ltd, Centenary Souvenir (Sheffield, 1905). Brief, illustrated house history.

Dyson, B.R., *A Glossary of Words and Dialect Formerly Used in the Sheffield Trades* (Sheffield, 1936). Fascinating dictionary of the local cutlery patois.

Fallon, J.P., *Marks of London Goldsmiths and Silversmiths 1837–1914* (London, 1992). Indispensable because it covers the history of several Sheffield firms, which had London offices.

Gatty, A., *Sheffield Past and Present* (Sheffield, 1873).

Goins, J.E., *Goins' Encyclopedia of Cutlery Markings* (Knoxville, TN, 1986). A knife collector's 'Bible' which does a creditable job of covering Sheffield marks.

Grayson, R. (with K. Hawley,), *Knifemaking in Sheffield: The Hawley Collection* (Sheffield, 1995). Brief, paperback account which accompanied an exhibition at the Ruskin Gallery.

Great Industries of Great Britain (London, 1886). Notable for an excellent chapter on Sheffield cutlery by Charles Hibbs. The engravings are outstanding.

Hartley, F., *Where Sparrows Coughed: Growing up in Sheffield in the 1940s and 1950s* (Sheffield, 1989).

Hatfield, J., and J. Hatfield, *The Oldest Sheffield Plater* (Huddersfield, 1974). Biography of Boulsover.

Hayward, J.F., *English Cutlery: Sixteenth to Eighteenth Century* (London, 1957). Brief, illustrated account, which features the Victoria and Albert Museum Collection (containing a few Sheffield knives).

Hey, D., *The Fiery Blades of Hallamshire: Sheffield and Its Neighbourhood, 1660–1740* (Leicester, 1991). Standard account of the rise of the knife industry.

Himsworth, J.B., *The Story of Cutlery: From Flint to Stainless Steel* (London, 1953). Dated, but still unsurpassed as an illustrated overview. The author was a director of the cutlers B. Worth & Sons and wrote from extensive personal knowledge.

Housley, H., *Grinders and Buffers: A Boyhood in the Sheffield Cutlery Industry* (Sheffield, 1988). Personal reminiscences. Paperback.

Hunter, J., *Hallamshire: The History and Topography of the Parish of Sheffield in the County of York*. Revised edn. by Arthur Gatty (Sheffield, 1869). Local antiquarian tome, written by a man who spent most of his life in Bath. For the industrial detail—which is not great—we are indebted to local worthy Gatty.

The Industries of Sheffield: Business Review (n.d., c. 1887). Despite its uncritical approach and boosterish tone, the profiles of leading cutlery firms often provide indispensable information.

Jenkins, C., and S. McLarence, *On the Knife Edge: The Inside Story of the Sheffield Cutlery Industry* (Sheffield, 1989). A series of interviews with little mesters, which updates Valerie Answer. Despite the fact that some of those included are not really little mesters, the interviews with knifemakers Ernest Mills and Stan Shaw, Bill Winfield (forger), and Doris Walsh (acid-etcher), are revealing.

Karsten, W.C., *Silver Folding Fruit Knives* (Knoxville, TN, 1986). Brief, illustrated paperback by a knowledgeable American collector.

Keane, J. *Six Months in Mecca* (London, 1881).

Krause, M. and J. Putsch, *Schneidwarenindustrie in Europa: Reisen zu den Werkstatten eines alten Gewerbes* (Cologne, 1994). Illustrated account of the European cutlery industry by the Industrial Museum in Solingen. A section looks at the decline of the Sheffield industry.

Krumholz, P.L., *A History of Shaving and Razors* (Bartonville, IL, 1987). A collectors' guide, with many Sheffield firms and trade marks.

Leader, R.E., *Reminiscences of Old Sheffield: Its Streets and People* (Sheffield, 2nd edn. 1876).

—*History of the Company of Cutlers in Hallamshire in the County of York* (Sheffield, 1905–6). Antiquarian work in two volumes, the second of which is devoted to a list of freemen and apprentices.

Leng, W.C. & Co, *First List of Corporate, Registered and Distinctive Trade Marks Used in Sheffield and District* (Sheffield, c. 1880).

Levine, B., *Levine's Guide to Knives and Their Values* (Northbrook, IL, 3rd edn, 1993). The best of the collectors' books, this encyclopedia for the collector includes information on many Sheffield patterns and firms.

—*Pocket-Knives: The Collector's Guide to Identifying, Buying and Enjoying Vintage Pocket-knives* (London, 1993). Glossy and accessible account.

Lloyd, G.I.H., *The Cutlery Trades: An Historical Essay in the Economics of Small-Scale Production* (1913). Still the standard work on the subject. Although the approach is rather dry, one keeps returning to it.

Magnusson, L., *The Contest for Control: Metal Industries in Sheffield, Solingen, Remscheid and Eskilstuna during Industrialization* (Oxford, 1994). The Sheffield chapter is poorly edited and contains errors of fact and interpretation. A missed opportunity to supersede Lloyd.

Men of the Period (London, 1896). Delightfully dated Victorian profiles of leading Sheffield cutlers and steelmakers.

Mensforth, E. (ed.), *Extracts from the Records of the Cutlers' Company* (Sheffield, 1972). Mostly facsimile documents.

Miller's Silver and Sheffield Plate Marks (London, 1993, repr., 1994).

Moore, S., *Penknives and Other Folding Knives* (Aylesbury, 1988). A photographic album in the well-known Shire series.

—*Table Knives and Forks* (Aylesbury, 1995).

Mosely Industrial Commission to the United States of America (Manchester, 1903).

Nether Edge Neighbourhood Group, *They Lived in Sharrow and Nether Edge* (Sheffield, 1988). Fascinating details of the personal lives of George Wostenholm and John Rodgers.

Olive, M. (compiler), *Central Sheffield* (Bath, 1994). Superior photographic essay of old Sheffield, with a section on cutlery.

Parker, J.F., *The Official Guide to Collector Knives* (New York, 9th edn 1987). Covers Bowie knives and some Sheffield makers.

Parry, D., *200 Years of Sheffield Cutlery and Edge Toolmaking* (Sheffield, n.d.).

Pawson & Brailsford's Illustrated Guide to Sheffield and Neighbourhood (Sheffield, 1862, 1879). A period piece, filled with excellent illustrations, advertisements and company information.

Peach, L.G., *The Company of Cutlers in Hallamshire in the County of York, 1906–1956* (Sheffield, 1960). Disappointing and uncritical update of Leader. The author's treatment of trade mark defence (which he depicts as one of the Company's great glories) sheds an unintentional light on the reasons for the decline of the Sheffield cutlery industry.

Pearce, M., *Sheffield Penknives* (Sheffield, 1976). A brief, illustrated Sheffield City Museums Information Sheet: No. 13.

Pickford, I., *Silver Flatware: English, Irish and Scottish 1660–1980* (Woodbridge, Suffolk, 1983). Well-produced collectors' book, with some information on table-knives.

Pike, W.T., *Sheffield at the Opening of the 20th Century* (Brighton, 1901). Brief biographies of leading Sheffielders, including some cutlers.

Platts, H., *The Knife Makers Who Went West* (Longmont, Colorado, 1978). Concerns Charles Platts and family, who emigrated from Sheffield in the 1860s, and founded a knifemaking dynasty in America. Excellent illustrations.

Pollard, S., *Three Centuries of Sheffield Steel: The Story of a Family Business* (Sheffield, 1954). Based on the Marsh Bros records now in Sheffield Archives, this is the best history of a 19th-century Sheffield cutlery firm.

—*A History of Labour in Sheffield* (Liverpool, 1959). Erudite (as usual with this author) and loaded with facts and references on cutlery.

—(ed), *The Sheffield Outrages* (Bath, 1971). Parliamentary documents and analysis.

Pryor, Edward & Son Ltd, *Making a Mark* (Sheffield, 6th edn, 1957).

Pybus, S., et al, *Cutlery: A Bibliography* (Sheffield, 2nd edn, 1982). Indispensable.

—'*Damned Bad Place, Sheffield*' (Sheffield, 1994). Compilation of visitors' accounts of Sheffield, with several cutlery references.

Records of British Business and Industry, 1760–1914: Metal Processing and Engineering (London, 1994). Handy HMSO listing of the few cutlery documents surviving.

Rees, D.M., *Yorkshire Craftsmen at Work* (Clapham, 1981). Section on the little mesters, including the late George Watts, Rowland Swinden and the late Eric Wragg, plus a few workers in the ancillary trades, such as pearl- and horn-cutting.

Rodgers, Joseph & Sons, *Under Five Sovereigns* (Sheffield, 1911). Short, illustrated house history, which surprisingly does not have a picture of a single knife.

Ruskin Gallery, *The Cutting Edge: An Exhibition of Sheffield Tools* (Sheffield, 1992). Features the tool collection of Ken Hawley, which contains some fine nineteenth-century Sheffield knives.

Sheffield and Rotherham Up-to-Date (Sheffield, 1897). More contemporary profiles of cutlery firms.

Sheffield City Library, *Catalogue of Business and Industrial Records* (Sheffield, 1977).

Sheffield and District Who's Who (Sheffield, 1905).

Sheffield Silver 1773–1973 (Sheffield, 1973). Catalogue of an Exhibition to Mark the Bicentenary of the Sheffield Assay Office, Sheffield City Museum, 24th July–13th September 1973.

Singleton, H.R., *A Chronology of Cutlery* (Sheffield, 1965). As seen through the collection at Weston Park, Sheffield. Brief, but illustrated.

Smith, J., *Explanation or Key, to the Various Manufactories of Sheffield, with Engravings of Each Article.* Ed. J.S. Kebabien, (Vermont, 1975).

Smithurst, P., *The Cutlery Industry* (Aylesbury, 1987). Shire Publications photo album, confined mostly to the 19th-century heyday.

Southern & Richardson, *A Century of Progress, 1828–1928* (Sheffield, 1928). Short house history.

Stainton, J.H., *The Making of Sheffield, 1865–1914* (Sheffield, 1924). More biographies.

Steerwood, R., and P. Machan, *Made in Sheffield: A Photographic Survey of Little Mester Workshops* (Sheffield, 1986). Fine photographs, brief text.

Stephens, F.J., *Fighting Knives: An Illustrated Guide to Fighting Knives and Military Survival Weapons of the World* (London, 1980).

Swann-Morton Ltd, *The First Fifty Years* (Sheffield, 1982). Brief history of a scalpel manufacturer.

Taylor, W., *The Sheffield Horn Industry* (Sheffield, 1927).

Thorp, R.W., *Bowie Knife* (Albuquerque: University of New Mexico, 1948). Pioneering study, which mixes fact with fancy.

Turner, C.A., *A Sheffield Heritage: An Anthology of Photographs and Words of the Cutlery Craftsmen* (Sheffield, 1978).

Turner, Thomas, & Wingfield Rowbotham, *Handicrafts that Survive: Centenary Souvenir 1802–1902* (Sheffield, 1902). Unashamed celebration of the old Sheffield ways, containing many valuable photographs.

Tweedale, G., *Giants of Sheffield Steel* (Sheffield, 1986). Brief biographies, including William Butcher and George Wostenholm. Further research has shown some inaccuracies in the Butcher profile.

—*Sheffield Steel and America: A Century of Commercial and Technological Interdependence, 1830–1930* (Cambridge, 1987). Academic account, dismally printed by Cambridge University Press on poor-quality paper.

—*Stan Shaw: Master Cutler* (Sheffield, 1993). Illustrated biography of one of the last little mesters.

—*Steel City: Entrepreneurship, Strategy and Technology in Sheffield, 1743–1993* (Oxford, 1995). Describes Sheffield cutlery manufacture and its linkages with the city's cluster of steel trades.

Washer, R., *The Sheffield Bowie and Pocket-Knife Makers 1825–1925* (Nottingham: T.A. Viner, 1974). Promising title for a disappointing book, which is poorly researched and includes photographs of counterfeit knives captioned as authentic.

White, J.E., *Fourth Report of the Children's Employment Commission* (London, 1865).

Whitham, J.H., and A. Sykes, (eds) *Register of Trade Marks of the Cutlers' Company of Sheffield* (London, 1953).

Whitham, J.H., and D. Vickers, (eds) *Register of Trade Marks of the Cutlers' Company of Sheffield* (London, 1919).

White's Hardware Trade marks (London, 1892). Ed. by. Herbert Hughes. Comprehensive guide.

Williamson, W.R., *I*XL Means I Excel: A Short History of the I*XL Bowie Knife* (1974). Illustrated history of Wostenholm's and the Bowie knife by an American collector.

Articles

Beauchamp, V., 'The Cutlery Workshops: A New Survey', *The Cutting Edge: Magazine of the South Yorkshire Industrial History Society*, No. 11 (1995).

'A Day at the Sheffield Cutlery Works', *The Penny Magazine* (London: vol. 13, 27th April 1844). Excellent early industrial reportage.

Farnsworth, K., 'The Craftsman Who Can't Find Time to Retire', *Quality* 28 (September/ October 1981). Interview with Ernest Mills.

Garlick, P.C., 'An Old Sheffield Cutlery Firm: The House of Nowill, 1786–1825', *Transactions of Hunter Archaeological Society* 7 (1955).

Geroski, P., and A. Vlassopoulos, 'A Market Leader in a Declining Industry: Richardson Sheffield', *Economic Review* 8 (1990).

Hawley, K., 'More About Stainless', *The Cutting Edge* (1991). Markings on stainless knives.

Hayter, R., and J. Patchell, 'Different Trajectories in the Social Divisions of Labour: The Cutlery Industry in Sheffield, England, and Tsubame, Japan', *Urban Studies* 30 (1993).

Higgins, D., and G. Tweedale, 'Asset or Liability?: Trade marks in the Sheffield Cutlery and Tool Trades', *Business History* (July 1995).

Holley, A.L., 'An Essay on Pen and Pocket Cutlery', *Poor's American Railroad Journal* (New York, May, June, July, 1850; reprinted in the *National Knife Magazine*, 1983–4). Holley was a famous American engineer, whose father established a cutlery factory in Connecticut. He recruited many Sheffield cutlers. This account, not surprisingly, is based on the Sheffield trades.

Palmer, H.J., 'Cutlery and Cutlers at Sheffield', *The English Illustrated Magazine* (Aug. 1884). Reprinted in Sheffield by MDE Publications, 1986, with Michael D. Everett as the 'compiler', who neglects to give the original author a credit.

Taylor, J., 'Richards: Solingen Comes to Sheffield', *Edges* (c. 1990).

—'The Slaters of Sheffield', *Edges* (Spring 1993).

Taylor, S., 'The Industrial Structure of the Sheffield Trades', in C. Binfield, R. Childs, G. Harper, D. Hey, D. Martin, and G. Tweedale, (eds), *The History of the City of Sheffield, 1843–1993* (Sheffield, 1993). Vol. 2.

Townsend, H., 'The Cutlery Trade', in D. Burn (ed.), *The Structure of British Industry* (Oxford, 1958). Detailed economic analysis of the industry in the 1950s.

Tweedale, G. 'The Razor Blade King of Sheffield: The Forgotten Career of Paul Kuehnrich', *Transactions of Hunter Archaeological Society* 16 (1991).

—'Strategies for Decline: George Wostenholm & Son and the Sheffield Cutlery Industry', Transactions of Hunter Archaeological Society 17 (1993).

Unwin, J., 'Apprenticeships and freedoms: The Computer Analysis of the Records of the Cutlers' Company in Sheffield', *Local Historian* 25 (Nov. 1995).

Williams, E., 'Low Cost Imports from the Far East have Decimated Sheffield Trade', Tableware International (Nov/Dec 1975)

Collectors' publications

The major market for antique knife-collecting is in America, where since the 1940s and 1950s there has been a growing interest in old Sheffield knives. The knife-collecting fraternity in the USA supports several magazines, the chief of which are: *National Knife Magazine* (run by the National Knife Collectors' Association, Chattanooga); *Blade Magazine* (and *Edges*) (published by Krause Pub- lications, Iola, WI); and *Knife World* (published by Knife World Publications, Knoxville). Of these, *Blade Magazine* has the largest circulation and can be seen on American newsstands (and less frequently In Europe), though it is now very much angled at the custom-knife market. However, all these periodicals occasionally have articles on antique Sheffield knives and firms.

Films and videos

Archival film of the cutlery industry is rare. Ibberson's made a short promotional film (silent, with separate commentary added later) in 1926, entitled 'The Making of 'Violin' Brand Cutlery'. It shows the making of table- and pocket-knives. Another advertising film made in about 1930, features the Western Works of Christopher Johnson & Co. Again, various stages in the manufacture of table- and pocket-knives are demonstrated.

In the late 1970s, the Department of Audio Visual Communications of Sheffield Polytechnic (now Sheffield Hallam University) filmed various branches of the 'dying crafts'. Amongst them were forging and knife-grinding.

The Kelham Island 'little mesters' were featured in a Channel 4 series called 'Changing Times', first broadcast on 20th August 1986 and repeated on 5th October 1987 (copy at Kelham Island Industrial Museum).

The 'little mesters', loosely defined, were also featured in the 'First Tuesday' series (ITV, 23rd February 1988), which was distinguished by its failure to feature either Graham Clayton, Rowland Swinden or Stan Shaw. The latter, though, is one of the subjects in the 'Masters of Metalworking' video series produced in 1993 by K. Hawley and the Ruskin Gallery (running time 22 minutes).

Copies and information on these films can be found at the Department of Local Studies, Sheffield City Library.